A Hamilton

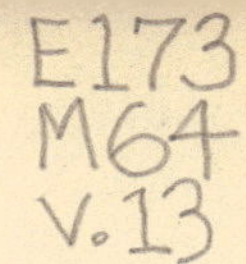

GREAT DEBATES IN AMERICAN HISTORY

From the Debates in the British Parliament on the Colonial Stamp Act (1764–1765) to the Debates in Congress at the Close of the Taft Administration (1912–1913)

EDITED BY

MARION MILLS MILLER, LITT.D. (PRINCETON)

Editor of "The Life and Works of Abraham Lincoln," etc.

IN FOURTEEN VOLUMES

EACH DEALING WITH A SPECIFIC SUBJECT, AND CONTAINING A SPECIAL INTRODUCTION BY A DISTINGUISHED AMERICAN STATESMAN OR PUBLICIST

VOLUME THIRTEEN

FINANCE: PART ONE

With an Introduction by THEODORE E. BURTON, LL.D.
Senator from Ohio

CURRENT LITERATURE PUBLISHING COMPANY
NEW YORK

CONTENTS OF VOLUME THIRTEEN

ILLUSTRATIONS IN VOLUME THIRTEEN

INTRODUCTION

The Need for Currency Reform[1]

An examination of the subject of currency reform will fail to convince us of the necessity of any increase in the aggregate volume of money in circulation. With one exception, that of France, the quantity of money per capita in the United States is greater than in any prominent commercial nation in the world. On December 31, 1909, the average per inhabitant in this country was $35.21. In France it is $37.85, due principally to the fact that the use of checks as substitutes for currency is much less. If we include with the amount in circulation the $150,000,000 gold reserve and the Government assets in our national treasury, our average amount would be $38.45 per capita, being greater than that of any prominent nation in the world. But, whichever method of determining the per capita circulation is chosen, the amount is greater by nearly $15 than in the period of maximum inflation in the Civil War, and greater by almost an equal amount than in the very prosperous years of 1880 and 1881; greater also by approximately $10 than twelve years ago, and this notwithstanding the constantly increasing use of checks and other substitutes for currency.

The most distinctive feature of our currency may be expressed in a word, and that is its motley character. Many other features, closely connected with this one, affect our whole system. To explain in detail, we have,

[1] Adapted from an address delivered in Philadelphia before the American Academy of Political and Social Science, December 8, 1910.

first of all, what are called the greenbacks, legal tender notes, amounting to $346,000,000. That amount was fixed in the year 1878. From 1862, the date of their first issue, until 1879 they were not redeemable in gold, but since that time a gold reserve has been maintained for their redemption, the amount of which was fixed at $150,000,000 in the year 1900. The next variety of currency is the national bank notes, which now amount to $726,000,000, according to the statement of December 1, 1910. These rest upon the security of Government bonds. The greenbacks are the direct obligation of the Government. The national bank notes are indirectly the obligation of the Federal Government. Indeed, they are more than this, since, whenever a national bank note is presented to our treasury, it must be exchanged by the Government for greenbacks or other legal tender. The total amount of greenbacks and national bank notes together is $1,072,000,000. In addition to this amount there are outstanding 564,000,000 of silver dollars, which rest in part on the credit of the Government. On the silver dollar there are written the words ''In God we trust.'' The intrinsic value of this silver dollar, according to the latest quotation of silver, is 42.8 cents, the remaining 57.2 cents depending upon the credit of the Government. This is semi-fiat money, and it would cause very great embarrassment in our circulation, except for the fact that it supplies the demand for currency in small denominations. In almost every country a certain amount of what is called token currency is required. The national authority assumes as its prerogative the coinage of fractional silver and derives a profit from it. For instance, in this country there are outstanding $156,000,000 of fractional silver and token coins. Only $84,000,000 in silver dollars are actually in circulation, the balance of $480,000,000 being represented by what are known as silver certificates. These are mostly in denominations of one, two, and five dollars. The national banks are forbidden to issue bills below $5, and the greenbacks, which are legal tender, are not issued below $5. Our people very much prefer to handle bills rather than coin, so in providing denominations of $1, $2, and $5 the silver certificates are very useful.

The best feature of our currency system I have not yet mentioned. We have in this country $1,700,000,000 of gold coins, nearly one-half of the whole amount of our currency, which at the present time is approximately $3,500,000,000. The $1,700,000,000 of gold, of course, circulates anywhere on the globe, since it has intrinsic value. You may melt one of these gold coins in a crucible into a shapeless mass and after that operation is finished it has as much value as it had before. This would not be true of the silver dollar which I hold in my hand. It would be worth only 42.8 cents if melted.

The principal disadvantages of our system are, first, that too much of our currency rests upon the credit of the Government. While it is true that the man who accepts a silver dollar, a silver certificate, a greenback, or a national bank note has absolute confidence in it because it is backed by the Government, nevertheless the system by which the Government issues so large a share of the currency is a vicious one. The experiment of issuing legal tender paper money has been tried by almost every nation in the world, and it has been abandoned by practically every one of the most advanced countries except our own. Nothing but the very exceptional credit of the United States saves us from disaster because of this situation.

It is true that the greenbacks served a very useful purpose during the Civil War, but what we need now is a currency adapted to our present needs, not one based upon historical or sentimental reasons. We want the best monetary system that can possibly be devised.

Briefly stated, the argument against such issues is that when a government issues currency it is in response to its own and not to business needs. Its expenditures should, under any rational system, approximately balance its income, but when its outgo is more than its income, then there arises the temptation to issue its paper currency, and that is just the very worst thing to do. In doing this the Government uses its right to create debt, to create issues of money, just at the time when such obligations ought not to be created. In a well-managed bank or financial institution circulation is small when its assets are small, and circulation is large, or should be large, when its assets are large. The quantity of money should respond to the demands of trade. Now it is not likely that we shall have any great calamity by reason of this quantity of Government money to which I have referred, but if there should be a crisis like the Civil War; if there should be a period in which our crops failed year after year; if there should be an enormous increase in the expenses of Government, a tremendous strain would be placed upon our financial system. Also, there should be an adjustment of the amount of paper currency to the increase or decrease of the gold supply. If there should ever be a cessation or material decrease in the present constantly increasing production of gold there would be such a readjustment in the course of exchanges as would necessitate considerable alteration in our currency system.

A rational currency system is one in which the quantity of money may be increased or decreased according to the demands of trade, and there is no criterion of these demands so correct as the quantity of business that is done. When there is a large quantity of wheat to be harvested and the supply of bills to pay for it is small, then is the time when it is proper and rational to issue an additional amount of currency. I do not wish to be understood as saying we should make a sudden change in our system; all changes should be made slowly. Custom, so potent in all monetary systems, has adapted itself to the present situation, however faulty it may be. But I do advocate that, little by little, step by step, with no retrogression, we should move away from this system under which the Government supports with its credit $346,000,000 directly, $726,000,000 indirectly, and $564,000,000 in part.

What our currency system lacks most and what any reform must supply is elasticity. The present system is one of rigidity. Those amounts of currency which I have mentioned remain practically the same year in and year out. Everyone knows that the demand for currency is different at different times. More is needed at the end of the week than in the mid-week, and more at the end of the month than in the middle of the month. Then there are annual disbursements, semiannual disbursements, and quarterly dividends to be paid. At certain times in the fall the crops must be marketed. Then you have what is called in England "the autumn drain." The degree of activity in business also varies greatly in different years. The volume of currency should expand and contract automatically to meet these business demands. But under our present system the amount of currency has no elasticity, no flexibility, except that which may be brought about by imports or exports of gold and by increasing or decreasing the quantity of national bank notes, and the volume of these latter does not respond to the needs of business. The law as it now stands forbids decreasing the national bank notes by more than $9,000,000 a month. Undoubtedly the lack of elasticity is the most serious defect in our present currency system.

What is required, first of all, is the enactment into law of a definite policy under which the quantity of currency can be diminished as well as increased. There is no reason for having $3,500,000,000 in circulation when it is not all needed. The result is necessarily harmful, as I can readily show you. Our bankers naturally wish to utilize all the currency in their vaults. They desire to obtain an income from their money on deposit in seasons of slack demand as well as in seasons of large demand. In any monetary system like ours the tendency is to make the total stock of currency sufficient to meet only the minimum demands. Thus when an increased demand arises, as inevitably it must, there is a scarcity or insufficiency of currency which threatens disaster. Now what happens? After great quantities of money have been loaned out and probably used for stock speculation or in other equally doubtful enterprises, there arises an insistent demand for currency for harvesting the enormous crops of the country. And thus, at this time of the year, when we need all of the money in circulation, we find that it has already been absorbed. This causes a stringency in the money market. This will always happen under an inflexible currency system like ours. You will notice, if you follow the stock market in these seasons of slack demand, that usually stocks command higher prices. The reason is that the speculator can borrow money at cheap rates, and consequently the number of stock buyers is increased.

The principal facts or objects to be considered in the solution of this problem are, first, the need for contraction as well as expansion; second, the amount of circulation should be adjusted to the volume of trade; finally, there should be absolute security for every note issued. I may have personally a partiality for notes based upon negotiable paper and the liquid assets of banks rather than upon bonds or other permanent securities, but, whichever method you have, be sure that the note will be a good one, so that no man when he rises in the morning and reads in the newspapers that a certain bank has failed need fumble through his pocketbook to see whether he has any bills of that bank.

There are numerous obstacles to a reform in our currency. In the first place, there is no other field in which the visionary or the crank has such an opportunity as in questions pertaining to money and finance. Secretary Windom remarked to me twenty years ago: "There are a great many men scattered through the country, sitting on dry goods boxes, who may not be able to manage their own business affairs, but who are convinced that they could manage the Federal treasury a great deal better than it is now being managed." Again, there are a great many selfish interests which come to the front when there is any attempt toward judicious reform. Senator Sherman once said he never had taken part in the passage of any financial measure with which he was entirely satisfied. It was always necessary to make concessions to some one to get the bill passed.

Another difficulty is that for the last fifty years or more there has been a demand that the Government pursue a policy which would result in high prices for crops and at the same time low prices for what we buy

—that is, the Government is expected to make high prices for the seller and low prices for the consumer. I do not know how any system of currency or banking can perform this miracle. People have come, however, to associate a plentiful supply of money with good times. The issue of greenbacks was accompanied by great prosperity and a period of industrial reawakening throughout the country, and from that day to this people have thought that they were more prosperous when there was a large supply of money in circulation. But in any judicious system there must be provision for contraction as well as for expansion, and this has been exceedingly difficult to obtain in the face of adverse public opinion.

Perhaps you may not have realized that in the last fifty years, whenever laws relating to currency were passed, the providing of a good system was never the main object. In 1862, when the greenbacks were issued, it was not to provide a good monetary supply, but to save the very life of the Government in the midst of a rebellion. Then a year or two later came the national banks. The main object in establishing them was not to obtain a perfect monetary system, but to supersede the variety of issues of the State banks, and, in addition, to aid the sale of the bonds of the Government. Then we come to the silver acts of 1878 and 1890. They were passed not for the purpose of providing us with good currency, but in response to the demands of those who were shouting for more money—some of whom doubtless were anxious to pay their debts in a depreciated medium —and of those who were interested in silver mines and desired to sell their output to the Government.

As good citizens we should appreciate rightly all these difficulties and conflicting interests, my fellow citizens, and undertake this problem of currency reform with an eye single to the prosperity of the country, resolved to place our monetary system on a par with the very best systems of other great nations.

Theodore E. Burton

CHAPTER I

Public Credit

Report of Alexander Hamilton, Secretary of the Treasury, on Public Credit—Debate on the Report: Shall Discrimination Be Made in Favor of Original Holders of National Obligations and against Purchasers of the Same?—Proposition of James Madison [Va.] in Favor of Original Holders—It Is Voted Down after Debate—Speeches in the Debate: in Favor of the Proposition, by James Jackson [Ga.]; Against It, by Elias Boudinot [N. J.]—Debate on the Assumption of State Debts by the Federal Government; Speeches in the Debate by Theodore Sedgwick [Mass.] and Fisher Ames [Mass.]; The Debts Are Assumed—Motion of Thomas Fitzsimons [Pa.] That the Secretary of the Treasury Report a Plan for the Redemption of the Public Debt—Debate on Whether or Not This Is a Proper Ministerial Function: in Favor, William Vans Murray [Md.] and Mr. Ames; Opposed, John Francis Mercer [Md.] and Mr. Madison—Resolutions of William B. Giles [Va.] against Hamilton—They Are Defeated—Hamilton's Report on Redeeming the Public Debt—Debate: in Favor of the Plan, Mr. Ames and Mr. Sedgwick; Opposed to It, Mr. Madison.

AT the opening of the second session of the First Congress President Washington especially recommended that provision be made for the support of the public credit, which had been the chief reason for the formation of the new Government.

The report of Alexander Hamilton, Secretary of the Treasury, respecting public credit, was submitted to the House on January 15, 1790. It showed that the public debt was more than $54,000,000. The foreign debt, due chiefly to France and Holland, with interest, was about $13,250,000; the domestic liquidated debt, with interest, was more than $40,000,000, and the unliquidated, $2,000,000.

The Secretary recommended the assumption of the debts of the several States to be paid equally with those of the Union, as "a measure of sound policy and substantial justice." These were estimated at twenty-five millions of dollars. Doubts were expressed by the Secretary whether, in addition to all other expenses, it was in the power of the United States to make a secure and effectual provision for the payment of the interest of so large a sum on the terms of the original contracts. He therefore submitted to the House several plans for the modification, security, and payment of the domestic debt.

One proposition was to lower the rate of interest on the whole debt, another to postpone the payment of the interest on a portion of the principal to a distant day. No new modification, however, was to be made without the assent of the creditors.

This important subject was under the consideration of Congress until the 4th of August, 1790, when a law was passed, making a new loan of the whole of the domestic debt.

By the same act Congress assumed twenty-one millions and a half of the State debts; and this sum was apportioned among the States, having regard to the amount of the debts of each. The sum thus assumed was also to be lent to the United States by individuals holding certain evidences of State debts.

Says Timothy Pitkin in his "Political History of the United States":

Congress was much divided as to the mode and manner of providing for the security and payment of so large a debt, deemed of little value under the old Confederation, and particularly on the question of assuming the payment of the State debts. Unfortunately the public debt had become an object of extensive speculation. That some provision would be made for the payment of this debt, under the new Government, was the general expectation, and the propriety of making a discrimination between the original holders and the purchasers had been suggested in private circles as well as in the public newspapers. The idea of making such a discrimination was opposed by Secretary Hamilton as unjust, impolitic, and ruinous to public credit.

In an early stage of the proceedings on his report this question was submitted to the House of Representatives. James Madison [Va.] proposed that the purchasers should receive the highest average price at which the debt had been sold, and the original holders the residue, both to have interest at six per cent. The Government was to have no advantage from this arrangement.

In favor of the proposition it was, among other things, urged that the case was in many respects so extraordinary that the usual maxims were not strictly applicable. The debt originally contracted, it was said, was to be paid in gold and silver, but, instead of this, paper had been substituted, which the creditors were compelled to take. This paper they had parted with, either from necessity or a well-grounded distrust of the public. In either case they had been injured, and suffered loss from the default of the debtor, and in justice the debtor ought not to take advantage of this default. The original debt had never been discharged, because the paper had been forced upon the creditors. A composition, therefore, between the purchasers and the original holders, by allowing the former an average price at which the debt had been sold and paying the latter the residue, would do equal justice to both. In opposition to the measure it was said in the first place that the discrimination proposed was a violation of the original contract on the part of the public. That, by the terms of the certificates given to the original creditors, the debt was made payable to assignees or to bearer; and, of course, the contract was made with the purchaser as well as with the original holder. That it was impossible for Government to examine into the private transactions between the original creditor and his assignee. The debt had been purchased at the market price, and the creditor had parted with his security for what he deemed an equivalent; and, however unfortunate might be the situation of some, who from necessity had been obliged to part with their securities, redress could not be afforded them in the manner contemplated. In most instances the purchaser had placed greater confidence in the Government than the original holder, and had run the risk of eventual payment, which, but for a change in the Federal Government, would perhaps never have been made.

The impolicy of the measure was also strongly urged as tending greatly to impair, if not totally destroy, public credit hereafter.

The interest of individuals, as well as the community, required that a public debt should be transferable; and its value in market would depend on a variety of circumstances. If Government should thus interfere, in case of transfers, all confidence in public engagements would be destroyed. It was likewise said that great injustice would be done in carrying the plan into effect in the manner proposed. That many of the original certificates were issued to persons who, in fact, had no interest in them, being for the benefit of others to whom, for various considerations, they were to transfer the same. That the immediate purchasers had, in many instances, suffered as much as or more than the original holders, and that no provision was proposed for them. The proposition was voted down by a large majority.

The following speeches, by James Jackson of Georgia and Elias Boudinot of New Jersey, are presented as typical of the debate. They bear upon the general subject of partial repudiation of the public debt as justified by an unfair advantage obtained by those speculating in the debt.

Speculation and Repudiation

House of Representatives, January 28, 1790

Mr. Jackson.—I know, sir, that there are, and will be, speculations in the funds of every nation possessed of public debt; but they are not such as the present report has given rise to, by the advantage those at the seat of government obtained of learning the plan contemplated by the principal of the Treasury Department, before others had heard a word thereof. If we had either received this report privately, or not sat in a large city, then, sir, none of these speculations would have arisen, because Congress could have devised means of diffusing the information so generally as to prevent any of its ill effects. Under these impressions, I am led to express my ardent wish to God that we had been on the banks of the Susquehanna or Potomac, or at any place in the woods, and out of the neighborhood of a populous city; all my unsuspecting fellow citizens might then have been warned of their danger and guarded themselves against the machinations of the speculators. To some gentlemen characters of this kind may appear to be of utility; but I, sir, view them in a different light; they are as rapacious wolves seeking whom they may devour, and preying upon the misfortunes of their fellow men, taking an undue advantage of their necessities.

Look at the gallant veteran, who nobly led your martial bands in the hour of extreme danger, whose patriotic soul acknowledged no other principle than that his life was the property of his country, and who evinced it by his repeated exposures to a vengeful enemy. See him deprived of those limbs which he sacrificed in your service! And behold his virtuous and tender wife sustaining him and his children in a wilderness, lonely, exposed to the arms of savages, where he and his family have been driven by this useful class of citizens, these speculators, who have drained from him the pittance which a grateful country had afforded him, in reward for his bravery and toils, and a long catalogue of merits. Nor is their insatiable avarice yet satisfied, while there remains a single class of citizens who retain the evidence of their demands upon the public; the State debts are to become an object for them to prey upon, until other citizens are driven into scenes of equal distress. Is it not the duty of the House to check this spirit of devastation? It most assuredly is. If, by the ill-timed promulgation of this report, we have laid the foundation for the calamity, ought we not to counteract it?

Jackson was replied to by a man of equally generous impulses but of calmer judgment, the wise and kindly Elias Boudinot, ex-President of Congress, and philanthropist.

Mr. Boudinot.—I would be sorry if, on this occasion, the House should decide that speculations in the funds are violations of either the moral or political law. A government hardly exists in which such speculation is disallowed; but it must, at the same time, be admitted that everything of this kind has proper bounds, which may be too small or too great. If you will not permit your creditor to transfer his debt, you deprive the commonwealth of a great part of her credit and capital; on the other hand, if speculation is carried on to such a degree as to divert the funds of productive labor into the pursuit of visionary objects, or destroy them, the community clearly loses the use of so much of its capital, which is a considerable evil. I agree with gentlemen that the spirit of speculation has now risen to an alarming height; but the only way to prevent its future effect is to give the public funds a degree of stability as soon as possible.

We should pay an ill compliment to the understanding and honor of every true American were we to adduce many arguments to show the baseness or bad policy of violating our national faith or omitting to pursue the measures necessary to preserve it. A bankrupt, faithless Republic would be a novelty in the political world, and appear, among reputable nations, like a common prostitute among chaste and respectable matrons.

I conceive, Mr. Chairman, after duly considering the momentous circumstances I have brought to your attention, there is no man possessed of the principles of common honesty, within the sound of my voice, that will hesitate to conclude with me that we are bound by every principle of honor, justice, and policy to fund the debt of the United States, which has been one great means, under heaven, of securing to us our independence. I presume, sir, on this point we shall have no dispute. All that remains, then, for our consideration is the manner and means of accomplishing it.

We must view it as a debt of honor, from the nature of the contract, from the objects effected, and the happy state we are now in. The principles of interest call loudly upon us to complete the business so happily begun. The Secretary, in the report before us, observes, with great justice, that exigencies are to be expected to occur in the affairs of nations, in which there will be a necessity for borrowing, and particularly in a country like this, possessed of little moneyed capital. How much, then, is it our interest to secure our public credit on a stable and sure foundation? Besides this, it is our interest in another point of view; by this means we shall introduce a medium into circulation which will give a spring to the agriculture, commerce, and manufactures of the Union.

Our policy also guides us into the adoption of some such measure as is proposed in the report. A punctual performance of our public engagements will invite moneyed men, in the days of distress, to lend us every pecuniary aid. Our debt undoubtedly is large; but not so large as might have been reasonably expected, considering the magnitude of the object we have successfully accomplished; but it can by no means be considered so large as to prevent us from an attempt to discharge it.

Let us then adopt the motion now on your table, or something like it; not, perhaps, immediately, because it might be supposed to preclude that discussion which the subject requires, as the most important that has or can come before us.

Assumption of State Debts[1]

House of Representatives, February 15–May 28, 1790

The assumption of the State debts, however, was a subject which gave rise to more serious debate, and created divisions both in and out of Congress, the effects of which were long felt in the administration of the general Government.

The debts of the several States were very unequal. Those of Massachusetts and South Carolina amounted to more than ten millions and a half, while the debts of all the other States were only estimated at between fourteen and fifteen millions. The first proposition on this subject in the House of Representatives was to assume the whole of these debts. This was at first adopted, in committee of the whole, by a small majority. Afterward, when the members from North Carolina took their seats, the subject was recommitted, and negatived by a majority of two—31 to 29. Propositions were afterward made to assume specific sums from each, but were negatived. These various propositions occasioned long and violent debates among the members from different States, and led to an inquiry into the origin of the State debts and to a comparative view of the different exertions and expenses of the States themselves in their struggle for independence. The assumption of specific sums from each was finally carried in the Senate, by a majority of two, and was concurred in by the House by a majority of six.

Those in favor of the assumption contended that it was a measure of *justice* as well as *policy*. That it was

[1] Abridged from Timothy Pitkin's "Political History of the United States."

just in respect to the creditors themselves, as well as to the States. These debts, it was said, were incurred for services rendered, supplies furnished, or loans made, not for the particular benefit of the individual States, but for the benefit of the Union, for the common cause in which all were embarked. Justice, therefore, required that the persons to whom they were due should be placed on the same footing with those who had a direct claim on the United States; and that both should be paid out of a common fund. That, although some States might be able to provide ample funds for the payment of their debts, yet others, destitute of like resources, burdened with a larger debt, occasioned, perhaps, by greater exertions in the common cause, might be unable to make adequate provision. One class of creditors, therefore, who happened to live in a large State, abounding in wealth and resources, and, perhaps, with a comparatively small debt, might be paid in full, while another, equally meritorious, living in a small State, having a larger debt and destitute of resources, might receive little or nothing. It would be just in respect to the States, as in this way each would bear its proportion of the expenses incurred for one common object. It was to be considered also, it was said, that no inconsiderable proportion of the State debts were incurred at a time when the United States had little or no credit. It was also strongly contended that, as the Constitution had transferred to Congress the principal funds on which the States had relied for payment of their debts, it was just that the debts should follow the funds.

The policy of the measure, its advocates said, was not less apparent than its justice.

A provision for these debts by the States themselves would necessarily create an interference between the general and State Governments in their revenue systems highly injurious, if not ruinous, to both. The United States having the *exclusive* power to lay imposts, most of the States must have recourse to excises and direct taxes. These, it was said, must be very unequal in different States in consequence of the inequality of their debts. Great burdens, therefore, would be thrown on those States whose exertions had been greatest in the common cause, and jealousies and dissatisfaction must be the necessary consequence. In those States where recourse was had to direct taxes a greater burden would be thrown on the landed interest, and this would produce emigration to other States less oppressed with taxes of this description. Where resort was had to excises, which would be laid on foreign as well as domestic articles, greater inducements would be held out to smuggling, materially affecting the revenue of the United States. In addition to this, commercial advantages might be greater in some States than in others, and a transfer of capital from one State to another be thereby encouraged. The collection of the same amount of taxes, it was said, might be made with less expense under the direction of one government than under several; and, by having the general management of the revenues of the country in their hands, the National Legislature would be enabled more fully to promote domestic industry and improvement throughout every part of the union.

In the course of the debates on this interesting question it was stated by the advocates of the assumption that a difference in the amount of State debts did not arise solely from a difference in exertions during the war, but that the debts of some States were lessened by the avails of confiscated property and from territorial acquisitions. And it was asked: whether those by whose offences a confiscation of property had been incurred had not offended against United America and not merely against that State where the offence was committed, and which alone received the benefit of the confiscation? And whether the acquisition of territory was not owing to the exertions of the national force, under national direction?

The opponents of the measure were not less decided in opinion that it was both *unjust* and *impolitic,* whether it went to a general or a partial assumption.

They denied that the State debts should be considered, in any way, the debts of the Union, or that the United States were under obligations to discharge any part of them, except the balance which, on a final settlement, should be found due to particular States. If they were the debts of the United States, in the hands of individuals, it was asked whether they were not equally so when in the State treasuries; whether the United States were not equally bound to provide for them in both situations. Before the adoption of the Constitution, it was said, they had never been so considered. They contended, also, that, not being the debts of the Union, Congress were not warranted by the Constitution in assuming the payment of them.

As to the policy of the measure, its opponents said, among other things, if a public debt was a public evil the assumption would increase and perpetuate the evil; that the United States and the individual States together could discharge a debt of eighty millions much sooner than the United States alone; that, after the general Government had resorted to all the means of revenue in its power, the individual States would have other financial resources still remaining. It was also particularly urged that each State could raise money in a way most convenient for itself and to which it had been accustomed. Some of the States, they said, were hostile to excises, others to direct taxes, and no general system of internal taxation could be established which was adapted to the circumstances of each State, or which would give general satisfaction.

Some of the States had, by their exertions, paid a greater proportion of their debts than others, and it would be unjust, they alleged, to compel them to contribute to the payment of the debts of delinquent States. In answer to the suggestion that, unless the measure should be carried, great dissatisfaction would exist in some of the States, it was said that much greater dissatisfaction would follow from its adoption. A majority of the people of the United States, it was believed, was opposed to it, and the discordant interests as well as jealousies among the States, now too much felt, would be thereby greatly increased.

The opposers of the assumption also stated that the adoption of the measure would render State creditors more dependent on the general Government; that it would greatly lessen the influence and importance of the States, and tend to consolidate the Union. The debts of Massachusetts, South Carolina, and Connecticut, as reported by the Secretary, amounted to about one-half of those of all the others. These States, therefore, felt a deep interest in the question. The legislature of South Carolina, in January, 1790, instructed their Representative in Congress to solicit the National Legislature to assume their debt, "it having been incurred," as they said, "in consequence of the war between the United States and Great Britain."

In the course of the debate Theodore Sedgwick, of Massachusetts, declared that Shay's Rebellion, which had then just taken place in Massachusetts, was occasioned by the burden of taxes necessarily imposed on the people of that State to pay a debt incurred merely for national purposes. Fisher Ames, of the same State, in his usual strain of eloquence asked, "but were the State debts contracted for the war? It appears by the books in the public offices that they were. Will anyone say that the whole expense of defending our common liberty ought not to be a common charge? Part of this charge was contracted by Massachusetts before Congress assumed the exercise of its powers. The first ammunition that repulsed the enemy at Lexington and made such havoc at Bunker Hill was purchased by the State and appears in the form of the State debt." The States of Virginia, North Carolina, and Georgia were most strenuous in their opposition.

This interesting question was finally decided in the Senate, 14 to 12. In this body the States of Massachusetts, Connecticut, New York, New Jersey, and South Carolina were unanimously in the affirmative; Rhode Island, Virginia, North Carolina, and Georgia, with equal unanimity in the negative, and Pennsylvania, Delaware, and Maryland divided.

In February, 1791, an act was passed for the establishment of a national bank [see chapter II.].

On November 19, 1792, Thomas Fitzsimons [Pa.] introduced a resolution in the House, directing the Secretary of the Treasury to report a plan for the redemption of the public debt. This resolution was opposed by John F. Mercer [Md.] and Mr. Madison, and supported by William Vans Murray [Md.] and Mr. Ames.

On Ministerial Functions

House of Representatives, November 19-21, 1792

Mr. Mercer.—No question, he conceived, was of more importance than that involved in the motion before the House. He conceived it improper to commit to any man what he was bound himself to do. He conceived the power of the House to originate plans of finance, to lay new burdens on the people intrusted to them by their constituents, as incommunicable.

Mr. Madison drew a distinction between the deliberative functions of the House and the ministerial functions of the Executive powers. The deliberative functions, he conceived, should be first exercised before the ministerial began to act. It should be decided by the House, in the first instance, he conceived, whether the debt should be reduced by imposing new taxes, or by varying the burdens, or by new loans. The fundamental principles of any measure, he was of opinion, should be decided in the House, perhaps even before a reference to a select committee. He did not pretend to determine whether the motion now before the House might not involve a reference of a ministerial nature merely. But he well knew, he said, that the act establishing the Treasury Department had been so construed as to give it a greater latitude than was contemplated when the law passed, much against the opinion of a great portion of the people. In the infancy of our Government that latitude perhaps might be necessary; but he saw no necessity for it at present.

Mr. Murray conceived that the distinction drawn by the gentleman from Virginia [Mr. Madison] between deliberative and ministerial functions was qualified by the nature of things. It is qualified, he said, in this instance, by the law which establishes the Treasury Department. That law makes it the duty of the Secretary to digest and report plans to ameliorate our finances, without any call from the House. True, the business of the House is to deliberate; but, by reference, neither is the power of the House to deliberate infringed, nor does it give the Secretary a right legislatively to deliberate, but to deliberate ministerially; and it was important, he conceived, in a government framed like ours, that such officers should have the power to deliberate in that manner. The result of their deliberations was not obligatory on the House, no further than it was warranted by wisdom.

MR. MERCER.—The House may require from the heads of departments the exposition of the documents and information that arise in the administration of government. But I want no *opinions* from them. If these are to influence us, they are wrong; if not to influence, they are useless. This mode of procedure, of *originating* laws with the Secretary, destroys the responsibility; it throws it on a man not elected by the people, and over whom they have no control.

MR. AMES.—What is the clause of the Constitution opposed to the receiving a plan of a sinking fund from the Secretary? Bills for raising revenue shall originate in this House. I verily believe the members of this House, and the citizens at large, would be very much surprised to hear this clause of the Constitution formally and gravely stated as repugnant to the reference to the Treasury Department for a plan, if they and we had not been long used to hear it.

To determine the force of this amazing constitutional objection, it will be sufficient to define terms.

What is a bill? It is a term of technical import, and surely it cannot need a definition; it is an act of an inchoate state, having the form but not the authority of the law.

What is originating a bill? Our rules decide it. Every bill shall be introduced by a motion for leave, or by a committee.

The opposers of this proposition surely will not adopt a construction of the Constitution. They have often told us we are to be guided by a strict adherence to the letter; that there is no end to the danger of constructions.

The letter is not repugnant; and will it be seriously affirmed that, according to the spirit and natural meaning of the Constitution, the report of the Secretary will be a revenue bill, or any other bill, and that this proposition is originating such a bill? If it be, where shall we stop? If the idea of such a measure, which first passes through the mind, be confounded with the measure subsequent to it, what confusion will ensue? The President, by suggesting the proposition, may as well be pretended to originate a revenue bill; even a newspaper plan would be a breach of the exclusive privilege of this House, and the liberty of the press, so justly dear to us, would be found unconstitutional. Yet if, without any order of the House, the draft of an act were printed, and a copy laid before every member in his seat, no person will venture to say that it is a bill—that it is originated, or can be brought under cognizance of the House, unless by a motion.

I rely upon it that neither the letter of the Constitution, nor any meaning that it can be tortured into, will support the objection which has so often been urged with solemn emphasis and persevering zeal.

We may repeat it, what color is there for saying that the Secretary *legislates?* Neither my memory nor my understanding can discern any. I am well aware that no topic is better calculated to make popular impressions; but I cannot persuade myself that they will charge us with neglect or violation of duty, for putting ourselves into a situation to discharge it in the best and most circumspect manner.

Mr. Madison.—I insisted that a reference to the Secretary of the Treasury on subjects of loans, taxes, and provisions for loans, etc., was in fact a delegation of the authority of the legislature, although it would admit of much sophistical argument to the contrary.

The funding system generally, the assumption of the State debts, the national bank, and duties on domestic spirits had already been made objects of the most severe attack, and the Secretary of the Treasury, who was considered as the author of them, had become very unpopular in some parts of the Union.

The difference between the heads of the departments of State and Treasury on some important questions which had been agitated in the Cabinet was well known and felt in Congress and elsewhere. Thomas Jefferson was considered by the Federalists as hostile to the Constitution, and was accused of being opposed to the Administration of which he was a member, and of taking measures to reduce the powers of the general Government within too narrow limits. By the anti-Federalists, on the other hand, Alexander Hamilton was viewed not only as the author of the funding system, the national bank, and other measures deemed either unconstitutional or highly injurious to the public interest, but was also charged with hostility to republican principles and State rights.

Giles's Resolution Against Hamilton

During this session an inquiry was instituted in the House of Representatives into the official conduct of the Secretary of the Treasury. This was commenced by William B. Giles [Va.]—who was instigated, it is thought, by Madison—by calling for information from the President and Secretary relative to loans negotiated in pursuance of the acts of 1790, and the management and application of these loans, as well as the application and management of the revenue generally. The resolutions introduced for the purpose of obtaining this information were adopted by the House. The object of the mover was disclosed in his remarks in support of them at the end of which he said: "Candor, however, induces me to acknowledge that impressions resulting from my inquiries into this subject have been made upon my mind by no means favorable to the arrangements made by the gentleman at the head of the Treasury Department."

The report of the Secretary, in answer to this call for information, evinced that his pride was not a little wounded by the remarks of Mr. Giles. "The resolutions," he said, "to which I am to answer were not moved without a pretty copious display of the reasons on which they were founded. These reasons are of a nature to excite attention, to beget alarm, to inspire doubts.

"Deductions of a very extraordinary complexion may, without forcing the sense, be drawn from them. I feel it incumbent upon me to meet the suggestions which have been thrown out with decision and explicitness."

Having endeavored to show the fallacy of the statements made by the mover of the resolutions, in conclusion he observed: "Thus have I not only furnished a just and affirmative view of the real situation of the public accounts, but have likewise shown, I trust, in a conspicuous manner, fallacies enough in the statements from which the inference of an unaccounted for balance is drawn to evince that it is one tissue of error."

Soon after this report was made Mr. Giles submitted

to the House several resolutions containing charges against the Secretary. The subject of them was that he had failed to give Congress information, in due time, of moneys drawn from Europe; that he had violated the law of the 4th of August, 1790, by an unauthorized application of money borrowed under it; that he had drawn part of the money into the United States without any instructions from the President; that he had exceeded his authority in making loans under the acts; that, without instructions from the President, he had drawn more of the money borrowed in Holland than he was authorized by those acts, and that he had been guilty of indecorum to the House in undertaking to judge its motives in calling for information. The charges contained in these resolutions being considered either frivolous or unsupported, the resolutions themselves were negatived by large majorities. In the spring of 1794 Giles again brought forward his charges against Hamilton, moving for an investigation into his official conduct. An investigating committee was appointed, of which Giles was made chairman. It completely exonerated Hamilton.

Hamilton's Report on Public Credit

On January 15, 1795, the Secretary of the Treasury submitted a plan to Congress for the redemption of the public debt.

The subject of making provision for the redemption of the public debt in accordance with the recommendation of the President in his message occasioned much debate as well as great division in the House of Representatives.

It was a favorite measure with the Secretary of the Treasury as well as with the President. The former, on the 15th of January, 1795, submitted to Congress a plan for this purpose, drawn with his usual ability.

The Secretary proposed an increase of the sinking fund by adding to it duties on imports and tonnage, on spirits distilled within the United States, and on stills, the avails of the sales of the public lands, the dividends on bank stock belonging to the United States, and the interest of the money which should be redeemed, together with all moneys which should be received from debts due to the United States antecedent to the Constitution, and all surpluses of the amount of revenues which should remain at the end of every calendar year beyond the amount of appropriations charged upon them, and which, during the session of Congress commencing next thereafter, should not be especially appropriated. This fund was to be applied to the payment of the six per cent. and deferred stock, according to the right reserved to the United States, that is, to the payment of eight per cent. on account of the principal and interest; and was to continue until the whole should be paid and redeemed; and, after such redemption, the same fund was to continue appropriated until the residue of the debt of the United States, foreign and domestic, funded and unfunded, should be redeemed and discharged. The faith of the United States was to be firmly pledged to the creditors for the inviolable application of this fund to the payment of the debts until the same should be fully completed; and for this purpose the fund was to be vested in the commissioners of the sinking fund as *"property in trust."*

The importance of this measure for the purpose of preventing the evils arising from a great accumulation of debt was pressed upon Congress by the Secretary in a manner calculated to produce conviction.

"There is no sentiment which can better deserve the serious attention of the legislature of a country than the one expressed in the speech of the President, which indicates the danger to every government from the progressive accumulation of debt. A tendency to it is perhaps *the natural disease* of all governments; and it is not easy to conceive anything more likely than this to lead to great and convulsive revolutions of empires. On the one hand, the exigencies of a nation creating new causes of expenditure, as well from its own, as from the ambition, rapacity, injustice, intemperance, and folly of other nations, proceed in increasing and rapid succession. On the other, there is a general propensity in those who administer the affairs of government, founded in the constitution of man, to shift off the burden from the present to a future day; a propensity which may be expected to be strong in proportion as the form of the state is popular."

The difficulties arising from this propensity in a republican government, as well as the inconsistency of those who, to obtain popularity, will loudly declaim against the accumulation of debt, and in favor of its reduction as *abstract questions;* and yet, from the same motives, will as loudly declaim against the very means which can alone prevent the one and effect the other, were stated by the Secretary with great perspicuity.

"To extinguish a debt which exists, and to avoid contracting more, are ideas almost always favored by public feeling and opinion, but to pay taxes for the one or the other purpose, which are the only means to avoid the evil, is always more or less unpopular. These contradictions are in human nature. And the lot of a country would be enviable indeed in which there were not always men ready to turn them to the account of their own popularity, or to some other sinister account. Hence it is no uncommon spectacle to see the same man clamoring for occasions of expense, when they happen to be in unison with the present humor of the community, well or ill directed; declaiming against a public debt, and for the reduction of it; yet vehement against every plan of taxation which is proposed to discharge old debts, or to avoid new, by defraying the expenses of exigencies as they emerge."

Act to Redeem the Public Debt

An act was finally passed on this subject during this session, substantially in accordance with the plan suggested by Secretary Hamilton, though Congress were divided on the question of pledging the internal duties. The funds appropriated for the reimbursement and redemption of the debt were by law *vested* in the commissioners of the sinking fund, *in trust* for that object, and the faith of the United States was pledged that the funds should inviolably so remain appropriated and vested until the whole debt should be paid.

These funds were to be applied to the payment of eight per cent. per annum on account of the principal and interest of the six per cent. deferred stock, and the surplus to the payment of the other debts, foreign and domestic. In pursuance of this compact with the public creditors the six per cent. stock was fully paid in the year 1818 and the deferred stock in 1824.

The total amount of the unredeemed debt of the United States (including the assumed debt) in 1795 was $76,096,468.17.

The chief supporters of Hamilton's plan were Fisher Ames [Mass.] and Theodore Sedgwick [Mass.]; the chief opponent was James Madison [Va.], who particularly objected to pledging the internal duties.

Redemption of the Public Debt

House of Representatives, December 23, 1794-March 2, 1795

Mr. Ames.—I am one of those who believe a nation ought to cherish public credit, for the same reason that it ought to have strength; for, in critical situations, credit is strength, and the want of it may happen to be not only weakness, but subjugation and ruin. And it is my belief that, although it may answer for a time to pay the interest, and neglect the principal, yet, at last, and in the course of affairs, it will appear that a nation which neglects to pay its debts will have no credit. That would be the case with an individual. Besides, if we neglect the interval of peace and prosperity to pay off, lessen, and, if possible, to extinguish the debt, we cannot expect, for any length of time, to avoid the occasion of adding to it. We have had eleven years of peace, one-half of which term, for want of a government, our debt was augmenting at least twelve or fifteen millions of dollars. It has been funded four years nearly, and less than three millions are yet paid off. Are we to hope for peace always? A blessing so great has been hitherto denied, perhaps in benevolence as well as wisdom, to the prayers of devotion and the tears of philanthropy, and, from all we know of the nature and history of man, we have reason to believe, if not to desire, that war will sometimes fall to the lot of a nation. Peace is the time to prepare for it, by extinguishing the burdens of the last war, by exhibiting, as a basis of present exultation, and, as a ground of future confidence and credit, the novel spectacle of a great nation which has freed itself from debt.

It is true the opposers of the resolution are not bound to adopt the plan nor to continue these very duties, but they are bound by more than common sanctions to go even beyond the description of persons whom they have accused, in some plan, and to provide other taxes. No puny operation, no halfway measures will do. They stand pledged for some strong system, some efficient funds to bring into activity at least all the present revenue faculties of the country.

That bugbear, the irredeemable quality, so artificially conjured up to terrify the country, opposes no obstacle to the redemption of all this great amount—a mass of debt far exceeding the most extravagant conjectures of the product of the revenue for many years to come. And here let me observe, the argument almost solely opposed to the resolution is this: We have revenue enough, without the temporary taxes. Let it be allowed that we have, for argument's sake, what follows? That we have too much revenue with the temporary taxes. Will our money rust in the treasury chest for want of debt to employ it upon? Shall we not make greater progress with all the present taxes than with only a part of them? Is it a time to refuse the aid of these temporary taxes when we are finding out a new way for employing the product? Shall we, with any color of wisdom, go on at the same instant to extend our expenses and to diminish the income of the taxes? The argument that these taxes are not wanted is utterly hostile to the professions we make of paying off the public burdens as fast as possible. If the statement to support this reasoning is true, it is not so much an objection as an encouragement to our progress in the plan, as it proves, by the documents adduced on one side, that the other has under-reckoned the calculations of success.

It is objected against the resolution that fluctuations of the revenue laws are undesirable. It is true that shifting, unsteady laws are a public evil, and they are always felt as such by the dealers in the taxed articles. The first effect of a tax is a little to stagnate and derange the business of the dealers, but soon the current finds its way again, and the tax becomes a part of the price, a part of the settled order of things, which a hasty repeal would derange anew. This argument, it is said, requires that all resource laws should be permanent. Where there is a permanent occasion for taxes, and the proper objects of taxation are known to be selected, the fluctuation of the revenue laws would be an evil, and therefore it would be proper to make them permanent. But when the call for taxes is temporary, or the mode of collection untried, the limitation of the bill to a short period may be no less proper.

Continuation of these taxes, it is said, will destroy manufacture of the commodities. If we regard the experience of other nations, we shall not find cause to dread the destruction of manufactures in consequence of taxes. Is England exempted from taxes, and yet where do manufactures flourish more? The truth is, in an increasing, thriving society, taxes are absorbed, and distributed over the whole mass of the community. No problem has been oftener debated than where the taxes ultimately fall, and yet experience has invariably refuted the gloomy anticipations of interested theory. The language that infant manufactures are not to be crushed is more declamatory than correct. They are not to be crushed; nor will the manufactures of snuff and loaf sugar fall, if the operation of the tax should be like that of other taxes, or of similar taxes in other countries.

A great object is before us, and if, after all, its attainment shall appear to be obstructed by much seeming and some real difficulty and embarrassment, still we owe it to our country, as well as to our own engagements, to proceed. Let us endeavor to overcome the prejudices of the over-apprehensive, and to conciliate the interests of the manufacturers with those of the public. In our other taxes we suppose it is done, and why should it be despaired of in this case? Greater difficulties than any that a calm and unprejudiced mind will discern in the plan before us ought to be expected, and readily acquiesced in, rather than to abandon the great object of freeing the nation from debt. It is worth some exertion and sacrifice. If we should effect it, any hopes of the destinies of our Government would brighten. There is nothing in the magnitude of the debt to discourage us, and still less in the prosperous circumstances and good dispositions of our citizens. It depends on ourselves whether we realize their expectations by acting in conformity with our own professions.

Mr. Madison.—Permanent taxes such as on property should be applied to permanent purposes, such as reducing the public debt, and temporary taxes, such as on manufactures, to temporary objects, such as the military establishment. If excises were to be preferred in reducing the public debt, it was in vain to hope they could be limited to a few trifling subjects, such as manufactured snuff and sugar. They must be extended to all the manufactures. The whole country would be covered in fact with excises. Every manufactory must be made to contribute, and even then it would not be possible to draw forth as much revenue as would be paid in the other mode. He was aware that objections and prejudices existed against a tax laid on property. He regretted that such a difference of opinion prevailed, not only in Congress, but in different parts of the Union, on this subject. He was persuaded, nevertheless, that a tax on property was not only a more economical, and in every respect a more eligible resource, than a general system of excises, yielding the same amount of revenue, but that, on the whole, a majority of the people of America would be found less averse to it. He could speak with confidence on this point, as far as his own communications extended. Much, he thought, of the dislike to a tax on property might be removed by taking different objects in different States, as might be most convenient or acceptable to them.

This was perfectly consistent with the Constitution, which did not require uniformity in this instance. In some States a tax on land, in others a tax on other articles of property, or partly on land and partly on other articles, might be most satisfactory; and the tax laws of the States would always assist in digesting the regulations for the purpose. He supposed that if this course should be taken a million or even two millions of dollars or more could be raised in a year, and that the people would be willing to make such an exertion, rather than be saddled with a permanent debt; whereas he did not believe that an excise system, if extended to every article manufactured in the country, could be made to produce anything like such a sum.

All that was aimed at at this time with respect to the debt would be attained by allotting the temporary part of the revenue to temporary purposes.

Mr. Sedgwick.—Now is the time to reduce our public debt. When we compare our own debt with the more enormous ones of some other countries, we are too apt to console ourselves with its comparative smallness. Yet I would call your attention to the fact that, in the year of 1697, when there were more anxious forebodings of ruin from that source than perhaps at any period since, the debt of Great Britain was comparatively less than ours is now. Had the Government then, in earnest, attempted a reduction, it might have been effectually done, with less annual revenue than is now required, in time of peace, for their ordinary expenditure.

Whenever a provision for the public credit shall be beyond the public faculties, confusion and ruin must be the consequence. That cause has destroyed the strongest government in Europe. This we all hope will prove a blessing. The same event here would blast the best hopes of the lovers of mankind.

Among all the causes which have operated to prevent the reduction of public debts, none has been more influential than that of diverting revenues appropriated to that purpose to other objects. If our appropriations of this kind shall be violated, we may despair of our country being ever discharged of its load of debts. To secure us against this evil, provision must be made, concomitantly with a sinking fund, for the other necessary expenses of government, and also an allowance made for those unforeseen and contingent demands which cannot be computed, but which will always occur. Otherwise we may be assured, unless America is to be exempted from the evils which have afflicted other countries, that our intention, however patriotic, will be defeated by a diversion of our permanent appropriations to temporary purposes. Our legislators may feel interested in the continuance of the debt; they may want energy of character; they may be indolent; they may meanly dread a loss of popularity, from imposing necessary burdens, or all these may combine to form a precedent, which, being once established, we may bid adieu to hope.

I will take the liberty of stating some of the reasons which have struck my mind with the greatest force why we should honestly unite in the attempt to reduce the public debt.

1. A debt, as an embarrassment to the faculties of a country, is an evil. To this there are, at some times, and in some countries, causes which counteract this evil, perhaps, in some instances, overbalance it; but I am confident those causes do not here operate to an extent which should induce us, for a moment, to suspend our efforts to reduce the debt.

2. A very cogent reason, and one which will influence every true patriot, is that our debt has been made a principal and ostensibly almost the only source of party. No man, then, who wishes a union of councils, a fraternity of sentiments, will seek for plausible reasons to defeat this important measure.

3. The experience of other countries has demonstrated a general disinclination in governments to liberate the pledged funds of the community. Every extraordinary demand accumulates, of course, the debt, and in the end must prove ruinous. It will be vain for us to profess ourselves the friends of republican government, and the admirers of our political institutions, if we are not, by the examples of others, warned against this evil.

4. A great portion of our debt is owned by foreigners, and from the value of capital here, compared with other countries,

we have reason to fear the evil will increase. It must be unnecessary to dwell on the impoverishing effects of a continued drain of specie from the community.

5. The proposed measure will, in my opinion, beyond any expedient which could be devised, tend to fix the market price of our six per cent. stock at par. This would make that species of debt less a subject, and more an instrument of commerce; and instead of acquiring it would supply the place of capital; and it would also enable the Government to employ beneficially our surplus of revenues in purchases in the market.

7. This measure will make us financially independent. Whatever our exigencies may be, we may be compelled to rely on our ordinary resources, without much aid from borrowing; for, from the smallness and value of capital here, we ought not to rely on domestic loans; and the uncertain issue of the troubles in Europe would prove it madness to depend on foreign aid.

CHAPTER II

Constitutionality of a National Bank

[The First United States Bank Charter]

Chartering of the First National Bank—Debate: in Favor, Fisher Ames [Mass.]; Opposed, James Madison [Va.]—Expiration of the Bank's Charter—Debate in the Senate on Its Renewal: in Favor, William H. Crawford [Ga.] and John Pope [Ky.]; Opposed, William B. Giles [Va.] and Henry Clay [Ky.]; Charter Is Not Renewed.

UPON the recommendation of Alexander Hamilton, Secretary of the Treasury, Congress, on February 25, 1791, chartered a national bank to aid in the management of the national finances. The preamble of the act declared that:

"The bank will be conducive to the successful conducting of the national finances, give facility to the obtaining of loans for the use of the Government in sudden emergencies, and will also be productive of considerable advantage to trade and industry in general."

The capital stock of the bank was ten millions of dollars, two millions to be subscribed for the benefit of the United States, and the residue by individuals. One-fourth of the sums subscribed by individuals was to be paid in gold and silver, and three-fourths in the public debt. By the act of incorporation it was to be a bank of discount as well as deposit, and its bills, which were payable in gold and silver on demand, were made receivable in all payments to the United States. The bank was located at Philadelphia, with power in the directors to establish offices of discount and deposit only, wherever they should think fit, within the United States.

The duration of the charter was limited to the 4th of March, 1811, and the faith of the United States was pledged that, during that period, no other bank should be established under their authority. One of the fundamental articles of the incorporation was that no loan should be made to the United States for more than one hundred thousand dollars, or to any particular State for more than fifty thousand, or to any foreign prince or State, unless previously authorized by a law of the United States. The books were opened for subscriptions in July, 1791, and a much larger sum subscribed than was allowed by the charter; and the bank went into successful operation. This measure was not adopted without warm and violent debates.

On the Establishment of a National Bank

House of Representatives, February 2-7, 1791

It was said in opposition, in the first place, that Congress had no power under the Constitution to create this or any other corporation; in the second place, that so large a moneyed institution would, in its effects, be highly injurious to the community.

Its advocates, on the other hand, contended generally that the establishment of an institution of this kind, though not within the express words of the Constitution, was among the incidental powers contemplated by that part of the instrument which enabled Congress to make all laws *necessary* and *proper* for carrying into execution the powers expressly granted.

An institution of this kind, they said, was necessary and proper for the attainment of the important ends contemplated in the Constitution; and that similar establishments, in all well-regulated communities, had been found necessary in the management of their finances and for the attainment of the great ends of civil government. In answer its opponents said that the Constitution was not only silent on the subject, but that no such power was intended to be granted by the framers of that instrument; that, in the general convention, a proposition to give Congress power to create corporations was made and negatived. It was a power, they said, too important to be assumed by implication; nor could they agree to so broad a construction as was given by the advocates of the measure to the words "*necessary* and *proper*," as used in the Constitution. No means they considered to be *necessary* for the purpose of carrying into execution the *specified powers*, except those without which the powers granted would be *nugatory*, or the ends contemplated *absolutely unattainable*.

The leaders in the debate were James Madison [Va.] and Fisher Ames [Mass.], respectively opposing and advocating the bank.

The bill was passed by a vote of 39 to 20. President Washington before approving the bill requested the opinions of the members of his Cabinet, in writing, as to its constitutionality. The Secretary of State [Thomas Jefferson] and Attorney-General [Edmund Randolph] were of the opinion that the bill was unconstitutional, while the Secretaries of the Treasury [Alexander Hamilton] and of War [Henry Knox] were of a different opinion and concurred with the majority in Congress. After mature deliberation the President put his signature to the bill.

Expiration of the National Bank Charter

The charter of the Bank of the United States expiring by law on March 4, 1811, on December 16, 1810, William Findley [Pa.] presented in the House of Representatives a petition from the stockholders of the bank, signed by David Lenox, the president, praying the renewal of its charter. The petition was referred to a select committee, which, on January 4, 1811, reported a bill to renew the act of incorporation. The question came before the House on January 16, and was debated exhaustively until January 24, when, by a vote of 65 to 64, the bill was defeated.

In this debate the constitutional arguments which were advanced developed those which had been presented when the bank was chartered in 1790. The chief advocate of the bank was a dead man, the great Secretary of the Treasury, Alexander Hamilton, copies of whose pam-

THE GHOST OF A DOLLAR, OR THE BANKER'S SURPRISE

From the collection of the New York Public Library

phlets, "On the Constitutionality of a National Bank," were distributed among the Representatives by agents of the bank.

The petition for the renewal of the charter was presented in the Senate on December 18, 1810, and referred to a select committee, which in due time presented a bill to renew the act of incorporation. The Senate debated the bill from February 11 to February 20, 1811, when it was defeated by the casting vote of the presiding officer, George Clinton [N. Y.], Vice-President of the United States.

Senator Benton remarks in his "Debates of Congress":

> Thus terminated the existence of the first bank of the United States; but there was a fatal defect in terminating it in not providing a general currency in place of its notes, by reviving the gold currency, and in not creating an independent treasury for keeping the public moneys. Those who terminated the existence of the second bank [in 1834] avoided these errors, and thereby avoided all the evils and embarrassments which followed the termination of the first one.

In the debate in the Senate the chief advocates of the bank were William H. Crawford, of Georgia, and John Pope, of Kentucky; the chief opponents were William B. Giles, of Virginia, and Henry Clay, of Kentucky.

Senator Clay, while joining with the strict construction Republicans in this measure, showed the beginning of his opposition to that party by twitting Senator Giles, its protagonist, upon the contradictions into which he was led by an extreme application of his theory, yet, by his own opposition to the bank, Senator Clay laid a far more substantial basis for the charge of inconsistency against himself, since in 1816 he supported the application for a new charter.[1]

Senator Pope showed his animosity toward his fellow Kentuckian, Senator Clay, by a rather demagogic "insinuendo" (to employ a useful term coined in later years by a Representative from North Carolina) against his colleague, who had been elected to fill a vacancy in the Senate by an opposing faction in the State.

[1] See page 54 ss.

Constitutionality of a National Bank

Senate, February 11-20, 1811

Senator Crawford.—The object of the Constitution was twofold: first, the delegation of certain general powers, of a national nature, to the Government of the United States; and, second, the limitation or restriction of the State sovereignties. Upon the most thorough examination of this instrument I am induced to believe that many of the various constructions given to it are the result of a belief that it is absolutely perfect. It has become so extremely fashionable to eulogize this Constitution, whether the object of the eulogist is the extension or contraction of the powers of the Government, that whenever its eulogium is pronounced I feel an involuntary apprehension of mischief. Upon the faith of this imputed perfection it has been declared to be inconsistent with the entire spirit and character of this instrument to suppose that after it has given a general power it should afterward delegate a specific power fairly comprehended within the general power. A rational analysis of the Constitution will refute in the most demonstrative manner this idea of its perfection.

In the present case, if there be any who, under the conviction that the Constitution is perfect, are disposed to give it a construction that will render it wholly imbecile, the public welfare requires that the veil should be rent, and that its imperfection should be disclosed to public view. By this disclosure it will cease to be the object of adoration, but it will nevertheless be entitled to our warmest attachment.

The eighth section of the first article of the Constitution contains five grants of general power. Under the power to coin money it is conceived that Congress would have a right to provide for the punishment of counterfeiting the money after it was coined, and that this power is fairly incidental to, and comprehended in, the general power. The power to raise armies and provide and maintain a navy comprehends, beyond the possibility of doubt, the right to make rules for the government and regulation of the land and naval forces; and yet in these three cases the Constitution, after making the grant of general power, delegates specifically the powers which are fairly comprehended within the general power. Under the power to regulate commerce, Congress has exercised the power of erecting light-houses, as incident to that power, and fairly comprehended within it. Under the power to establish post-offices and post roads, Congress has provided for the punishment of offences against the Post-Office Department. If the Congress can exercise an incidental power not granted in one case, it can in all cases of a similar kind. But it is said that the enumeration of certain powers excludes all other powers not enumerated. This is true so far as original substantive grants of power are concerned, but it is not true when applied to express grants of power, which are strictly incidental to some original and substantive grant of power. If all incidental powers are excluded except the few which are enumerated this would exclude from all claim to constitutionality nearly one-half of your laws, and, what is still more to be deprecated, would render your Constitution equally imbecile with the old Articles of Confederation.

When we come to examine the fourth article, the absurdity of this rule of construction, and also of the idea of perfection which has been attributed to the Constitution, will be equally manifest. This article appears to be of a miscellaneous character and very similar to the codicil of a will. The first three articles provide for the three great departments of government called into existence by the Constitution, but some other provisions just then occur, which ought to have been included in one or the other of the preceding articles, and these provisions are incorporated and compose the fourth article.

In the first section express authority has been given to Congress to prescribe the manner in which the records, etc., should be proved, and also the effect thereof, but in the other two [relating to extradition of criminals and return of fugitive slaves and bond servants] no authority is given to Congress, and yet the bare inspection of the three cases will prove that the interference of Congress is less necessary in the first than in the two remaining cases. According, however, to the rule of construction contended for, Congress cannot pass any law to carry the Constitution into effect in the two last cases selected, because express power has been given in the first and is withheld in the two last. Congress has nevertheless passed laws to carry those provisions into effect, and this exercise of power has never been complained of by the people or the States.

But it is said the advocates of the bank differ among themselves in fixing upon the general power to which the right to create a bank is incidental, and that this difference proves that there is no incidentality, to use a favorite expression, between that and any one of the enumerated general powers. The same reason can be urged, with equal force, against the constitutionality of every law for the erection of light-houses. Let the advocates of this doctrine lay their finger upon the power to which the right of erecting light-houses is incidental. It can be derived with as much apparent plausibility and reason from the right to lay duties as from the right to regulate commerce. Who is there, now, in this body who has not voted for the erection of a light-house? And no man in the nation, so far as my knowledge extends, has ever complained of the exercise of this power. The right to erect light-houses is exercised because the commerce of the nation or the collection of duties is greatly facilitated by that means; and, sir, the right to create a bank is exercised because the collection of your revenue and the safe-keeping and easy and speedy transmission of your public money are not simply facilitated, but because these important objects are more perfectly secured by the erection of a bank than they can be by any other means in the power of human imagination to devise. We say, therefore, in the words of the Constitution, that a bank is necessary and proper to enable the Government to carry into complete effect the right to lay and collect taxes, imposts, duties, and excises. We do not say that the existence of the Government absolutely depends upon the operations of a bank, but that a national bank enables the Government to manage its fiscal concerns more advantageously than it could do by any other means. The terms necessary and proper, according to the construction given to every part of the Constitution, impose no limitation upon the powers previously delegated. If these words had been omitted in the clause giving authority to pass laws to carry into execution the powers vested by the Constitution in the national Government, still Congress would have been bound to pass laws which were necessary and proper, and not such as were unnecessary and improper. Every legislative body, every person invested with power of any kind, is morally bound to use only those means which are necessary and proper for the correct execution of the powers delegated to them. But it is contended that, if a bank is necessary and proper for the management of the fiscal concerns of the nation, yet Congress has no power to incorporate one, because there are State banks which may be resorted to. Can it be seriously contended that, because the Constitution has in some cases made the Government of the United States dependent upon the State governments, in all which cases it has imposed the most solemn obligations upon them to act, that it will be necessary and proper for Congress to make itself dependent upon them in cases where no such obligation is imposed? The Constitution has defined all the cases where this Government ought to be dependent upon the State governments; and it would be unwise and improvident for us to multiply these cases by legislative acts, especially where we have no power to compel them to perform the act for which we have made ourselves their dependents. In forming a permanent system of revenue, it would be unwise in Congress to rely, for its collection and transmission from one extreme of this extensive empire to the other, upon any accidental circumstance, wholly beyond their power or control. There are State banks in almost every State in the Union, but their existence is wholly independent of this Government, and their dissolution is equally so. The Secretary of the Treasury [Albert Gallatin] has informed you that he conceives a bank is necessary to the legitimate exercise of the powers vested by the Constitution in the Government. His testimony is entitled to great weight in the decision of this question, at least with those gentlemen who have no knowledge of the practical effects of the operation of the bank in the collection, safe-keeping, and transmission of your revenue. In the selection of means to carry any of your constitutional powers into effect, you must exercise a sound discretion; acting under its influence, you will discover that what is proper at one time may be extremely unfit and improper at another. The original powers granted to the Government by the Constitution can never change with the varying circumstances of the country, but the means by which those powers are to be carried into effect must necessarily vary with the varying state and circumstances of the nation. We are, when acting to-day, not to inquire what means were necessary and proper twenty years ago, not what were necessary and proper at the organization of the Government, but our inquiry must be, what means are necessary and proper this day. The Constitution, in relation to the means by which its powers are to be executed, is one eternal *now*. The state of things now, the precise point of time when we are called upon to act, must determine our choice in the selection of means to execute the delegated powers.

Senator Giles.—The gentleman from Georgia [Senator Crawford] proceeded to remark that in taking a review of the Constitution he found general as well as incidental powers enumerated therein. I did not see the precise application the gentleman intended to make of this remark, but I have been induced to review the Constitution in reference to this subject, and it does appear to me that the classification and definition of powers are as well arranged as human wisdom could devise. I know that nothing is perfect which is the work of man; that no language is capable of perfect definition. But, as far as definition can be drawn from language, I conceive the Constitution exhibits as perfect an example as is in existence. In the next place, the gentleman remarked that there were a number of cases in which Congress had departed from the particular enumerated powers in the Constitution, and had resorted to implication or construction for the derivation of its powers. The remark is perfectly correct, and I am very ready to admit that there is no such thing as carrying into effect enumerated powers in any instrument whatever without the intervention of certain derivative and implied powers. But, if the gentleman had succeeded in showing that there had been aberrations by the Congress of the United States from the enumerated powers of the Constitution, would he think it correct to use those aberrations as precedents for still further aberrations? Ought they not rather to be considered as mementoes on the part of Congress to induce them to tread with more care, and, if they find that their former errors could not be supported by a fair and candid construction of the Constitution, to restrain the laws within its wholesome provisions?

I will now, Mr. President, proceed to examine those instances which the gentleman has presented of the supposed aberrations of the Congress of the United States from the enumerated powers, and I think it will not be difficult to show that there is not a single instance quoted but which is deducible from a fair and correct interpretation of the express words of the Constitution, giving them their common and appropriate meaning.

The first instance presented to our consideration by the honorable gentleman from Georgia [Senator Crawford] of the exercise of a power by Congress not enumerated in the Constitution was the erection of light-houses. The gentleman from Massachusetts [Senator Lloyd] superadded the instance of the erection of custom-houses.

I think Congress possesses the power to erect light-houses and custom-houses by the express words of the Constitution; for both of these descriptions of houses must necessarily be included within the term "needful buildings." But, if this term "needful buildings" had not been expressed in the Constitution, I should not hesitate to admit with these gentlemen that the erection of light-houses and custom-houses might properly be deduced from the power to lay and collect taxes, duties, etc., which are particular grants of power enumerated in the Constitution. Because custom-houses are appropriately necessary to the collection of duties, and have always been deemed indispensable for that object, as are light-houses to the due regulation of commerce.

The gentlemen, reasoning from a supposed analogy, have asked, if Congress can derive the right to erect light-houses and custom-houses from their necessary agency in effectuating the particular powers to which they are said to be appendant or appurtenant, why may it not in the same way derive the right of granting charters of incorporation for the same objects? The question is admitted to be a fair one; and, if a clear distinction cannot be made in the two cases, it will be admitted either that Congress may constitutionally establish a bank or that it has heretofore transcended its powers in erecting custom-houses, etc. A clear and most obvious distinction appears to me to exist in the cases suggested by the gentlemen to be analogous, arising from the striking difference in the nature and essential character of these powers. A custom-house is in its nature incidental and subservient to the collection of duties. It is one of the common, necessary, and proper means to effect that end. It is believed that in no commercial country in the world are duties collected without them. Besides, the erection of custom-houses does not involve in it the exercise of any other higher or consequential powers. The same remarks will apply to light-houses, as among the common, necessary, and proper means for the regulation of commerce, etc.

Is the incorporation of a bank of this character? No. It wants that connection, affiliation, and subserviency to some enumerated power which are clearly pointed out in relation to the two powers to which it has been said to be analogous. Besides, does granting a charter of incorporation to a bank involve no other higher or consequential power than merely erecting a needful building for collecting duties, etc.? It certainly does. It involves the power to grant charters of incorporation generally; and in this respect, principally, its character is essentially different from both of the powers cited by the gentleman. The power to grant charters of incorporation is not an incidental, subordinate, substantive power. It is a distinct, original, substantive power. It is also susceptible of the clearest definition; and, not being among the enumerated powers, it seems to me that Congress can have no fair claim to its exercise in any case. If Congress had been expressly authorized to grant charters of incorporation generally, then granting a charter of incorporation to a bank would have been an instance, or among the means, of carrying into effect that enumerated power, and would have been as much connected and affiliated with it as is the erection of custom-houses with the collection of duties. I do not mean to exaggerate the consequences which might result from an assumption of the power to grant charters of incorporation, etc. It is sufficient for me to say that it is a power of primary importance; that it involves as many incidental powers in its exercise as any one of the enumerated powers; that it is equal, if not paramount, to any; and, therefore, in my judgment, cannot be assumed by fair construction as incidental and subservient to any; and, of course, not as among the necessary and proper means for carrying any into effect.

Senator Clay.—As this subject, at the memorable period when the charter was granted, called forth the best talents of the nation; as it has, on various occasions, undergone the most thorough investigation; and as we can hardly expect that it is susceptible of receiving any further elucidation, it was to have been hoped that we should have been spared a useless debate. This was the more desirable because there are, I conceive, much superior claims upon us for every hour of the small portion of the session yet remaining to us. Under the operation of these motives, I had resolved to give a silent vote, until I felt myself bound, by the defying manner of the arguments advanced in support of the renewal, to obey the paramount duties I owe my country and its Constitution; to make one effort, however feeble, to avert the passage of what appears to me a most unjustifiable law.

After my honorable friend from Virginia [Senator Giles] had instructed and amused us with the very able and ingenious argument which he delivered on yesterday, I should have still forborne to trespass on the Senate but for the extraordinary character of his speech. He discussed both sides of the question, with great ability and eloquence, and certainly demonstrated to the satisfaction of all who heard him both that it was constitutional and unconstitutional, highly proper and improper to prolong the charter of the bank. The honorable gentleman appeared to me in the predicament in which the celebrated orator of Virginia, Patrick Henry, is said to have been once placed. Engaged in a most extensive and lucrative practice of the law, he mistook in one instance the side of the cause on which he was retained and addressed the court and jury in a very splendid and convincing speech in behalf of his antagonist. His distracted client came up to him while he was progressing, and, interrupting him, bitterly exclaimed, "You have undone me! you have ruined me!"—"Never mind, give yourself no concern,'' said the adroit advocate; and, turning to the court and jury, continued his argument by observing, ''May it please your honors, and you, gentlemen of the jury, I have been stating to you what I presume my adversary may urge on his side. I will now show you how fallacious his reasoning and groundless his pretensions are.'' The skillful orator proceeded, satisfactorily refuted every argument he had advanced, and gained his cause! A success with which I trust the exertion of my honorable friend will on this occasion be crowned.

The gentleman from Georgia [Senator Crawford], after wandering throughout the whole Constitution in quest of some congenial spot whereon to fasten, has at length located it on that provision which authorizes Congress to lay and collect taxes, etc. In 1791 the power is referred to one part of the instrument; in 1811 to another. Sometimes it is alleged to be deducible from the power to regulate commerce. Hard pressed here, it disappears, and shows itself under the grant to coin money. The sagacious Secretary of the Treasury [Alexander Hamilton] in 1791 pursued the wisest course—he has taken shelter behind general, high-sounding, and imposing terms. He has declared in the preamble to the act establishing the bank that it will be very conducive to the successful conducting of the national finances; will tend to give facility to the obtaining of loans, and will be productive of considerable advantage to trade and industry in general. No allusion is made to the collection of taxes. The power to charter companies is not specified in the Constitution, and I contend is of a nature not transferable by mere implication. It is one of the most exalted attributes of sovereignty. In the exercise of this gigantic power we have seen an East India Company created, which has carried dismay, desolation, and death throughout one of the largest portions of the habitable world. A company which is, in itself, a sovereignty—which has subverted empires and set up new dynasties—and has not only made war, but war against its legitimate sovereign! Under the influence of this power, we have seen arise a South Sea company, and a Mississippi company, that distracted and convulsed all Europe, and menaced a total overthrow of all credit and confidence, and universal bankruptcy. Is it to be imagined that a power so vast would have been left by the wisdom of the Constitution to doubtful inference? In deducing the power to create corporations from the power to collect taxes, the relation and condition of principal and incident are prostrated and destroyed. The accessory is exalted above the principal. As well might it be said that the great luminary of day is an accessory, a satellite to the humblest star that twinkles forth its feeble light in the firmament of heaven![1]

Suppose the Constitution had been silent as to an individual department of this Government, could you, under the power to lay and collect taxes, establish a judiciary? I presume not; but, if you could derive the power by mere implication, could you vest it with any other authority than to enforce the collection of the revenue? A bank is made for the ostensible purpose of aiding in the collection of the revenue, and, while it is engaged in this, the most inferior and subordinate of all its functions, it is made to diffuse itself through society, and to influence all the great operations of credit, circulation, and commerce. Like the Virginia justice, you tell the man whose turkey has been stolen that your book of precedents furnishes no form for his case, but then you will grant him a precept to search for a cow, and when looking for that he may possibly find his turkey! You say to this corporation, we cannot authorize you to discount —to emit paper—to regulate commerce, etc. No! Our book has no precedents of that kind. But then we can authorize you to collect the revenue, and, while occupied with that, you may do whatever else you please!

What is a corporation such as the bill contemplates? It is a splendid association of favored individuals, taken from the mass of society, and invested with exemptions and surrounded by immunities and privileges.

I contend that the States have the exclusive power to regulate contracts, to declare the capacities and incapacities to contract, and to provide as to the extent of responsibility of debtors to their creditors. If Congress have the power to erect an artificial body and say it shall be endowed with the attributes of an individual—if you can bestow on this object of your own creation the ability to contract, may you not, in contravention of State rights, confer upon slaves, infants, and *femmes couvertes* the ability to contract? And, if you have the power to say that an association of individuals shall be responsible for their debts only in a certain limited degree, what is to prevent an extension of a similar exemption to individuals? Where is the limitation upon this power to set up corporations? You establish one, in the heart of a State, the basis of whose capital is money. You may erect others whose capital shall consist of land, slaves, and personal estate, and thus the whole property within the jurisdiction of a State might be absorbed by these political bodies. The existing bank contends that it is beyond the power of a State to

[1] Senator Clay was evidently not strong on astronomy.

tax it, and, if this pretension be well founded, it is in the power of Congress, by chartering companies, to dry up the whole of the sources of State revenue. The United States own a great deal of land in the State of Ohio; can this Government, for the purpose of creating an ability to purchase it, charter a company? Aliens are forbidden, I believe, in that State, to hold real estate—could you, in order to multiply purchasers, confer upon them the capacity to hold land, in derogation of the local law? I imagine this will hardly be insisted upon; and yet there exists a more obvious connection between the undoubted power, which is possessed by this Government, to sell its land and the means of executing that power, by increasing the demand in the market, than there is between this bank and the collection of a tax. This Government has the power to levy taxes—to raise armies—provide a navy—make war—regulate commerce—coin money, etc. It would not be difficult to show as intimate a connection between a corporation, established for any purpose whatever, and some one or other of those great powers, as there is between the revenue and the bank of the United States.

It is urged by the gentleman from Massachusetts [Senator Lloyd] that, as this nation progresses in commerce, wealth, and population, new energies will be unfolded, new wants and exigencies will arise, and hence he infers that powers must be implied from the Constitution. But, sir, the question is, shall we stretch the instrument to embrace cases not fairly within its scope, or shall we resort to that remedy, by amendment, which the Constitution prescribes?

Gentlemen contend that the construction which they give to the Constitution has been acquiesced in by all parties, and under all administrations; and they rely particularly on an act which passed in 1804, for extending a branch to New Orleans, and another act, of 1807, for punishing those who should forge or utter forged paper of the bank. With regard to the first law, passed no doubt upon the recommendation of the Treasury Department, I would remark that it was the extension of a branch to a Territory, over which Congress possesses power of legislation almost uncontrolled, and where, without any constitutional impediment, charters of incorporation may be granted. As to the other act, it was passed no less for the benefit of the community than the bank—to protect the ignorant and unwary from counterfeit paper, purporting to have been emitted by the bank.

When gentlemen attempt to carry this measure, upon the ground of acquiescence or precedent, do they forget that we are not in Westminster Hall? In courts of justice, the utility of uniformity of decision exacts of the judge a conformity to the adjudication of his predecessor. In the interpretation and administration of the law this practice is wise and proper; and without it, everything depending upon the caprice of the judge, we should have no security for our dearest rights. It is far otherwise when applied to the source of legislation. Here no rule exists but the Constitution; and to legislate upon the ground merely that our predecessors thought themselves authorized, under similar circumstances, to legislate is to sanctify error and perpetuate usurpation. But, if we are to be subjected to the trammels of precedents, I claim, on the other hand, the benefit of the restrictions under which the intelligent judge cautiously receives them. It is an established rule that to give to a previous adjudication any effect the mind of the judge who pronounced must have been awakened to the subject, and it must have been a deliberate opinion formed after full argument. In technical language, it must not have been *sub silentio.* Now, the acts of 1804 and 1807, relied upon as pledges for rechartering this company, passed not only without any discussions whatever of the constitutional power of Congress to establish a bank, but, I venture to say, without a single member having had his attention drawn to this question. I had the honor of a seat in the Senate [1] when the latter law passed, probably voted for it; and I declare, with the utmost sincerity, that I never once thought of that point; and I appeal confidently to every honorable member who was then present to say if that was not his situation.

This doctrine of precedents, applied to the legislature, appears to me to be fraught with the most mischievous consequences. The great advantage of our system of government over all others is that we have a written Constitution defining its limits and prescribing its authorities; and that, however for a time faction may convulse the nation, and passion and party prejudice sway its functionaries, the season of reflection will recur when calmly retracing their deeds, and all aberrations from fundamental principle will be corrected. But once substitute practice for principle, the expositions of the Constitution for the text of the Constitution, and in vain shall we look for the instrument in the instrument itself. It will be as diffused and intangible as the pretended constitution of England; and it must be sought for in the statute book, in the fugitive journals of Congress, and in reports of the Secretary of the Treasury. What would be our condition if we were to take the interpreta-

[1] Senator Clay was then as now filling a vacancy.

tions given to that sacred book which is or ought to be the criterion of our faith for the book itself? We should find the Holy Bible buried beneath the interpretations, glosses, and comments of councils, synods, and learned divines, which have produced swarms of intolerant and furious sects, partaking less of the mildness and meekness of their origin than of a vindictive spirit of hostility toward each other. They ought to afford us a solemn warning to make that Constitution, which we have sworn to support, our invariable guide.

I conceive, then, sir, that we are not empowered by the Constitution nor bound by any practice under it to renew the charter of this bank and I might here rest the argument. But, as there are strong objections to the renewal upon the score of expediency, and as the distresses which will attend the dissolution of the bank have been greatly exaggerated, I will ask your indulgence for a few moments longer. That some temporary inconvenience will arise I shall not deny; but most groundlessly have the recent failures in New York been attributed to the discontinuance of this bank. As well might you ascribe to that cause the failures of Amsterdam and Hamburg, of London and Liverpool. The embarrassments of commerce, the sequestration in France, the Danish captures—in fine, the belligerent edicts—are the obvious sources of these failures. Their immediate cause is the return of bills upon London, drawn upon the faith of unproductive or unprofitable shipments. Yes, sir, the protests of the notaries of London, not those of New York, have occasioned these bankruptcies.

The power of a nation is said to consist in the sword and the purse. Perhaps, at last, all power is resolvable into that of the purse, for with it you may command almost everything else. The specie circulation of the United States is estimated by some calculators at ten millions of dollars; and, if it be no more, one moiety is in the vaults of this bank. May not the time arrive when the concentration of such a vast portion of the circulating medium of the country in the hands of any corporation will be dangerous to our liberties? By whom is this immense power wielded? By a body who, in derogation of the great principle of all our institutions, responsibility to the people, is amenable only to a few stockholders, and they chiefly foreigners. Suppose an attempt to subvert this Government, would not the traitor first aim, by force or corruption, to acquire the treasure of this company? Look at it in another aspect. Seven-tenths of its capital are in the hands of foreigners, and these foreigners chiefly English subjects. We are possibly upon the eve of a rupture with that nation. Should such an event occur, do you apprehend that the English Premier would experience any difficulty in obtaining the entire control of this institution? Republics, above all other nations, ought most studiously to guard against foreign influence. All history proves that the internal dissensions excited by foreign intrigue have produced the downfall of almost every free government that has hitherto existed; and yet gentlemen contend that we are benefited by the possession of this foreign capital. If we could have its use, without its attending abuse, I should be gratified also. But it is in vain to expect the one without the other. Wealth is power, and, under whatsoever form it exists, its proprietor, whether he lives on this or the other side of the Atlantic, will have a proportionate influence. It is argued that our possession of this English capital gives us a certain influence over the British Government. If this reasoning be sound, we had better revoke the interdiction as to aliens holding land, and invite foreigners to engross the whole property, real and personal, of the country. We had better at once exchange the condition of independent proprietors for that of stewards. We should then be able to govern foreign nations, according to the arguments of gentlemen on the other side. But let us put aside this theory, and appeal to the decisions of experience. Go to the other side of the Atlantic, and see what has been achieved for us there by Englishmen holding seven-tenths of the capital of this bank. Has it released from galling and ignominious bondage one solitary American seaman, bleeding under British oppression? Did it prevent the unmanly attack upon the *Chesapeake?* Did it arrest the promulgation, or has it abrogated the Orders in Council—those orders which have given birth to a new era in commerce? In spite of all its boasted effects, are not the two nations brought to the very brink of war? Are we quite sure that, on this side of the water, it has had no effect favorable to British interests? It has often been stated, and, although I do not know that it is susceptible of strict proof, I believe it to be a fact, that this bank exercised its influence in support of Jay's treaty; and may it not have contributed to blunt the public sentiment, or paralyze the efforts of this nation against British aggression?

The Duke of Northumberland is said to be the most considerable stockholder in the Bank of the United States. A late Lord Chancellor of England, besides other noblemen, was a large stockholder. Suppose the Prince of Essling, the Duke of Cadore, and other French dignitaries owned seven-eighths of the capital of this bank, should we witness the same exertions (I allude not to any made in the Senate) to recharter it? So far from it, would not the danger of French influence be resounded throughout the nation?

Senator Pope.—My honorable friend from Georgia [Senator Crawford] has been reminded of the Macedonian phalanx. I trust, sir, we shall ever be found associated with a phalanx American, Republican, in heart and sentiment. I will not sacrifice the interest of my constituents for fear of being called hard names. The epithets of quidism, quadroonism, or any other ism which malice or policy may suggest shall not drive me from the course called for by the public good. I am proud that I represent a people just, generous, and independent, not to be carried away by unmeaning clamor. Before they discard a public servant, they will view him both on a political theater and in the walks of private life. They know, too well, that those are not always the best Christians who sing hallelujahs on the house top, nor have they forgotten the celebrated Sempronius, who, on the approach of Cæsar, thundered war in the Roman Senate, and at the same time was secretly coöperating with the traitor to overthrow the liberties of the Roman people.

Deeply impressed, Mr. President, with the opinion that the rejection of this bill will give at least a temporary check to the prosperity of the rising State from which I come, I shall give my negative to the motion to strike out the first section. Yes, sir, not only the interest but importance of that State in the Union is about to be sacrificed. When I look beyond the mountains, and remember that Kentucky has nurtured me almost from my cradle, that she has bestowed on me her choicest honors, my bosom is filled with emotions of gratitude which impel me to say on this, as on all other occasions, Kentucky, I am only thine!

CHAPTER III

National Bank Currency

[THE SECOND UNITED STATES BANK]

Proposals for Bank Charters, 1814-16—Bank of the United States of America Chartered in 1816—Debate in the House on the Effect of a National Bank on Currency: in Favor of the Bank, John C. Calhoun [S. C.], Henry Clay [Ky.]; Opposed, John Randolph [Va.], Daniel Webster [N. H.].

THE question of chartering a national bank came up again during the closing years of Madison's Administration. In January, 1814, sundry citizens of New York petitioned the House of Representatives for such a charter, but the committee to whom the matter was referred reported adversely, saying:

> That the power to create corporations within the territorial limits of the States, without the consent of the States, is neither one of the powers delegated by the Constitution of the United States, nor essentially necessary for carrying into effect any delegated power.

John C. Calhoun [S. C.] then, in the following month (on February 4, 1814), proposed that the Committee of Ways and Means be instructed to inquire into the expediency of establishing a national bank in the District of Columbia, to do which, he said, came undoubtedly within the constitutional powers of Congress. On February 21 John W. Taylor [N. Y.], chairman of the committee, reported a bill to charter such a bank. Discussion of the report was deferred until the next session, when it was brought before the House on November 14, 1814, and discussed until November 28, when it was rejected by a vote of 49 to 104, owing to certain objectionable features.

The bill was then amended by the removal of certain

of these features. On December 8 it was ordered by the Senate to the third reading, and reported to the House of Representatives. The House referred it to a committee, which made other amendments, and reported it on January 6, 1815. It was passed on the following day by a vote of 120 to 38.

President Madison returned the bill to the Senate unsigned, and stated his objections to it. The nature of the bill may be inferred from the President's summary of his objections:

"On the whole, when it is considered that the proposed establishment will enjoy a monopoly of the profits of a national bank for a period of twenty years; that the monopolized profits will be continually growing, with the progress of the national population and wealth; that the nation will, during the same period, be dependent on the notes of the bank for that species of circulating medium, whenever the precious metals may be wanted, and at all times for so much thereof as may be an eligible substitute for a specie medium; and that the extensive employment of the notes in the collection of the augmented taxes will, moreover, enable the bank greatly to extend its profitable issues of them, without the expense of specie capital to support their circulation; it is as reasonable as it is requisite that the Government, in return for these extraordinary concessions to the bank, should have a greater security for attaining the public objects of the institution than is presented in the bill, and particularly for every practicable accommodation, both in the temporary advances necessary to anticipate the taxes, and in those more durable loans which are equally necessary to diminish the resort to taxes."

The Senate, on February 2, 1815, voted, 15 to 19, to pass the bill, and so failed to overrule the President's veto. On February 17, by a vote of 74 to 73, the House of Representatives indefinitely postponed the bill.

On the assembling of Congress in December, 1815, President Madison, in his message, after referring to the disordered condition of national finances due to the War of 1812, said:

"It is essential to every modification of the finances that the benefits of a uniform national currency should be restored to the community. The absence of the precious metals will, it is believed, be a temporary evil; but, until they can again be rendered the general medium of exchange, it devolves on the wisdom of Congress to provide a substitute, which shall equally engage the confidence and accommodate the wants of the citizens throughout the Union. If the operation of the State banks cannot produce this result, the probable operation of a national bank will merit consideration.''

This part of the President's message was referred by the House of Representatives to a special committee, of which John C. Calhoun was appointed chairman. On January 8, 1816, he reported a bill to establish The Bank of the United States, with a capital of $35,000,000, $7,000,000 to be subscribed by the Government and $28,000,000 to be subscribed for by individuals, companies, or corporations. The question came up for discussion in the House on February 26, and was debated until March 14, when it was passed by a vote of 80 to 71. It was brought forward in the Senate on March 25, and debated until April 3, when it was passed by a vote of 22 to 12. The act was approved by the President on April 10.

In all the later discussions of a national bank the constitutional arguments of the former were repeated, and hence need not be reproduced here. However, in the interim a special need had arisen for reformation of the *currency,* which, owing to the War of 1812, consisted wholly of paper, fluctuating greatly in value.

The effect of the establishment of a national bank in remedying this evil was the new feature in the later debates, and the arguments on this point are therefore presented. The leading speakers in behalf of the bank as an instrumentality tending toward a stable currency were Mr. Calhoun and Henry Clay [Ky.]. The leading opponent of the bank as not removing the evil complained of and as creating other evils was Daniel Webster [N. H.]. John Randolph [Va.], while denouncing the bill as proposing a ''monstrous alliance between the bank and the Government,'' was so opposed to the evils of private banking that he was ready ''almost in his heart'' to vote for the bill.

It will be noted that Henry Clay reversed his attitude on the bank question. For some reason his speech in Congress on the establishment of the second bank was not reported. However, on his return to Kentucky he delivered an address to his constituents justifying his course, which repeated the arguments of the speech, and therefore has been here substituted for it.

The Effect of a National Bank on Currency

House of Representatives, February 26–March 14, 1816

Mr. Calhoun said: The state of our circulating medium is opposed to the principles of the Federal Constitution. The power was given to Congress by that instrument in express terms to regulate the currency of the United States. In point of fact, that power, though given to Congress, is not in their hands. The power is exercised by banking institutions, no longer responsible for the correctness with which they manage it. Gold and silver have disappeared entirely, there is no money but paper money, and that money is beyond the control of Congress. No one who refers to the Constitution can doubt that the money of the United States was intended to be placed entirely under the control of Congress. The only object the framers of the Constitution could have in view in giving to Congress the power "to coin money, regulate the value thereof, and of foreign coin" must have been to give a steadiness and fixed value to the currency of the United States. The state of things at the time of the adoption of the Constitution affords an argument in support of this construction. There then existed a depreciated paper currency, which could be regulated and made uniform only by giving a power for that purpose to the general Government. The States could not do it. Taking into view the prohibition against the States issuing bills of credit, there was a strong presumption this power was intended to be exclusively given to Congress.

There has been an extraordinary revolution in the currency of the country. By a sort of undercurrent the power of Congress to regulate the money of the country has caved in, and upon its ruin have sprung up those institutions which now exercise the right of making money for the United States—for gold and silver are not the only money, but whatever is the medium of purchase and sale, in which bank paper alone is now employed, and has, therefore, become the money of the country. A change, great and wonderful, has taken place, which divests you of your rights, and turns you back to the condition of the Revolutionary War, in which every State issued bills of credit, which were made a legal tender and were of various value.

This, then, is the evil. We have in lieu of gold and silver a paper medium, unequally but generally depreciated, which affects the trade and industry of the nation; which paralyzes the national arm; which sullies the faith, both public and private, of the United States; a paper no longer resting on gold and silver as its basis. We have indeed laws regulating the currency of foreign coin, but they are under present circumstances a mockery of legislation, because there is no coin in circulation. The right of making money—an attribute of sovereign power, a sacred and important right—is exercised by two hundred and sixty banks, scattered over every part of the United States, not responsible to any power whatever for their issues of paper. The next and great inqiury is, how this evil is to be remedied. Restore these institutions to their original use; cause them to give up their usurped power; cause them to return to their legitimate office of places of discount and deposit; let them be no longer mere paper machines; restore the state of things which existed anterior to 1813, which was consistent with the just policy and interests of the country; cause them to fulfill their contracts, to respect their broken faith, resolve that everywhere there shall be a uniform value to the national currency, your constitutional control will then prevail.

A national bank paying specie itself would have a tendency to make specie payments general, as well by its influence as by its example. It will be the interest of the national bank to produce this state of things, because otherwise its operations will be greatly circumscribed, as it must pay out specie or national bank notes; for I presume one of the first rules of such a bank would be to take the notes of no bank which did not pay in gold and silver. A national bank of thirty-five millions, with the aid of those banks which are at once ready to pay specie, would produce a powerful effect all over the Union. Further, a national bank would enable the Government to resort to measures which would make it unprofitable to banks to continue the violation of their contracts, and advantageous to return to the observance of them. The leading measures of this character would be to strip the banks refusing to pay specie of all the profits arising from the business of the Government, to prohibit deposits with them, and to refuse to receive their notes in payment of dues to the Government.

The evil is a deep one; almost incurable, because connected with public opinion, over which banks have a great control; they have, in a great measure, a control over the press. For proof of which I refer to the fact that the present wretched state of the circulating medium has scarcely been denounced by a single paper within the United States. The derangement of a circulating medium is a joint thrown out of its socket; let it remain for a short time in that state and the sinews will be so knit that it cannot be replaced; apply the remedy soon, and it is an operation easy, though painful. The evil grows, while the resistance to it becomes weak; and, unless checked at once, will become irresistible.

Mr. Webster said: It is a mistaken idea, which I have heard uttered on this subject, that we are about to reform the national currency. No nation has a better currency than the United States; there is no nation which has guarded its currency with more care; for the framers of the Constitution, and those who enacted the early statutes on this subject, were hard-money men; they had felt and therefore duly appreciated the evils of a paper medium; they therefore sedulously guarded the currency of the United States from debasement. The legal currency of the United States was gold and silver coin. This was a subject in regard to which Congress had run into no folly.

What, then, is the present evil? Having a perfectly sound national currency—and the Government have no power, in fact, to make anything else current but gold and silver—there has grown up in different States a currency of paper issued by banks, setting out with the promises to pay gold and silver, which they have been wholly unable to redeem. The consequence is that there is a mass of paper afloat, of perhaps fifty millions, which sustains no immediate relation to the legal currency of the country—a paper which will not enable any man to pay money he owes to his neighbor, or his debts to the Government. The banks have issued more money than they can redeem, and the evil is severely felt. In consequence of the immense paper issues having banished specie from circulation, the Government has been obliged, in direct violation of existing statutes, to receive the amount of their taxes in something which is not recognized by law as the money of the country, and which is, in fact, greatly depreciated. This is the evil.

In my opinion, any remedy now to be applied to this evil must be applied to the depreciated mass of paper itself; it must be some measure which will give heat and life to this mortified mass of the body politic. The evil is not to be remedied by introducing a new paper circulation; there can be no such thing as two media in circulation, the one credited and the other discredited. All bank paper derives its credit solely from its relation to gold and silver; and there is no remedy for the state of depreciation of the paper currency but the resumption of specie payments. If all the property of the United States was pledged for the redemption of these fifty millions of paper, it would not thereby be brought up to par; or, if it did, that would happen which has never yet happened in any other country. An issue of treasury notes would have no better effect than the establishment of a new bank paper. At a period anterior to the time of the reformation of the coin of England, when the existing coin had been much debased by clipping, an attempt had been made to correct the currency thus vitiated by throwing a quantity of sound coin into circulation with the debased; the result was that the sound coin disappeared, was hoarded up, because more valuable than that of the same nominal value which was in general circulation.

The establishment of a national bank not being in my opinion the proper remedy, I shall proceed to examine what is. The solvency of the banks is not questioned. There can be no doubt, if the banks would unite in the object, they might in three weeks resume the payment of specie, and render the adoption of any measure by this House wholly unnecessary. The banks are making, out of the present state of things, extravagant profits, which ought to be curtailed. The Bank of Pennsylvania, as exhibited in the return to the legislature of that State, is receiving interest on nearly three times the amount of its capital. This I consider an extraordinary fact. That bank has been pronounced by the legislature to be in "a flourishing state." It is so to the stockholders in the bank, I doubt not; but how is it to those who are affected by the depreciation of it—to the man who comes into an office for life, and relinquishes all his prospects and profits for a fixed salary, not to be diminished during his continuance in office; to the poor pensioner whose wounds received in his country's service are yet bleeding?

These banks not emanating from Congress, what engine is Congress to use for remedying the existing evil? Their only legitimate power is to interdict the paper of such banks as do not pay specie from being received at the custom-house. With a receipt of forty millions a year, if the Government is faithful to itself and to the interests of the people, they can control the evil. In the end the taxes must be paid in the legal money of the country, and the sooner that is brought about the better.

Mr. Randolph.—The present time is one of the most disastrous I have ever witnessed in the Republic, and this bill proves it. The proposal to establish this great bank is like a crutch, and, as far as I understand it, it is a broken one: it would tend, instead of remedying the evil, to aggravate it. The evil of the times is a spirit engendered in this Republic, fatal to Republican principles, fatal to Republican virtue; a spirit to live by any means but those of honest industry; a spirit of profusion—in other words, the spirit of Catiline himself, *alieni avidus, sui profusus*—a spirit of expediency, not only in public but private life; the system of Diddler in the farce, living any way and well—wearing an expensive coat, and drinking the finest wines, at anybody's expense. This bank, I imagine (I am far from ascribing to the gentleman from South Carolina any such views), is to a certain extent a modification of the same system. Connected, as it is to be, with the Government, whenever it went into operation a scene would be exhibited on the great theater of the United States at the contemplation of which I shudder. If we mean to transmit our institutions unimpaired to posterity, if some now living wish to continue to live under the same institutions by which they are now ruled—and, with all its evils, real or imaginary, I presume no man would question that we live under the easiest government on the globe—we must put bounds to the spirit which seeks wealth by every path but the plain and regular path of honest industry and honest fame. This is one of the grounds on which I am hostile to this bill.

If the existing laws do not compel men to pay their debts, the establishment of a bank will not. Let us not disguise the fact; we think we are living in the better times of the Republic. We deceive ourselves; we are almost in the days of Sylla and Marius; yes, we have almost got down to the time of Jugurtha. It is unpleasant to put one's self in array against a great leading interest in a community, be they a knot of land speculators, paper jobbers, or what not; but every man you meet in this House or out of it, with some rare exceptions, which only serve to prove the rule, is either a stockholder, president, cashier, clerk, or doorkeeper, runner, engraver, papermaker, or mechanic in some other way to a bank. The gentleman from Pennsylvania might dismiss his fears for the State banks, with their one hundred and seventy millions of paper on eighty-two millions of capital. However great the evil of their conduct might be, who is to bell the cat—who is to take the bull by the horns? You might as well attack Gibraltar with a pocket pistol as to attempt to punish them. There are very few who dare to speak truth to this mammoth; the banks are so linked together with the business of the world that there are very few men exempt from their influence. The true secret is the banks are creditors as well as debtors; and, if we were merely debtors to them for the paper in our pockets, they would soon, like Robert Morris, go to jail (figuratively speaking) for having issued more paper than they were able to pay when presented to them. We are tied hand and foot, and bound to conciliate this great mammoth,[1] which is set up to worship in this Christian land. Thus, while our Government denounces hierarchy—will permit no privileged order for conducting the service of the only true God —while it denounces nobility, etc., a privileged order of new men has grown up under it, the pressure of whose foot I at this moment feel on my neck. If anything could reconcile me to this monstrous alliance between the bank and the Government, I could, if the object could be attained of compelling these banks to fulfil their engagements, almost find in my heart to go with the gentleman in voting for it.

The stuff uttered on all hands, and absolutely got by rote by the haberdashers' boys behind the counters in the shops, that the paper now in circulation will buy anything you want as well as gold and silver, is answered by saying that you want to buy silver with it. The present mode of banking goes to demoralize society; it is as much swindling to issue notes with intent not to pay as it is burglary to break open a house. If they are unable to pay, the banks are bankrupts; if able to pay, and will not, they are fraudulent bankrupts. But a man might as well go to Constantinople to preach Christianity as to get up here and preach against banks. I despair, almost, of remedying the evil they cause when I see so many men of respectability directors, stockholders, debtors of the banks. To pass this bill would be like getting rid of the rats by setting fire to the house; whether any other remedy could be devised I do not now undertake to pronounce. The banks have lost all shame, and exemplify a beautiful and very just observation of one of the finest writers that men banded together in a common cause will collectively do that at which every individual of the combination would spurn.

Mr. Clay said: When I was a member of the Senate of the

[1] Randolph evidently used this word instead of "mammon" to suggest magnitude and monstrosity, as well as worship of wealth.

United States, I was induced to oppose the renewal of the charter to the old Bank of the United States by three general considerations: The first was that I was instructed to oppose it by the legislature of the State. What were the reasons that operated with the legislature, in giving the instruction, I do not know. I infer either that the legislature did not believe a bank to be unconstitutional or that it had formed no opinion on that point, from the fact that, although the two late Senators from this State, as well as the present Senators, voted for a national bank, the legislature, which must have been well apprised that such a measure was in contemplation, did not again interpose, either to protest against the measure itself or to censure the conduct of those Senators. From this silence on the part of a body which has ever fixed a watchful eye upon the proceedings of the general Government, I have a right to believe that the legislature of Kentucky now sees, without dissatisfaction, the proposal to establish a national bank; and that its opposition to the former one was upon grounds of expediency, applicable to that corporation alone, or no longer existing.

When the application was made to renew the old charter of the Bank of the United States, such an institution did not appear to me to be so necessary to the fulfillment of many of the objects specifically enumerated in the Constitution as to justify Congress in assuming, by construction, a power to establish it; it was supported mainly upon the ground that it was indispensable to the treasury operations. But the local institutions in the several States were, at that time, in prosperous existence, confided in by the community, having a confidence in each other, and maintaining an intercourse and connection the most intimate. Many of them were actually employed by the treasury to aid that department in a part of its fiscal arrangements; and they appeared to me to be fully capable of affording to it all the facility that it ought to desire in all of them. They superseded, in my judgment, the necessity of a national institution. But how stood the case in 1816, when I am called upon again to examine the power of the general Government to incorporate a national bank? A total change of circumstances is presented—events of the utmost magnitude have intervened.

A general suspension of specie payments has taken place, and this has led to a train of consequences of the most alarming nature. I behold, dispersed over the immense extent of the United States, about three hundred banking institutions, enjoying, in different degrees, the confidence of the public, shaken as to them all, under no direct control of the general Government, and subject to no actual responsibility to the State authorities. These institutions are emitting the actual currency of the United States; a currency consisting of a paper on which they neither paid interest nor principal, while it was exchanged for the paper of the community on which both were paid. I see these institutions, in fact, exercising what has been considered at all times, and in all countries, one of the highest attributes of sovereignty—the regulation of the current medium of the country. They are no longer competent to assist the treasury in either of the great operations of collection, deposit, or distribution of the public revenues. In fact, the paper which they emit, and which the treasury, from the force of events, finds itself constrained to receive, is constantly obstructing the operations of that department; for it accumulates where it is not wanted, and cannot be used where it is wanted for the purposes of government without a ruinous and arbitrary brokerage. Every man who pays, or receives from, the Government pays or receives as much less than he ought to as is the difference between the medium in which the payment is made and specie. Taxes are no longer uniform. In New England, where specie payments have not been suspended, the people are called upon to pay larger contributions than where they are suspended. In Kentucky, as much more is paid by the people in their taxes than is paid, for example, in the State of Ohio, as Kentucky paper is worth more than Ohio paper.

Considering, then, that the state of the currency is such that no thinking man can contemplate it without the most serious alarm; that it threatens general distress, if it does not ultimately lead to convulsion and subversion of the Government, it appears to me to be the duty of Congress to apply a remedy, if a remedy can be devised. A national bank, with other auxiliary measures, is proposed as that remedy. I am determined to examine the question with as little prejudice as possible arising from my former opinion; I know that the safest course, if I were to pursue a cold, calculating prudence, is to adhere to that opinion, right or wrong. I am perfectly aware that, if I change or seem to change it, I shall expose myself to some censure; but, looking at the subject with the light shed upon it by events happening since the commencement of the war, I can no longer doubt. A bank appears not only necessary, but indispensably necessary, in connection with another measure, to remedy the evils of which all are but too sensible. I prefer to the suggestions of the pride of consistency the evident interests of the community, and determine to throw myself upon their candor and justice. That which appeared to me in 1811, under the state of things then existing, not to be necessary to the general Government seems now to be necessary, under the present state of things. Had I then foreseen what now exists, and no objection had lain against the renewal of the charter, other than that derived from the Constitution, I should have voted for the renewal.

CHAPTER IV

President Jackson's War on the United States Bank

President Jackson's Message on Rechartering the Second United States Bank—Arraignment of the Bank by Senator Thomas H. Benton [Mo.]: "The Power Greater Than the Government"—Debate in the Senate on Renewal of the Bank's Charter: in Favor, George M. Dallas [Pa.], Daniel Webster [Mass.]—Bill Is Passed—The President Vetoes It; His Message—Debate in the Senate on the Veto: in Favor, Hugh L. White [Tenn.]; Opposed, Senator Benton, Senator Webster, Henry Clay [Ky.].

PRESIDENT JACKSON was of autocratic temper, brooking no superior to his will. He used his appointing power to build up what in later political parlance would be called a "Jackson machine." He dominated his Cabinet, dictating the policy of the Administration. Indeed, those with whom he chiefly conferred were men outside of his official family, who composed what was known as the "Kitchen Cabinet." He used the veto power of his office more freely and arbitrarily than his predecessors, overriding, indeed, the precedents set by them (see his veto of the Maysville Turnpike bill, Volume X, page 157), and thus subordinated Congress to the legislative power incident in the Executive.

Accordingly, when he saw the growth of new power in the country, the President first attempted to utilize it for his own aggrandizement, and then, on failure to do so, to crush it. This power was the Bank of the United States, which, by 1829, had become an extensive system composed of the parent bank at Philadelphia and twenty-five branch banks scattered over the country, but most thickly in New England and the Middle Atlantic States.

In June, 1829, the engineers of the Jackson "machine" in New Hampshire urged Nicholas Biddle, president of the bank, to remove the president of the branch at Portsmouth and appoint a Jackson man in his place. Biddle flatly refused to do so. The Secretary of the Treasury, Samuel D. Ingham, then brought official pressure to bear, but in vain, Biddle declaring that the bank did not "acknowledge the slightest responsibility whatsoever to the Secretary of the Treasury touching the political opinions and conduct of its officers, that being a subject on which they never consult, and have no desire to know, the views of any Administration."

In his next message to Congress (December 8, 1829) President Jackson made the first move in his warfare against the bank. He said:

The charter of the Bank of the United States expires in 1836, and its stockholders will most probably apply for a renewal of their privileges. In order to avoid the evils resulting from precipitancy in a measure involving such important principles, and such deep pecuniary interests, I feel that I cannot, in justice to the parties interested, too soon present it to the deliberate consideration of the legislature and the people. Both the constitutionality and the expediency of the law creating this bank are well questioned by a large portion of our fellow citizens; and it must be admitted by all that it has failed in the great end of establishing a uniform and sound currency.

Under these circumstances, if such an institution is deemed essential to the fiscal operations of the Government, I submit to the wisdom of the legislature whether a national one founded upon the credit of the Government and its revenues might not be devised, which would avoid all constitutional difficulties and at the same time secure all the advantages to the Government and country that were expected to result from the present bank.

At the instigation of the President resolutions were offered, during the ensuing session, against the bank, but were laid on the table by a vote of 86 to 66.

During the congressional recess the President continued his fight on the bank through the Administration press. At the opening of the next session he repeated his former observations in regard to the bank, and amplified his argument in favor of a Treasury bank.

Not being a corporate body, having no stockholders, debtors, or property, and but few officers, it would not be obnoxious to

"SHINPLASTER" CARICATURE OF BENTON, JACKSON, AND VAN BUREN

From the collection of the New York Historical Society

the constitutional objections which are urged against the present bank; and having no means to operate on the hopes, fears, or interests of large masses of the community, it would be shorn of the influence which makes that bank formidable. The States would be strengthened by having in their hands the means of furnishing the local paper currency through their own banks; while the Bank of the United States, though issuing no paper, would check the issues of the State banks, by taking their notes in deposit, and for exchange, only so long as they continue to be redeemed with specie. In times of public emergency, the capacities of such an institution might be enlarged by legislative provisions.

These suggestions are made, not so much as a recommendation, as with a view of calling the attention of Congress to the possible modifications of a system which cannot continue to exist in its present form without occasional collisions with the local authorities, and perpetual apprehensions and discontent on the part of the States and the people.

On February 2, 1831, Thomas H. Benton [Mo.], a spokesman of the Administration, introduced in the Senate a resolution "that the charter of the Bank of the United States ought not to be renewed," and advocated its adoption in a powerful speech, arraigning the bank not only for its actual, but also its potential, abuses.

"The Power Greater than the Government"

Speech of Senator Benton Against the National Bank

First: Mr. President, I object to the renewal of the charter of the Bank of the United States, because I look upon the bank as an institution too great and powerful to be tolerated in a government of free and equal laws. Its power is that of the purse; a power more potent than that of the sword; and this power it possesses to a degree and extent that will enable the bank to draw to itself too much of the political power of this Union; and too much of the individual property of the citizens of these States. The money power of the bank is both direct and indirect.

The direct power of the bank is now prodigious, and, in the event of the renewal of the charter, must speedily become boundless and uncontrollable. The bank is now authorized to own effects, lands inclusive, to the amount of fifty-five millions of dollars, and to issue notes to the amount of thirty-five millions more. This makes ninety millions; and, in addition to this vast sum, there is an opening for an unlimited increase; or there is a dispensation in the charter to issue as many more notes as Congress, by law, may permit. This opens the door to boundless emissions; for what can be more unbounded than the will and pleasure of successive Congresses? The indirect power of the bank cannot be stated in figures; but it can be shown to be immense. In the first place, it has the keeping of the public moneys, now amounting to twenty-six millions per annum (the Post Office Department included), and the gratuitous use of the undrawn balances, large enough to constitute in themselves the capital of a great State bank. In the next place, its promissory notes are receivable, by law, in purchase of all property owned by the United States, and in payment of all debts due them; and this may increase its power to the amount of the annual revenue, by creating a demand for its notes to that amount. In the third place, it wears the name of the United States, and has the Federal Government for a partner; and this name and this partnership identify the credit of the bank with the credit of the Union. In the fourth place, it is armed with authority to disparage and discredit the notes of other banks, by excluding them from all payments to the United States; and this, added to all its other powers, direct and indirect, makes this institution the uncontrollable monarch of the moneyed system of the Union. To whom is all this power granted? To a company of private individuals, many of them foreigners. By whom is all this power to be exercised? By a directory of seven (it may be), governed by a majority of four (it may be), and none of these elected by the people, or responsible to them. Where is it to be exercised? At a single city, distant a thousand miles from some of the States, receiving the produce of none of them (except one); no interest in the welfare of any of them (except one); no commerce with the people; with branches in every State; and every branch subject to the secret and absolute orders of the supreme central head; thus constituting a system of centralism, hostile to the federative principle of our Union, encroaching upon the wealth and power of the States, and organized upon a principle to give the highest effect to the greatest power. This mass of power, thus concentrated, thus ramified, and thus directed, must necessarily become, under a prolonged existence, the absolute monopolist of American money, the sole manufacturer of paper currency, and the sole authority (for authority it will be) to which the Federal Government, the State governments, the great cities, corporate bodies, merchants, traders, and every private citizen must of necessity apply for every loan which their exigencies may demand. "The rich ruleth the poor, and the borrower is the servant of the lender."

It is to no purpose that gentlemen may come forward, and vaunt the character of the United States Bank, and proclaim it too just and merciful to oppress the State. I must be permitted to repudiate both the pledge and the praise. The security is insufficient and the encomium belongs to Constantinople. "The Sultan is too just and merciful to abuse his power."

Secondly. I object to the continuance of this bank, because its tendencies are dangerous and pernicious to the Government and to the people.

What are the tendencies of a great moneyed power connected with the Government and controlling its fiscal operations? Are they not dangerous to every interest, public and private—political as well as pecuniary?

Such a bank tends to create public debt, by facilitating public loans and substituting unlimited supplies of paper for limited supplies of coin. The British debt is born of the Bank of England, which was chartered in 1694, and was nothing more nor less in the beginning than an act of Parliament for the incorporation of a company of subscribers to a government loan.

It tends to aggravate the inequality of fortunes; to make the rich richer, and the poor poorer; to multiply nabobs and paupers; and to deepen and widen the gulf which separates Dives from Lazarus. A great moneyed power is favorable to great capitalists; for it is the principle of money to favor money. It is unfavorable to small capitalists; for it is the principle of money to eschew the needy and unfortunate. It is injurious to the laboring classes; because they receive no favors, and they have the price of the property they wish to acquire raised to the paper maximum, while their wages remain at the silver minimum.

It tends to make and to break fortunes, by the flux and reflux of paper. Profuse issues and sudden contractions perform this operation, which can be repeated, like planetary and pestilential visitations, in every cycle of so many years; at every periodical return, transferring millions from the actual possessors of property to the Neptunes who preside over the flux and reflux of paper.

Thirdly. I object to the renewal of the charter, on account of the exclusive privileges and anti-republican monopoly which it gives to the stockholders. It gives, and that by an act of Congress, to a company of individuals, the following exclusive legal privileges:

1. The imposing name, the incalculable credit, and the great and continuing revenues of the United States are given up to the use of this company, and constitute in themselves an immense capital to bank upon. The revenues of the Union are twenty-six millions of dollars, including the post office; and all this is so much capital in the hands of the bank, because the revenue is received by it, and is payable in its promissory notes.

2. To pay the revenues of the United States in their own notes. Other banks depend upon their credit for the receivability of their notes; but this favored institution has law on its side, and a chartered right to compel the reception of its paper by the Federal Government. The immediate consequence of this extraordinary privilege is that the United States becomes virtually bound to stand security for the bank, as much so as if she had signed a bond to that effect; and must stand forward to sustain the institution in all emergencies, in order to save her own revenue. This is what has already happened, some ten years ago, in the early progress of the bank, and when the immense aid given it by the Federal Government enabled it to survive the crisis of its own overwhelming mismanagement.

3. To hold the moneys of the United States in deposit, without making compensation for the use of the undrawn balances. This is a right which I deny; but, as the bank claims it, and, what is more material, enjoys it; and as the people of the United States have suffered to a vast extent in consequence of this claim and enjoyment, I shall not hesitate to set it down to the account of the bank. Let us then examine the value of this privilege and its effect upon the interest of the community; and, in the first place, let us have a full and accurate view of the amount of these undrawn balances from the establishment of the bank to the present day. Here it is! Look! Read!

Here Mr. Benton exhibited a table of the quarterly amounts of public money in the bank, averaging about four millions of dollars, and equivalent to a permanent deposit or loan without interest to that amount.

See, Mr. President, what masses of money, and always on hand. The paper is covered all over with millions; and yet, for all these vast sums, no interest is allowed; no compensation is made to the United States. The Bank of England, for the undrawn balances of the public money, has made an equitable compensation to the British Government; namely, a permanent loan of half a million sterling, and a temporary loan of three millions for twenty years, without interest. Yet, when I moved for a like compensation to the United States, the proposition was utterly rejected by the Finance Committee, and treated as an attempt to violate the charter of the bank. At the same time it is incontestable that the United States have been borrowing these undrawn balances from the bank and paying an interest upon their own money.

4. To discredit and disparage the notes of all other banks, by excluding them from the collection of the federal revenue. In consequence of this exclusion they are also excluded from all the land offices, eleven in number, which deposit in the Branch Bank of St. Louis; and, being excluded from the land offices, they cease to be current money among the people. If a traveler or emigrant brings these notes to the country, or receives them in remittance; if a trader accepts them in exchange for produce, they are "*shaved*" out of their hands, and sent out of the country. This is a pecuniary injury done to the Northwest; it may be more—it may be a political injury also; for it contributes to break the communication between the two quarters of the Union, and encourages the idea that nothing good can come from the South—not even money! This power to disparage the notes of all other banks is a power to injure them; and, added to all the other privileges of the Bank of the United States, is a power to destroy them! The President (Mr. Biddle) answers, as the whole world would answer to a question of oppression, that it never had; and this response was as much as the interrogatory required. But it did not content the president of the bank; he chose to go further, and to do honor to the institution over which he presided, by showing that it was as just and generous as it was rich and powerful. He, therefore, adds the following words, for which, as a seeker after evidence to show the alarming and dangerous character of the bank, I return him my unfeigned thanks: "There are very few banks which might not have been destroyed by an exertion of the power of the bank."

This is enough! proof enough! not for me alone, but for all who are unwilling to see a moneyed domination set up—a moneyed oligarchy established in this land, and the entire Union subjected to its sovereign will. The power to destroy all other banks is admitted and declared; the inclination to do so is known to all rational beings to reside with the power! Policy may restrain the destroying faculties for the present; but they exist; and will come forth when interest prompts and policy permits. They have been exercised; and the general prostration of the Southern and Western banks attests the fact. They will be exercised (the charter being renewed), and the remaining State banks will be swept with the besom of destruction. Not that all will have their signs knocked down and their doors closed up. Subjugation, in preference to destruction, will be the fate of many. Every planet must have its satellites; every tyranny must have its instruments; every knight is followed by his squire; even the king of beasts, the royal quadruped, whose roar subdues the forest, must have a small subservient animal to spring his prey. Just so of this imperial bank, when installed anew in its formidable and lasting power. The State banks spared by the sword will be passed under the yoke. They will become subordinate parts in the great machine; and thus the entire moneyed power of the Union will fall into the hands of one single institution, whose inexorable and invisible mandates, emanating from a center, would pervade the Union, giving or withholding money according to its own sovereign will and absolute pleasure. To a favored State, to an individual, or a class of individuals, favored by the central power, the golden stream of Pactolus would flow direct. To all such the munificent mandates of the High Directory would come, as the fabled god made his terrestrial visit of love and desire, enveloped in a shower of gold. But to others—to those not favored—and to those hated—the mandates of this same directory would be as "the planetary plague which hangs its poison in the sick air"; death to them! death to all who minister to their wants! What a state of things! What a condition for a confederacy of States! What grounds for alarm and terrible apprehension, when, in a confederacy of such vast extent, so many independent States, so many rival commercial cities, so much sectional jealousy, such violent political parties, such fierce contests for power, there should be but one moneyed tribunal before which all the rival and contending elements must appear! but one single dispenser of money, to which every citizen, every trader, every merchant, every manufacturer, every planter, every corporation, every city, every State, and the Federal Government itself must apply, in every emergency, for the most indispensable loan! and this, in the face of the fact that, in every contest for human rights, the great moneyed institutions of the world have uniformly been found on the side of kings and nobles, against the lives and liberties of the people.

5. To hold real estate, receive rents, and retain a body of

tenantry. This privilege is hostile to the nature of our republican Government, and inconsistent with the nature and design of a banking institution. Republics want freeholders, not landlords and tenants. Instead of remaining bankers, the corporators may turn land speculators; instead of having money to lend, they may turn you out tenants to vote. To an application for a loan, they may answer, and answer truly, that they have no money on hand; and the reason may be that they have laid it out in lands. The bank is now the greatest moneyed power in the Union; in the event of the renewal of its charter, it will soon be the sole one. Sole dispenser of money, it will soon be the chief owner of property. To unlimited means of acquisition would be united perpetuity of tenure; for a corporation never dies, and is free from the operation of the laws which govern the descent and distribution of real estate in the hands of individuals. Having all the money, it would be the sole lender; mortgages being the road to loans, all borrowers must travel that road. When birds enough are in the net, the fowler draws his string, and the heads are wrung off. So when mortgages enough are taken, the loans are called in; discounts cease; curtailments are made; failures to pay ensue; writs issue; judgments and executions follow; all the mortgaged premises are for sale at once; and the attorney of the bank appears at the elbow of the marshal, sole bidder, and sole purchaser.

What is the legal effect of this vast capacity to acquire, and this legal power to retain, real estate? Is it not the creation of a new species of mortmain? And of a kind more odious and dangerous than the mortmain of the church which it baffled the English Parliament so many ages to abolish. The mortmain of the church was a power in an ecclesiastical corporation to hold real estate, independent of the laws of distribution and descent: the mortmain of the bank is a power in a lay corporation to do the same thing. The evil of the two tenures is identical; the difference between the two corporations is no more than the difference between partners and money changers; the capacity to do mischief incomparably the greatest on the part of the lay corporators. The church could only operate upon the few who were thinking of the other world; the bank, upon all who are immersed in the business or the pleasures of this. The means of the church were nothing but prayers; the means of the bank is money! The church received what it could beg from dying sinners; the bank may extort what it pleases from the whole living generation of the just and unjust. Such is the parallel between the mortmain of the two corporations. They both end in monopoly of estates and perpetuity of succession; and the bank is the greatest monopolizer of the two. Monopolies and perpetual succession are the bane of republics. Our ancestors took care to provide against them, by abolishing entails and primogeniture. All the States abolished the anti-republican tenures; but Congress reëstablishes them, and in a manner more dangerous and offensive than before the revolution. They are now given, not generally, but to few; not to natives only, but to foreigners also; for foreigners are large owners of this bank. And thus the principles of the revolution sink before the privileges of an incorporated company. The laws of the States fall before the mandates of a central directory in Philadelphia. Foreigners become the landlords of free-born Americans; and the young and flourishing towns of the United States are verging to the fate of the family boroughs which belong to the great aristocracy of England.

6. To deal in pawns, merchandise, and bills of exchange. This bank, in addition to all its other attributes, is an incorporated company of pawnbrokers! The allegation staggers belief, but a reference to the charter will dispel incredulity. The bank is forbidden to deal in merchandise—proviso, unless in the case of goods pledged for money lent, and not redeemed to the day; and, proviso, again, unless for goods which shall be the proceeds of its lands. With the help of these two provisos it is clear that the limitation is undone; it is clear that the bank is at liberty to act the pawnbroker and merchant to any extent that it pleases. It may say to all the merchants who want loans, Pledge your stores, gentlemen! They must do it, or do worse; and, if any accident prevents redemption on the day, the pawn is forfeited, and the bank takes possession. On the other hand, it may lay out its rents for goods; it may sell its real estate, now worth three millions of dollars, for goods. Bills of exchange are also subjected to the traffic of this bank. It is a traffic unconnected with the trade of banking, dangerous for a great bank to hold, and now operating most injuriously in the South and West. It is the process which drains these quarters of the Union of their gold and silver, and stifles the growth of a fair commerce in the products of the country. The merchants, to make remittances, buy bills of exchange from the branch banks, instead of buying produce from the farmers. The bills are paid for in gold and silver; and, eventually, the gold and silver are sent to the mother bank, or to the branches in the Eastern cities, either to meet these bills, or to replenish their coffers, and to furnish vast loans to favorite States or indi-

viduals. Under this system the best of the Western banks sunk ten years ago. Under this system the entire West is now undergoing a silent, general, and invisible drain of its hard money; and, if this is not quickly arrested, these States will soon be, as far as the precious metals are concerned, no more than the empty skin of an immolated victim.

7. To establish branches in the different States without their consent, and in defiance of their resistance. No one can deny the degrading and injurious tendency of this privilege. It derogates from the sovereignty of a State; tramples upon her laws; injures her revenue and commerce; lays open her government to the attacks of centralism; impairs the property of her citizens; and fastens a vampire on her bosom to suck out her gold and silver. The Southern States, with three-fifths of the marketable productions of the Union, are not able to sustain thirty specie-paying banks; while the minority of the States north of the Potomac, without any of the great staples for export, have above four hundred of such banks. These States, without rice, without cotton, without tobacco, without sugar, and with less flour and provisions, to export, are saturated with gold and silver, while the Southern and Western States, with all the real sources of wealth, are in a state of the utmost destitution.

The *National Intelligencer* of this morning exults on the quantity of gold and silver in the vaults of the United States Bank. It declares that institution to be "overburdened" with gold and silver; and well may it be so overburdened, since it has lifted the load entirely from the South and West.

8. Exemption of the stockholders from individual liability on the failure of the bank. This privilege derogates from the common law, is contrary to the principle of partnerships, and injurious to the rights of the community. When a bank fails, its assets are always less than its debits; so that responsibility fails the instant that liability accrues. Let no one say that the Bank of the United States is too great to fail. One greater than it and its prototype has failed, and that in our own day, and for twenty years at a time: the Bank of England failed in 1797, and the Bank of the United States was on the point of failing in 1819. The same cause, namely, stockjobbing and overtrading, carried both to the brink of destruction; the same means saved both, namely, the name, the credit, and the helping hand of the governments which protected them. Yes, the Bank of the United States may fail; and its stockholders live in splendor upon the princely estates acquired with its notes, while the in-

dustrious classes, who hold these notes, will be unable to receive a shilling for them. This is unjust. It is a vice in the charter. The true principle in banking requires each stockholder to be liable to the amount of his shares; and subjects him to the summary action of every holder on the failure of the institution, till he has paid up the amount of his subscription. This is the true principle. It has prevailed in Scotland for the last century, and no such thing as a broken bank has been known there in all that time.

9. To have the United States for a partner. Sir, there is one consequence, one result of all partnerships between a government and individuals, which should of itself, and in a mere mercantile point of view, condemn this association on the part of the Federal Government. It is the principle which puts the strong partner forward to bear the burthen whenever the concern is in danger. The weaker members flock to the strong partner at the approach of the storm, and the necessity of venturing more to save what he has already staked leaves him no alternative. He becomes the Atlas of the firm, and bears all upon his own shoulders. This is the principle: what is the fact? Why, that the United States has already been compelled to sustain the Federal bank; to prop it with her revenues and her credit in the trials and crisis of its early administration. I pass over other instances of the damage suffered by the United States on account of this partnership; the immense standing deposits for which we receive no compensation; the loan of five millions of our own money, for which we have paid a million and a half in interest; the five per cent. stock note, on which we have paid our partners four million seven hundred and twenty-five thousand dollars in interest; the loss of ten millions on the three per cent. stock, and the ridiculous catastrophe of the miserable *bonus,* which has been paid to us with a fraction of our own money: I pass over all this, and come to the point of a direct loss, as a partner, in the dividends upon the stock itself. Upon this naked point of profit and loss, to be decided by a rule in arithmetic, we have sustained a direct and heavy loss. The stock held by the United States, as everybody knows, was subscribed, not paid. It was a stock note, deposited for seven millions of dollars, bearing an interest of five per cent. The inducement to this subscription was the seductive conception that, by paying five per cent. on its note the United States would clear four or five per cent. in getting a dividend of eight or ten. This was the inducement; now for the realization of this fine conception. Let us see it. Here it is: an official return from

the Register of the Treasury of interest paid, and of dividends received. The account stands thus:

Interest paid by the United States,	$4,725,000
Dividends received by the United States,	4,629,426
Loss to the United States,	$95,574

Disadvantageous as this partnership must be to the United States in a moneyed point of view, there is a far more grave and serious aspect under which to view it. It is the political aspect, resulting from the union between the bank and the Government. This union has been tried in England, and has been found there to be just as disastrous a conjunction as the union of church and State. It is the conjunction of the lender and the borrower, and holy writ has told us which of these categories will be master of the other. But suppose they agree to drop rivalry, and unite their resources. Suppose they combine and make a push for political power: how great is the mischief which they may accomplish!

I wish to secure the Union from all chance of harm from this bank. I wish to provide against its friendship, as well as its enmity—against all danger from its hug, as well as from its blow.

10. To have foreigners for partners. This, Mr. President, will be a strange story to be told in the West. The downright and upright people of that unsophisticated region believe that words mean what they signify, and that "the Bank of the United States" is the Bank of the United States. How great then must be their astonishment to learn that this belief is a false conception, and that this bank (its whole name to the contrary nowithstanding) is just as much the bank of foreigners as it is of the Federal Government. The report of the Committee of Ways and Means, in the House of Representatives, for the last session of Congress, admits that foreigners own seven millions of the stock of this bank; and everybody knows that the Federal Government owns seven millions also.

Thus it is proved that foreigners are as deeply interested in this bank as the United States itself. In the event of a renewal of the charter they will be much more deeply interested than at present; for a prospect of a rise in the stock to two hundred and fifty, and the unsettled state of things in Europe, will induce them to make great investments. It is to no purpose to say that the foreign stockholders cannot be voters or directors. The answer to that suggestion is this: the foreigners have the money;

they pay down the cash, and want no accommodations; they are lenders, not borrowers; and in a great moneyed institution such stockholders must have the greatest influence.

If I have shown it to be dangerous for the United States to be in partnership with its own citizens, how much stronger is not the argument against a partnership with foreigners? What a prospect for loans when at war with a foreign power, and the subjects of that power large owners of the bank here, from which alone, or from banks liable to be destroyed by it, we can obtain money to carry on the war! What a state of things if, in the division of political parties, one of these parties, and the foreigners, coalescing, should have the exclusive control of all the money in the Union, and, in addition to the money, should have bodies of debtors, tenants, and bank officers stationed in all the States, with a supreme and irresponsible system of centralism to direct the whole! Dangers from such contingencies are too great and obvious to be insisted upon. They strike the common sense of all mankind, and were powerful considerations for the old whig republicans for the non-renewal of the charter of 1791. Mr. Jefferson and the whig republicans staked their political existence on the non-renewal of that charter. They succeeded; and, by succeeding, prevented the country from being laid at the mercy of British and ultra federalists for funds to carry on the last war. It is said the United States lost forty millions by using depreciated currency during the last war. That, probably, is a mistake of one-half. But be it so! For what are forty millions compared to the loss of the war itself—compared to the ruin and infamy of having the Government arrested for want of money—stopped and paralyzed by the reception of such a note as the younger Pitt received from the Bank of England in 1795, withdrawing its assistance from the Government?

11. Exemption from due course of law for violations of its charter.—It is the right of every citizen to set the laws in motion against every offender; and it is the constitution of the law, when set in motion, to work through, like a machine, regardless of powers and principalities, cutting down the guilty which may stand in its way. Not so in the case of this bank. In its behalf there are barriers erected between the citizen and his oppressor, between the wrong and the remedy, between the law and the offender. Instead of a right to sue out a *scire facias* or a *quo warranto,* the injured citizen, with an humble petition in his hand, must repair to the President of the United States, or to Congress, and crave their leave to do so.

If leave is denied (and denied it will be whenever the bank has a peculiar friend in the President, or a majority of such friends in Congress, the convenient pretext being always at hand that the general welfare requires the bank to be sustained), he can proceed no further. Thus the administration of justice is subject to be strangled in its birth for the shelter and protection of this bank. But this is not all. Another and most alarming mischief results from the same extraordinary privilege. It gives the bank a direct interest in the presidential and congressional elections; it gives it need for friends in Congress and in the presidential chair. Its fate, its very existence may often depend upon the friendship of the President and Congress; and, in such cases, it is not in human nature to avoid using the immense means in the hands of the bank to influence the elections of these officers.

An impartial President or Congress might let the laws take their course; those of a different temper might interpose their veto. What a crisis for the bank! It beholds the sword of Damocles suspended over its head! What an interest in keeping those away who might suffer the hair to be cut.

12. To have all these unjust privileges secured to the corporators as a monopoly by a pledge of the public faith to charter no other bank.—This is the most hideous feature in the whole mass of deformity. If these banks are beneficial institutions, why not several? one, at least, and each independent of the other, to each great section of the Union? If malignant, why create one? The restriction constitutes the monopoly, and renders more invidious what was sufficiently hateful in itself. It is, indeed, a double monopoly, legislative as well as banking; for the Congress of 1816 monopolized the power to grant these monopolies. It has tied up the hands of its successors; and if this can be done on one subject, and for twenty years, why not upon all subjects, and for all time?

Fourthly. I object, Mr. President, to the renewal of the bank charter, because this bank is an institution too costly and expensive for the American people to keep up.

Let no one cavil at this head of objection, under the belief that the Bank of the United States supports itself, like the hibernal bear, by sucking its own paws; or that it derives its revenues, as a spider spins its web, from the recesses of its own abdomen. Such a belief would be essentially erroneous, and highly unbecoming the intelligence of the nineteenth century. The fact is that the bank lives upon the people; that all its expenses are made out of the people; all its profits derived from, and all its losses reimbursed by, them. This is the naked truth; by consequence every shilling held, or issued, by the bank, over and above the capital stock, is a tax upon the people. In the case of every other tax, in all the contributions levied for the purposes of Government, there is some alleviation of the burden—some restitution of the abducted treasure—some return to the people—some reinfusion of strength into their ranks—in the customary reimbursement of the revenue. The Government usually pays it back, or a portion of it for salaries, services, and supplies. But, in the case of the bank tax, there is nothing of this reimbursement. The bank refunds nothing; but all the money it makes out of the people is gone from them forever. It goes into a corner of the Union, and remains there; it goes into private hands, and becomes individual property. The stockholders divide it among themselves. Twice, in every year, they make the division of these modern *spolia opima*—these dearest spoils—not of the enemy's general killed in battle, but of American citizens fleeced at home. This is a grievous aggravation of the amount of the tax. It is the aggravation which renders taxation insupportable. It is "absenteeism" in a new and legalized form. It is the whole mischief of that system of absenteeism, which drains off the wealth of Ireland to fertilize England, France, and Italy, leaving Ireland itself the most distressed and exhausted country in Europe, instead of remaining, as God created it, one of the richest and most flourishing. Eternal drawing out, and no bringing back, is a process which no people, or country, can endure. It is a process which would exhaust the resources of nature herself. The earth would be deprived of its moisture, and changed into a desert, if the exhalations of the day did not return in dews at night. The vast ocean itself, with all its deep and boundless waters, would be sucked up and dried away, if the vapors drawn up by the sun did not form into clouds, and descend in rain and snow. So will any people be exhausted of their wealth, no matter how great that wealth may be, whose miserable destiny shall subject them to a system of taxation which is forever levying, and never refunding: a system whose cry is that of the horse leech, more! more! more!—whose voice is that of the grave, give! give! give! —whose attribute is that of the grave also, never to render back!—and such precisely is the system of taxation to which the people of these States are now subjected by the federal bank.

I am willing to see the charter expire, without providing any substitute for the present bank. I am willing to see the currency of the Federal Government left to the hard money mentioned and intended in the Constitution; I am willing to have a hard-money government, as that of France has been since the time of *assignats* and *mandats.* Every species of paper might be left to the State authorities, unrecognized by the Federal Government, and only touched by it for its own convenience when equivalent to gold and silver. Such a currency filled France with the precious metals, when England, with her overgrown bank, was a prey to all the evils of unconvertible paper. It furnished money enough for the imperial Government when the population of the empire was three times more numerous, and the expenses of government twelve times greater, than the population and expenses of the United States; and, when France possessed no mines of gold or silver, and was destitute of the exports which command the specie of other countries. The United States possess gold mines, now yielding half a million per annum, with every prospect of equaling those of Peru. But this is not the best dependence. We have what is superior to mines, namely, the exports which command the money of the world; that is to say, the food which sustains life, and the raw materials which sustain manufactures. Gold and silver is the best currency for a republic; it suits the men of middle property and the working people best; and, if I was going to establish a workingman's party, it should be on the basis of hard money; a hard-money party against a paper party.

The Senate by an adverse vote refused leave for the introduction of the resolution.

In his message at the opening of the next session of Congress (December 6, 1831) the President stated that, after discharging his constitutional duty by bringing the matter before the national legislature, he now left the question of renewing the bank's charter to the people. This was in effect a notice that he would make it a leading issue in the coming presidential campaign.

The National Republican party, at its convention on December 12, 1831, accepted the challenge, and nominated as its candidates Henry Clay [Ky.] and John Sergeant [Pa.], prominent advocates of the bank, upon a platform approving the institution as wholly beneficial and as essential to the business of the country.

Owing to the fact that Congress at this time was in favor of the bank, Clay instigated the officers of the institution to apply for a new charter even though the old one had four years to run.

Clay reasoned, in his own interest, that the passage of the bill would give him an advantage over Jackson by doubly fortifying his defensive position. He already counted on wresting the Democratic State of Pennsylvania from his opponent, owing to the universal sentiment in that State in favor of the bank, which had been expressed in a unanimous endorsement of the institution by the legislature.

The application for the new charter was made in the Senate on January 9, 1832, through George M. Dallas [Pa.]. It came up for discussion on May 23.

Renewal of the Bank Charter

Senate, May 23, 1832

Senator Dallas upheld the motion, saying:

The committee could not be insensible, not merely to the inutility, but to the positively disastrous consequences, to the people, and to their Government, of substituting, for the present, another Bank of the United States; of compelling this to close its enormous business, or to transfer it to other hands; of leaving the immense interests of the industrious, enterprising, and prosperous people of our country, to the extent of more than a hundred millions of dollars, to be rapidly, if not suddenly, shifted in arrangement, responsibility, and connection; or of again committing the monetary system of the entire Confederacy to the charge of local and detached and conflicting State institutions, over which no control whatever could be exercised. Such an unnecessary, involuntary, forced diversion of the great streams of commercial and moneyed operations could not be effected without incalculable and incurable injury to every class, and especially to the laborious, and most worthy, and most useful class, and without sacrificing many of the great purposes of government for which the Constitution was formed. Wherefore, indeed, should such an experiment be made? The practical operations of the existing bank, under its now matured system, have attained every desired object. The currency is uniform, and representing a metallic basis; it is better for all purposes than gold or silver. The collection and distribution of the nation's revenue are gently, safely, and satisfactorily effected. Facilities of every description had been experienced in the financial movements of the Government. Salutary checks and remedies had been applied to the irregularities and fluctuations of foreign and domestic exchanges. And in all parts of the country, particularly in the progressive and enterprising regions of the West, capital and accommodation, at all times and without stint, had, in a manner alike salutary and judicious, been accorded to the people.

Daniel Webster [Mass.] also spoke in favor of the bank, particularly as a means of giving stability to the currency. He said:

The influence of the bank, Mr. President, on the interests of the Government, and the interests of the people, may be considered in several points of view. It may be regarded as it affects the currency of the country; as it affects the collection and disbursement of the public revenue; as it respects foreign exchanges; as it respects domestic exchanges; and as it affects, either generally or locally, the agriculture, commerce, or manufactures of the Union.

First, as to the currency of the country. This is, at all times, a most important political object. A sound currency is an essential and indispensable security for the fruits of industry and honest enterprise. Every man of property or industry, every man who desires to preserve what he honestly possesses, or to obtain what he can honestly earn, has a direct interest in maintaining a safe circulating medium; such a medium as shall be a real and substantial representative of property, not liable to vibrate with opinions, not subject to be blown up or blown down by the breath of speculation, but made stable and secure, by its immediate relation to that which the whole world regards as of permanent value. A disordered currency is one of the greatest of political evils. It undermines the virtues necessary for the support of the social system, and encourages propensities destructive of its happiness. It wars against industry, frugality, and economy; and it fosters the evil spirits of extravagance and speculation. Of all the contrivances for cheating the laboring classes of mankind, none has been more effectual than that which deludes them with paper money. This is the most effectual of inventions to fertilize the rich man's field by the sweat of the poor man's brow. Ordinary tyranny, oppression, excessive taxation, these bear lightly on the happiness of the mass of the community, compared with fraudulent currencies, and the robberies committed by depreciated paper. Our own history has recorded for our instruction enough, and more than enough, of the demoralizing tendency, the injustice, and the intolerable oppression on the virtuous and well-disposed of a degraded paper currency, authorized by law, or in any way countenanced by Government.

We all know, sir, that the establishment of a sound and uniform currency was one of the great ends contemplated in the adoption of the present Constitution. It cannot well be questioned that it was intended by that Constitution to submit the whole subject of the currency of the country, all that regards the actual medium of payment and exchange, whatever that should be, to the control and legislation of Congress. But, notwithstanding this apparent purpose in the Constitution, the truth is that the currency of the country is now, to a very great extent, practically and effectually under the control of the several State governments; if it be not more correct to say that it is under the control of the banking institutions created by the States: for the States seem first to have taken possession of the power, and then to have delegated it.

Whether the States can constitutionally exercise this power, or delegate it to others, is a point which I do not intend, at present, either to concede or to argue. It is much to be hoped that no controversy on the point may ever become necessary. But it is a matter highly deserving of consideration that, although clothed by the Constitution with exclusive power over the metallic currency, Congress, unless through the agency of a bank established by its authority, has no control whatever over that which, in the character of a mere representative of the metallic currency, fills up almost all the channels of pecuniary circulation.

In the absence of a Bank of the United States, the State banks become effectually the regulators of the public currency. Their numbers, their capital, and the interests connected with them give them, in that state of things, a power which nothing is competent to control.

I am of opinion, sir, that a well-conducted national bank has an exceedingly useful and effective operation on the general paper circulation of the country. I think its tendency is manifestly to restrain, within some bounds, the paper issues of other institutions. If it be said, on the other hand, that these institutions in turn hold in check the issues of the national bank, so much the better. Let that check go to its full extent. An over-issue by the bank itself no one can desire. But it is plain that, by holding the State institutions, which come into immediate contact with itself and its branches, to an accountability for their issues, not yearly or quarterly, but daily and hourly, an important restraint is exercised. Be it remembered always that what it is to expect from others it is to perform itself; and that its own paper is at all times to turn into coin by the first touch of its own counter.

The bill passed the Senate on June 11, 1832, by a vote of 28 to 20, and the House on July 3 by a vote of 109 to 76. It was charged that the bank had secured its passage by making loans to Congressmen, and a partisan anti-bank committee of investigation, subsequently appointed by the Democratic Speaker of the House, Andrew Stevenson [Va.], reported that, for three years, from 54 to 59 Congressmen had been so accommodated.

The Opposition felt that it had won a decisive victory in the passage of the bill, because no veto was to be expected, since the Supreme Court, in the case of McCulloch *vs.* Maryland (4 Wheat. 316), had declared that the act of April 10, 1816, incorporating the Bank of the United States, was in "pursuance of the Constitution."

But their expectation was confuted, at once and with great effectiveness, by a message from the President on July 10, 1832, vetoing the bill, and presenting bold and cogent reasons for this action. After a long argument against the abuses of the bank, he said:

Veto of the National Bank

Message of President Jackson, July 10, 1832

It is maintained by the advocates of the bank that its constitutionality, in all its features, ought to be considered as settled by precedent, and by the decision of the Supreme Court. To this conclusion I cannot assent. Mere precedent is a dangerous source of authority, and should not be regarded as deciding questions of constitutional power, except where the acquiescence of the people and the States can be considered as well settled. So far from this being the case on this subject, an argument against the bank might be based on precedent. One Con-

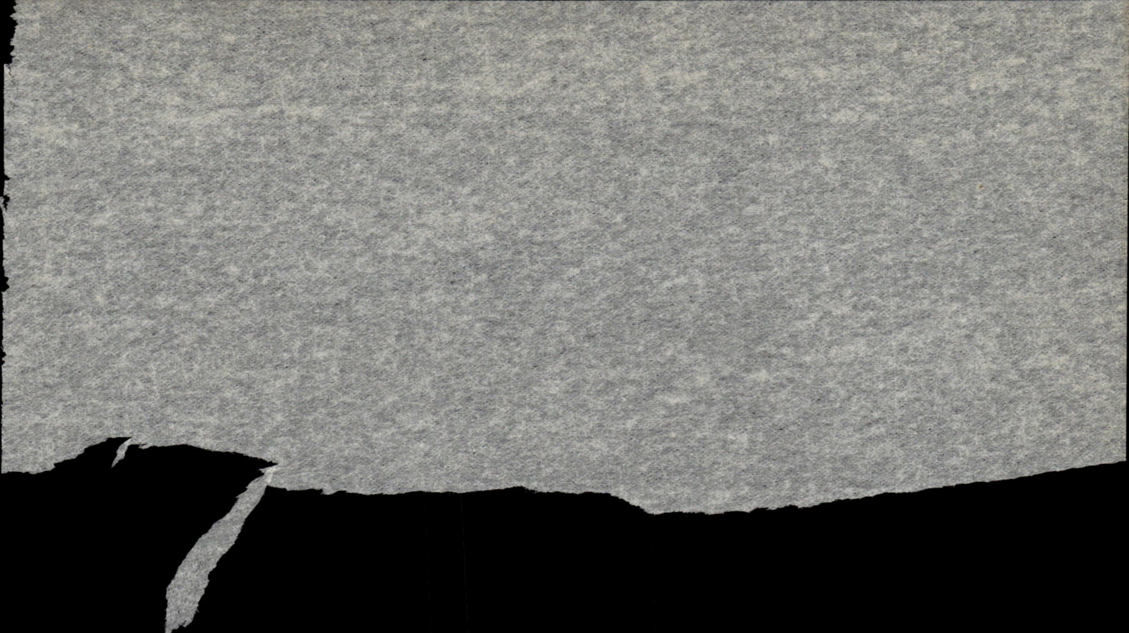

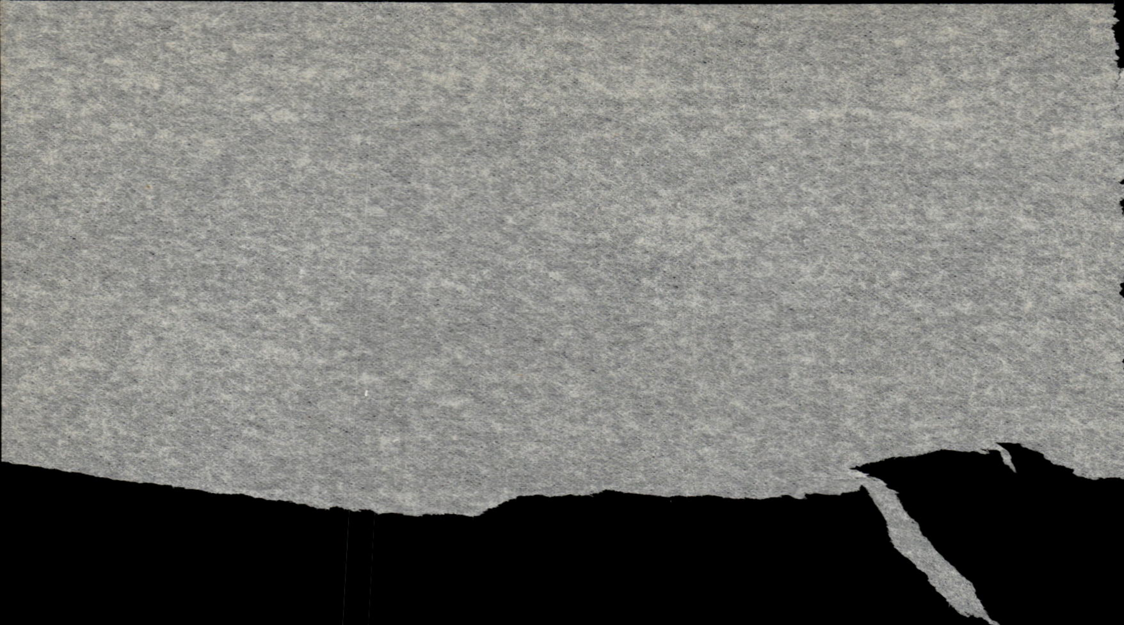

Andrew Jackson

gress, in 1791, decided in favor of a bank; another, in 1811, decided against it. One Congress, in 1815, decided against a bank; another, in 1816, decided in its favor. Prior to the present Congress, therefore, the precedents drawn from that source were equal. If we resort to the States, the expressions of legislative, judicial, and executive opinions against the bank have been, probably, to those in its favor as four to one. There is nothing in precedent, therefore, which, if its authority were admitted, ought to weigh in favor of the act before me.

If the opinion of the Supreme Court covered the whole ground of this act, it ought not to control the coördinate authorities of this Government. The Congress, the Executive, and the court must each for itself be guided by its own opinion of the Constitution. Each public officer who takes an oath to support the Constitution swears that he will support it as he understands it, and not as it is understood by others. It is as much the duty of the House of Representatives, of the Senate, and of the President to decide upon the constitutionality of any bill or resolution which may be presented to them for passage or approval as it is of the supreme judges, when it may be brought before them for judicial decision. The opinion of the judges has no more authority over Congress than the opinion of Congress has over the judges; and on that point the President is independent of both. The authority of the Supreme Court must not, therefore, be permitted to control the Congress or the Executive, when acting in their legislative capacities, but to have only such influence as the force of their reasoning may deserve.

But, in the case relied upon, the Supreme Court have not decided that all the features of this corporation are compatible with the Constitution. It is true that the court have said that the law incorporating the bank is a constitutional exercise of power by Congress. But taking into view the whole opinion of the court, and the reasoning by which they have come to that conclusion, I understand them to have decided that, inasmuch as a bank is an appropriate means for carrying into effect the enumerated powers of the general Government, therefore the law incorporating it is in accordance with that provision of the Constitution which declares that Congress shall have power "to make all laws which shall be necessary and proper for carrying those powers into execution." Having satisfied themselves that the word "necessary," in the Constitution, means "needful," "requisite," "essential," "conducive to," and that "a bank" is a convenient, a useful, and essential instrument in the prosecution of the Government's "fiscal operations," they conclude that to "use one must be within the discretion of Congress"; and that "the act to incorporate the Bank of the United States is a law made in pursuance of the Constitution." "But," say they, "where the law is not prohibited, and is really calculated to effect any of the objects intrusted to the Government, to undertake here to inquire into the degree of its necessity would be to pass the line which circumscribes the judicial department, and to tread on legislative ground."

The principle here affirmed is that the "degree of its necessity," involving all the details of a banking institution, is a question exclusively for legislative consideration. A bank is constitutional; but it is the province of the legislature to determine whether this or that particular power, privilege, or exemption is "necessary and proper" to enable the bank to discharge its duties to the Government; and from their decision there is no appeal to the courts of justice. Under the decision of the Supreme Court, therefore, it is the exclusive province of Congress and the President to decide whether the particular features of this act are "necessary and proper," in order to enable the bank to perform, conveniently and efficiently, the public duties assigned to it as a fiscal agent, and therefore constitutional, or unnecessary and improper, and therefore unconstitutional.

In this manner President Jackson checked, to the aggrandizement of his own office, the power of the Supreme Court, which, since the accession of John Marshall to the Supreme Bench in 1801, had been extending its authority above that of both the legislative and executive branches of the Government.

A debate ensued in the Senate on the message, in which Daniel Webster [Mass.] and Henry Clay [Ky.] denounced the President's action, and Hugh L. White [Tenn.] and Thomas H. Benton [Mo.] defended it.

On the President's Veto

Senate, July 11-12, 1832

Senator Webster.—Mr. President, we have arrived at a new epoch. We are entering on experiments with the Government and the Constitution of the country, hitherto untried, and of fearful and appalling aspect. This message calls us to the contemplation of a future which little resembles the past. Its principles are at war with all that public opinion has sustained, and all which the experience of the Government has sanctioned. It denies first principles. It contradicts truths heretofore received as indisputable. It denies to the judiciary the interpretation of law, and demands to divide with Congress the origination of statutes. It extends the grasp of Executive pretension over every power of the Government. But this is not all. It presents the Chief Magistrate of the Union in the attitude of arguing away the powers of that Government over which he has been chosen to preside; and adopting, for this purpose, modes of reasoning which, even under the influence of all proper feeling toward high official station, it is difficult to regard as respectable. It appeals to every prejudice which may betray men into a mistaken view of their own interests; and to every passion which may lead them to disobey the impulses of their understanding. It urges all the specious topics of State rights and national encroachment, against that which a great majority of the States have affirmed to be rightful, and in which all of them have acquiesced. It sows, in an unsparing manner, the seeds of jealousy and ill will against that government of which its author is the official head. It raises a cry that liberty is in danger, at the very moment when it puts forth claims to power heretofore unknown and unheard of. It affects alarm for the public freedom, when nothing so much endangers that freedom as its own unparalleled pretences. This, even, is not all. It manifestly seeks to influence the poor against the rich. It wantonly attacks whole classes of the people for the purpose of turning against them the prejudices and resentments of other classes. It is a State paper which finds no topic too exciting for its use; no passion too inflammable for its address and its solicitation. Such is the message. It remains now for the people of the United States to choose between the principles here avowed and their Government. These cannot subsist together. The one or the other must be rejected. If the sentiments of the message shall receive general approbation, the Constitution will have perished even earlier than the moment which its enemies originally allowed for the termination of its existence. It will not have survived to its fiftieth year.

Senator White.—Mr. President, in submitting this message, one of the highest duties of the Chief Magistrate has been performed. Under peculiar and trying circumstances he has given his sentiments, plainly and frankly, as he believed his duty required.

When the excitement of the time in which we act shall have

passed away, and the historian and biographer shall be employed in giving his account of the acts of our most distinguished public men, and comes to the name of Andrew Jackson; when he shall have recounted all the great and good deeds done by this man in the course of a long and eventful life, and the circumstances under which this message was communicated shall have been stated, the conclusion will be that, in doing this, he has shown a willingness to risk more to promote the happiness of his fellow men, and to secure their liberties, than by the doing of any other act whatever.

Senator Clay.—The veto is an extraordinary power, which, though tolerated by the Constitution, was not expected by the convention to be used in ordinary cases. It was designed for instances of precipitate legislation, in unguarded moments. Thus restricted, and it had been thus restricted by all former Presidents, it might not be mischievous. During Mr. Madison's Administration of eight years there had occurred but two or three cases of its exercise. During the last Administration I do not now recollect that it was once. In a period little upward of three years the present Chief Magistrate has employed the veto four times. We now hear quite frequently, in the progress of measures through Congress, the statement that the President will veto them urged as an objection to their passage.

The veto is hardly reconcilable with the genius of representative government. It is totally irreconcilable with it, if it is to be frequently employed, in respect to the expediency of measures, as well as their constitutionality. It is a feature of our Government borrowed from a prerogative of the British King. And it is remarkable that in England it has grown obsolete, not having been used for upward of a century. At the commencement of the French revolution, in discussing the principles of their Constitution, in the national convention, the veto held a conspicuous figure. The gay, laughing population of Paris bestowed on the King the appellation of Monsieur Veto, and the Queen that of Madame Veto. The convention finally decreed that, if a measure rejected by the King should obtain the sanction of the two concurring legislatures, it should be a law, notwithstanding the veto. In the constitution of Kentucky, and perhaps in some of the State constitutions, it is provided that if, after the rejection of a bill by the governor, it shall be passed by a majority of all the members elected to both Houses it shall become a law, notwithstanding the governor's objections. As a coördinate branch of the Government, the Chief Magistrate has great weight. If, after a respectful consideration of his objections urged against a bill, a majority of all the members elected to the legislature shall still pass it, notwithstanding his official influence and the force of his reasons, ought it not to become a law? Ought the opinion of one man to overrule that of a legislative body twice deliberately expressed?

It cannot be imagined that the convention contemplated the application of the veto to a question which has been so long, so often, and so thoroughly scrutinized as that of the Bank of the United States, by every department of the Government, in almost every stage of its existence, and by the people, and by the State legislatures. Of all the controverted questions which have sprung up under our Government, not one has been so fully investigated as that of its power to establish a Bank of the United States. More than seventeen years ago, in January, 1815, Mr. Madison then said in a message to the Senate of the United States: "Waiving the question of the constitutional authority of the legislature to establish an incorporated bank, as being precluded, in my judgment, by repeated recognitions, under varied circumstances, of the validity of such an institution, in acts of the legislative, executive, and judicial branches of the Government, accompanied by indications, in different modes, of a concurrence of the general will of the nation." Mr. Madison, himself opposed to the first Bank of the United States, yielded his own convictions to those of the nation, and all the departments of the Government thus often expressed.

After the President had directed public attention to this question in 1829, it became not only a topic of popular conversation, but was discussed in the press, and employed as a theme in popular elections. It seemed as if a sort of general order had gone out from headquarters to the partisans of the Administration everywhere, to agitate and make the most of the question. They have done so: and their condition now reminds me of the fable invented by Dr. Franklin of the Eagle and the Cat, to demonstrate that Æsop had not exhausted inventions in the construction of his memorable fables. The eagle, you know, Mr. President, pounced, from his lofty flight in the air, upon a cat, taking it to be a pig. Having borne off his prize, he quickly felt most painfully the paws of the cat thrust deeply into his sides and body. While flying, he held a parley with the supposed pig, and proposed to let go his hold, if the other would let him alone. No, says puss, you brought me from yonder earth below, and I will hold fast to you until you carry me back; a condition to which the eagle readily assented.

The friends of the President, who have been for nearly three years agitating this question, now turn round upon their opponents who have supposed the President quite serious and in earnest in presenting it for public consideration, and charge them with prematurely agitating it. And that for electioneering purposes! The other side understands perfectly the policy of preferring an unjust charge in order to avoid a well-founded accusation.

Mr. President, we are about to close one of the longest and most arduous sessions of Congress under the present Constitution; and, when we return among our constituents, what account of the operations of their Government shall we be bound to communicate? We shall be compelled to say that the Supreme Court is paralyzed; that the Executive, through the Secretary of the Treasury, sent to Congress a tariff bill which would have destroyed numerous branches of our domestic industry, and led to the final destruction of all; that the veto has been applied to the Bank of the United States, our only reliance for a sound and uniform currency; that the Senate has been violently attacked for the exercise of a clear constitutional power; that the House of Representatives has been unnecessarily assailed; and that the President has promulgated a rule of action for those who have taken the oath to support the Constitution of the United States, that must, if there be practical conformity to it, introduce general nullification, and end in the absolute subversion of the Government.

Senator Benton turned the point of Dr. Franklin's fable in another direction than Senator Clay had done. He said:

An eagle towering in his pride of height was—not by a mousing owl, but by a pig under a jimpson weed—not hawked and killed, but caught and whipped. The opening he thought grand; the conclusion rather bathotic. The mistake of the sharp-eyed bird of Jove, he thought, might be attributed to old age dimming the sight, and to his neglect of his spectacles that morning. He was rather surprised at the whim of the cat in not choosing to fall, seeing that a cat (unlike a politician sometimes) always falls on its legs; but concluded it was a piece of pride in puss, and a wish to assimilate itself still closer to an aëronaut; and, having gone up pendant to a balloon, it would come down artistically, with a parachute spread over its head. It was a pretty fable, and well told; but the moral—the application? Æsop always had a moral to his fable; and Dr. Franklin, his imputed continuator in this particular, though not yet the rival of his master in fabulous reputation, yet had a large sprinkling of practical sense; and never wrote or spoke without a point and an application. And now, what is the point here? And the Senator from Kentucky has not left that to be inferred; he has told it himself. General Jackson is the eagle; the bank is the cat; the parley is the proposition of the bank to the President to sign its charter, and it will support him for the presidency—if not, will keep his claws stuck in his sides. But, Jackson, different from the eagle with his cat, will have no compromise or bargain with the bank. One or the other shall fall, and be dashed into atoms!

CHAPTER V

Censure of President Jackson

[FOR HIS REMOVAL OF GOVERNMENT DEPOSITS FROM THE UNITED STATES BANK]

President Jackson Removes Government Deposits from the United States Bank—The House Supports the President, and the Bank Terminates Its Existence as a National Institution—The Senate Censures the President for His Action—Debate on the Resolution of Censure: in Favor, Henry Clay [Ky.], John C. Calhoun [S. C.]; Opposed, Thomas H. Benton [Mo.]—The Resolution Is Expunged (1837).

IN his fourth annual message of December 4, 1832, President Jackson stated that the Bank of the United States was insolvent, and recommended that the Government's stock in it be sold. This recommendation was not followed by the old Congress, which was anti-Jackson in sentiment. The President thereupon took it upon himself to remove the Government's deposits of money from the bank (or, more strictly, to cease making new deposits, and drawing on the old for Government expenses), justifying his action by the unsafe condition of the bank's affairs, and its conversion into a "permanent electioneering machine" (Annual Message, December, 1833). The Secretary of the Treasury, William J. Duane, had refused to make the removal, whereupon the President replaced him with Roger B. Taney, who carried out the Executive orders. The funds were then deposited in certain State banks, which, because favoritism in their selection was charged, were called "pet banks."

This action of the President became the leading subject of controversy in the next Congress, which met on December 2, 1833. The new House was pro-Jackson, while the Senate remained opposed to the President.

The Senate censured the President for his action, and the House, after a debate continuing through almost the entire session, on April 4, 1834, voted (1) that the bank ought not to be rechartered, (2) that the deposits ought not to be restored, (3) that they should be left in the State banks, and (4) that the affairs of the bank should be investigated. Owing to the obstacles the bank placed in the way the investigation was fruitless. The bank, however, realized that it was doomed, and so applied for a charter from Pennsylvania, receiving which it subsided into a State bank.

The chief speakers in the Senate upon the censure of the President were Henry Clay [Ky.] and John C. Calhoun [S. C.] in favor of censure[1], and Thomas H. Benton [Mo.] opposed to it.

Censure of President Jackson for Removing the Bank Deposits

Senate Session of 1833-34

Senator Clay.—Mr. President, when Congress adjourned at the termination of the last session, there was one remnant of its powers—that over the purse—left untouched. The two most important powers of civil government are those of the sword and purse; the first, with some restrictions, is confided by the Constitution to the Executive, and the last to the legislative department. If they are separate, and exercised by different responsible departments, civil liberty is safe; but, if they are united in the hands of the same individual, it is gone. That clear-sighted and revolutionary orator and patriot, Patrick Henry, justly said, in the Virginia convention, in reply to one of his opponents, "'Let him candidly tell me where and when did freedom exist, when the sword and purse were given up from the people? Unless a miracle in human affairs interposed, no nation ever retained its liberty after the loss of the sword and the purse. Can you prove, by any argumentative deduction, that it is possible to be safe without one of them? If you give them up, you are gone."

Up to the period of the termination of the last session of Congress, the exclusive constitutional power of Congress over

[1] These two statesmen had entered into a coalition against the President.

the treasury of the United States had never been contested. Prior to the establishment of the present Bank of the United States, no treasury or place had been provided or designated by law for the safe keeping of the public moneys, but the treasurer was left to his own discretion and responsibility. When the existing bank was established, it was provided that the public moneys should be deposited with it, and, consequently, that bank became the treasury of the United States; for, whatever place is designated by law for the keeping of the public money of the United States, under the care of the treasurer of the United States, is, for the time being, the treasury. Its safety was drawn in question by the Chief Magistrate, and an agent was appointed a little more than a year ago to investigate its ability. He reported to the Executive that it was perfectly safe. His apprehensions of its solidity were communicated by the President to Congress, and a committee was appointed to examine the subject; they also reported in favor of its security. And finally, among the last acts of the House of Representatives, prior to the close of the last session, was the adoption of a resolution, manifesting its entire confidence in the ability and solidity of the bank.

After all these testimonies to the perfect safety of the public moneys in the place appointed by Congress, who could have supposed that the place would have been changed? Who could have imagined that, within sixty days of the meeting of Congress, and, as it were, in utter contempt of its authority, the change should have been ordered? Who would have dreamed that the treasurer should have thrown away the single key to the treasury, over which Congress held ample control, and accepted, in lieu of it, some dozens of keys, over which neither Congress nor he has any adequate control? Yet, sir, all this has been done; and it is now our solemn duty to inquire, 1st. By whose authority it has been ordered; and, 2d. Whether the order has been given in conformity with the Constitution and laws of the United States.

I agree, sir, and I am very happy whenever I can agree with the President, as to the immense importance of these questions. He says, in the paper which I hold in my hand, that he looks upon the pending question as involving higher considerations than the "mere transfer of a sum of money from one bank to another. Its decision may affect the character of our Government for ages to come." And, with him, I view it as "of transcendent importance, both in the principles and the consequences it involves." It is a question of all time, for posterity as well as for us—of constitutional government or monarchy—of liberty or slavery. As I regard it, I hold the bank as nothing, as perfectly insignificant, faithful as it has been in the performance of all its duties. I hold a sound currency as nothing, essential as it is to the prosperity of every branch of business, and to all conditions of society, and efficient as the agency of the bank has been in providing the country with a currency as sound as ever existed, and unsurpassed by any in Christendom. I consider even the public faith, sacred and inviolable as it ever should be, as comparatively nothing. All these questions are merged in the greater and mightier question of the constitutional distribution of the powers of the Government, as affected by the recent executive innovation. The real inquiry is, Shall all the barriers which have been erected by the caution and wisdom of our ancestors, for the preservation of civil liberty, be prostrated and trodden under foot, and the sword and the purse be at once united in the hands of one man? Shall the power of Congress over the treasury of the United States, hitherto never contested, be wrested from its possession, and be henceforward wielded by the Chief Magistrate?

The President says that "upon him has been devolved, by the Constitution and the suffrages of the American people, the duty of superintending the operation of the executive departments of the Government and seeing that the laws are faithfully executed." If there existed any such double source of executive power, it has been seen that the Treasury Department is not an executive department; but that, in all that concerns the public treasury, the Secretary is the agent or representative of Congress, acting in obedience to their will, and maintaining a direct intercourse with them. By what authority does the President derive power from the mere result of an election? In another part of this same cabinet paper he refers to the suffrages of the people as a source of power, independent of a system in which power has been most carefully separated, and distributed between three separate and independent departments. We have been told a thousand times, and all experience assures us, that such a division is indispensable to the existence and preservation of freedom. We have established and designated offices, and appointed officers in each of those departments, to execute the duties respectively allotted to them. The President, it is true, presides over the whole; specific duties are often assigned by particular laws to him alone, or to other officers under his superintendence. His parental eye is presumed to survey the whole extent of the system in all its movements;

but has he power to come into Congress, and to say such laws only shall you pass; to go into the courts, and prescribe the decisions which they may pronounce; or even to enter the offices of administration, and, where duties are specifically confided to those officers, to substitute his will to their duty? Or has he a right, when those functionaries, deliberating upon their own solemn obligations to the people, have moved forward in their assigned spheres, to arrest their lawful progress, because they have dared to act contrary to his pleasure? No, sir; no, sir. His is a high and glorious station, but it is one of observation and superintendence. It is to see that obstructions in the forward movement of government, unlawfully interposed, shall be abated by legitimate and competent means.

What security have the people against the lawless conduct of any President? Where is the boundary to the tremendous power which he has assumed? Sir, every barrier around the public treasury is broken down and annihilated. From the moment that the President pronounced the words, "This measure is my own; I take upon myself the responsibility of it," every safeguard around the treasury was prostrated, and henceforward it might as well be at the Hermitage.[1] The measure adopted by the President is without precedent. I beg pardon—there is one; but we must go down for it to the commencement of the Christian era. It will be recollected by those who are conversant with Roman history that, after Pompey was compelled to retire to Brundusium, Cæsar, who had been anxious to give him battle, returned to Rome, "having reduced Italy," says the venerable Plutarch, "in sixty days—[the exact period between the day of the removal of the deposits and that of the commencement of the present session of Congress, without the usual allowance of any days of grace]—in sixty days, without bloodshed." The biographer proceeds:

"Finding the city in a more settled condition than he expected, and many senators there, he addressed them in a mild and gracious manner [as the President addressed his late Secretary of the Treasury], and desired them to send deputies to Pompey with an offer of honorable terms of peace, &c. As Metellus, the tribune, opposed his taking money out of the public treasury, and cited some laws against it—[such, sir, I suppose, as I have endeavored to cite on this occasion]—Cæsar said, 'Arms and laws do not flourish together. If you are not pleased at what I am about, you have only to withdraw. [Leave the office, Mr. Duane!] War, indeed, will not tolerate much liberty of

[1] The name of Andrew Jackson's home in Tennessee.

speech. When I say this, I am renouncing my own right; for you, and all those whom I have found exciting a spirit of faction against me, are at my disposal.' Having said this, he approached the doors of the treasury, and, as the keys were not produced, he sent for workmen to break them open. Metellus again opposed him, and gained credit with some for his firmness; but Cæsar, with an elevated voice, threatened to put him to death if he gave him any further trouble. 'And you know very well, young man,' said he, 'that this is harder for me to say than to do.' Metellus, terrified by the menace, retired; and Cæsar was afterward easily and readily supplied with everything necessary for that war."

For more than fifteen years, Mr. President, I have been struggling to avoid the present state of things. I thought I perceived, in some proceedings, during the conduct of the Seminole war, a spirit of defiance to the Constitution and to all law. With what sincerity and truth—with what earnestness and devotion to civil liberty I have struggled the Searcher of all human hearts best knows. With what fortune, the bleeding Constitution of my country now fatally attests.

I have, nevertheless, persevered; and, under every discouragement, during the short time that I expect to remain in the public councils I will persevere. And if a bountiful Providence would allow an unworthy sinner to approach the throne of grace, I would beseech Him, as the greatest favor He could grant to me here below, to spare me until I live to behold the people, rising in their majesty, with a peaceful and constitutional exercise of their power, to expel the Goths from Rome; to rescue the public treasury from pillage, to preserve the constitution of the United States; to uphold the Union against the danger of the concentration and consolidation of *all* power in the hands of the Executive; and to sustain the liberties of the people of this country against the imminent perils to which they now stand exposed.

The eyes and the hopes of the American people are anxiously turned to Congress. They feel that they have been deceived and insulted; their confidence abused; their interest betrayed; and their liberties in danger. They see a rapid and alarming concentration of all power in one man's hands. They see that, by the exercise of the positive authority of the Executive, and his negative power exerted over Congress, the will of one man alone prevails, and governs the republic. The question is no longer what laws will Congress pass, but what will the Executive not veto? The President, and not Congress, is addressed for legislative action. We have seen a corporation, charged with the execution of a great national work, dismiss an experienced, faithful, and zealous president, afterwards testify to his ability by a voluntary resolution, and reward his extraordinary services by a large gratuity, and appoint in his place an executive favorite, totally inexperienced and incompetent, to propitiate the President. We behold the usual incidents of approaching tyranny. The land is filled with spies and informers, and detraction and denunciation are the orders of the day. People, especially official incumbents in this place, no longer dare speak in the fearless tones of manly freemen, but in the cautious whispers of trembling slaves. The premonitory symptoms of depotism are upon us; and if Congress do not apply an instantaneous and effective remedy, the fatal collapse will soon come on, and we shall die—ignobly die—base, mean, and abject slaves; the scorn and contempt of mankind; unpitied, unwept, unmourned!

Senator Benton.—The Senator from Kentucky calls upon the people to rise and drive the Goths from the capitol. Who are those Goths? They are General Jackson and the Democratic party,—he just elected President over the Senator himself, and the party just been made the majority in the House—all by the vote of the people. It is their act that has put these Goths in possession of the capitol to the discomfiture of the Senator and his friends; and he ought to be quite sure that he felt no resentment at an event so disastrous to his hopes, when he has indulged himself with so much license in vituperating those whom the country has put over him.

The Senator from Kentucky says the eyes and the hopes of the country are now turned upon Congress. Yes, Congress is his word, and I hold him to it. And what do they see? They see one House of Congress—the one to which the Constitution gives the care of the purse, and the origination of impeachments, and which is fresh from the popular elections; they see that body with a majority of above fifty in favor of the President and the Secretary of the Treasury, and approving the act which the Senator condemns. They see that popular approbation in looking at one branch of Congress, and the one charged by the Constitution with the inquisition into federal grievances. In the other branch they see a body far removed from the people, neglecting its proper duties, seizing upon those of another branch, converting itself into a grand inquest, and trying offences which itself prefers; and in a spirit which bespeaks a zeal quickened by the sting of personal mortification. He says the country feels itself deceived and betrayed—insulted and wronged—its liberties endangered—and the treasury robbed; the representatives of the people in the other House say the reverse of all this—that the President has saved the country from the corrupt domination of a great corrupting bank, by taking away from her the public money which she was using in bribing the press, subsidizing members, purchasing the venal, and installing herself in supreme political power.

The Senator wishes to know what we are to do? What is our duty to do? I answer, to keep ourselves within our constitutional duties—to leave this impeachment to the House of Representatives—leave it to the House to which it belongs, and to those who have no private griefs to avenge—and to judges, each of whom should retire from the bench, if he happened to feel in his heart the spirit of a prosecutor instead of a judge. The Senate now tries General Jackson; it is subject to trial itself—to be tried by the people, and to have its sentence reversed.

The coalition between Clay and Calhoun against the President was openly acknowledged by both Senators, Clay at the beginning of the debate announcing that he counted on the support of the "Nullifiers," and Calhoun responding as follows:

Senator Calhoun.—The Senator from Kentucky [Mr. Clay] anticipates with confidence that the small party who were denounced at the last session as traitors and disunionists [1] will be found, on this trying occasion, standing in the front rank, and manfully resisting the advance of despotic power. I heard the anticipation with pleasure, not on account of the compliment which it implied, but the evidence which it affords that the cloud which has been so industriously thrown over the character and motive of that small but patriotic party begins to be dissipated. The Senator hazarded nothing in the prediction. That party is the determined, the fixed, and sworn enemy to usurpation, come from what quarter and under what form it may—whether from the Executive upon the other departments of this Government, or from this Government on the sovereignty and rights of the States. The resolution and fortitude with which it maintained its position at the last session, under so many difficulties and dangers, in defence of the States against the encroachments of the general Government, furnished evi-

[1] See Volume V, chapter III.

dence not to be mistaken that that party, in the present momentous struggle, would be found arrayed in defence of the rights of Congress against the encroachments of the President. And let me tell the Senator from Kentucky that, if the present struggle against executive usurpation be successful, it will be owing to the success with which we, the nullifiers—I am not afraid of the word—maintained the rights of the States against the encroachment of the general Government at the last session.

The Senator from Kentucky read a striking passage from one of the most pleasing and instructive writers in any language [Plutarch], the description of Cæsar forcing himself, sword in hand, into the treasury of the Roman commonwealth. We are at the same stage of our political revolution, and the analogy between the two cases is complete, varied only by the character of the actors and the circumstances of the times. That was a case of an intrepid and bold warrior, as an open plunderer, seizing forcibly the treasury of the country, which, in that republic, as well as ours, was confined to the custody of the legislative department of the Government. The actors in our case are of a different character—artful, cunning, and corrupt politicians, and not fearless warriors. They have entered the treasury, not sword in hand, as public plunderers, but, with the false keys of sophistry, as pilferers, under the silence of midnight. The motive and the object are the same, varied in like manner by circumstances and character. "With money I will get men, and with men money," was the maxim of the Roman plunderer. With money we will get partisans, with partisans votes, and with votes money, is the maxim of our public pilferers. With men and money Cæsar struck down Roman liberty, at the fatal battle of Pharsalia, never to rise again; from which disastrous hour all the powers of the Roman republic were consolidated in the person of Cæsar, and perpetuated in his line. With money and corrupt partisans a great effort is now making to choke and stifle the voice of American liberty, through all its natural organs; by corrupting the press; by overawing the other departments; and, finally, by setting up a new and polluted organ, composed of officeholders and corrupt partisans, under the name of a national convention, which, counterfeiting the voice of the people, will, if not resisted, in their name dictate the succession. When this deed is done, the revolution will be completed, and all the powers of our republic, in like manner, will be consolidated in the President, and perpetuated by his dictation.

Senator Calhoun nevertheless showed his independence by differing from his new colleague on their ancient point of difference, the tariff, and claimed that it was the action of the "Nullifiers" which had strengthened Clay in his present position. Since Clay had to submit to this humiliating view of the situation as the price of Calhoun's support, the Senator from South Carolina gained the "whip-hand" in the coalition.

The revolution, in the midst of which we are, began, not as supposed by the Senator from Kentucky, shortly before the commencement of the present session, but many years ago, with the commencement of the restrictive system, and terminated its first stage with the passage of the force bill of the last session, which absorbed all the rights and sovereignty of the States, and consolidated them in this Government. While this process was going on, of absorbing the reserved powers of the States, on the part of the general Government, another commenced, of concentrating in the Executive the powers of the other two—the legislative and judicial departments of the Government; which constitutes the second stage of the revolution, in which we have advanced almost to the termination.

To the interposition of the State of South Carolina we are indebted for the adjustment of the tariff question; without it, all the influence of the Senator from Kentucky over the manufacturing interest, great as it deservedly is, would have been wholly incompetent, if he had even thought proper to exert it, to adjust the question. The attempt would have prostrated him, and those who acted with him, and not the system. It was the separate action of the State that gave him the place to stand upon, created the necessity for the adjustment, and disposed the minds of all to compromise.

I will venture to add to these remarks another, in connection with the point under consideration, not less true. We are not only indebted to the cause which I have stated for our present strength in this body against the present usurpation of the Executive, but if the adjustment of the tariff had stood alone, as it ought to have done, without the odious bill which accompanied it—if those who led in the compromise had joined the State-rights party in their resistance to that unconstitutional measure, and thrown the responsibility on its real authors, the Administration, their party would have been so prostrated throughout the entire South, and their power, in consequence, so reduced, that they would not have dared to attempt the present measure; or, if they had, they would have been broken and defeated.

The President replied as follows to the censure:

Protest Against Censure

President Jackson

The resolution [of censure] charges in substance that, in certain proceedings relating to the public revenue, the President has usurped authority and power not conferred upon him by the Constitution and laws, and that in doing so he violated both. Any such act constitutes a high crime—one of the highest, indeed, which the President can commit—a crime which justly exposes him to impeachment by the House of Representatives, and, upon due conviction, to removal from office, and to the complete and immutable disfranchisement prescribed by the Constitution.

The resolution, then, is in substance an impeachment of the President; and in its passage amounts to a declaration by a majority of the Senate that he is guilty of an impeachable offence. As such it is spread upon the journals of the Senate—published to the nation and to the world—made part of our enduring archives—and incorporated in the history of the age. The punishment of removal from office and future disqualification does not, it is true, follow this decision; nor would it have followed the like decision, if the regular forms of proceeding had been pursued, because the requisite number did not concur in the result. But the moral influence of a solemn declaration, by a majority of the Senate, that the accused is guilty of the offence charged upon him has been as effectually secured as if the like declaration had been made upon an impeachment expressed in the same terms. Indeed, a greater practical effect has been gained, because the votes given for the resolution, though not sufficient to authorize a judgment of guilty on an impeachment, were numerous enough to carry that resolution.

The President of the United States, therefore, has been by a majority of his constitutional triers, accused and found guilty of an impeachable offence; but in no part of this proceeding have the directions of the Constitution been observed.

The impeachment, instead of being preferred and prosecuted by the House of Representatives, originated in the Senate, and was prosecuted without the aid or concurrence of the other House. The oath or affirmation prescribed by the Constitution was not taken by the Senators; the Chief Justice did not preside; no notice of the charge was given to the accused; and no opportunity afforded him to respond to the accusation, to meet his accusers face to face, to cross-examine the witnesses, to procure counteracting testimony, or to be heard in his defence. These safeguards and formalities were not only practically disregarded, in the commencement and conduct of these proceedings, but in their result I find myself convicted by less than two-thirds of the members present of an impeachable offence.

For the reasons which have been stated, I do hereby solemnly protest against the aforementioned proceedings of the Senate, as unauthorized by the Constitution; contrary to its spirit and to several of its express provisions; subversive of that distribution of the powers of government which it has ordained and established; destructive of the checks and safeguards by which those powers were intended, on the one hand, to be controlled, and, on the other, to be protected; and calculated, by their immediate and collateral effects, by their character and tendency, to concentrate in the hands of a body not directly amenable to the people a degree of influence and power dangerous to their liberties, and fatal to the constitution of their choice.

The resolution of the Senate contains an imputation upon my private as well as upon my public character; and, as it must stand forever on their journals, I cannot close this substitute for that defence which I have not been allowed to present in the ordinary form without remarking that I have lived in vain if it be necessary to enter into a formal vindication of my character and purposes from such an imputation. In vain do I bear upon my person enduring memorials of that contest in which American liberty was purchased; in vain have I since periled property, fame, and life in defence of the rights and privileges so dearly bought; in vain am I now, without a personal aspiration, or the hope of individual advantage, encountering responsibilities and dangers, from which, by mere inactivity in relation to a single point, I might have been exempt—if any serious doubts can be entertained as to the purity of my purposes and motives. If I had been ambitious, I should have sought an alliance with that powerful institution which even now aspires to no divided empire. If I had been venal, I should have sold myself to its designs. Had I preferred personal comfort and official ease to the performance of my arduous duty, I should have ceased to molest it. In the history of conquerors and usurpers, never, in the fire of youth, nor in the vigor of manhood, could I find an attraction to lure me from the path of duty; and now I shall scarcely find an inducement to commence the career of ambition, when gray hairs and a decaying frame, instead of inviting to toil and battle, call me to the contemplation of other worlds, where conquerors cease to be honored, and usurpers expiate their crimes. The only ambition I can feel is to acquit myself to Him to whom I must soon render an account of my stewardship, to serve my fellow-men, and live respected and honored in the history of my country. No; the ambition which leads me on is an anxious desire and a fixed determination to return to the people, unimpaired, the sacred trust they have confided to my charge—to heal the wounds of the Constitution and preserve it from further violation; to persuade my countrymen, so far as I may, that it is not in a splendid government, supported by powerful monopolies and aristocratical establishments, that they will find happiness, or their liberties protected, but in a plain system, void of pomp—protecting all, and granting favors to none—dispensing its blessings like the dews of heaven, unseen and unfelt, save in the freshness and beauty they contribute to produce. It is such a government that the genius of our people requires—such a one only under which our States may remain for ages to come united, prosperous, and free. If the Almighty Being who has hitherto sustained and protected me will but vouchsafe to make my feeble powers instrumental to such a result, I shall anticipate with pleasure the place to be assigned me in the history of my country, and die contented with the belief that I have contributed in some small degree to increase the value and prolong the duration of American liberty.

To the end that the resolution of the Senate may not be hereafter drawn into precedent, with the authority of silent acquiescence on the part of the Executive Department; and to the end, also, that my motives and views in the Executive proceeding denounced in that resolution may be known to my fellow-citizens, to the world, and to all posterity, I respectfully request that this message and protest may be entered at length on the journals of the Senate.

The resolution, after many debates in which Senators Benton and William R. King [Ala.] led in defence of the President, and Webster, Clay, and Calhoun were the chief opponents, was expunged from the Senate journal on January 14, 1837, by a vote of 24 to 19.

CHAPTER VI

Paper Money or Specie?

[President Jackson's Treasury Circular]

Inflation of the Currency by State Bank Notes—President Jackson on the Evils of Such a Currency—The Treasury Circular Ordering Payments in Specie for Public Lands—Thomas Ewing, Sr. [O.] Moves in the Senate to Rescind the Order—Debate on the Resolution: in Favor, Senator Ewing, Daniel Webster [Mass.]; Opposed, Thomas H. Benton [Mo.]—William C. Rives [Va.] Moves in the Senate That Only Bank Notes of Large Denominations and Payable in Specie Be Accepted by the Government—Debate on a Bill Based on the Resolution: in Favor, Senator Rives, Robert J. Walker [Miss.]; Opposed, Senator Benton—Bill Is Carried, but Receives the President's "Pocket" Veto.

THE demise of the Bank of the United States left the State banks the only available receptacle of the public funds, and these were in a condition far from sound, owing to the liberality of their charters, which permitted them to issue notes to an extent far beyond their actual capital, thus flooding the country with paper money, which caused a general increase in the price of all property and great and sudden fluctuations in land values in particular. An era of land speculation began which promised to end in disaster.

Accordingly, finance became a chief subject of interest with Congress. In 1835 the national legislature took preparatory steps to bring the currency back to the hard money system intended by the Constitution, by greatly increasing the output of the mint (incidentally increasing the ratio of silver and gold to 16 to 1 from 15 to 1), and by passing various acts forbidding the receipt or payment on public account of the small notes of the State banks. In his annual message of December 6, 1836, President Jackson spoke of the problem as follows:

Evil Effects of Inflation of the Currency

President Jackson

Variableness must ever be the characteristic of a currency, of which the precious metals are not the chief ingredient, or which can be expanded or contracted without regard to the principles that regulate the value of those metals as a standard in the general trade of the world. With us, bank issues constitute such a currency, and must ever do so, until they are made dependent on those just proportions of gold and silver, as a circulating medium, which experience has proved to be necessary, not only in this, but in all other commercial countries. Where those proportions are not infused into the circulation, and do not control it, it is manifest that prices must vary according to the tide of bank issues, and the value and stability of property must stand exposed to all the uncertainty which attends the administration of institutions that are constantly liable to the temptation of an interest distinct from that of the community in which they are established.

The progress of an expansion, or rather a depreciation, of the currency, by excessive bank issues, is always attended by a loss to the laboring classes. This portion of the community have neither time nor opportunity to watch the ebbs and flows of the money market. Engaged from day to day in their useful toils, they do not perceive that, although their wages are nominally the same, or even somewhat higher, they are greatly reduced, in fact, by the rapid increase of a spurious currency; which, as it appears to make money abound, they are at first inclined to consider a blessing. It is not so with the speculator, by whom this operation is better understood, and is made to contribute to his advantage. It is not until the prices of the necessaries of life become so dear that the laboring classes cannot supply their wants out of their wages that the wages rise and gradually reach a justly proportioned rate to that of the products of their labor. When thus, by the depreciation in consequence of the quantity of paper in circulation, wages as well as prices become exorbitant, it is soon found that the whole effect of the adulterations is a tariff on our home industry for the benefit of the countries where gold and silver circulate and maintain uniformity and moderation in prices. It is then perceived that the enhancement of the price of land and labor produces a corresponding increase in the price of products, until

THE MODERN BALAAM AND HIS ASS

[Caricature of Jackson and Van Buren, and, for the first time, of the Democratic Donkey]

From the collection of the New York Historical Society

these products do not sustain a competition with similar ones in other countries, and thus both manufactured and agricultural productions cease to bear exportation from the country of the spurious currency, because they cannot be sold for cost. This is the process by which specie is banished by the paper of the banks. Their vaults are soon exhausted to pay for foreign commodities; the next step is a stoppage of specie payment—a total degradation of paper as a currency—unusual depression of prices, the ruin of debtors, and the accumulation of property in the hands of creditors and cautious capitalists.

It was in view of these evils, together with the dangerous power wielded by the Bank of the United States, and its repugnance to our Constitution, that I was induced to exert the power conferred upon me by the American people to prevent the continuance of that institution. But, although various dangers to our republican institutions have been obviated by the failure of that bank to extort from the Government a renewal of its charter, it is obvious that little has been accomplished except a salutary change of public opinion toward restoring to the country the sound currency provided for in the Constitution. In the acts of several of the States prohibiting the circulation of small notes, and the auxiliary enactments of Congress at the last session, forbidding their reception or payment on public account, the true policy of the country has been advanced, and a larger portion of the precious metals infused into our circulating medium. These measures will probably be followed up in due time by the enactment of State laws, banishing from circulation bank notes of still higher denominations; and the object may be materially promoted by further acts of Congress, forbidding the employment, as fiscal agents, of such banks as continue to issue notes of low denominations, and throw impediments in the way of the circulation of gold and silver.

The effects of an extension of bank credits and over-issues of bank paper have been strikingly illustrated in the sales of the public lands. From the returns made by the various registers and receivers in the early part of last summer, it was perceived that the receipts arising from the sales of the public lands were increasing to an unprecedented amount. In effect, however, these receipts amounted to nothing more than credits in bank. The banks let out their notes to speculators; they were paid to the receivers, and immediately returned to the banks to be sent out again and again, being mere instruments to transfer to speculators the most valuable public land, and pay the Government by a credit on the books of the banks. Those credits on the books of some of the Western banks, usually called deposits, were already greatly beyond their immediate means of payment and were rapidly increasing. Indeed, each speculation furnished means for another; for no sooner had one individual or company paid in their notes than they were immediately lent to another for a like purpose; and the banks were extending their business and their issues so largely as to alarm considerate men, and render it doubtful whether these bank credits, if permitted to accumulate, would ultimately be of the least value to the Government. The spirit of expansion and speculation was not confined to the deposit banks, but pervaded the whole multitude of banks throughout the Union, and was giveing rise to new institutions to aggravate the evil.

The safety of the public funds, and the interest of the people, generally, required that these operations should be checked and it became the duty of every branch of the general and State governments to adopt all legitimate and proper means to produce that salutary effect. Under this view of my duty, I directed the issuing of the order [1] which will be laid before you by the Secretary of the Treasury, requiring payment for the public lands sold to be made in specie, with an exception until the fifteenth of the present month in favor of actual settlers. This measure has produced many salutary consequences. It checked the career of the Western banks, and gave them additional strength in anticipation of the pressure which has since pervaded our Eastern as well as the European commercial cities. By preventing the extension of the credit system, it measurably cut off the means of speculation, and retarded its progress in monopolizing the most valuable of the public lands. It has tended to save the new States from a non-resident proprietorship, one of the greatest obstacles to the advancement of a new country and the prosperity of an old one. It has tended to keep open the public lands for entry by emigrants, at Government prices, instead of their being compelled to purchase of speculators at double or treble prices. And it is conveying into the interior large sums in silver and gold, there to enter permanently into the currency of the country, and place it on a firmer foundation.

The President accordingly recommended Congress to take further steps in this direction, especially in preventing the excessive issue of bank paper.

[1] On July 11, 1836.

On December 14 Thomas Ewing, Sr. [Ohio] introduced in the Senate resolutions rescinding the order of the Secretary of the Treasury mentioned by the President in his message. Upon these an extended debate took place, in which the order was attacked by Senator Ewing and Daniel Webster [Mass.], and defended by Thomas H. Benton [Mo.]

The Treasury Circular

Senate, December 14-21, 1836

Senator Ewing.—It was foreseen, prior to the commencement of the last session of Congress, that there would be a very large surplus of money in the public treasury beyond the wants of the country for all their reasonable expenditures. It was also well understood that the land bill, or some other measure for the distribution of this fund, would be again presented to Congress; and, if the true condition of the public treasury were known and understood, that its distribution, in some form or other, would be demanded by the country. On the other hand, it seems to have been determined by the party, and some of those who act with it thoroughly, that the money should remain where it was, in the deposit banks, so that it could be wielded at pleasure by the Executive.

Senators, in the course of the debate which afterward sprung up on the land bill, denied, and most unequivocally, that there was any surplus, or that there would be any; and, when some of us offered an estimate of what would be the receipts into the treasury in the current year, we were told that it would be very difficult to fasten that estimate upon us at this session of Congress.

But when the true state of things became too obvious to be any longer successfully contested; when it became apparent to everyone here and to the public that there was a large amount of public money lying in the deposit banks, and likely to remain there for years, an injury to the public, and beneficial to nobody, except bankers and brokers, the deposit bill passed, after a desperate struggle, and then came this measure—the treasury order—intended to destroy its effect.

This order was issued not by the advice of Congress nor under the sanction of any law. It was delayed until Congress was fairly out of the city, and all possibility of interference by legislation was removed, and then came forth this new and last expedient. It was known that these funds, received for public lands, had become a chief source of revenue, and it may have occurred to some that the passage of a treasury order of this kind would have a tendency to embarrass the country; and, as the bill for the regulation of the deposits had just passed, the public might be brought to believe that all the mischief occasioned by the order was the effect of the distribution bill. It has, indeed, happened that this scheme has failed; the public understand it rightly, but that was not by any means certain at the time the measure was devised. It was not then foreseen that the people would as generally see through the contrivance as it has since been found that they do.

There may have been various other motives which led to the measure. Many minds were probably to be consulted, for it is not to be presumed that a step like this was taken without consultation, and guided by the will of a single individual alone. That is not the way in which these things are done. No doubt one effect hoped for by some was that a check would be given to the sales of the public lands. The operation of the order would naturally be to raise the price of land by raising the price of the currency in which it was to be paid for. But, while this would be the effect on small buyers, those who purchased on a large scale would be enabled to sell at an advance of ten or fifteen per cent. over what would have been given if the United States lands had been open to purchasers in the ordinary way. Those who had borrowed money of the deposit banks and paid it out for lands would thus be enabled to make sales to advantage, and by means of such sales make payment to the banks who found it necessary to call in their large loans, in order to meet the provisions of the deposit bill. The order, therefore, was likely to operate to the common benefit of the deposit banks and the great land dealers, while it counteracted the efforts of the obnoxious deposit bill.

There may have been yet another motive actuating some of those who devised this order. There was danger that the deposit banks, when called upon to refund the public treasure, would be unable to do it; indeed, it was said on this floor that the immediate effect of the distribution bill would be to break those banks. Now this treasury order would operate to collect the specie of the country into the land offices, whence it would immediately go into the deposit banks, and would prove an acceptable aid to them while making the transfers required by law. These seem to me to have been among the real motives which led to the adoption of that order.

Senator Benton.—The treasury order was a measure of regulation upon the State banks, intended to save the finances and the currency, as well as the public lands. The Bank of the United States regulated the State banks by the simple process of excluding their paper from the Federal receipts and expenditures. She excluded them to make room for her own notes; and this is the extent of her skill and of her merit in all this boasted regulation of local currencies of which we hear so much. The Federal Government has only to do the same, and the State bank issues are repelled upon their sources, and become comparatively harmless. It is receivability for Federal dues; it is receivability at the land offices, customhouses, and post offices, which gives them wings to fly over the continent, and enables them to pass, without regard to the credit or solvency of the bank from which they come. It is the Federal Government indorsement which does the mischief; and this indorsement, for all the purposes of false credit and want of responsibility, is given to the whole issue of every bank whose paper is made receivable for public dues. The experiment has been tried, and local paper has failed as a national currency, and out of that failure arose the second United States Bank. It will fail again, and again, and forever! There is no safety for the Federal revenues but in the total exclusion of local paper, and that from every branch of the revenue—customs, lands, and post office. There is no safety for the national finances but in the constitutional medium of gold and silver. After forty years of wandering in the wilderness of paper money, we have approached the confines of the constitutional medium. Seventy-five millions of specie in the country, with the prospect of an annual increase of ten or twelve millions for the next four years, three branch mints to commence next spring, and the complete restoration of the gold currency announce the success of President Jackson's great measures for the reform of the currency, and vindicate the Constitution from the libel of having prescribed an impracticable currency. The success is complete; and there is no way to thwart it, but to put down the treasury order, and to reopen the public lands to the inundation of paper money. Of this, it is not to be dissembled, there is great danger. Four deeply interested classes are at work to do it—speculators, local banks, United States Bank, and politicians out of power. They may succeed, but he (Mr. B.) would not despair. The darkest hour of night is just before the break of day; and, through the gloom ahead, he saw the bright vision of the constitutional currency erect, radiant, and victorious. Through regulation or explosion success must eventually come. If reform measures go on, gold and silver will be gradually and temperately restored; if reform measures are stopped, then the paper system runs riot, and explodes from its own expansion. Then the Bank of the United States will exult on the catastrophe, and claim its own reëstablishment, as the only adequate regulator of the local banks. Then it will be said the specie experiment has failed! But no; the contrary will be known, that the specie experiment has not failed, but it was put down by the voice and power of the interested classes, and must be put up again by the voice and power of the disinterested community.

SENATOR WEBSTER.—What is meant by the "constitutional currency," about which so much is said? What species, or forms, of currency does the Constitution allow, and what does it forbid? It is plain enough that this depends on what we understand by currency. Currency, in a large and, perhaps, in a just sense, includes not only gold and silver and bank notes, but bills of exchange also. It may include all that adjusts exchanges, and settles balances, in the operations of trade and business. But if we understand by currency the legal money of the country, that which constitutes a lawful tender for debts, and is the statute measure of value, then, undoubtedly, nothing is included but gold and silver. Most unquestionably there is no legal tender, and there can be no legal tender, in this country, under the authority of this Government or any other, but gold and silver, either the coinage of our own mints, or foreign coins, at rates regulated by Congress. This is a constitutional principle, perfectly plain, and of the very highest importance. The States are expressly prohibited from making anything but gold and silver a tender in payment of debts; and, although no such express prohibition is applied to Congress, yet, as Congress has no power granted to it, in this respect, but to coin money, and to regulate the value of foreign coins, it clearly has no power to substitute paper, or anything else, for coin, as a tender in payment of debts and in discharge of contracts.

The only question, therefore, is, what is the law, or what was the law, when the Secretary issued his order?

The Secretary considers that that which has been uniformly done for twenty years, that is to say, the receiving of payment for the public lands in the bills of specie-paying banks, is against law. He calls it an "indulgence," and this "indulgence" the order proposes to continue for a limited time, and in favor of a particular class of purchasers. If this were an indulgence, and against law, one might well ask, how has it happened that it should have continued so long, especially through recent years, marked by such a spirit of thorough and searching reform? It might be asked, too, if this be illegal, and an indulgence only, why continue it longer, and especially why continue it as to some, and refuse to continue it as to others?

But, sir, it is time to turn to the statute, and to see what the legal provision is. On the 30th of April, 1816, a resolution passed both Houses of Congress. It was in the common form of a joint resolution, and was approved by the President. It provides that, "from and after the 20th day of February next (1817), no duties, taxes, debts, or sums of money, accruing or becoming payable to the United States, ought to be collected or received otherwise than in the legal currency of the United States, or treasury notes, or notes of the Bank of the United States, or *in notes of banks which are payable in specie on demand,* in the said legal currency of the United States."

The honorable member from Missouri has, indeed, himself furnished a complete answer to the Secretary's idea; that is to say, he defends the order on grounds not only differing from, but totally inconsistent with, those assumed by the Secretary. He does not consider the receipt of bank notes hitherto, or up to the time of issuing the order, as an indulgence, but as a lawful right while it lasted. Thus his argument entirely deprives the Secretary of the only ground assigned by him for the treasury order.

I am, therefore, of opinion that the treasury order of the 11th of July is against the plain words and meaning of the law of 1816; against the whole practice of the Government under that law; against the honorable gentleman's own opinion, as expressed in his resolution of the 23d of April; and not reconcilable with the necessity which was supposed to exist for the passage of the act of last session.

On January 10, 1837, Senator William C. Rives [Va.] proposed, as a substitute for Senator Ewing's motion, the resolution that thereafter all sums of money due the United States should be paid in specie, or in bank notes which were payable in specie on demand, subject to the restriction that notes of low denomination should not be received, there being a stated gradual increase in the minimum amount of the receivable notes. The resolutions of Ewing and Rives were referred to the Committee on Public Lands, which reported Rive's resolution with the proviso that the public deposits should be withdrawn from those banks which refused to receive and credit to the United States notes receivable under the act.

Senator Rives and Robert J. Walker [Miss.] defended the resolution, and Senator Benton opposed it. Rives's speech is valuable chiefly for its clear presentation of economic laws, notably Sir Thomas Gresham's law that "bad money drives good out of circulation," as amplified by Adam Smith. Rives held that paper and specie could both be used, if they were not of the same denomination. Benton insisted on hard money alone, whence he received the nickname of "Old Bullion."[1]

Relations of Paper Money and Specie

Senate, January 10-28, 1837

Senator Rives.—In discussing the question of a reform of the currency, it is necessary to settle our ideas clearly as to two things: first, the nature and extent of the end to be aimed at; secondly, the means by which it is to be attained. If I am asked what is the end I propose, whether I am in favor of a specie circulation exclusively, and the total suppression of bank paper, I answer No. Even if such an object were desirable, it is plainly impracticable. In the present state of commercial progress and refinement throughout the world, it would probably be impracticable anywhere; but in this country, and under our system of government especially, it is obviously wholly unattainable. Whether right or wrong, we find twenty-six independent State legislatures possessed of the power to create banking corporations. Whatever speculative doubts may exist in the minds of some as to the constitutional validity of this power, the States now actually possess and exercise it, as they have invariably done from the foundation of the Government, and there is not the slightest probability that they will ever be divested of it. In every sober and practical scheme of policy we must proceed upon the assumption that this independent State power will remain. How, then, can the banking system

[1] This name also squinted at "billon," precious metal containing a large alloy of baser, which Senator Benton suggested should be used in our currency (see page 123).

be suppressed by this Government? Such a notion, if entertained anywhere, would indeed be Utopian and visionary.

My object, then, would be, not the destruction of the banking system and the total suppression of bank paper, but an efficient regulation of it, and its restriction to safe and proper limits; not the exclusive use of specie as a circulating medium, but such a substantial enlargement and general diffusion of it, in actual circulation, as would make it the practical currency of common life, the universal medium of ordinary transactions; in short, the money of the farmer, the mechanic, the laborer, and the tradesman; while the merchant should be left in the enjoyment of the facilities of a sound and restricted paper currency for his larger operations. Such a reformation in the currency as this would, in my opinion, be productive of the most beneficial results. It would give security to the industrious classes of society for the products of their labor, against the casualties incident to the paper system. The laborer, in returning to the bosom of his family from his weekly toil, would no longer find his slumbers broken by the apprehension that the hard earnings of the week, perhaps the accumulation of long years of honest industry, might be dissipated in a moment by the explosion of a bank, or the bursting of some paper bubble. It would give security, to a great extent, to the whole body of the community against those disastrous fluctuations in the value of property and contracts which arise from the ebbs and flows of an unrestricted paper currency. It would give security to the banks themselves, by providing them, in the daily internal circulation of the country, an abundant and accessible fund for recruiting their resources, whenever they should be exposed to an extraordinary pressure.

This, sir, is the happy state of things we might promise ourselves from replacing (as it is the aim of the proposition which I have had the honor to submit to do) all bank bills, under the denomination of twenty dollars, with a solid circulation of gold and silver. Is there anything wild, anything visionary, anything pernicious, in such a system of currency as this? It has the sanction, Mr. President, of the profoundest writers on questions of political economy, and has received the practical assent of the wisest nations. I am well aware that it would ill become me to present for the consideration of the Senate any scheme which was not thus tested and approved. Of all the writers who have treated and examined questions of this character, none possess so high an authority as the author of the "Wealth of Nations." It has been well and justly said that Adam Smith had done for the science of political economy what Bacon and Newton had done for physical science, and Sydney and Locke for the science of government and the fundamental principles of civil and political liberty. His work, appearing contemporaneously with the American Revolution, was deeply imbued with the free spirit and the large and vigorous thought which so remarkably distinguished that great era. He came forth as the zealous and powerful champion of free trade, the inflexible opponent of monopoly and restriction, in all their multiplied forms, the ardent advocate of everything that is liberal, generous, and popular, in the institutions of society and the intercourse of nations. No work has ever exercised so large an influence for good on the policy and destiny of nations; and none, I am sure, considering the stamp of liberty as well as wisdom impressed upon it, is better entitled to the respect of an assembly of American legislators. Adam Smith, by a strange mistake, has been held up, rather opprobriously, as the advocate of a paper system—as the founder, in fact, of the paper school! Sir, there can be no greater mistake than this. While he recognized the utility of a judicious system of banking, in liberating and putting into productive employment capital which would otherwise remain dead and inactive, and the facilities it is calculated to afford to commerce, he yet insists that the general circulation of the country should be gold and silver.

As the general principles he has laid down on the subjects of banking and currency continue still to be appealed to by the enlightened writers who have followed him, as affording the soundest exposition of those subjects, whatever modifications of subordinate points may have been made by subsequent inquirers, I will give to the Senate, and principally in the words of Adam Smith himself, an outline of his system of currency. After speaking of the advantages to be expected from a judicious and properly conducted system of banking, he says expressly that "the commerce and industry of a country are not so secure when suspended, as it were, on the Dædalian wings of paper money, as when they travel about on the solid ground of gold and silver." He says, therefore, it is the policy of wise governments "to guard, not only against that excessive multiplication of paper money which ruins the very banks which issue it, but even against that multiplication of it which enables them to fill the greater part of the circulation of the country with it." He then proceeds to show that "the circulation of every country may be considered as divided into two different branches: the circulation of the dealers with one another, and the circulation between the dealers and consumers." His next position is, "that paper money may be so regulated as either to confine itself very much to the circulation between the different dealers, or to extend itself likewise to a great part of that between the dealers and consumers." The regulation is effected by fixing the denomination of the notes permitted to be issued. "It were better," he adds, "that no bank notes were issued in any part of the kingdom for a smaller sum than five pounds. Paper money would then confine itself to the circulation between the different dealers"; and, where this is the case, he says, "there is always plenty of gold and silver. But where it extends itself to a considerable part of the circulation between dealers and consumers it banishes gold and silver almost entirely from the country." The system of Adam Smith, then, resolves itself into this: that the circulation between dealer and dealer may be of paper, but that the circulation between dealer and consumer should be of the precious metals; that this result ought to be secured by prohibiting the issue of bank notes for a less sum than five pounds, and that, if such a restriction be adopted, there "will always be plenty of gold and silver" in circulation, performing all the offices of exchange in the "ordinary transactions" of society, while the use of paper would be confined to commercial operations of a larger scale.

Instead of being the advocate, far less the founder, of an unrestricted paper system, Smith urges the necessity of confining it to commercial accommodation in the larger transactions between dealer and dealer. He is in favor of the suppression of all bank notes under five pounds; whereby gold and silver will fill the ordinary channels of circulation, and become, in fact, the common practical currency of the country.

It is in vain to expect to bring gold and silver coins into circulation, without a previous suppression of all notes of corresponding denominations. The reason is obvious. If there exist in any country two distinct currencies, both of them answering equally well the purposes of domestic circulation, but one of them possessing only a local value, confined to the country of its emission, while the other has a universal and equal value throughout the world, the latter will necessarily go abroad into the commerce of the world, in quest of the riches and productions of foreign nations, leaving the former at home to perform an office which it does equally as well, though it would be wholly without use or value abroad. The total incompatibility, therefore, of a paper and metallic currency of the same denominations has grown into an axiom. Edmund Burke (whose sagacity in questions of this sort is well known), at the memorable period of the bill brought forward by Mr. Pitt for the suspension of specie payments by the Bank of England, in 1797, in a letter written during his last illness to Mr. Canning, which the latter gentleman brought most touchingly to the notice of the House of Commons, in a debate of great interest and instruction, on this whole subject, at a much more recent period (1826), used these memorable words: "Tell Mr. Pitt that, if he consents to the issue of one-pound notes, he will never see a guinea again." The prophecy, sir, became history. No one saw a guinea in circulation in England while the bank continued the issue of one-pound notes.

Mr. Burke's remark also applies most forcibly to our present situation. We have voted the metallic money, we have coined it, but it will not circulate. We have coined at our own mint, within little more than two years, ten millions of gold. But where is it? In the vaults of the banks, or hoarded by individuals! and we shall never see it in circulation until we have opened the way for it by a previous suppression of the small notes.

Senator Benton.—We stand upon a constitution which recognizes nothing but gold and silver for money; we stand upon a legislation of near fifty years, which recognizes nothing but gold and silver for money. Now, for the first time, we have a statutory enactment proposed to recognize the paper of a wilderness of local banks for money, and in so doing to repeal all prior legislation by law, and the Constitution by fact. This is an era in our legislation. It is statute law to control all other law, and is not a resolution to aid other laws, and to express the opinions of Congress.

Mr. B. said, the effects of this statute would be to make a paper government—to insure the exportation of our specie—to leave the State banks without foundations to rest upon—to produce a certain catastrophe in the whole paper system—to revive the pretensions of the United States Bank—and to fasten, for a time, the Adam Smith system upon the Federal Government and the whole Union.

Mr. B. objected, totally, to the idea of continuing to receive paper money for the dues of the Federal Government. This bill was intended to be a permanent law; there was no limitation of time in it. It was intended to continue paper money forever as the currency of the Federal Government. There was no longer any plea of necessity to justify such a gross departure from the Constitution. It is not now as it was in 1816, when the joint resolution of that year was passed. Then, there was less specie in the country than ever was known; now there is more than ever was known. The joint resolution of 1816 was a great advance upon the existing state of things at that time: the same resolution would be a retrograde movement, and a great falling back at the present day. We have now near eighty millions of specie; that sum is far beyond any possible demand that the collection of the revenues in specie could demand. Everybody knows that it does not require an amount of money equal to the whole amount of annual payments to make those payments. This might be the case if every creditor ate all the money which he received; but as he does not eat it, but pays it over to somebody else, it follows that the same piece of money performs many payments in the course of the year; and, consequently, that a sum far below the amount of annual payments will be sufficient to effect all those payments. A proportionate supply, then, is all that is wanted; and that proportion is fixed by political economists at the one-tenth.

It is the faculty of issuing paper currency which makes banks dangerous to the country, and the height to which this danger has risen in the United States, and the progress which it is making should rouse and alarm the whole community. It is destroying all standard of value. It is subjecting the country to demoralizing and ruinous fluctuations of price. It is making a lottery of property, and making merchandise of money, which has to be bought by the ticket holders in the great lottery at two and three per cent. a month. It is equivalent to the destruction of weights and measures, and like buying and selling without counting, weighing, or measuring. It is the realization, in a different form, of the debasement and arbitrary alteration of the value of coins practiced by the kings of Europe in former ages, and now by the Sultan of Turkey. It is extinguishing the idea of fixed, moderate, annual interest. Great duties are thus imposed upon the legislator; and the first of these duties is to revive and favor the class of banks of discount and deposit; banks to make loans, keep money, transfer credits on books, buy and sell exchange, deal in bullion; but to issue no paper. This class of banks should be revived and favored; and the United States could easily revive them by confiding to them the public deposits. The next great duty of the legislator is to limit the issues of banks of circulation, and make them indemnify the community in some little degree, by refunding, in annual taxes, some part of their undue gains.

The amount of capital reported by the banks to have been paid in is about $300,000,000; and the quantity of paper money which they are authorized by their charters to issue is about $750,000,000. How much of this is actually issued can never be known with any precision; for such are the fluctuations in the amount of a paper currency, flowing from 750 fountains, that the circulation of one day cannot be relied upon for the next. This, upon its face, and without recourse to any other evidence, is proof that our banking system, as a whole, is unsolid and delusive, and a frightful imposition upon the people. Nothing but specie can form the capital of a bank; there are not above sixty or seventy millions of specie in the country, and of that the banks have not the one-half. Thirty millions in specie is the extent; the remainder of the capital must have been made up of that undefinable material called "specie funds," or "funds equivalent to specie," the fallacy of which is established by the facts already stated, and which show that all the specie in the country put together is not sufficient to meet the one-fifth part of these "specie funds," or "funds equivalent to specie." The equivalent, then, does not exist! credit alone exists; and any general attempt to realize these "specie funds," and turn them into specie, would explode the whole banking system, and cover the country with ruin. There may be some solid and substantial banks in the country, and undoubtedly there are better and worse among them; but as a whole—and it is in that point of view the community is interested—as a whole, the system is unsolid and delusive; and there is no safety for the country until great and radical reforms are effected.

Mr. B. said this was a faint sketch of the banking system as carried on in the United States, where every bank is a coiner of paper currency, and where every town, in some States, must have its banks of circulation (while such cities as Liverpool and Manchester have no such banks), and where the paper money of all these machines receives wings to fly over the whole continent, and to infest the whole land, from its universal receivability by the Federal Government in payment of all dues at their customhouses, land offices, post offices, and by all the district attorneys, marshals, and clerks, employed under the Federal judiciary. The improvidence of the States, in chartering such institutions, is great and deplorable; but their error was trifling, compared to the improvidence of the Federal Government in taking the paper coinage of all these banks for the currency of the Federal Government, maugre that clause in the Constitution which recognizes nothing but gold and silver for currency, and which was intended forever to defend and preserve this Union from the evils of paper money.

Mr. B. averred, with a perfect knowledge of the fact, that the banking system of the United States was on a worse footing than it was in any country upon the face of the earth; and that, in addition to its deep and dangerous defects, it was also the most expensive and burdensome, and gave the most undue advantages to one part of the community over another. He had no doubt but that this banking system was more burdensome to the free citizens of the United States than ever the feudal system was to the villeins, and serfs, and peasants of Europe. And what did they get in return for this vast burden? A pestiferous currency of small paper! when they might have a gold currency without paying interest, or suffering losses, if their banks, like those in Liverpool and Manchester, issued no currency except as bills of exchange. And with how much real capital is this banking system, so burdensome to the people of the United States, carried on? About $30,000,000! Yes; on about $30,000,000 of specie rests the $300,000,000 paid in, and on which the community are paying interest, and giving profits to bankers, and blindly yielding their faith and confidence, as if the whole $30,000,000 was a solid bed of gold and silver, instead of being, as it is, one-tenth part specie, and nine-tenths paper credit!

Sir, I have performed a duty to myself, not pleasant, but necessary. This bill is to be an era in our legislation and in our political history. It is to be a point upon which the future age will be thrown back, and from which future consequences will be traced. I separate myself from it; I wash my hands of it; I oppose it. I am one of those who promised gold, not paper. I promised the currency of the Constitution, not the currency of corporations. I did not join in putting down the Bank of the United States, to put up a wilderness of local banks. I did not join in putting down the paper currency of a national bank, to put up a national paper currency of a thousand local banks. I did not strike Cæsar, to make Antony master of Rome.

Senator Walker.—Congress, no more than a State legislature, can make anything but gold or silver a tender in payment of debts by one citizen to another; but that Congress, or a State legislature, or an individual, may waive their constitutional rights, and receive bank paper or drafts, in payment of any debt, is a principle of universal adoption in theory and practice, and never doubted by anyone until at the present session by the Senator from Missouri. The distinction of the Senator in this respect was as incomprehensible to him (Mr. W.) as he believed it was to every Senator, and, indeed, was discernible only by the magnifying powers of a solar microscope. It was a point-no-point, which, like the logarithmic spiral, or asymptote of the hyperbolic curve, might be forever approached without reaching; an infinitesimal, the ghost of an idea, not only without length, breadth, thickness, shape, weight, or dimensions, but without position—a mere imaginary nothing, which flitted before the bewildered vision of the honorable Senator, when traversing, in his fitful somnambulism, that tesselated pavement of gold, silver, and billion,[1] which that Senator delighted to occupy. Sir, the Senator from Missouri might have heaped mountain-high his piles of metal; he might have swept, in his Quixotic flight, over the banks of the States, putting to the sword their officers, stockholders, directory, and legislative bodies by which they were chartered; he might, in his reveries, have demolished their charters, and consumed their paper by the fire of his eloquence; he might have transacted, in fancy, with a metallic currency of twenty-eight millions in circulation, an actual annual business of fifteen hundred millions, and Mr. W. would not have disturbed his beatific visions, nor would any other Senator—for they were visions only that could never be realized—but when, descending from his ethereal flights, he seized upon the Committee on Public Lands as criminals, arraigned them as violators of the Constitution, and prayed Heaven for deliverance from them, Mr. W. could be silent no longer. Yes, even then he would have passed lightly over the ashes of the theories of the honorable Senator, for, if he desired to make assaults upon any, it would be upon the living, and not the dead; but that Senator, in the opening of his (Mr. W.'s) address, had rejected the olive branch which, upon the urgent solicitation of mutual friends, against his own judgment, he had extended to the honorable Senator. The Senator from Missouri had thus, in substance, declared his "voice was still for war." Be it so; he thanked God that he was not so abject or degraded as to submit, with impunity, to unprovoked attacks or unfounded accusations from any quarter. Could he thus submit, he would be unfit to represent the noble, generous, and gallant people, whose rights and interests it was his pride and

[1] A coin composed of both gold and silver which Senator Benton had proposed.

glory to endeavor to protect, whose honor and character were dearer to him than life itself, and should never be tarnished by any act of his, as one of their humble representatives upon this floor.

The bill was passed by Congress, but so late in the session that the President did not have the constitutional period of ten days for considering it. He therefore virtually vetoed it by retaining it without action, a disposition which became known about that time as the "pocket" veto.

CHAPTER VII

Divorce of Bank and State

[THE SUBTREASURY BILL]

Panic of 1837—President Van Buren Calls Congress in Special Session—Administration Bill to Issue Treasury Notes: Opposed, in Senate, by Daniel Webster [Mass.]; Defended by Thomas H. Benton [Mo.]; Carried—Administration Bill to Establish Independent Treasury: in Favor, Silas Wright [N. Y.] (Mover); John C. Calhoun [S. C.], Senator Benton, Robert J. Walker [Miss.], James Buchanan [Pa.]; Opposed, William C. Rives [Va.], Nathaniel P. Tallmadge [N. Y.], Henry Clay [Ky.], Senator Webster; Carried—Bill Is Lost in the House—It Is Reintroduced in the Senate (1838)—Bill Is Passed 1840; Repealed 1842; Re-Enacted 1846.

PRESIDENT VAN BUREN entered office during a period of financial disaster. In November, 1836, the liquidation of several English banks caused the ruin of three mercantile houses doing an extensive business with the United States, and precipitated a financial, industrial and agricultural panic in this country. The Dry Dock Bank of New York, one of the Federal deposit banks, stopped cash payments early in May, 1837, and on the 10th of the month all the other banks in the city followed suit. The suspension quickly became general throughout the country; many mercantile houses were ruined, and many factories closed their doors, and land and agricultural products slumped greatly in value. The Government was blamed for this condition, and great pressure was brought to bear, from every direction, upon the new Administration to change the financial policy it had inherited from the old, especially to rescind the treasury circular of July 11, 1836, ordering payment for the public lands to be made in specie, and to reëstablish a national bank.

President Van Buren refused to rescind the order or

to endorse the reëstablishment of the bank, but yielded to the pressure in so far as to call a special session of Congress to relieve the situation. Congress met on September 4, 1837. In his message the President outlined an entirely new organization of administering the finances, recommending an entire dissolution of the connection of the Government with banks of issue, and the establishment of an independent treasury system. He also recommended the passage of a "uniform law concerning bankruptcies of corporations, and other bankers" as a "salutary check on the issues of paper money, and an effectual remedy given to the citizen, in a way at once equal in all parts of the Union, and fully authorized by the Constitution." In order to provide for the needs of the Government, in view of the approaching deficit in revenue due to the general suspension of specie payments, the President advised that the fourth instalment of the deposit to be made with the States be withheld, and a temporary issue of treasury notes or warrants be made to supply the deficiency until the incoming revenue should be sufficient to redeem them.

Senator Daniel Webster [Mass.] assailed the proposed issue of treasury notes as a return to the old Continental currency, and taunted the Democratic party with so early a failure in its policy for getting back to hard money.

Senator Thomas H. Benton [Mo.] defended the issue as being one of "notes to raise loans, and to be laid by as investments, and not as notes for currency to be pushed into circulation by the power of the Government."

A bill for the issue of the notes passed the Senate on September 18 by a vote of 42 to 5, Webster voting in its favor, and Henry Clay [Ky.] against it.

A bill imposing additional duties on public officers as depositaries for receiving the public money (Independent or Sub-Treasury system) was introduced in the Senate on September 19, by Silas Wright [N. Y.], chairman of the Finance Committee. Leading speakers in favor of the bill were John C. Calhoun [S. C.]—who thereby realigned himself with the Democratic party, breaking his coalition with Henry Clay, now that its cause, a common antagonism toward Andrew Jackson, had passed—Senator Benton, Robert J. Walker [Miss.], James Buchanan

THE REJECTED MINISTER

"WE CAN NEVER MAKE HIM PRESIDENT WITHOUT FIRST MAKING HIM VICE-PRESIDENT"

Jackson Bearing Van Buren to the Presidency

From the collection of the New York Historical Society

[Pa.], and Senator Wright. Chief of the opponents of the bill were William C. Rives [Va.], Nathaniel P. Tallmadge [N. Y.], Senator Clay, and Senator Webster. The bill passed the Senate on October 4, 1837, by a vote of 26 to 20. It then went to the House, where, after full debate (in which, however, no arguments additional to those of the Senate were adduced), it was, on October 14, laid on the table by a vote of 119 to 107.

The Sub-Treasury Bill

Senate, September 19–October 4, 1837

Senator Calhoun.—An extraordinary course of events, with which all are too familiar to need recital, has separated, in fact, the Government and the banks. What relation shall they bear hereafter? Shall the banks again be used as fiscal agents of the Government? be the depositories of the public money? And, above all, shall their notes be considered and treated as money, in the receipts and expenditures of the Government? This is the great and leading question; one of the first magnitude, and full of consequences. I have given it my most anxious and deliberate attention; and have come to the conclusion that we have reached the period when the interests both of the Government and the banks forbid a reunion.

If, Mr. President, there be any one point fully established by experience and reason, I hold it to be the utter incompetency of the State banks to furnish, of themselves, a sound and stable currency. They may succeed in prosperous times, but the first adverse current necessarily throws them into utter confusion. Nor has any device been found to give them the requisite strength and stability, but a great, central, and controlling bank, instituted under the authority of this Government.

But there are difficulties in the way of a national bank, no less formidable than a reconnection with the State banks. It is utterly impracticable, at present, to establish one. There is reason to believe that a majority of the people of the United States are deliberately and unalterably opposed to it. At all events, there is a numerous, respectable, and powerful party (I refer to the old State Rights party), who are, and ever have been, from the beginning of the Government, opposed to the bank; and whose opinions, thus long and firmly entertained, ought at least to be so much respected as to forbid the creation of one, without an amendment of the Constitution. To this must be added the insuperable difficulty, that the Executive branch of the Government is openly opposed to it, and pledged to interpose his veto, on constitutional grounds, should a bill pass to incorporate one. For four years, at least, then, it will be impracticable to charter a bank. What must be done in the meantime? Shall the treasury be reorganized to perform the functions which have been recently discharged by the banks, or shall the State institutions be again employed until a bank can be created?

My opposition to a reunion with the banks is not confined to objections limited to national or State banks. It goes beyond, and comprehends others of a more general nature, relating to the currency, which to me are decisive. I am of the impression that the connection has a most pernicious influence over bank currency; that it tends to disturb that stability and uniformity of value which are essential to a sound currency; and are among the leading causes of that tendency to expansion and contraction which experience has shown is incident to bank notes as a currency. They are, in my opinion, at best, without the requisite qualities to constitute a currency, even when unconnected with the Government; and are doubly disqualified by reason of that connection, which subjects them to sudden expansions and contractions, and exposes them to fatal catastrophes, such as the present.

I will explain my views. A bank note circulates, not merely on account of the credit of the institution by which it is issued, but because Government receives it, like gold and silver, in all its dues, and thus adds its own credit to that of the bank. It, in fact, virtually indorses on the note of every specie-paying bank, "receivable by Government in its dues." To understand how greatly this adds to the circulation of bank notes, we must remember that Government is the great money dealer of the country, and the holder of immense public domains; and that it has the power of creating a demand against every citizen, as high as it pleases, in the shape of a tax, or duty, which can be discharged, as the law now is, only by bank notes or gold and silver. This, of course, cannot but add greatly to the credit of bank notes, and contribute much to their circulation.

It follows, as a necessary consequence, that, to the extent of this influence, the issues of the banks expand and contract with the expansion and contraction of the fiscal action of the Government; with the increase of its duties, taxes, income, and expenditure; with the deposits in its vaults acting as additional capital, and the amount of bank notes withdrawn, in consequence, from circulation; all of which must directly affect the amount of their business and issues; and bank currency must of course partake of all those vibrations to which the fiscal action of the Government is necessarily exposed, and, when great and sudden, must expose the system to catastrophes such as we now witness.

It is often easy to prevent what cannot be remedied, which the present instance strongly illustrates. If the Administration had formed a true conception of the danger in time, what has since happened might have then been easily averted. The near approach of the expiration of the charter of the United States Bank would have afforded ample means of staying the desolation, if it had been timely and properly used. I saw it then, and proposed to renew the charter, for a limited period, with such modifications as would have effectually resisted the increasing expansion of the currency; and, at the same time, gradually and finally, wear out the connection between the bank and the Government:—to use the expression I then used, "to unbank the banks"; to let down the system easily, and so to effect the separation between the bank and the Government as to avoid the possibility of that shock which I then saw was inevitable without some such remedy. The moment was eminently propitious. The precious metals were flowing in on us from every quarter, and the vigorous measures I proposed to adopt in the renewal of the charter would have effectually arrested the increase of banks and checked the excess of their discounts and issues; so that the accumulating mass of gold and silver, instead of being converted into bank capital, and swelling the tide of paper circulation, would have been substituted in the place of bank notes, as a permanent and wholesome addition to the currency of the country.

But neither the Administration nor the opposition sustained me, and the precious opportunity passed unseized. I then clearly saw the coming calamity was inevitable, and it has neither arrived sooner, nor is it greater, than what I expected.

That the connection between the banks and the Government, the receiving and paying away their notes as cash, and the use of the public money from the time of the collection to the disbursement, is the source of immense profit to the banks, cannot be questioned. It is impossible to ascertain with any precision to what extent their issues and circulation depend upon it, but it certainly constitutes a large proportion. A single illustration may throw light upon this point. Suppose the Government were to take up the veriest beggar in the street, and enter into a contract with him, that nothing should be received in payment of its dues or for the sales of its public lands in future, except gold and silver and his promissory notes, and that he should have the use of the public funds from the time of their collection until their disbursement. Can anyone estimate the wealth which such a contract would confer? His notes would circulate far and wide over the whole extent of the Union; would be the medium through which the exchanges of the country would be performed; and his ample and extended credit would give him a control over all the banking institutions and moneyed transactions of the community. The possession of a hundred millions would not give a control more effectual. I ask, would it be fair, would it be equal, would it be consistent with the spirit of our institutions, to confer such advantages on any individual? And, if not on one, would it be if conferred on any number? And, if not, why should it be conferred on any corporate body of individuals? How can they possibly be entitled to benefits so vast, which all must acknowledge could not be justly conferred on any number of unincorporated individuals?

The union between bank and Government is not only a main source of that dangerous expansion and contraction in the banking system, which I have already illustrated, but is also one of the principal causes of that powerful and almost irresistible tendency to the increase of banks, which even its friends see and deplore. We have made banking too profitable—far, very far, too profitable; and, I may add, influential. One of the most ample sources of this profit and influence may be traced, as I have shown, to the connection with the Government; and is, of course, among the prominent causes of the strong and incessant tendency of the system to increase, which even its friends see must finally overwhelm either the banks or the institutions of the country. There can be but one safe and consistent remedy for this; the rendering banking, as a business, less profitable and influential; and the first and decisive step toward this is a disseverance between the banks and the Government.

I pass over other important objections to the connection; the corrupting influence and the spirit of speculation which it spreads far and wide over the land. Who has not seen and deplored the vast and corrupting influence brought to bear upon the legislatures to obtain charters, and the means necessary to participate in the profits of the institutions. This gives a control to the Government, which grants such favors, of a most extensive and pernicious character; all of which must continue to spread and increase, if the connection should continue, until the whole community must become one contaminated and corrupted mass.

There is another, and a final reason, which I shall assign against the reunion with the banks. We have reached a new era with regard to these institutions. He who would judge of the future by the past, in reference to them, will be wholly mistaken. The year 1833 marks the commencement of this era.

That extraordinary man who had the power of imprinting his own feelings on the community then commenced his hostile attacks, which have left such effects behind, that the war then commenced against the banks, I clearly see, will not terminate, unless there be a separation between them and the Government—until one or the other triumphs—till the Government becomes the bank, or the bank the Government. In resisting their union I act as the friend of both. I have, as I have said, no unkind feelings toward the banks. I am neither a bank man nor an anti-bank man. I have had little connection with them. Many of my best friends, for whom I have the highest esteem, have a deep interest in their prosperity, and as far as friendship or personal attachment extends, my inclination would be strongly in their favor. But I stand up here as the representative of no particular interest. I look to the whole, and to the future as well as the present; and I shall steadily pursue that course which, under the most enlarged view, I believe to be my duty. In 1834 I saw the present crisis. I in vain raised a warning voice, and endeavored to avert it. I now see, with equal certainty, one far more portentous. If this struggle is to go on—if the banks will insist upon a reunion with the Government, against the sense of a large and influential portion of the community—and, above all, if they should succeed in effecting it, a reflux flood will inevitably sweep away the whole system. A deep popular excitement is never without some reason, and ought ever to be treated with respect; and it is the part of wisdom to look timely into the cause, and correct it before the excitement shall become so great as to demolish the object, with all its good and evil, against which it is directed.

The only safe course for both Government and banks is to remain as they are, separated—each in the use of its own credit and in the management of its own affairs. The less the control and influence of the one over the other, the better. Confined to their legitimate sphere—that of affording temporary credit to commercial and business men, bank notes would furnish a safe and convenient circulation in the range of commerce and business, within which the banks may be respectively situated, exempt almost entirely from those fluctuations and convulsions to which they are now so exposed; or, if they should occasionally be subject to them, the evil would be local and temporary, leaving undisturbed the action of the Government, and the general currency of the country, on the stability of which the prosperity and safety of the community so much depend.

I am of the impression, to make this great measure successful and secure it against reaction, some stable and safe medium of circulation, to take the place of bank notes in the fiscal operations of the Government, ought to be issued. I intend to propose nothing. It would be impossible, with so great a weight of opposition, to pass any measure without the entire support of the Administration. I then intend merely to throw out suggestions, in order to excite the reflection of others on a subject so delicate, and of so much importance—acting on the principle that it is the duty of all in so great a juncture to present their views without reserve.

It is, then, my impression that, in the present condition of the world, a paper currency, in some form, if not necessary, is almost indispensable in financial and commercial operations of civilized and extensive communities. In many respects it has a vast superiority over a metallic currency, especially in great and extended transactions, by its greater cheapness, lightness, and the facility of determining the amount. The great desideratum is to ascertain what description of paper has the requisite qualities of being free from fluctuation in value, and liability to abuse, in the greatest perfection. I have shown, I trust, that the bank notes do not possess these requisites in a degree sufficiently high for this purpose. I go further. It appears to me, after bestowing the best reflection I can give the subject, that no convertible paper—that is, no paper whose credit rests upon a *promise to pay*—is suitable for currency. It is the form of credit proper in private transactions between man and man, but not for a standard of value, to perform exchanges generally, which constitute the appropriate functions of money or currency. The measures of safety in the two cases are wholly different. A promissory note, or convertible paper, is considered safe so long as the drawer has ample means to meet his engagements; and, in passing from hand to hand, regard is had only to his ability and willingness to pay. Very different is the case in currency. The aggregate value of the currency of a country necessarily bears a small proportion to the aggregate value of its property. It follows that an increase in the amount of the currency, by the addition of a paper circulation of no intrinsic value, but increases the nominal value of the aggregate property of the country in the same proportion that the increase bears to the whole amount of currency; so that, if the currency be doubled, the nominal value of the property will also be doubled. Hence it is that, when the paper currency of a country is in the shape of promissory notes, there is a constant tendency to excess. And hence, with other causes, there is the constant tendency to an excessive issue of bank notes in prosperous times, when so large a portion of the community are anxious to obtain accommodation, and who are disappointed when negotiable paper is refused by the banks—not reflecting that it would not be safe to discount beyond the limits of a safe circulation, however good the paper offered.

On what, then, ought a paper currency to rest? I would say, on demand and supply simply, which regulates the value of everything else—the constant demand which the Government has on the community for its necessary supplies. A medium, resting on this demand, which simply obligates the Government to receive it in all of its dues, to the exclusion of everything else, except gold and silver—and which shall be optional with those who have demands on Government to receive or not, would, it seems to me, be as stable in its value as those metals themselves, and be as little liable to abuse as the power of coining. It would contain within itself a self-regulating power. It could only be issued to those who had claims on the Government, and to those only with their consent, and, of course, only at or above par with gold and silver, which would be its habitual state; for, so far as the Government was concerned, it would be equal, in every respect, to gold and silver, and superior in many, particularly in regulating the distant exchanges of the country. Should, however, a demand for gold and silver from abroad, or other accidental causes, depress it temporarily, as compared with the precious metals, it would then return to the treasury, and as it could not be paid out during such depression, its gradual diminution in the market would soon restore it to an equality, when it would again flow out into the general circulation. Thus there would be a constant alternate flux and reflux into and from the treasury, between it and the precious metals; but, if at any time a permanent depression in its value be possible from any cause, the only effect would be to operate as a reduction of taxes on the community, and the only sufferer would be the Government itself. Against this its own interest would be a sufficient guaranty.

Nothing but experience can determine what amount and of what denominations might be safely issued; but it may be safely assumed that the country would absorb an amount greatly exceeding its annual income. Much of its exchanges, which amount to a vast sum, as well as its banking business, would revolve about it, and many millions would thus be kept in circulation beyond the demands of the Government. It may throw some light on this subject to state that North Carolina, just after the Revolution, issued a large amount of paper, which was made receivable in dues to her. It was also made a legal tender, but which, of course, was not obligatory after the adoption of the Federal Constitution. A large amount, say between four and five hundred thousand dollars, remained in circulation after that period, and continued to circulate for more than twenty years at par with gold and silver during the whole time, with no other advantage than being received in the revenue of the State, which was much less than $100,000 per annum.

No one can doubt that the fact of the Government receiving and paying away bank notes in all its fiscal transactions is one of the principal sources of their great circulation; and it was mainly on that account that the notes of the late Bank of the United States so freely circulated all over the Union. I would ask, then, why should the Government mingle its credit with that of private corporations? No one can doubt but that the Government credit is better than that of any bank—more stable and more safe. Why then should it mix it up with the less perfect credit of those institutions? Why not use its own credit to the amount of its own transactions? Why should it not be safe in its own hands, while it shall be considered safe in the hands of eight hundred private institutions scattered all over the country, and which have no other object but their own private profits, to increase which, they almost constantly extend their business to the most dangerous extremes? And why should the community be compelled to give six per cent. discount for the Government credit blended with that of the banks, when the superior credit of the Government could be furnished separately, without discount, to the mutual advantage of the Government and the community? Why, let me ask, should the Government be exposed to such difficulties as the present, by mingling its credit with the banks, when it could be exempt from all such by using by itself its own safer credit? It is time the community, which has so deep an interest in a sound and cheap currency, and the equality of the laws between one portion of the citizens and the country and another, should reflect seriously on these things; not for the purpose of oppressing any interest, but to correct gradually disorders of a dangerous character, which have insensibly, in the long course of years, without being perceived by anyone, crept into the State.

Having now presented my views of the course and the

measures which the permanent policy of the country, looking to its liberty and lasting prosperity, requires, I come finally to the question of relief. The patient lies under a dangerous disease, with a burning thirst and other symptoms, which distress him more than the vital organs which are attacked. The skillful physician first makes himself master of the nature of the disease, and then determines on the treatment necessary for the restoration of health. This done, he next alleviates the distressing symptoms, as far as is consistent with the restoration of health, and no further. Such shall be my course.

After the best reflection, I am of the opinion that the Government can do but little in the way of relief, and that it is a case which must be mainly left to the constitution of the patient, who, thank God, is young, vigorous, and robust, with a constitution sufficient to sustain and overcome the severest attack. I dread the doctor and his drugs much more than the disease itself. The distress of the country consists in its indebtedness, and can only be relieved by payment of its debts. To effect this, industry, frugality, economy, and *time* are necessary. I rely more on the growing crop—on the cotton, rice, and tobacco of the South—than on all the projects or devices of politicians. I am utterly opposed to all coercion by this Government. But Government may do something to relieve the distress. It is out of debt, and is one of the principal creditors both of the banks and of the merchants, and should set an example of liberal indulgence. This I am willing to give freely. I am also prepared to vote freely the use of Government credit, in some safe form, to supply any deficit in the circulation during the process of recovery, as far as its financial wants will permit. I see not what more can be safely done.

We have, Mr. President, arrived at a remarkable era in our political history. The days of legislative and executive encroachments, of tariffs and surpluses, of bank and public debt, and extravagant expenditure are past for the present. The Government stands in a position disentangled from the past, and freer to choose its future course than it ever has been since its commencement. We are about to take a fresh start. I move off under the State Rights banner, and go in the direction in which I have been so long moving. I seize the opportunity thoroughly to reform the Government; to bring it back to its original principles; to retrench and economize, and rigidly to enforce accountability. I shall oppose, strenuously, all attempts to originate a new debt; to create a national bank; to reunite the political and money powers (more dangerous than Church and State) in any form or shape; to prevent the disturbances of the compromise, which is gradually removing the last vestige of the tariff system; and, mainly, I shall use my best efforts to give an ascendency to the great conservative principle of State sovereignty, over the dangerous and despotic doctrine of consolidation. I rejoice to think that the Executive Department of the Government is now so reduced in power and means that it can no longer rely on its influence and patronage to secure a majority. Henceforward it can have no hope of supporting itself but on wisdom, moderation, patriotism, and devoted attachment to the Constitution, which I trust will make it, in its own defence, an ally in effecting the reform which I deem indispensable to the salvation of the country and its institutions.

SENATOR RIVES.—Sir, I have always been taught to believe—my honorable colleague and myself learned it from the bill of rights of our own State as soon as we were capable of reading—that a common interest between the governors and the governed is a fundamental principle of free institutions, and that the best means of "restraining the former from oppression is to make them feel and participate in the burdens of the latter." Let the Government share the same fate with the citizen, and you give it the strongest of all motives to watch over the general interests. On the other hand, place it in a position different from that of the great body of the community, especially in so vital a matter as that of its revenue and pecuniary support, and you make it at once callous and indifferent to the sufferings of the people, and even give it an interest to perpetuate those sufferings. You destroy all sympathy on the part of the Government with the people, and you alienate the confidence and affections of the people from the Government.

What, sir, is at this moment the ungracious attitude in which the Government is placed toward the people? Its officers and contractors are paid in gold and silver, or in treasury drafts made receivable in discharge of public dues, and therefore nearly equivalent to gold and silver, while the community at large are left to conduct their business as they may, in an irredeemable paper currency. Does not this operate as a virtual increase of the salaries of public officers, in the midst of general distress affecting all the rest of the community? The gold and silver which they receive is at a premium of ten or twelve per cent., and the treasury drafts at seven or eight per cent., above the actual and common currency of the country. This premium is, I repeat, an addition of so much to the amount of their salaries; for, in a practical sense, there has as yet been no depreciation in the value of current bank notes. They pass for as much in the ordinary business of life—in the payment of debts, in the purchase of necessaries and conveniences, of whatever is worn, drunk, or eaten—as they ever did. The premium, then, which the public officers and contractors obtain on their gold and silver and treasury drafts is so much clear gain to them. And at whose expense is it acquired? Is it not at that of the great body of the people, the ultimate taxpayers and supporters of the Government? Does anyone suppose that the importing merchant, who has to give ten or twelve per cent. for the gold and silver, and seven or eight per cent. for the treasury drafts, with which he pays his duties to the Government, does not add an equal amount, with the usual profit upon it, to the price of his goods? It is, then, the consumer at last, or, in other words, the great body of the people, who are subject to increased taxation for the benefit of the officeholder and the contractor.

Sir, this is a state of things which I do not wish to see perpetuated. It is contrary to the genius and fundamental principles of our republican system. Of all schemes of policy I can conceive, that which proposes a permanent distinction between the Government and the people in their pecuniary interests—one currency, and that the better one, for the Government, and another and inferior currency for the people—such a system of discrimination is, to my mind, of all others, the most injurious and revolting in principle, the most heartless in character, and the most despotic in its tendencies. It is like quartering the Government, as a foreign enemy, on the heart of the country. You intrench it behind a frowning fortification, surround it with battlements, and lay the country, far and near, under contribution for the support of this garrison of officeholders. Desolation and oppression are without, while the tenants of the citadel are reveling in luxury and profusion within. I am not willing, for one, to see the Government of my country placed in this anti-social, if not belligerent, attitude toward the people. I am not willing that this favored land, to which the nations of the earth are looking for a successful example of the practical enjoyment of free institutions, should exhibit such a spectacle of inequality and oppression in the eyes of the world.

Much reliance, Mr. President, has been placed on the popular catchword of divorcing the Government from all connection with banks. Nothing is more delusive and treacherous than catchwords. How often has the revered name of liberty been invoked, in every quarter of the globe, and every age of the world, to disguise and sanctify the most heartless despot-

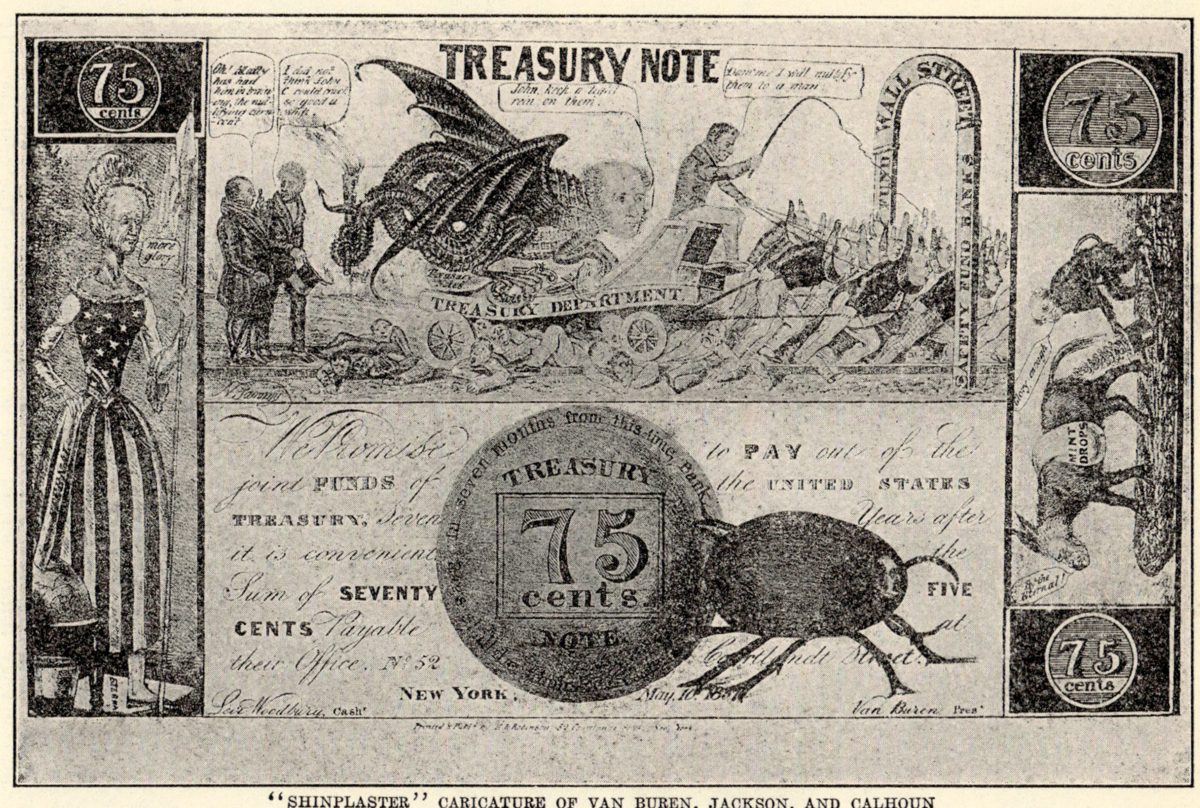

"SHINPLASTER" CARICATURE OF VAN BUREN, JACKSON, AND CALHOUN

From the collection of the New York Historical Society

ism. Let us beware that, in attempting to divorce the Government from all connection with banks, we do not end with divorcing the Government from the people.

Senator Tallmadge.—The banks are now as able, with the aid and confidence of the Government, to perform all the duties required of them as they were before. We have the testimony of the President and the Secretary of the Treasury that they performed them as well as the Bank of the United States. They are capable of doing the same again in the same way. I am not, therefore, prepared to say that, on account of the calamity which has befallen the country, the experiment has failed, and they ought not to be employed a second time. No, sir; such a catastrophe may not occur again in the course of a century. One reason assigned for it now was the existence of an enormous surplus in the treasury. This cause is not likely to exist hereafter, for every man is willing to bring down our receipts to the measure of our wants; and under that, as a general rule, such a catastrophe might never happen again. The banks have abundance of means to meet all their engagements. Such being the case, all that is necessary is to create confidence, to restore confidence, and they will be found able to perform all that is required of them. Let that confidence be extended to them by the Government in good faith, and let them be placed on their former footing. Let the Government pursue a system which has been tried, and which we know will prove effectual, instead of attempting an "untried expedient," the disastrous consequences of which cannot be anticipated, and which, I fear, imagination can scarcely depict.

This new experiment consists in a "divorce of bank and state." This is a mere catchphrase, which was originally introduced by artful and designing politicians to impose upon the credulity and honesty of the people. Many have adopted it without reflecting or inquiring as to its import or its consequences. First impressions are favorable to it; it summons to our recollection our early impressions of a "divorce of church and state." But it is the duty of wise statesmen and discreet politicians to consider well the evils which must follow the adoption of any system heretofore untried and of doubtful policy, however euphonious the phrase may be which designates its character before the people.

The proposition contained in these few catchwords strikes at the very foundation of the credit system of the country. It does not stop with the destruction of bank credit, but strangles, in its withering grasp, commercial credit also. It establishes a depreciated paper currency for the people, and an appreciated specie currency for the incumbents of office, and for Government contractors. It gives the baser currency to the master, and the "better currency" to the servant. In a Government like ours it is impossible long to preserve our institutions or our liberties if such distinctions are to prevail. It separates the Government of the people from the people themselves, as if those whom the people have chosen to direct their affairs were of a superior order, or distinct class in society, endowed with peculiar privileges beyond the rest of the community. It has a tendency to alienate the affections of the people from the Government. They will come to consider it not as a Government identified with their feelings and interests, but as something foreign to them. This is not all. The Government itself will lose in a measure the idea of dependence on the people. This want of dependence is too much felt already. Put this additional power into its hands, and the identity of interests which exists, or ought to exist between them, is done away.

Under this system, the specie of the country will be drawn from circulation, and from the vaults of the banks, where it is the basis of circulation and of confidence, and deposited in these sub-treasury vaults, till the country is left without a sufficient circulating medium to transact its ordinary business. The farmer, the merchant, the manufacturer, and the mechanic will be unable to command the means to pursue their ordinary avocations, no matter what their property may be. They may be rich in houses and lands, in goods and merchandise, in manufactures and machinery, in materials, in tools and implements of trade, nay, they may possess the best of bonds and mortgages, and every species of stock which has heretofore been deemed equivalent to money, and still they will be unable to carry on their ordinary business for want of a circulating medium by which to transact it. Credit is the poor man's capital, as well as the auxiliary of the rich. Deprive him of this, and his habits of industry, his character for probity, his good name and reputation avail him nothing. He has no means by which he can rise above the ordinary occupation of a day laborer. With a growing family, and the increased expense of living, he is doomed to abject poverty, without the slightest hope of ever gaining that standing and that condition in society which a "well-regulated credit system" always holds out to the enterprising, the honest, the industrious portion of the community.

The tendency of this scheme is to bring the country virtually to an exclusive metallic currency. Whatever gentlemen may say on this subject, this wild and visionary theory is gaining ground with a certain portion of our population. It is propagated by reason of the countenance which it is supposed to receive from men in high places. Meetings have been held in New York and elsewhere, at which an exclusive metallic currency has been resolved on as the only true policy. All paper money of every description has been repudiated, as contrary to the genius of our Government and the spirit of our institutions. In the same resolutions, men in elevated stations have been applauded by name for maintaining the same doctrines. The proceedings of such meetings have been responded to in terms of approbation, thereby tacitly acquiescing in all the principles set forth in them, and thus giving currency to them with the people. It is the belief that such principles are recognized by those to whose approval they are submitted that excites the alarm and apprehension which pervade the rational and thinking portion of the community. It is this, too, which gives countenance to the idea that the sub-treasury scheme is intended to bring about an exclusive metallic currency.

Gentlemen are very anxious, apparently, for this divorce, as they are pleased to term it. I would remind them, however, that, while they are talking of a divorce, they are getting up an incestuous union between members of the same family—a marriage which is unlawful; and which I would say comes within the Levitical decrees, and therefore ought to be forbidden.

This union which is now proposed is a most unsafe and dangerous one. It reminds me of an anecdote of a captain of a packet with whom I was acquainted, who informed me that he always found it indispensably necessary, for the safety of his ship's stores, to have his cook and his steward of different families, and if possible of different colors, and, if he could get up a fight between them, it was all the better; for, if they were connected together in a common bond of interest or affection, the stores were apt to be wasted. So here, I think our stores, the stores of the ship of state, will not be safe, if a union take place between the Government and the public treasury, which ought to be separated in different sets of hands, and those, too, antagonistic hands.

I do not wish to disparage our public officers or those who may be employed under this system. But I look at human nature as it is. I look at the temptations to which they are exposed. The confidence of individuals in their own integrity may be unbounded, and they will never suspect it till put to the test of such temptations as will be presented under this system. I mean no unnecessary or improper disparagement when I say I have no faith in the safety of the public money if this scheme goes into operation. There is danger in every stage of it. And no opportunity will pass unimproved where the temptation is sufficiently presented. There is no safety in it.

> "You may as well spread out the unsunn'd heaps
> Of miser's treasure by an outlaw's den,
> And tell me it is safe, as bid me hope
> Danger will wink on opportunity."

SENATOR BENTON.—I am for restoring to the Federal treasury the currency of the Constitution. I am for carrying back this Government to the solidity projected by its founders. This is a great object in itself—a reform of the first magnitude—a reformation with healing on its wings, bringing safety to the Government and blessings to the people. The currency is a thing which reaches every individual and every institution.

Great are the evils, political, pecuniary, and moral, which have flowed from this departure from our Constitution. Through the Federal Government alone—through it, not by it—two millions and a half of money have been lost in the last four months. Thirty-two millions of public money was the amount in the deposit banks when they stopped payment; of this sum twenty-five millions have been paid over to Government creditors, or transferred to the States. But how paid, and how transferred? In what? In real money, or its equivalent? Not at all! But in the notes of suspended banks—in notes depreciated, on an average, ten per cent. Here then were two and a half millions lost. Who bore the loss? The public creditors and the States. Who gained it? for where there is a loss to one there must be a gain to another. Who gained the two and a half millions thus sunk upon the hands of the creditors and the States? The banks were the gainers; they gained it; the public creditors and the States lost it; and to the creditors it was a forced loss. It is in vain to say that they consented to take it. They had no alternative. It was that or nothing. The banks forced it upon the Government; the Government forced it upon the creditor. Consent was out of the question. Power ruled, and that power was in the banks; and they gained the two and a half millions which the States and the public creditors lost.

The Senator from New York [Mr. Tallmadge] has predicted

an argument in favor of the local banks on account of the small amount of the public money which has been lost in their hands; but here is two and a half millions in a single operation, and without going back to the period of bank stoppages in 1819 and 1814. He confines himself to direct losses, but that is a most imperfect view of the question. The full view embraces, besides direct losses, all that are incidental to the use of depreciated paper money; increased prices—disappointed operations by sea and land in time of war—and embarrassed operations in time of peace; per centums shaved off at every step; the ignorant, the helpless, the necessitous imposed upon; and one vast scene of pushing off bad paper on each other exhibited all over the country.

I do not pretend to estimate the moneyed losses, direct or indirect, to the Government alone, from the use of local bank notes, in the last twenty-five years, including the war, and covering three general suspensions. Leaving the people out of view, as a field of losses beyond calculation, I confine myself to the Federal Government, and say its losses have been enormous, prodigious, and incalculable. We have had three general stoppages of the local banks in the short space of twenty-two years. It is at the average rate of one in seven years; and who is to guarantee us from another, and from the consequent losses, if we continue to receive their bills in payment of public dues. Another stoppage must come, and that, reasoning from all analogies, in less than seven years after the resumption. Many must perish in the attempt to resume, and would do better to wind up at once, without attempting to go on, without adequate means, and against appalling obstacles. Another revulsion must come. Thus it was after the last resumption (in 1817). Why was it that, within two years after resumption, both in England and in our America, these disastrous revulsions ensued? Loss of confidence was the cause; and that loss resulting, not from the act of Government, but from the conduct of the banks themselves. The banks had failed, and, therefore, could fail. The people had seen them fail, and, therefore, they feared they might do so again. There was no confidence in them; no more than the coachman places in the balking horse when he comes to the hill. The gentleman from Virginia [Mr. Rives] wishes the Government to do something to reanimate confidence in these banks. Could a law of Congress inspire confidence into his coachman, and give him faith in the balking horse? No more can it be done in relation to these banks. They have stopped, universally and simultaneously, in a season of profound peace and general prosperity—no war, no pestilence, no famine—with four times as much specie in the country as ever was in it before; and this stoppage has killed confidence. It is dead by the act of the banks, and cannot be legislated into existence again by act of Congress. Confidence is a plant of voluntary and not of forced existence. It is said by an eminent man to be a plant of slow growth. We all know it to be so; and we know, besides, that, when this plant is once pulled up by the roots, it rarely takes root again in the same place.

The Senators from New York and Virginia [Messrs. Tallmadge and Rives] push this point of confidence a little further; they address a question to me, and ask if I would lose confidence in all steamboats, and have them all discarded, if one or two blew up in the Mississippi? I answer the question in all frankness and say that I should not. But if, instead of one or two in the Mississippi, all the steamboats in the Union should blow up at once—in every creek, river, and bay—while all the passengers were sleeping in confidence, and the pilots crying out all is well; if the whole should blow up from one end of the Union to the other just as fast as they could hear each other's explosions; then, indeed, I should lose confidence in them, and never again trust wife, or child, or my own foot, or anything not intended for destruction, on board such sympathetic and contagious engines of death. I answer further, and tell the gentlemen that, if only one or two banks had stopped last May in New York, I should not have lost all confidence in the remaining nine hundred and ninety-nine; but when the whole thousand stopped at once; tumbled down together—fell in a lump—lie there—and when one of their number, by a sign with the little finger, can make the whole lie still, then, indeed, confidence is gone! And this is the case with the banks. It did not take a national calamity—a war to stop them! They fell in time of peace and prosperity! We read of people in the West Indies and in South America who rebuild their cities on the same spot where earthquakes have overthrown them; we are astonished at their fatuity; we wonder that they will build again on the same perilous foundations. But these people have a reason for their conduct; it is that their cities are destroyed only by earthquakes; and, when there is no earthquake, they are safe. But suppose their cities fell down without any commotion in the earth or the air—fell in a season of perfect calm and serenity—and after that the survivors should go to building again in the same place; would not all the world say that they were demented and were doomed to destruction? So of the Government of the United States by these banks. If it continues to use them, and to receive their notes for revenue, after what has happened, and in the face of what now exists, it argues fatuity and a doom to destruction.

Resume when they will, or when they shall, and the longer it is delayed the worse for themselves, the epoch of resumption is to be a perilous crisis to many. This stopping and resuming by banks is the realization of the poetical description of the descent into hell, and the return from it. *Facilis descensus Averni—sed revocare gradum—hoc opus, hic labor est.* Easy is the descent into the regions below, but to return! this is work, this is labor indeed! Our banks have made the descent; they have gone down with ease; but to return—to ascend the rugged steps, and behold again the light above—how many will falter and fall back again into the gloomy regions below!

Banks of circulation are banks of hazard and of failure. It is an incident of their nature. Those without circulation rarely fail. That of Venice has stood seven hundred years; those of Hamburg, Amsterdam, and others have stood for centuries. The Bank of England, the great mother of banks of circulation, besides an actual stoppage of a quarter of a century, has had her crisis and convulsion in average periods of seven or eight years, for the last half century—in 1783, '93, '97, 1814, '19, '25, '36—and has been saved from repeated failure only by the powerful support of the British Government and profuse supplies of exchequer bills. Her numerous progeny of private and joint stock banks of circulation have had the same convulsions; and, not being supported by the Government, have sunk by hundreds at a time. All the banks of the United States are banks of circulation; they are all subject to the inherent dangers of that class of banks, and are, besides, subject to new dangers peculiar to themselves. From the quantity of their stock held by foreigners, the quantity of other stocks in their hands, and the current foreign balance against the United States, our paper system has become an appendage to that of England. As such, it suffers from sympathy when the English system suffers. In addition to this, a new doctrine is now broached—that our first duty is to foreigners! and, upon this principle, when the banks of the two countries are in peril, ours are to be sacrificed to save those of England!

The power of a few banks over the whole presents a new feature of danger in our system. It consolidates the banks of the whole Union into one mass, and subjects them to one fate, and that fate to be decided by a few, without even the knowledge of the rest. An unknown divan of bankers sends forth an edict which sweeps over the empire, crosses the lines of States with the facility of a Turkish firman, prostrating all State institutions, breaking up all engagements, and leveling all law before it. This is consolidation of a kind which the genius of Patrick Henry had not even conceived. But, while this firman is thus potent and irresistible for prostration, it is impotent and powerless for resurrection. It goes out in vain, bidding the prostrate banks to rise. A veto power intervenes. One voice is sufficient to keep all down; and thus we have seen one word from Philadelphia[1] annihilate the New York proposition for resumption, and condemn the many solvent banks to the continuation of a condition as mortifying to their feelings as it is injurious to their future interests.

But what excuse, what apology, what justification have we for surrendering, abandoning, and losing the precise advantage for which the present Constitution was formed? What was that advantage—what the leading and governing object which led to the abandonment of the old confederation and induced the adoption of the present form of government? It was revenue! independent revenue! a revenue under the absolute control of this Government, and free from the action of the States. This was the motive, the leading and governing motive, which led to the formation of this Government. The reason was that the old Confederation, being dependent upon the States, was often left without money. This state of being was incompatible with its existence; it deprived it of all power; its imbecility was a proverb. To extricate it from that condition was the design and the cardinal design of the new Constitution. An independent revenue was given to it—independent even of the States. Is it not suicidal to surrender that independence, and to surrender it, not to States, but to money corporations? What does history record of the penury and moneyed destitution of the old Confederation, comparable to the annihilation of the revenues of this Government in May last, when the banks shut down, in one night, upon a revenue in hand of thirty-two millions; even upon that which was in the names of disbursing officers, and refuse a nine-pence or a picaillon[2] in money from that day to this? The old Confederation was often reduced low—often near empty-handed—but never saw itself stripped in an instant, as if by enchantment, of tens of millions and heard the shout of triumph thundered over its head, and the notes of

[1] From Nicholas Biddle, President of the Bank of the United States.
[2] Picayune.

exultation sung over its supposed destruction! Yet this is what we have seen—what we now see—from having surrendered to corporations our moneyed independence, and unwisely abandoned the precise advantage which led to the formation of this Federal Government.

I do not go into the moral view of this question. It is too obvious, too impressive, too grave, to escape the observation of anyone. Demoralization follows in the train of an unconvertible paper money. The whole community becomes exposed to a moral pestilence. Every individual becomes the victim of some imposition, and, in self-defence, imposes upon some one else. The weak, the ignorant, the uninformed, the necessitous are the sufferers; the crafty and the opulent are the gainers. The evil augments until the moral sense of the community, revolting at the frightful accumulation of fraud and misery, applies the radical remedy of total reform.

Thus pecuniary, political, and moral considerations require the Government to retrace its steps, to return to first principles, and to restore its fiscal action to the safe and solid path of the Constitution. Reform is demanded. It is called for by every public and by every private consideration. Now is the time to make it. The connection between bank and State is actually dissolved. It is dissolved by operation of law, and by the delinquency of these institutions. They have forfeited the right to the deposits, and lost the privilege of paying the revenue in their notes, by ceasing to pay specie. The Government is now going on without them, and all that is wanting is the appropriate legislation to perpetuate the divorce which, in point of fact, has already taken place. Now is the time to act; this the moment to restore the constitutional currency to the Federal Government; to restore the custody of the public moneys to national keepers; and to avoid, in time to come, the calamitous revulsions and perilous catastrophes of 1814, 1819, and 1837.

Senator Clay.—We are told that it is necessary to separate, divorce the Government from the banks. Let us not be deluded by sounds. Senators might as well talk of separating the Government from the States, or from the people, or from the country. We are all—people—States—Union—banks—bound up and interwoven together, united in fortune and destiny, and all, all entitled to the protecting care of a parental government. You may as well attempt to make the Government breathe a different air, drink a different water, be lit and warmed by a different sun from the people! A hard-money government and a paper-money people! A Government, an official corps—the servants of the people—glittering in gold, and the people themselves, their masters, buried in ruin, and surrounded with rags.

No prudent or practical government will in its measures run counter to the long-settled habits and usages of the people. Religion, language, laws, the established currency and business of the whole country cannot be easily or suddenly uprooted. After the denomination of our coin was changed to dollars and cents many years elapsed before the old method of keeping accounts, in pounds, shillings, and pence, was abandoned. And to this day there are probably some men of the last century who adhere to it. If a fundamental change becomes necessary, it should not be sudden, but conducted by slow and cautious degrees. The people of the United States have always been a paper-money people. It was paper money that carried us through the Revolution, established our liberties, and made us a free and independent people. And, if the experience of the Revolutionary War convinced our ancestors, as we are convinced, of the evils of an irredeemable paper medium, it was put aside only to give place to that convertible paper which has so powerfully contributed to our rapid advancement, prosperity, and greatness.

The proposed substitution of an exclusive metallic currency, to the mixed medium with which we have been so long familiar, is forbidden by the principles of eternal justice. Assuming the currency of the country to consist of two-thirds of paper and one of specie, and assuming also that the money of a country, whatever may be its component parts, regulates all values, and expresses the true amount which the debtor has to pay to his creditor, the effect of the change upon that relation and upon the property of the country would be most ruinous. All property would be reduced in value to one-third of its present nominal amount; and every debtor would, in effect, have to pay three times as much as he had contracted for. The pressure of our foreign debt would be three times as great as it is, while the six hundred millions, which is about the sum now probably due to the banks from the people, would be multiplied into eighteen hundred millions.

There are more specific objections to this project of subtreasuries, which deserve to be noticed. The chief is the fearful increase of Executive patronage.

Hundreds and thousands of new officers are to be created; for this bill is a mere commencement of the system, and all are to be placed under the direct control of the President.

The Senator from South Carolina [Mr. Calhoun] thinks

that the Executive is now weak, and that no danger is to be apprehended from its patronage. I wish to God I could see the subject in the same light that he does. I wish that I could feel free from that alarm at Executive encroachments by which he and I were so recently animated. When and how, let me ask, has that power, lately so feared and formidable, suddenly become so weak and harmless? Where is that corps of one hundred thousand officeholders and dependents whose organized strength, directed by the will of a single man, was lately held up in such vivid colors and powerful language by a report made by the Senator himself? When were they disbanded? What has become of proscription? Its victims may be exhausted, but the spirit and the power which sacrificed them remain unsubdued. What of the dismissing power? What of the vote? Of that practice of withholding bills, contrary to the Constitution, still more reprehensible than the abuses of the veto? Of treasury orders, put in force and maintained in defiance and contempt of the legislative authority? And, although last, not least, of that expunging power which degraded the Senate, and placed it at the feet of the Executive?

Which of all these enormous powers and pretensions has the present Chief Magistrate disavowed? So far from disclaiming any one of them, has he not announced his intention to follow in the very footsteps of his predecessor? And has he not done it? Was it against the person of Andrew Jackson that the Senator from South Carolina so ably coöperated with us? No, sir, no, sir, no. It was against his usurpations, as we believed them; against his arbitrary administration; above all, against that tremendous and frightful augmentation of the power of the Executive branch of the Government, that we patriotically but vainly contended. The person of the Chief Magistrate is changed, but there stands the Executive power, perpetuated in all its vast magnitude, undiminished, reasserted, and overshadowing all the other departments of the Government. Every trophy which the late President won from them now decorates the Executive mansion. Every power which he tore from a bleeding Constitution is now in the Executive armory, ready, as time and occasion may prompt the existing incumbent, whoever he may be, to be thundered against the liberties of the people.

Whatever may have been the motives or the course of others, I owe it to myself and to truth to say that, in deprecating the election of General Andrew Jackson to the office of Chief Magistrate, it was not from any private considerations, but because

I considered it would be a great calamity to my country; and that, in whatever opposition I made to measures of his Administration, which more than realized my worst apprehensions, I was guided solely by a sense of public duty. And I do now declare my solemn and unshaken conviction that, until the Executive power, as enlarged, extended, and consolidated by him, is reduced within its true constitutional limits, there is no permanent security for the liberties and happiness of this people.

Pass this bill, and whatever divorce its friends may profess to be its aim, that perilous union of the purse and the sword, so justly dreaded by our British and Revolutionary ancestors, becomes absolute and complete. And who can doubt it who knows that over the Secretary of the Treasury at Washington, and every sub-treasurer, the President claims the power to exercise uncontrolled sway?

Senator Walker.—Sir, the Senator from South Carolina [Mr. Calhoun] is right; and I hail him back with pleasure, on this question, to the ranks of the Democracy, of which he was so long the pride and ornament. Well may he who has on this floor so repeatedly opposed the augmentation of Executive power—well may he support the bill now under consideration; because it not only adds nothing to Executive patronage, but takes from it that alarming patronage and power that it could have acquired through the deposit bank system.

Vague and general denunciation we have indeed had, but how one iota of power or patronage will be conferred on the President by this bill, in addition to that which he already possesses, has not been designated; but, were it so conferred, the bank patronage, of which this bill deprives him, would be infinitely greater.

The President's message is against the extension of Executive patronage. Its cardinal doctrine is this: "A limitation of the expenses of the Government to its actual wants, and of the revenue to those expenses." This, then, is the President's doctrine, openly avowed in his message—reduction of the expenses and of the revenue, economy in all public expenditures, and no "interference with the pursuits of the citizen." "No special favors to individuals or any classes of them, to create systems of agriculture, manufactures, or trade." These are the doctrines of the message; and do they enlarge Executive patronage? How is Executive patronage enlarged? It is chiefly by extending the powers of this Government, and augmenting its revenues; for every increase of the powers and revenue of the Government is an augmentation of the power of the Executive functionary. This the message avoids; but what measures would the Senator from Kentucky give us to reduce Executive patronage? His policy would give us a quadruple alliance between the surplus, the bank, the tariff, and internal improvements, all certainly tending to, and terminating in, a national debt, to create a new tariff. The tariff to regulate the whole industry of the whole people of the Union and build up vast manufacturing establishments by the extension and perversion of the taxing power of this Government. A great national bank, to grow rich upon the revenue deposited from the proceeds of the tariff, deriving its profits from Government moneys, and, of course, the ally of the Administration which feeds and created it. The internal improvement policy, growing and extending with the increase of the tariff, and making roads and canals in some favored States, by taxes collected from the whole people; and, lastly, to give universality to the principle, the surplus—the annual surplus for distribution, from sales, by townships and counties at an entry, to speculators in the public lands—a system calculated to debauch and corrupt the States; to break down every feeling of State independence; to feed them annually, from the public treasury, mere stipendiaries upon our bounty; supporting even their State governments and State officers from the revenues of this Government. And at the head of this mighty system, this consolidation of all powers in this Government, would stand the Executive of those powers—the President of the United States, a monarch in everything but a name. And, sir, this league of State banks, confederated by the Government, and fed by the tariff, increasing its deposits and profits, would be the next most potent ally of these systems. It would station some hundred bank fortresses throughout the States, armed and equipped by Government deposits, and extending Executive power and influence. All this President Van Buren would avoid. No, sir, no; it is not the principle or policy of this Administration—Give us patronage and we will make ourselves popular.

It is said this bill, separating the Government from the banks, will divorce the Government from the people. Are the banks the people? No, sir; this bill will elevate the people, and the Government of the people, and of the States, above the banks, and prevent them from arresting the Government, as they now do, by withholding the public revenue. It will have a still greater tendency to elevate the people above the banks, by diminishing, by its incidental operation, the amount of bank paper, and increasing the circulation of gold and silver—for the payment of it into the treasury will be as constantly flowing out, enriching and fertilizing the whole country.

We have been told that the terms divorce of bank and state, as reminding the people of the divorce of church and state, are popular catchwords. I have not used these terms, although I firmly believe that the union of bank and state would soon prove as fatal to liberty as the union of church and state; but, let me ask, are not the terms used upon the other side—one currency for the people, and another for the Government—and the terms separating the Government from the people, mere popular catchwords, which will not bear, as we have seen, the slightest examination. It is said this bill will destroy credit by impairing confidence in banks. Have we not had too much confidence in banks, and have they not proved the greatest and universal destroyers of all credit and all confidence? Yes, these very banks, by their expansions, contractions, and failures, destroyed all confidence and all credit, not only in themselves, but also between man and man, and almost between nation and nation. It is the banks that render prices, confidence, and credit fluctuating and uncertain; and, before their existence, the page of history tells that confidence and credit, between man and man, were infinitely more universal, and that protest of bills of exchange and mercantile failures were then almost wholly unknown. Specie was not hoarded nor credit withheld from honest industry, but universally extended, unchecked by that overthrow of all confidence and all credit, arising from expansions, contractions, and explosions of the bank paper system. We are told that confidence, confidence is the magic word, and the Government has only to breathe into these banks the breath of confidence, and all will be well. Sir, if these banks, limited and restrained by the State legislatures, ought to be continued, I would rather, by the ultimate incidental operation of this bill, push a little more of their paper out of circulation, and much more specie into the vaults, than all the false and delusive confidence that could be excited by the Government indorsement of eight hundred and twenty-three suspended State banks.

While this measure will have a most beneficial effect upon the whole country, it is to me an inexpressible gratification that to the sunny South it will prove a fountain of wealth and prosperity. The war of overexpanded credit upon labor and its products, aided by a great national bank at some distant capital, or by the concentration at or near the same point of the great Northern banking capital, sustained by the Government deposits and indorsements, must cease, and paper credit and the products of labor, left a fair field, without artificial aid, will find labor and its products rising in the scale of importance and influence, and leaving the great staple States a fair opportunity of carrying out their own exports, and introducing their own imports, and the balances in gold and silver, the real, solid, substantial business of their banks, being more safely augmented than all the ruinous aid they can ever receive from Government patronage. And now, sir, if the distinguished Senators opposed to the Administration on this floor will go home to their constituents and explain the full and precise effects of this measure, they can, in aiding the establishment of a sound credit on sound principles—aiding in inspiring a just confidence in the relief this great measure will ultimately extend to all the great interests of the country—they can have almost a moneyed millennium dawn upon the country at once. I appeal to them, then, as patriots, with hearts overflowing with sympathy for the distress of the country, as we have so repeatedly heard on this floor, to unite with us in producing this great, this glorious result; and the thanks of millions of grateful freemen will give them more real happiness, more genuine consolation, and more true and durable applause than all the party triumphs that could adorn the proudest political conquerors. Let them imitate the noble example of the distinguished Senator and statesman from South Carolina, in laying down, in support of this bill, his personal and political prejudices as a burnt offering upon the patriot's altar of his country's good, and for them, also, the swelling heart of a mighty nation will throb with love and gratitude. But should they esteem it their duty to determine otherwise—should their inspiring eloquence and great intellectual power be exerted in appeals to the people against this measure—should it be represented as a tropical tornado, about to sweep in its destructive career over all the great and cherished institutions of our common country, panics and pressures may follow for a time; but soon, yes, very soon, the great principles involved in this bill must and will triumph, and it will then go forth with healing on its wings, hailed by the approving voice of the people. The measure itself will be justly viewed as a third declaration of American independence, and the day of its passage be celebrated in all time to come as a great and glorious national jubilee.

Senator Webster.—Mr. President, the honorable member from South Carolina [Mr. Calhoun] remarked the other day with great frankness and good humor that, in the political classifications of the times, he desired to be considered as nothing but an "honest nullifier." And I am very much afraid, sir, that (whatever he may think of it himself) it has been under the influence of those sentiments which belong to his character as a nullifier that he has so readily and so zealously embraced the doctrines of the President's message. In my opinion, the message, the bill before us, and the honorable member's amendment form, together, a system, a code of practical politics, the direct tendency of which is to nullify and expunge, or, perhaps, more correctly speaking, by a united and mixed process of nullification and expunging, to abolish a highly important and useful power of the Government. It strikes down the principle upon which the Government has been administered, in regard to the subject of the currency, through its whole history; and it seeks to obliterate, or to draw black lines around, that part of the Constitution on which this principle of administration has rested. The system proposed, in my opinion, is not only anti-commercial, but anti-constitutional also, and anti-union in a high degree.

Now, sir, when we look at the message, the bill, and the proposed amendment, their single, exclusive, and undivided object is found to be relief to the Government. Not one single provision is adopted or recommended with direct reference to the relief of the people. They all speak of revenue, of finance, of duties and customs, of taxes and collections; and the evils which the people suffer by the derangement of the currency and the exchanges, and the breaking up of commercial credit, instead of being put forth as prominent and leading objects of regard, are dismissed with a slight intimation, here and there, that, in providing for the superior and paramount interests of Government, some incidental or collateral benefits may, perhaps, accrue to the community. But is Government, I ask, to care for nothing but itself? Is self-preservation the great end of Government? Has it no trust powers? Does it owe no duties but to itself? If it keeps itself in being does it fulfill all the objects of its creation? I think not. I think Government exists, not for its own ends, but for the public utility. It is an agency established to promote the common good by common counsels; its chief duties are to the people; and it seems to me strange and preposterous, in a moment of great and general distress, that Government should confine all its deliberations to the single object of its own revenues, its own convenience, its own undisturbed administration.

Now, sir, my present purpose chiefly is to maintain two propositions:

1. That it is the constitutional duty of this Government to see that a proper currency, suitable to the circumstances of the times, and to the wants of trade and business, as well as to the payment of debts due to Government, be maintained and preserved; a currency of general credit, and capable of aiding the operations of exchange, so far as those operations may be conducted by means of the circulating medium; and that there are duties, therefore, devolving on Congress, in relation to currency, beyond the mere regulation of the gold and silver coins.

2. That the message, the bill, and the proposed amendment, all, in effect, deny any such duty, disclaim all such power, and confine the constitutional obligation of Government to the mere regulation of the coins and the care of its own revenues.

Webster then argued at great length in favor of his propositions, showing that it was the duty of Congress to regulate the paper as well as the metallic currency, and that the proper regulation of the paper currency was a national bank; and concluded:

In every respect this project is objectionable. It is but another "experiment"; and those who recommend it so zealously were the authors of the last, and were equally full of confidence and assurance in regard to that.

Who invite us to try this experiment? What voices do we hear raised in its recommendation? Are they not the well-known voices which we heard so often when the late "experiment" was begun? We know of but one accession. The voice of the honorable member from South Carolina is heard, it is true, now mingling with the general strain; and that is all. Where, then, is the ground for confidence in this experiment, more than there was for it in the last?

This scheme, too, is against all our usages and all our habits. It locks up the revenue, under bolts and bars, from the time of collection to the time of disbursement. Our practice has been otherwise, and it has been a useful practice. In 1833 the Secretary of the Treasury admonished the deposit banks, since they had obtained the custody of the public funds, to accommodate the public, to loan freely, especially to importing merchants. And now a system is proposed to us, according to which any use of the public funds, by way of loan or accommodation to the public, is made a criminal offence, and to be prosecuted by indictment! Admirable, admirable consistency!

Senator Buchanan.—Mr. President: The exhaustion of the human system does not succeed a high degree of unnatural excitement with more unerring certainty than that a depression in the business of the country must follow excessive speculation. The one is a law of nature, the other a scarcely less uniform law of trade.

Whence this eternal vicissitude in the business of the country? What is the secret spring of all these calamities? I answer, the spirit of enterprise, so natural to American citizens, excited into furious action by the stimulus of excessive banking. It operates as does the inhaling of oxygen gas upon the human mind, urging it on to every extravagance and to every folly.

Senators have attributed some portion of the existing distress to the act of 1834, regulating the standard of our gold coins. They have not told us, and they cannot tell us, how this act could have produced such an effect. It was no party measure, and, upon its passage, there were but few, I believe seven, votes against it in the Senate. It was a measure of absolute necessity, if we desired that our own gold coins should ever circulate in this country. Before its passage a half eagle, as an article of merchandise, was intrinsically worth about five dollars and thirty-three cents in silver, while its standard value, as currency under our laws, was only five dollars. It is manifest, therefore, that eagles and half eagles never could have entered into general circulation had it not been for the passage of this act, which is now condemned. It was a mere adjustment of the relative value of gold to silver, according to the standard of other nations.

I have been utterly at a loss to conceive the cause of the hostility of Senators to this necessary measure, unless it be from a feeling similar to that which, it is said, made a distinguished gentleman desire to kill every sheep which came in his way. He could feel no personal hostility to these innocent and harmless animals; but was such a violent anti-tariff man that the sight of them always reminded him of our woolen manufacturers. Certainly no gentleman can entertain any objection to the eagle and half eagle themselves; but they may remind Senators of the efficient and untiring exertions of the Senator from Missouri [Mr. Benton] to introduce a gold currency into circulation. As gold, they may like these coins; but, as Bentonian mint drops, they are detestable.

Without the agency of any of these secondary causes the present distress must have come. It was inevitable as fate. No law of nature is more fixed than that our overbanking and our overtrading must have produced the disastrous results under which we are now suffering.

In this crisis all that the general Government can effect is, in the first place, to withhold its deposits from the banks, and thus refrain from contributing their funds to swell the torrent of wild speculation; and, in the second place, to restrain the extravagance of their credits and issues, in some small degree, by collecting and disbursing our revenue exclusively in specie, or in the notes of banks which will pay the balances due from them in specie, at short intervals. To accomplish these two purposes, as well as to render the public revenue more secure, are the objects of the bill and amendment now before the Senate.

The evils of a redundant paper circulation are now manifest to every eye. It alternately raises and sinks the value of every man's property. It makes a beggar of the man to-morrow who is indulging in dreams of wealth to-day. It converts the business of society into a mere lottery; while those who distribute the prizes are wholly irresponsible to the people. When the collapse comes, as come it must, it casts laborers out of employment, crushes manufacturers and merchants, and ruins thousands of honest and industrious citizens. Shall we, then, by our policy, any longer contribute to such fatal results? That is the question.

The system of extravagant banking benefits no person except the shrewd speculator, who knows how to take advantage of the perpetual fluctuation in prices which a redundant paper currency never fails to produce. He sees, in the general causes which operate upon the commercial world, when money is about to be scarce, and when it will become plenty. He studies the run as a gambler does that of the cards. He knows when to buy and when to sell, and thus often realizes a large estate in a few happy ventures. Those who have been initiated into the mysteries of the paper money market can thus accumulate rapid fortunes at the expense of their less skillful neighbors.

The question before the Senate is not whether we shall divorce the Government from the banks. The banks themselves have done that already. The alliance is already dissolved. The question now is, shall we, with all the experience of the past, restore this ill-fated union? No propitious divinities would grace the new nuptials; but the fatal sisters would be there ready again to cut the cord at the first approach of difficulty and danger.

Senator Wright.—Is it not most desirable to free the legislation of Congress from bank influence altogether? Will it not tend more than any other single act we could perform to take from our debates and deliberations that bitterness and acrimony which have too strongly characterized them for the last few years, but which, I am proud to say, have entered, in a much less degree, into the present debate in the Senate than into any similar debate for many years? For myself I feel that this consideration alone demands the passage of this bill; that it is entirely paramount to any objections I have yet heard urged against it; that it is as much superior to considerations of financial convenience and pecuniary profit, as are the purity and permanency of our political institutions to temporary advantages of a bargain or facilities of borrowing money.

Can it be desirable to preserve a connection which is the subject of incessant complaint on the part of the banks and their friends, and of constant embarrassment to the operations of the public treasury, and of imputation upon the most faithful and worthy public officers? I consider this connection of the fiscal affairs of the Government with the credit and business of the banks, and of business and commercial men, and the constant imputations brought upon the Government thereby, as promoting a political morality in the public mind most dangerous to our institutions; as doing more to weaken the confidence of the people in the Government of their choice than any and all other causes of distrust combined. If we would listen to the slander and misrepresentations of the times, we must believe that all our misfortunes, public and private, are imputable to our Government—all our prosperity to a resistance to its measures and its policy. And whence do these imputations come but from our connection with the banks? They all emanate from that source, and from no other. That connection is now dissolved by the operation of law and the voluntary action of the banks themselves; and I would say, let it be perpetual—let it never be renewed.

The Wright bill was introduced at the next session (the regular one beginning December 4, 1837) and passed by the Senate and voted down by the House.

In the debate in the Senate an exchange of personalities occurred between Henry Clay and John C. Calhoun, which is of special interest owing to the fact that they had for a number of years been close allies in opposition to President Jackson.

Senator Thomas H. Benton [Mo.] gives an account

of this forensic duel in his "Thirty Years' View" (Vol. II, page 97), to which the reader is referred.

The Wright bill to establish an independent treasury was again introduced in the session of 1838-39, and met its former fate. A new Congress assembled in 1839-40, in which a few sub-treasury Whigs held the balance of power, and the Wright bill passed both Houses, and became a law, by the approval of the President, on July 4, 1840—a date evidently chosen in order to help along the prophecy of Senator Walker that the enactment of the bill would be hailed as the "third Declaration of Independence" (the confirmation by the people of the Revolution of 1798 in electing Thomas Jefferson to the presidency in 1800 being considered the second). None of the evil results foretold by the Whigs came to pass; everything working smoothly under the new system.

However, in the session of 1841-42, the Whigs came into control of both the legislative and executive branches of the Government, and, being committed to the policy of a national bank, they repealed the sub-treasury act as the first step toward the bank's resurrection. For five years the Government's finances were conducted virtually at the discretion of the Secretary of the Treasury. The election in 1844 of James K. Polk to the presidency and of a Congress Democratic in both branches afforded an opportunity to reënact the sub-treasury bill, which became law on August 6, 1846, and has remained in force down to the present time. The ghost of the "murdered" national bank was effectually laid, never again rising to disturb the national councils.

CHAPTER VIII

The Whig Fight to Reëstablish a National Bank

Election of William Henry Harrison and John Tyler—Harrison's Inaugural Address—Death of Harrison—The Whigs in Congress Pass a National Bank Bill—It Is Vetoed by President Tyler—Debate in the Senate on the Veto: in Favor, William C. Rives [Va.]; Opposed, Henry Clay [Ky.]; Veto Is Sustained—Whig Mob "Shivarees" the President While Democratic Congressmen Are Congratulating Him—Humorous Remarks by Senator Clay on the Incident—Rejoinder by Senator James Buchanan [Pa.]—Second Attempt to Pass a Bank Bill—It Is Vetoed by the President and Lampooned by Senator Thomas H. Benton [Mo.]—Resignations of the Cabinet, Daniel Webster Excepted—Repudiation of the President by His Party—Representative Caleb Cushing [Mass.] in His Defence—Denunciation of Cushing by Representative Garrett Davis [Ky.].

IN 1840 William Henry Harrison [O.], the previous Whig candidate, and John Tyler [Va.], a former Democrat, were nominated by the Whigs as their candidates for President and Vice-President respectively against President Van Buren and Vice-President Johnson, who stood for reëlection. Harrison and Tyler were overwhelmingly elected by 234 votes out of 294.

In his inaugural address the President adverted to the sub-treasury policy of his predecessor, as follows:

The President's Power Over the Purse

Inaugural Address of William Henry Harrison

By making the President the sole distributor of all the patronage of the Government the framers of the Constitution do not appear to have anticipated at how short a period it would become a formidable instrument to control the free operations of the State governments. Of trifling importance at first, it had, early in Mr. Jefferson's Administration, become so powerful as to create great alarm in the mind of that patriot, from the potent influence it might exert in controlling the freedom of the elective franchise. If such could have been the effects of its influence, how much greater must be the danger at this time, quadrupled in amount, as it certainly is, and more completely under the control of the Executive will than their construction of their powers allowed, or the forbearing characters of all the early Presidents permitted them to make? But it is not by the extent of its patronage alone that the Executive Department has become dangerous, but by the use which it appears may be made of the appointing power to bring under its control the whole revenue of the country. The Constitution has declared it to be the duty of the President to see that the laws are executed, and it makes him the Commander-in-Chief of the armies and navy of the United States. If the opinion of the most approved writers upon that species of mixed government, which, in modern Europe, is termed *monarchy,* in contradistinction to *despotism,* is correct, there was wanting no other addition to the powers of our Chief Magistrate to stamp a monarchical character on our Government but the control of the public finances. And to me it appears strange, indeed, that anyone should doubt that the entire control which the President possesses over the officers who have the custody of the public money, by the power of removal with or without cause, does, for all mischievous purposes at least, virtually subject the treasure also to his disposal. The first Roman Emperor, in his attempt to seize the sacred treasure, silenced the opposition of the officer to whose charge it had been committed by a significant allusion to his sword. By a selection of political instruments for the care of the public money, a reference to their commissions by a President would be quite as effectual an argument as that of Cæsar to the Roman knight. I am not insensible of the great difficulty that exists in devising a proper plan for the safe-keeping and disbursement of the public revenues, and I know the importance which has been attached by men of great abilities and patriotism to the divorce, as it is called, of the treasury from the banking institutions. It is not the divorce which is complained of, but the unhallowed union of the treasury with the Executive Department which has created such extensive alarm. To this danger to our republican institutions, and that created by the influence given to the Executive through the instrumentality of the Federal officers, I propose to apply all the remedies which may be at my command. It was certainly a great error in the framers of the Constitution not to have made the officer at the head of the Treasury Department entirely independent of the Executive. He should at least have been removable only upon the demand of the popular branch of the legislature. I have determined never to remove a Secretary of the Treasury without communicating all the circumstances attending such removal to both Houses of Congress.

At the instigation of Senator Henry Clay President Harrison convened Congress in extra session to revise the treasury system, but died before the date set, which was May 31, 1841.[1]

President Tyler entered into office with a majority of his party in both Houses of Congress, and therefore with the prospect of conducting a harmonious and successful Administration. In the short space of three months he was at odds with the leading members of the party, who accused him of violating its principles, coining from his name a new synonym for the word "apostatize"—namely, "Tylerize." Being unyielding in character Tyler destroyed all hope of rendering his term of office notable for anything other than discord and failure.

The chief message for the passage of which Senator Clay had instigated the special session of Congress was the establishment of a national bank. Because both Harrison and Tyler had opposed such a bank when they were members of the Democratic party, this issue had been kept in the background during the presidential campaign—as, indeed, had been almost every important issue, the campaign being conducted along personal lines by opposing the rough democratic character of the Western Indian fighter, General Harrison ("Tippecanoe," as he was called from his famous victory), to the suave and supposedly aristocratic temperament of the "Fox of Kinderhook," as Van Buren was termed, and by visibly impressing this contrast upon the voters in the form of replicas of the log cabin in which Harrison had lived, and the free distribution of "hard cider," his favorite beverage—it being represented that his opponent lived in a lordly mansion and drank only foreign wines.

Senator Clay called upon Thomas Ewing, Sr., Secre-

[1] The date of President Harrison's death was April 4, 1841, just one month after his inauguration.

tary of the Treasury, for a plan of a national bank. The Secretary drafted the bill with a special view to removing every constitutional objection to the bank, and so to enable the President to sign the act without laying himself open to the charge of inconsistency, but in the course of the bill through committee it acquired features which caused the President, when it had been passed (by a vote of 26 to 23 in the Senate and 128 to 98 in the House), to veto the bill, giving his reasons for the action, and saying:

Entertaining the opinions alluded to, and having taken this oath, the Senate and the country will see that I could not give my sanction to a measure of the character described without surrendering all claim to the respect of honorable men—all confidence on the part of the people—all self-respect—all regard for moral and religious obligations; without an observance of which no government can be prosperous and no people can be happy. It would be to commit a *crime* which I would not wilfully commit to gain any earthly reward, and which would *justly* subject me to the ridicule and scorn of all virtuous men.

Senator Clay attacked the President for his action, and William C. Rives [Va.] defended him.

The Veto of the National Bank

Senate, August, 1841

Senator Clay.—On the 4th of April last, the lamented Harrison, the President of the United States, paid the debt of nature. President Tyler, who, as Vice-President, succeeded to the duties of that office, arrived in the city of Washington on the 6th of that month. He found the whole metropolis wrapped in gloom, every heart filled with sorrow and sadness, every eye streaming with tears, and the surrounding hills yet flinging back the echo of the bells which were tolled on that melancholy occasion. On entering the presidential mansion he contemplated the pale body of his predecessor stretched before him, and clothed in the black habiliments of death. At that solemn moment I have no doubt that the heart of President Tyler was overflowing with mingled emotions of grief, of patriotism and

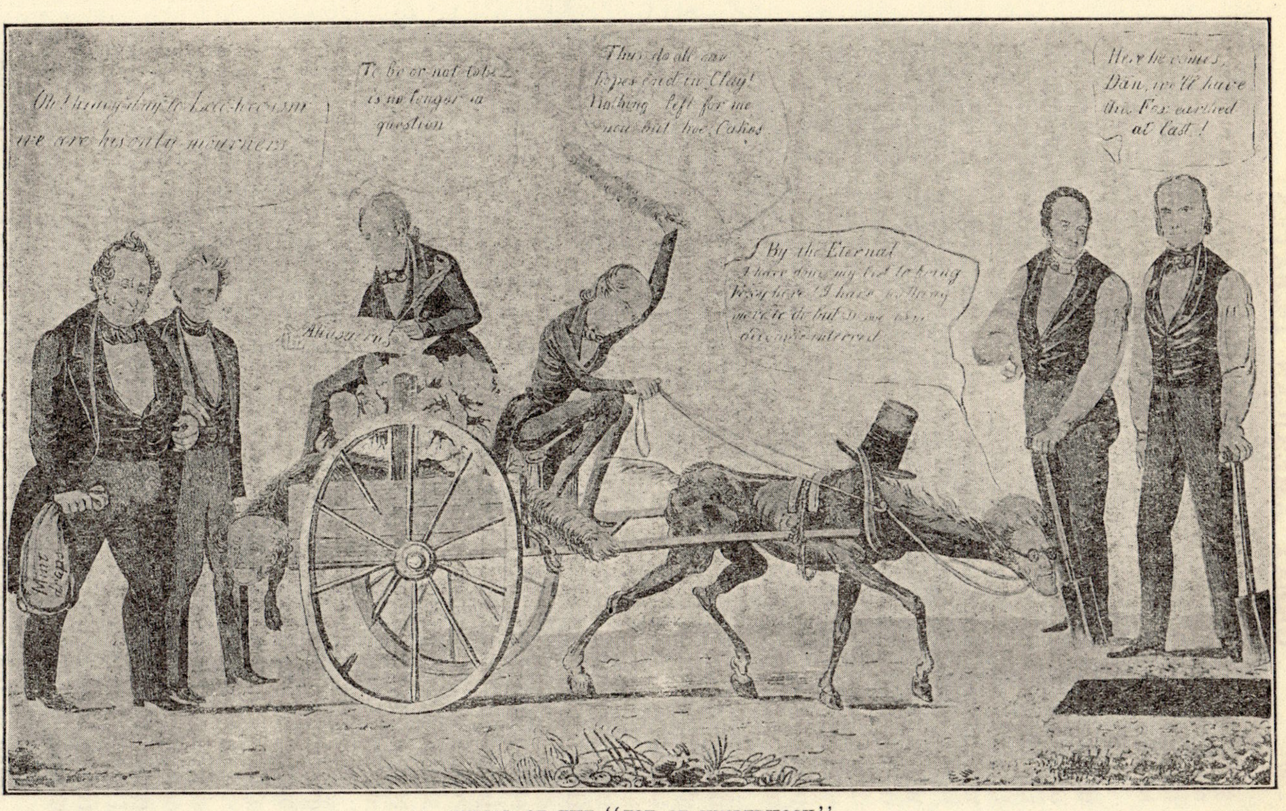

BURIAL OF THE "FOX OF KINDERHOOK"

Whig Caricature of Van Buren, Tyler, Jackson, Webster, Clay, Calhoun, et **al.**

From the collection of the New York Historical Society

gratitude—above all, of gratitude to that country by a majority of whose suffrages, bestowed at the preceding November, he then stood the most distinguished, the most elevated, the most honored of all living Whigs of the United States.

It was under these circumstances and in this probable state of mind that President Tyler, on the 10th day of the same month of April, voluntarily promulgated an address to the people of the United States. That address was in the nature of a coronation oath, which the chief of the state in other countries and under other forms takes upon ascending the throne. It referred to the solemn obligations and the profound sense of duty under which the new President entered upon the high trust which had devolved upon him by the joint acts of the people and of Providence, and it stated the principles and delineated the policy by which he would be governed in his exalted station. It was emphatically a Whig address from beginning to end—every inch of it was Whig, and was patriotic.

In that address the President, in respect to the subject-matter embraced in the present bill, held the following conclusive and emphatic language: "I shall promptly give my sanction to any constitutional measure which, originating in Congress, shall have for its object the restoration of a sound circulating medium, so essentially necessary to give confidence in all the transactions of life, to secure to industry its just and adequate rewards, and to reëstablish the public prosperity. In deciding upon the adaptation of any such measure to the end proposed, as well as its conformity to the Constitution, I shall resort to the fathers of the great republican school for advice and instruction, to be drawn from their sage views of our system of government, and the light of their ever-glorious example."

To this clause in the address of the President I believe but one interpretation was given throughout this whole country, by friend and foe, by Whig and Democrat, and by the presses of both parties. It was by every man with whom I conversed on the subject at the time of its appearance, or of whom I have since inquired, construed to mean that the President intended to occupy the Madison ground, and to regard the question of the power to establish a national bank as immovably settled. And I think I may confidently appeal to the Senate and to the country to sustain the fact that this was the contemporaneous and unanimous judgment of the public.

Entertaining this opinion of the address, I came to Washington at the commencement of the session with the most confident and buoyant hopes that the Whigs would be able to carry all their prominent measures, and especially a Bank of the United States, by far that one of the greatest immediate importance. I anticipated nothing but cordial coöperation between the two departments of government; and I reflected with pleasure that I should find at the head of the Executive branch a personal and political friend, whom I had long and intimately known and highly esteemed.

Upon the opening of the session, but especially on the receipt of the plan of a national bank, as proposed by the Secretary of the Treasury, fears were excited that the President had been misunderstood in his address, and that he had not waived but adhered to his constitutional scruples. Under these circumstances it was hoped that, by the indulgence of a mutual spirit of compromise and concession, a bank, competent to fulfill the expectations and satisfy the wants of the people, might be established.

In this hope the friends of the bank have been deceived, as the message before you indicates. I must think, and hope I may be allowed to say, with profound deference to the Chief Magistrate, that it appears to me he has viewed with too lively sensibility the personal consequences to himself of his approval of the bill; and that, surrendering himself to a vivid imagination, he has depicted them in much too glowing and exaggerated colors, and that it would have been most happy if he had looked more to the deplorable consequences of a veto upon the hopes, the interests, and the happiness of his country. Does it follow that a magistrate who yields his private judgment to the concurring authority of numerous decisions, repeatedly and deliberately pronounced, after the lapse of long intervals, by all the departments of government, and by all parties, incurs the dreadful penalties described by the President? Can any man be disgraced and dishonored who yields his private opinion to the judgment of the nation? In this case the country (I mean a majority), Congress, and, according to common fame, a unanimous Cabinet were all united in favor of the bill. Should any man feel himself humbled and degraded in yielding to the conjoint force of such high authority? Does any man, who at one period of his life shall have expressed a particular opinion, and at a subsequent period shall act upon the opposite opinion, expose himself to the terrible consequences which have been portrayed by the President? How is it with the judge, in the case by no means rare, who bows to the authority of repeated precedents, settling a particular question, while in his private judgment the law is otherwise? How is it with that numerous class of public men in this country, and with the two great parties that have divided it, who, at different periods, have maintained and acted on opposite opinions in respect to this very bank question?

How is it with James Madison, the father of the Constitution—that great man whose services to his country placed him only second to Washington—whose virtues and purity in private life—whose patriotism, intelligence, and wisdom in public councils stand unsurpassed? He was a member of the national convention that formed, and of the Virginia convention that adopted, the Constitution. No man understood it better than he did. He was opposed in 1791 to the establishment of the Bank of the United States upon constitutional ground; and in 1816 he approved and signed the charter of the late Bank of the United States. It is a part of the secret history connected with the first bank that James Madison had, at the instance of General Washington, prepared a veto for him in the contingency of his rejection of the bill. Thus stood James Madison when, in 1815, he applied the veto to a bill to charter a bank upon considerations of expediency, but with a clear and express admission of the existence of a constitutional power in Congress to charter one. In 1816, the bill which was then presented to him being free from the objections applicable to that of the previous year, he sanctioned and signed it. Did James Madison surrender "all claim to the respect of honorable men—all confidence on the part of the people—all self-respect—all regard for moral and religious obligations"? Did the pure, the virtuous, the gifted James Madison, by his sanction and signature to the charter of the late Bank of the United States, commit a crime which justly subjected him "to the ridicule and scorn of all virtuous men"?

Senator Rives.—What was the real issue before the Senate? Was it not the naked question between the bill and the objections to it, as compared with each other? I really had hoped that the honorable Senator, after announcing to us the issue in this very proper manner, would have confined his observations to it alone; and if he had done so I should not have troubled the Senate with a single word. But what has been the course of the honorable Senator? I do not reproach him with it. He, no doubt, felt it necessary, in order to vindicate his own position before the country, to inculpate the course taken by the President; and accordingly about two-thirds of his speech, howsoever qualified by expressions of personal kindness and respect, were taken up in a solemn arraignment of the President of the United States. Most of the allegations put forth by the Senator seem to arrange themselves under the general charge of perfidy —of faithlessness to his party and to the people.

Senator Rives went on to defend the President at all points, declaring the question of a bank was not an issue in the election—repelling the imputation of perfidy and arguing that General Harrison himself would have disapproved the same bill if he had lived and it had been presented to him.

Senator Clay rejoined to Senator Rives, and became more close and pointed in his personal remarks upon Mr. Tyler's conduct, commencing with Mr. Rives' lodgment in the "halfway house," *i. e.,* the pet bank system—which was supposed to have been a camping station in the transition from the Democratic to the Whig camp. He began thus:

I have no desire to prolong this unpleasant discussion, but I must say that I heard with great surprise and regret the closing remark, especially, of the honorable gentleman from Virginia, as, indeed, I did many of those which preceded it. That gentleman stands in a peculiar situation. I found him several years ago in the halfway house, where he seems afraid to remain, and from which he is yet unwilling to go. I had thought, after the thorough riddling which the roof of the house had received in the breaking up of the pet bank system, he would have fled somewhere else for refuge; but there he still stands, solitary and alone, shivering and pelted by the pitiless storm. The sub-treasury is repealed—the pet bank system is abandoned—the United States Bank bill is vetoed—and now, when there is as complete and perfect a reunion of the purse and the sword in the hands of the Executive as ever there was under General Jackson or Mr. Van Buren, the Senator is for doing nothing.

There was a rumor of a design to make a third party, of which the President was to be the head; and, as a part of the scheme, to foment a quarrel between him and Senator Clay, in which Clay was to be made the aggressor. Senator Clay brought this rumor to the notice of

Senator Rives, repelling the part which inculpated himself, and leaving the rest for Senator Rives to answer.

SENATOR CLAY.—Why, sir, what possible, what conceivable motive can I have to quarrel with the President, or to break up the Whig party? What earthly motive can impel me to wish for any other result than that that party shall remain in perfect harmony, undivided, and shall move undismayed, boldly, and unitedly forward to the accomplishment of the all-important public objects which it has avowed to be its aim? What imaginable interest or feeling can I have other than the success, the triumph, the glory of the Whig party? But that there may be designs and purposes on the part of certain other individuals to place me in inimical relations with the President, and to represent me as personally opposed to him, I can well imagine—individuals who are beating up for recruits, and endeavoring to form a third party, with materials so scanty as to be wholly insufficient to compose a decent corporal's guard. I fear there are such individuals, though I do not charge the Senator as being himself one of them. What a spectacle has been presented to this nation during this entire session of Congress! That of the cherished and confidential friends of John Tyler, persons who boast and claim to be, *par excellence,* his exclusive and genuine friends, being the bitter, systematic, determined, uncompromising opponents of every leading measure of John Tyler's administration! Was there ever before such an example presented in this or any other age, in this or any other country? I have myself known the President too long, and cherished toward him too sincere a friendship, to allow my feelings to be affected or alienated by anything which has passed here to-day. If the President chooses—which I am sure he cannot, unless falsehood has been whispered into his ears or poison poured into his heart—to detach himself from me, I shall deeply regret it, for the sake of our common friendship and our common country. I now repeat, what I before said, that, of all the measures of relief which the American people have called upon us for, that of a national bank and a sound and uniform currency has been the most loudly and importunately demanded.

The Senator says that, if placed in like circumstances, I would have been the last man to avoid putting a direct veto upon the bill, had it met my disapprobation; and he does me the honor to attribute to me high qualities of stern and unbending intrepidity. I hope that in all that relates to personal firmness—all that concerns a just appreciation of the insignificance of human life—whatever may be attempted to threaten or alarm a soul not easily swayed by opposition, or awed or intimidated by menace—a stout heart and a steady eye that can survey, unmoved and undaunted, any mere personal perils that assail this poor transient, perishing frame—I may, without disparagement, compare with other men. But there is a sort of courage which, I frankly confess it, I do not possess—a boldness to which I dare not aspire—a valor which I cannot covet. I cannot lay myself down in the way of the welfare and happiness of my country. That I cannot, I have not the courage to do. I cannot interpose the power with which I may be invested—a power conferred not for my personal benefit, not for my aggrandizement, but for my country's good—to check her onward march to greatness and glory. I have not courage enough, I am too cowardly for that. I would not, I dare not, in the exercise of such a trust, lie down and place my body across the path that leads my country to prosperity and happiness. This is a sort of courage widely different from that which a man may display in his private conduct and personal relations. Personal or private courage is totally distinct from that higher and nobler courage which prompts the patriot to offer himself a voluntary sacrifice to his country's good. Apprehensions of the imputation of the want of firmness sometimes impel us to perform rash and inconsiderate acts. It is the greatest courage to be able to bear the imputation of the want of courage. But pride, vanity, egotism, so unamiable and offensive in private life, are vices which partake of the character of crimes in the conduct of public affairs. The unfortunate victim of these passions cannot see beyond the little, petty, contemptible circle of his own personal interests. All his thoughts are withdrawn from his country, and concentrated on his consistency, his firmness, himself. The high, the exalted, the sublime emotions of a patriotism which, soaring toward Heaven, rises far above all mean, low, or selfish things, and is absorbed by one soul-transporting thought of the good and the glory of one's country, are never felt in his impenetrable bosom. That patriotism which, catching its inspiration from the immortal God, and leaving, at an immeasurable distance below, all lesser, groveling, personal interests and feelings, animates and prompts to deeds of self-sacrifice, of valor, of devotion, and of death itself—that is public virtue—that is the noblest, the sublimest of all public virtues!

Senator Rives.—The Senator from Kentucky says he found me several years ago in this halfway house, which, after the thorough riddling the roof had received in the breaking up of the pet bank system, he had supposed I would have abandoned. How could I find it in my heart, Mr. President, to abandon it when I found the honorable Senator from Kentucky (even after what he calls the riddling of the roof) so anxious to take refuge in it from the ruins of his own condemned and repudiated system, and where he actually took refuge for four long years, as I have already stated. When I first had the honor to meet the honorable Senator in this body, I found him not occupying the humble but comfortable halfway house which has given him shelter from the storm for the last four years, but a more lordly mansion, gaudy to look upon, but altogether unsafe to inhabit; old, decayed, rat-eaten, which has since tumbled to the ground with its own rottenness, devoted to destruction alike by the indignation of man and the wrath of heaven. Yet the honorable Senator, unmindful of the past, and heedless of the warnings of the present, which are still ringing in his ears, will hear of nothing but the instant reconstruction of this devoted edifice.

I owe it to myself, Mr. President, before I close, to say one or two words in regard to this gorgon of a cabal, which the Senators tells us, upon the authority of dame rumor, has been formed to break up the Cabinet, to dissolve the Whig party, and to form a new or third party. Although the Senator was pleased to acquit me of being a member of this supposed cabal, he yet seemed to have some lurking jealousies and suspicions in his mind on the subject. I will tell the honorable Senator, then, that I know of no such cabal, and I should really think that I was the last man that ought to be suspected of any wish or design to form a new or third party. I have shown myself at all times restive under mere party influence and control from any quarter. All party, in my humble judgment, tends, in its modern degeneracy, to tyranny, and is attended with serious hazard of sacrificing an honest sense of duty, and the great interests of the country, to an arbitrary lead, directed by other aims. I desire, therefore, to take upon myself no new party bonds, while I am anxious to fulfill, to the fullest extent that a sense of duty to the country will permit, every honorable engagement implied in existing ones. The Senator from Kentucky may rest satisfied that he will never see me in any Cabinet, under this or any other Administration. During the brief remnant of my public life, the measure of my ambition will be filled by the humble but honest part I may be permitted to take on this floor in consultations for the common good.

Having disposed of this rumor of a cabal, to the satisfaction, I trust, of the honorable Senator, I will tell him of another rumor I have heard, which, I trust, may be equally destitute of foundation. Rumor is busy in alleging that there is an organized dictatorship, in permanent session in this capitol, seeking to control the whole action of the Government, in both the legislative and executive branches, and sending deputation after deputation to the President of the United States to teach him his duty, and bring him to terms. I do not vouch for the correctness of this rumor. I humbly hope it may not be true; but, if it should unfortunately be so, I will say that it is fraught with far more danger to the regular and salutary action of our balanced Constitution, and to the liberties of the people than any secret cabal that ever has existed or ever will exist.

The Whig leaders attempted to pass the bill over the President's veto, but signally failed, the vote in the Senate, instead of yielding the requisite two-thirds majority, being a tie—24 to 24. That night a crowd of Whig partisans assembled before the executive mansion and hooted the President[1] while he was receiving congratulations from a number of Democratic Senators and Representatives. Levi Woodbury [N. H.] proposed in the Senate an inquiry into the disturbance, which was abandoned upon the discovery of the low and irresponsible character of the participants.

Senator Clay took occasion of this motion to animadvert on the assembly within the executive mansion on the night of the disturbance. Professing artfully that he had not been conclusively informed of the demonstration by the populace, he said:

I did hear that about eight or nine o'clock on that same night of the famous 16th of August there was an irruption on the President's house of the whole loco foco party[2] in Congress; and I did not know but that the alleged disorders might have grown out of or had some connection with that fact. I un-

[1] A serenade of this character was called at the time a "shivaree," a corruption of the French word "charivari."

[2] A Whig term for the Democrats, especially the extreme State Rights wing, derived from an incident (1835) in Tammany (New York) politics, where an attempt to break up a political meeting by blowing out the candles was frustrated by a number relighting them with friction matches —then a novelty and known as "loco-focos." The Whigs attempted to fasten this name upon their opponents by refusing to recognize them as "Democrats."

derstand that the whole party were there. No spectacle, I am sure, could have been more supremely amusing and ridiculous. If I could have been in a position in which, without being seen, I could have witnessed that most extraordinary reunion, I should have had an enjoyment which no dramatic performance could possibly communicate. I think that I can now see the principal *dramatis personæ* who figured in the scene. There stood the grave and distinguished Senator from South Carolina——

[Senator Calhoun here instantly rose, and earnestly insisted on explaining; but Senator Clay refused to be interrupted or to yield the floor.]

SENATOR CLAY.—There, I say, I can imagine stood the Senator from South Carolina—tall, careworn, with furrowed brow, haggard, and intensely gazing, looking as if he were dissecting the last and newest abstraction which sprung from metaphysician's brain, and muttering to himself, in half-uttered sounds, "This is indeed a real crisis!" Then there was the Senator from Alabama [Mr. King], standing upright and gracefully, as if he were ready to settle in the most authoritative manner any question of order, or of etiquette, that might possibly arise between the high assembled parties on that new and unprecedented occasion. Not far off stood the honorable Senators from Arkansas and from Missouri [Mr. Sevier and Mr. Benton], the latter looking at the Senator from South Carolina, with an indignant curl on his lip and scorn in his eye, and pointing his finger with contempt toward that Senator [Mr. Calhoun], while he said, or rather seemed to say, "He call himself a statesman! why, he has never even produced a decent humbug!"

SENATOR BENTON [interrupting].—The Senator from Missouri was not there.

SENATOR CLAY.—I stand corrected; I was only imagining what you would have said if you had been there. Then there stood the Senator from Georgia [Mr. Cuthbert], conning over in his mind on what point he should make his next attack upon the Senator from Kentucky. On yonder ottoman reclined the other Senator from Missouri on my left [Mr. Linn], indulging, with smiles on his face, in pleasing meditations on the rise, growth, and future power of his new colony of Oregon. The honorable Senator from Pennsylvania [Mr. Buchanan], I presume, stood forward as spokesman for his whole party; and, although I cannot pretend to imitate his well-known eloquence, I beg leave to make an humble essay toward what I presume to have been the kind of speech delivered by him on that august occasion:

"May it please your Excellency: A number of your present political friends, late your political opponents, in company with myself, have come to deposit at your Excellency's feet the evidences of our loyalty and devotion; and they have done me the honor to make me the organ of their sentiments and feelings. We are here more particularly to present to your Excellency our grateful and most cordial congratulations on your rescue of the country from a flagrant and alarming violation of the Constitution, by the creation of a Bank of the United States; and also our profound acknowledgments for the veto, by which you have illustrated the wisdom of your administration and so greatly honored yourself. And we would dwell particularly on the unanswerable reasons and cogent arguments with which the notification of the act to the legislature had been accompanied. We had been, ourselves, struggling for days and weeks to arrest the passage of the bill, and to prevent the creation of the monster to which it gives birth. We had expended all our logic, exerted all our ability, employed all our eloquence; but in spite of all our utmost efforts, the friends of your Excellency in the Senate and House of Representatives proved too strong for us. And we have now come most heartily to thank your Excellency that you have accomplished for us that against your friends, which we, with our most strenuous exertions, were unable to achieve."

I hope the honorable Senators on the other side of the chamber will pardon me for having conceived it possible that, amid the popping of champagne, the intoxication of their joy, the ecstasy of their glorification, they might have been the parties who created a disturbance, of which they never could have been guilty had they waited for their *"sober second thoughts."* I have no doubt the very learned ex-Secretary of the Treasury, who conducted that department with such distinguished ability, and such happy results to the country, and who now has such a profound abhorrence of all the taxes on tea and coffee, though, in his own official reports, he so distinctly recommended them, would, if appointed chairman of the committee, have conducted the investigation with that industry which so eminently distinguishes him; and would have favored the Senate with a report, marked with all his accustomed precision and ability, and with the most perfectly lucid clearness.

Senator Buchanan.—The honorable Senator has, with great power of humor, and much felicity of description, drawn for us a picture of the scene which he supposes to have been presented at the President's house on the ever-memorable evening of the veto. It was a happy effort; but, unfortunately, it was but a fancy sketch—at least so far as I am concerned. I was not there at all upon the occasion. But, I ask, what scenes were enacted on that eventful night at this end of the avenue? The Senator would have no cause to complain if I should attempt, in humble imitation of him, to present a picture, true to the life, of the proceedings of himself and his friends. Amid the dark and lowering clouds of that never-to-be-forgotten night a caucus assembled in one of the apartments of this gloomy building, and sat in melancholy conclave, deploring the unhappy fate of the Whig party. Some rose and advocated vengeance; "their voice was still for war." Others, more moderate, sought to repress the ardent zeal of their fiery compatriots, and advised to peace and prudence. It was finally concluded that, instead of making open war upon Captain Tyler, they should resort to stratagem, and, in the elegant language of one of their number, that they should endeavor "to head" him. The question was earnestly debated by what means they could best accomplish this purpose; and it was resolved to try the effect of the "Fiscality" now before us. Unfortunately for the success of the scheme, "Captain Tyler" was forewarned and forearmed by means of a private and confidential letter addressed by mistake to a Virginia coffee house. It is by means like this that "enterprises of great pith and moment" often fail. But so desperately intent are the Whig party still on the creation of a bank that one of my friends on this side of the House told me that a bank they would have, though its exchanges should be made in bacon hams, and its currency be small potatoes.

Other Senators took the imaginary scene, in which they had been made to act parts, in thoroughly good temper; and thus the debate on the first proposal of a charter to establish a Fiscal Bank was brought to a conclusion with more amicability than that with which it had been conducted.

A second attempt was made by the Whigs in the same year [1841] to establish a national bank, this time disguised as "The Fiscal Corporation of the United States"—a pretentious title which was much ridiculed by the Democrats. Thus Senator Thomas H. Benton [Mo.] exclaimed:

The Cat in the Meal Tub

Senator Benton

Heavens what a name! long as the moral law—half subtreasury and half national bank—and all fraudulent and deceptive, to conceal what it is; and entirely too long. The name is too long. People will never stand it. They cannot go through all that. We must have something shorter—something that will do for every-day use. Corporosity! that would be a great abridgment; but it is still too long. It is five syllables, and people will not go above two syllables, or three at most, and often hang at one, in names which have to be incontinently repeated. They are all economical at that, let them be as extravagant as they may be in spending their money. They will not spend their breath upon long names which have to be repeated every day. They must have something short and pointed; and, if you don't give it to them, they will make it for themselves. The defunct Fiscal Bank was rapidly taking the title of fiscality; and by alliteration, rascality; and, if it had lived, would soon have been compendiously and emphatically designated by some brief and significant title. The Fiscal Corporation cannot expect to have better luck. It must undergo the fate of all great men and of all great measures, overburdened with titles—it must submit to a short name. There is much virtue in a name; and the poets tell us there are many on whose conception Phœbus never smiled, and at whose birth no muse nor grace was present. In that predicament would seem to be this intrusive corporosity, which we have received from the other House, and sent to our young committee, and which has mutation of title without alteration of substance, and without accession of euphony or addition of sense. Some say a name is nothing—that a rose by any other name would smell as sweet. So it will; and a thorn by any other name would stick as deep. And so of these fiscals, whether to be called banks or corporations. They will still be the same thing—a thorn in our side—but a short name they must have. This corporosity must retrench its extravagance of title.

Senator Benton here told the story of a steamboat to which the owner, in honor of his sweetheart, a Louisiana girl of French parentage, had given the captivating designation of "La Belle Creole"—a name which was successively shortened to "Creole" (pronounced cree-owl) and to "Owl." This story was greeted with roars of laughter, one Senator exclaiming that it was a good name for a bank; that there had been an Owl-Creek Bank in Ohio once, now dead and insolvent, though in its day as good as the best.

Mr. B. continued. I do not know whether owl will do for this child of long name and many fathers; but we must have a name, and must continue trying till we get one. Let us hunt far and wide. Let us have recourse to the most renowned Æsop and his fables, and to that one of his fables which teaches us how an old black cat succeeded in getting at the rats again after having eaten up too many of them, and become too well known, under her proper form, to catch any more. She rolled herself over in a meal tub—converted her black skin into white—and walked forth among the rats as a new and innocent animal that they had never seen before. All were charmed to see her! but a quick application of teeth and claws to the throats and bellies of the rats let them see that it was their old acquaintance, the black cat; and that whitening the skin did not alter the instincts of the animal nor blunt the points of its teeth and claws. The rats, after that, called her the meal-tub cat and the mealy cat. May we not call this corporosity the meal-tub bank? A cattish name would certainly suit it in one particular; for, like a cat, it has many lives, and a cat, you know, must be killed nine times before it will die; so say the traditions of the nursery; and of all histories the traditions of children are the most veracious. They teach us that cats have nine lines. So of this bank. It has been killed several times, but here it is still, scratching, biting, and clawing. Jackson killed it in 1832; Tyler killed it last week. But this is only a beginning. Seven times more the *Fates* must cut the thread of its hydra life before it will yield up the ghost.

The meal tub! No insignificant or vulgar name. It lives in history, and connects its fame with kings and statesmen. We all know the Stuarts of England—an honest and bigoted race in the beginning, but always unfortunate in the end. The second Charles was beset by plots and cabals. There were many attempts or supposed attempts to kill him; many plots against him, and some very ridiculous; among the rest one which goes by the name of the meal-tub plot; because the papers which discovered it were found in the meal tub where the conspirators or their enemies had hid them.

When a small boy I went to school in a Scotch-Irish neighborhood and learned many words and phrases which I have not met with since, but which were words of great pith and power; among the rest shake-poke. Poke signifies bag, and is a phrase much used among the Scotch-Irish in America. A pig is carried to market in a poke, and, if you buy it without taking it out first, you may be "taken in." So corn is carried to a mill in a poke, and when brought home, ground into meal, the meal remains in the poke, in the houses of poor families, until it is used up. When the bag is nearly empty it is turned upside down and shaken; and the meal that comes out is called the shake-poke, that is to say, the last shake of the bag. By an easy and natural metaphor this term is also applied to the last child that is born in a family; especially if it is puny or a rickety concern. The last child, like the last meal, is called a shake-poke; and may we not call this *fiscalous corporation* a shake-poke also, and for the same reason? It is the last—the last at all events for the session! it is the last meal in their bag—their shake-poke! and it is certainly a rickety concern.

I do not pretend to impose a name upon this bantling; that is a privilege of paternity or of sponsorship, and I stand in neither relation to this babe. But a name of brevity—of brevity and significance—it must have; and, if the fathers and sponsors do not bestow it, the people will; for a long name is abhorred and eschewed in all countries. Remember the fate of John Barebone, the canting hypocrite in Cromwell's time. He had a very good name, John Barebone; but the knave composed a long verse, like Scripture, to sanctify himself with it, and intituled himself thus:—"Praise God, Barebone, for, if Christ had not died for you, you would be damned, Barebone." Now, this was very sanctimonious; but it was too long—too much of a good thing—and so the people cut it all off but the last two words, and called the fellow "damned Barebone," and nothing else but damned Barebone, all his life after. So let this corporosity beware: it may get itself damned before it is done with us, and Tyler, too.[1]

This bill, like the former, was passed by Congress, vetoed by the President, and failed to pass over the veto.

On account of his action on the bank bill, the members of the Cabinet, whom the President had inherited from

[1] A reference to the Whig campaign slogan: "Tippecanoe and Tyler too!"

Harrison, resigned on September 11, 1841, with the exception of Daniel Webster, Secretary of State, who refused to go out with the others on the patriotic ground that he was conducting "delicate and important affairs" in his department. The vacancies were filled by the President with Democrats and Whigs friendly to his interest. The Whigs in Congress met in caucus and issued a manifesto repudiating him. Representative Caleb Cushing [Mass.], in an able paper, rushed to the President's defence, attacking Henry Clay as a "dictator"—at the instigation, it was said, of Daniel Webster—and in the succeeding years of the Administration he supported the President through thick and thin, calling forth the following severe denunciation by Representative Garrett Davis [Ky.].

The Pupil of Machiavelli

Denunciation of Caleb Cushing by Representative Davis

The gentleman occupies a strange position, and puts forth extraordinary notions, considering the measures and principles which he always, until the commencement of this Administration, advocated with so much zeal and ability. I had read many of his speeches before I knew him. I admired his talents and attainments; I approved of the soundness of his views, and was instructed and fortified in my own. But he is wonderfully metamorphosed; and I think, if he will examine the matter deliberately, he will find it to be quite as true, that he has broken his neck politically in jumping his somersets, as that "the Whig party has knocked out its brains against the fixed fact." He tells us that party is nothing but an association of men struggling for power; and that he contemns measures—that measures are not principles. The gentleman must have beer reading the celebrated treatise, "The Prince," for such *dicta* are of the school of Machiavelli; and his sudden and total abandonment of all the principles as well as measures, to which he was as strongly pledged as any Whig, good and true, proves that he has studied his lesson to some purpose. At the extra session of 1837 he opposed the sub-treasury in a very elaborate speech. Now he is the unscrupulous advocate of the exchequer, a measure embodying both the sub-treasury and a great organized govern-

THE PEDLAR AND HIS PACK, OR THE DESPERATE EFFORT. AN OVERBALANCE

Caricature of Tyler's Defunct Cabinet, Webster Holding His Seat

From the collection of the New York Historical Society

ment bank, and fraught with more frightful dangers than his own excited imagination had pictured in the whole three years.

He was one of the stanchest supporters of a United States bank. He characterized "the refusal of the late President (Jackson) to sign the bill rechartering the bank, like the removal of the deposits, to be in defiance and violation of the popular will," and characterized as felicitous the periods of time when we possessed a national bank, and as calamitous the periods that we were without it. And yet, sir, he has denied that he was ever the supporter of a bank of the United States, and is now one of the most rabid revilers of such an institution.

He was for Mr. Clay's land bill; and he has abandoned and now contemns it. No man has been more frequent and unsparing in his denunciations of General Jackson; and now he is the sycophantic eulogist of the old hero. He was the unflinching defender of the constitutional rights and powers of Congress. This Administration has not only resorted to the most flagitious abuse of the veto power, but has renewed every other assault, open or insidious, of Presidents Jackson and Van Buren upon Congress, which he, at the time, so indignantly rebuked; and he now justifies them all. He has gone far ahead of the extremest parasites of executive power. John Tyler vetoed four acts of Congress which the gentleman had voted for, and strange, by his subtle sophistry, he defended each of the vetoes; and, most strange, when the House, in conformity to the provisions of the Constitution, voted again upon the measures, his vote was recorded in their favor, and to overrule the very vetoes of which he had just been the venal advocate."

CHAPTER IX

Treasury Notes

["greenbacks"]

Elbridge G. Spaulding [N. Y.] Introduces Bill in the House to Authorize a Large Issue of Treasury Notes ("Greenbacks")—Debate: in Favor, Mr. Spaulding; Opposed, George H. Pendleton [O.], Clement L. Vallandigham [O.]; the Bill Is Passed.

CONGRESS at various times during the session of 1861-62 appropriated vast sums of money for the prosecution of the war, and authorized repeated issues of treasury notes ("greenbacks") to pay the same.

On January 22, 1862, Elbridge G. Spaulding [N. Y.], from the Committee on Ways and Means, introduced in the House a bill to authorize $100,000,000 of such notes, and to fund the floating national debt. Such notes were to bear no interest and to be payable "at the pleasure of the United States"; no note should be for less than $5; such notes were to be receivable for all debts due the Government and for all debts of the Government due to individuals, corporations, etc., within the United States; they were to be "legal tender in payment of all debts, public and private, within the United States"; when deposited in multiples of $50 in the treasury, six per cent. bonds, payable in twenty years at the pleasure of the Government, were to be issued therefor, and when not less than $2,500 of these bonds were presented the Secretary of the Treasury, if he deemed it expedient, might issue therefor bonds whose principal and interest were payable in foreign lands in foreign currency; the treasury notes were to be lawful payment at par value for Government bonds thereafter to be issued.

To fund the public debt the Secretary of the Treasury was authorized to issue bonds to an amount not exceeding $500,000,000, bearing six per cent. interest, and redeemable at the pleasure of the Government twenty years from date; the denominations of the bonds were to be not less than $50, and the amount issued to each person or corporation not less than $2,500; the Secretary might, if he deemed it expedient, issue for these bonds similar ones payable in foreign lands in foreign currency; he was also authorized to pay creditors of the United States with the bonds, or to exchange them for lawful money of the United States, including treasury notes.

Treasury Notes

House of Representatives, January 28–February 25, 1862

In advocacy of the bill Mr. Spaulding, on January 28, said:

The bill before us is a war measure—a measure of *necessity,* and not of choice, presented by the Committee of Ways and Means, to meet the most pressing demands upon the treasury, to sustain the army and navy until they can make a vigorous advance upon the traitors and crush out the rebellion. These are extraordinary times, and extraordinary measures must be resorted to in order to save our Government and preserve our nationality.

At the extra session in July last Congress authorized the Secretary of the Treasury to borrow $250,000,000, for which he was authorized to issue coupon bonds, or registered bonds, or treasury notes, in such proportions of each as he might deem advisable. The bonds were to be issued for twenty years at a rate not exceeding seven per cent. interest per annum, payable half yearly; and the treasury notes were to be issued in denominations of not less than $50 each, at three years, with interest at seven and three-tenths per cent. per annum, payable half yearly, and exchangeable at any time for twenty-year six per cent. bonds. Or, at the option of the Secretary, he was permitted to issue $50,000,000 of the above loan in treasury notes, on demand, in denominations of not less than $5 each without interest, and made receivable in payment of salaries or other dues owing by the United States; or, in his discretion, he was authorized to issue treasury notes at one year, bearing interest at three and sixty-five hundredths per cent. per annum, exchangeable at any time in sums of $100 or upward for the three-year treasury notes bearing seven and three-tenths per cent. interest, but in the aggregate not to exceed $250,000,000. A further provision, however, was made, to wit: that the Secretary of the Treasury might negotiate any part of the loan for six per cent. twenty-year bonds *at a rate not less than the equivalent of par for bonds, bearing seven per cent. interest per annum half yearly, payable in twenty years.*

Under these provisions the Secretary of the Treasury has borrowed $203,516,500.

The total amount of the public debt up to the present time, and for which United States stock and treasury notes have been issued, is, liquidated and unliquidated, to July 1, 1863, $1,200,-000,000.

There is now over $100,000,000 of accrued indebtedness in different forms that should be paid at an early day.

With this large accrued indebtedness, and with the prospect that (unless this bill is adopted) the Government will put on the market to the highest bidder still further issues of bonds to the amount of two hundred and fifty to three hundred millions of dollars, to pay current expenses to July next, it is not expected that even the present price of United States stocks can be maintained if forced on the market at this time. We have this alternative, either to go into the market and sell our bonds for what they will command or to pass this bill, or find some other better mode, if one can be devised, to raise means to carry on the war. The Secretary has the means of defraying the daily expenses required to be disbursed from the treasury for only a few days longer. With the enormous expenditures of the Government, to pay the extraordinary expenses of the war, it requires no extended calculation to show that the treasury must be supplied from some source, or the Government must stop payment in a very few days.

You cannot borrow of capitalists any more money on twenty-year seven per cent. bonds, nor on your seven and three-tenths per cent. treasury notes, at the rates fixed by the act of July last. If you offer to the people, and put on the market, $300,000,000 more to the highest bidder, in the present aspect of affairs, they would not be taken except at ruinous rates of discount. That policy would depreciate the bonds already taken by the banks and the people, who are most loyal to the Government, and who came forward as your best friends and furnished the means so much needed during the last few months to organize your army and navy; and, besides, such depreciation would greatly increase the debt, by requiring a much larger amount of bonds to be issued than would be needed if your loans were taken at par. A loan put upon the market in the present depressed state of United States stocks, to be followed by other large loans, is not regarded as a favorable mode of providing means for maintaining the Government at the present time. If it had been adopted at first, it might possibly have been the best mode; but it is now too late to essay that plan, and I believe it would be ruinous to adopt it. I fear the twenty-year six per cent. bonds would, under the pressure, fall to seventy-five, seventy, sixty, and even fifty cents. This would be a ruinous mode of raising the means to carry on the Government.

What, then, is to be done? The Secretary of the Treasury [Salmon P. Chase] in his annual report does not recommend the issue of demand treasury notes, although he points out many advantages that would result to the Government from their issue. He suggests two plans: first, the issue of demand treasury notes; and, second, a national currency secured by a pledge of United States stocks, to be issued by banks and associations, with proper regulations for their redemption by the banks themselves.

On the propriety of the issue of treasury notes by the Government, to be put in circulation as money, the Secretary says:

> "The first of these plans was partially adopted at the last session of Congress, in the provision authorizing the Secretary to issue United States notes, payable in coin, to an amount not exceeding $50,000,000. That provision may be so extended as to reach the average circulation of the country, while a moderate tax, gradually augmented, on bank notes, will relieve the national from the competition of local circulation. It has been already suggested that the substitution of a national for a State currency, upon this plan, would be equivalent to a loan to the Government without interest, except on the fund to be kept in coin, and without expense, except the cost of preparation, issue, and redemption, while the people would gain the additional advantage of a uniform currency, and relief from a considerable burden in the form of interest on debt."

These remarks of the Secretary were made before the suspension of specie payments. The situation of the country is now very different from what it was two months ago. The circumstances have changed, and the Secretary and Congress will find it necessary, in the present exigency, to conform their action to what *can* be done, and not to what they would *like* to do were it otherwise practicable.

The second plan of the Secretary, and the one which he recommends for adoption, namely: a national currency, to be issued by banks, and secured by a pledge of United States stocks, the sub-Committee of Ways and Means have examined with considerable care. A bill has been prepared and printed for the use of the committee, which may, after some modification, be reported to this House for its action. The committee have come to the conclusion that, however meritorious this system may be in providing a way for funding the stocks of the United States, and however perfect the system may be made by Congress, it cannot, if adopted, be made available soon enough to meet the immediately impending necessities of the Government.

The new system of banking would necessarily go into operation slowly. The existing circulation of bank notes in the loyal States is supposed to be about one hundred and forty millions of dollars. This new currency, when issued, would come into competition with the existing circulation of the banks already established in the several States, and, in the present embarrassed condition of monetary affairs, several months must necessarily elapse before any considerable amount of United States stocks would be absorbed by banks under this proposed new law. As an ultimate mode of funding some part of the large amount of Government stock which has already been issued, and which must from time to time be issued, it may be very valuable; and the national currency issued upon it would no doubt obtain a wide circulation, and greatly facilitate the payment of taxes and other dues to the Government. But with a navy, and an army of six hundred thousand men in the field, requiring, with the other expenses of the Government, an average daily expenditure of more than $1,600,000, this new system of banking will not afford relief to the treasury in time to enable the Secretary to meet the pressing demands that are made upon him.

The duties received at the different customhouses, and the taxes levied at the extra session, or that may now be levied, will be wholly inadequate to meet the requirements of the treasury in the present emergency during the next six months. If you cannot borrow the money on the credit of the United States, except at ruinous rates of discount, and cannot make the new banking system available in time, and cannot realize the amount required from your tariff and tax bills, in what mode can the means be obtained and the Government be carried on? It is believed that the only way in which it can be done is by issuing treasury notes, payable on demand, and making them a legal tender in payment of all debts, public and private, and by adequate taxation to be imposed by new bills. This will bring into full exercise all the higher powers of Government under the Constitution. (See article one, section eight.)

The tables from the Census Bureau show that the true value of the property, real and personal, within the United States, is $16,159,616,068, and the assessed value is $12,006,756,585.

The power in the Constitution to "lay and collect taxes, duties, imposts, and excises" is general and unlimited. Congress has the power to levy and collect any amount of taxes that may be necessary to preserve its existence and pay all its *debts.* Government has a claim—a mortgage, in fact—on all this property to that extent. Will Congress do its duty by passing bills to collect these taxes? This is the vital question. Will Congress have the firmness and the courage to impose the necessary taxation to sustain the credit of the Government? Direct taxation, excises, and internal duties are new features within the United States. They will be heavy burdens on the people, but essential to sustain the circulation of demand treasury notes. The tax gatherer will be an unwelcome visitor to most people, but his face must soon be familiar.

Some members of Congress may hesitate to vote for the tax bills, fearing that they may not be in favor with their constituency at home. Under these circumstances will members of Congress meet the question boldly and firmly? Here is the whole property of the country at the will of Congress. You have the power to tax it to an unlimited extent if necessary to sustain the Government.

This is the *capital,* $16,000,000,000 in amount, on which your treasury notes and bonds rest. This claim of Government in the hands of Congress is direct and specific on the banks throughout the United States, including the gold and silver in their vaults; on commerce, on all kinds of production and business; on railroads, steamboats, and their passengers; on gas companies, on manufacturing companies of all kinds; in short, all real and personal estate of every kind is held subject to the payment of the treasury notes and bonds issued by the Government. Congress is clothed with this mighty power to sustain the nation at this time.

Will you hesitate to do your duty? This is what the people —the capitalist, the merchant, and all who confide in your demand notes—want to know. If they take these notes they want to know positively whether you will enforce the claim of the Government upon the property of the country to the full extent necessary to redeem the treasury notes, and pay punctually the interest on the bonds which they take of you to sustain the Government. Unless you are prepared to satisfy the country on this point, it is in vain to issue bonds or notes and expect them to pass currently among all the people. Unless this is done they will depreciate, and they ought to depreciate; but with ample taxation, cheerfully voted by Congress, they will be the very best security in the country, because the whole property of the country is held for their redemption. Congress has a plain duty to perform; it has ample power. This power should now be enforced.

In carrying on this existing war and putting down the rebellion it is necessary to bring into exercise all the sovereign power of the Government to sustain itself. The war power must be exercised to its full extent. The money power of the Government must be brought into requisition. The power to tax must be availed of. All the energies of the nation must be aroused and brought into action. The power of the Government and the means of the people must all be devoted to this great work. The Government must be preserved, and this nation of thirty-four States must be perpetuated. The life of the nation is in peril, and all we have and all we hope for must be devoted to maintain its existence, until peace and quiet are restored in every part of our common country.

This bill is a *necessary means* of carrying into execution the powers granted in the Constitution "to raise and *support* armies," and "to provide and *maintain* a navy.

In the present *crisis* of our national affairs it is necessary that the army should be "supported," and the navy "maintained." This necessity will not be questioned by any loyal member on this floor.

The Constitution provides that "*all the laws necessary and proper* for carrying into execution the foregoing powers" may be passed by Congress.

If the *end* be legitimate, and within the scope of the Constitution, all the *means* that are appropriate, which are plainly adapted to that end, and which are not prohibited, may be constitutionally employed to carry it into effect.

If a certain means to the exercise of any of the powers expressly given by the Constitution to the Government of the Union be an appropriate measure, not prohibited by the Constitution, the degree of its necessity is a question of *legislative discretion,* not of judicial cognizance.

The Government of the United States is not prohibited by the Constitution from issuing treasury notes on demand, and making them a *legal tender* in payment of all debts within its jurisdiction. The Constitution (article one, section ten) prohibits the *States* from making anything but gold and silver coin a legal tender in payment of debts; but this does not at all restrict the sovereign power of the United States. Congress has the power to coin money, "regulate the *value* thereof and of foreign coin." Gold and silver by long practice—a practice that has continued for centuries among all nations—have become the legal money of the world in all commercial transactions. Their real intrinsic value is not as great as that fixed upon it by governments. All governments fix the value of gold and silver; and without their government stamp gold and silver would be a simple commodity, like other things having intrinsic value. Some governments fix the value of coin higher, and some lower; just as each for itself chooses to determine. Any other metal or thing that should be stamped, and its value regulated by all the governments of the world, would pass equally well in all commercial transactions, as gold and silver, although not intrinsically as valuable. Exchequer bills or treasury notes, whose value is fixed by Government, and stamped as money, would pass as money in the payment of debts within the jurisdiction of the Government fixing such value.

In regulating the value of "coin"—either foreign or domestic—Congress may provide that gold and silver shall be of no greater value in the payment of debts, within the United States, than the treasury notes issued on the credit of this Government, which stamps such coin and fixes its value. These high powers of government have been frequently exercised by Great Britain during her continental wars, in making the Bank of England notes receivable for public dues, and virtually in payment of debts, by a suspension of specie payments within the United Kingdom; and other governments of Europe have exercised the same high prerogatives wherever necessary to preserve their existence. But we are not left to this argument alone for constitutional power to issue these demand notes and make them a legal tender in payment of debts.

Here the speaker read an opinion from Attorney-General Edward Bates, supporting the constitutional soundness of the proposition.

The Attorney-General, in an unofficial opinion, given to me at my solicitation, says:

"Certainly the Constitution contains no direct verbal prohibition, and I think it contains no inferential prohibition that can be fairly drawn from its expressed terms. The first article of the Constitution, section eight, grants to Congress specifically a great mass of powers. Section nine contains divers limitations upon Congress, upon the United States, and upon individuals; and section ten contains restrictions upon the several States. This last section is the only one that treats of *tender.* 'No *State* shall make anything but gold and silver coin a tender in payment of debts.' This applies to a *State* only, and not to the nation; and thus it has been always understood.

"With regard to the next preceding clause in the same section—'No State shall emit bills of credit;' the prohibition to emit *bills of credit* is quite as strong as the prohibition to make anything but gold and silver coin a legal tender, yet nobody doubts, Congress does not doubt, its power to issue bills of credit. Treasury notes *are* bills of credit, and I think one is just as much prohibited as the other. Neither is forbidden to Congress."

The Constitution provides that Congress shall have power to pass "all laws necessary and proper" for carrying into execution all the powers granted to the Government of the United States, or any department or officer thereof.

The word "necessary," as used, is not limited by the additional word "proper," but enlarged thereby.

"If the word *necessary* were used in the strict, rigorous sense, it would be an extraordinary departure from the usual course of the human mind, as exhibited in solemn instruments, to add another word, the only possible effect of which is to qualify that strict and rigorous meaning, and to present clearly the idea of a choice of means in the course of legislation. If no means are to be resorted to but such as are *indispensably* necessary, there can be neither sense nor utility in adding the word '*proper;*' for the *indispensable necessity* would shut out from view all consideration of the *propriety* of the means."—3 Story's "Commentaries," sec. 122.

Mr. Spaulding also read from the "Federalist," No. 23, in which Alexander Hamilton contended that the powers of the sword and purse in the Federal Government were unlimited.

Congress may judge of the necessity in the present exigency. It may decide whether it will authorize the Secretary of the Treasury to issue demand treasury notes, and make them a legal tender in payment of debts, or whether it will put its six or seven per cent. bonds on the market, at various rates of discount, and raise the money at any sacrifice the money lender may require to meet the pressing demands upon the treasury. In the one case the Government will be able to pay its debts at fair rates of interest; in the other it must go into the streets "shinning" for the means, like an individual in failing circumstances, and sure of being used up in the end by the avarice of those who may exact unreasonable terms. The Government needs and should have in her present peril the aid and protection of all patriotic citizens.

But, sir, knowing the power of money, and the disposition there is among men to use it for the acquisition of greater gain, I am unwilling that this Government, with all its immense power and resources, should be left in the hands of any class of men, bankers or money lenders, however respectable and patriotic they may be. The Government is much stronger than any of them. Its capital is much greater. It has control of the bankers' money, and all the brokers' money, and all the property of the thirty millions of people under its jurisdiction. Why, then, should it go into Wall street, State street, Chestnut street, or any other street begging for money? Their money is not as secure as Government money. All the gold they possess would not carry on the Government for ninety days. They issue only promises to pay, which, if Congress does its duty, are not half as secure as United States treasury notes based on adequate taxation upon all the property of the country.

Why then go into the streets at all to borrow money? I am opposed, in our present extremity, to all shifts of this kind. I prefer to assert the power and dignity of the Government, by the issue of its own notes, pledging the faith, the honor, and property of the whole loyal people of the country to maintain their circulation and provide for their redemption.

On the question of constitutional power we are not left without the recorded opinions of the ablest jurists in the country. (1 Kent's "Commentaries," 351-52; McCulloch *vs.* the State of Maryland, 4 Wheaton's R. 413-20.)

A suspension of specie payments is greatly to be deplored, but it is not a fatal step in an exigency like the present. The British Government and the Bank of England remained under suspension from 1797 to 1821-22, a period of twenty-five years. During this time England successfully resisted the imperial power of the Emperor Napoleon, and preserved her own imperiled existence. As a measure of necessity, she made the Bank of England notes virtually a legal tender by suspending the specie restriction. During all this time the people of Great Britain advanced in wealth, population, and resources. Gold is not as valuable as the productions of the farmer and mechanic, for it is not as indispensable as are food and raiment. Our army and navy must have what is far more valuable to them than gold and silver. They must have food, clothing, and the material of war. Treasury notes issued by the Government, on the faith of the whole people, will purchase these indispensable articles, and the war can be prosecuted until we can enforce obedience to the Constitution and laws, and an honorable peace be thereby secured. This being accomplished, I will be among the first to advocate a speedy return to specie payments, and all measures that are calculated to preserve the honor and dignity of the Government in time of peace, and which I regret are not practicable in the prosecution of this war.

An early and successful advance of our armies is of the utmost importance; we need such an advance to sustain the financial credit of the Government; we need it to prevent foreign intervention; we need it to rouse the flagging energies of the people; and, above all, we need it to vindicate the courage and invincibility of our brave soldiers, who are so anxious to be led on to victory.

On January 29 George H. Pendleton [O.] spoke against the bill.

I have examined, Mr. Chairman, with some care, every law authorizing the issue of treasury notes which has been passed from the foundation of the Government up to this hour, and I find that this bill differs from all of them in several essential particulars. Every other law authorizing the issue of treasury notes provided that they should bear some rate of interest, whereas these are to bear none; that they should be payable at a fixed time prescribed in the note, whereas these are only to be payable at the pleasure of the United States; that the notes thereby authorized should be receivable in payment of public debts only by those who were willing to receive them at par, while these notes are to be received by every public creditor who is not willing to forfeit his right to payment at all. These notes are to be made lawful money, and a legal tender in discharge of all pecuniary obligations, either by the Government or by individuals, a characteristic which has never been given to any note of the United States or any note of the Bank of the United States by any law ever passed. Not only, sir, was such a law never passed, but such a law was never voted on, never proposed, never introduced, never recommended by any department of the Government; the measure was never seriously entertained in debate in either branch of Congress.

If this bill shall pass, we are about to take a departure from the settled financial policy of the Government. We are about to launch ourselves, with sails all set, upon an ocean of experiment, upon which the wise men who administered the Government before we came into power, warned by the example of other nations, would not permit it even to enter. I believe that this Government has reached a crisis in its history. I believe that it is approaching a period in the history of its legislation which may determine the question of its continuance. By wisdom it may overcome the evils of secession; by its great powers and resources it may be able to defend itself against those in arms against it; but I firmly believe that it cannot maintain itself against the shock of the accumulated and manifold dangers which follow inevitably, closely in the wake of an illegal, unsound, and depreciated Government paper currency.

The feature of this bill which first strikes every thinking man even in these days of novelties, is the proposition that these notes shall be made a legal tender in discharge of all pecuniary obligations, as well those which have accrued in virtue of contracts already made as those which are yet to accrue in pursuance of contracts which shall hereafter be made. Do gentlemen appreciate the full import and meaning of that clause? Do they realize the full extent to which it will carry them? Every contract for the payment of money is in legal contemplation a contract for the payment of gold and silver coin. Every promissory note, every bill of exchange, every lease reserving rent, every loan of money reserving interest, every bond issued by this Government, is a contract to which the faith of the obligor is pledged that the amount, whether rent, interest, or principal, shall be paid in the gold and silver coin of the country. Every contract for the performance of some other thing than the payment of money carries with it, as the penalty of its infraction, that damages shall be assessed, and that these damages shall be paid, even if necessary at the end of an execution, in the gold and silver coin of the country. Every verdict which has been rendered, every judgment which has been entered up, every decree for the payment of money has been made upon that hypothesis. That is the measure of the obligation of the one party, and of the right of the other.

The provisions of this bill contemplate impairing the obligation of every contract of that kind, and disturbing the basis upon which every judgment and decree and verdict has been entered. It proposes to say to a party who has entered into a contract, "You shall be discharged from the obligations of that contract by doing something else than that which you have agreed to do.'' It proposes to say to every party with whom a contract has been made, ''Though you are entitled to demand one thing, you shall, perforce, remain satisfied with the doing of another.'' It proposes to say, ''Although you have agreed to pay gold and silver, you shall be discharged upon the payment of these notes; although you are entitled to demand gold and silver, you shall rest content with the reception of this paper.'' It proposes, in one word, to release the one party from the obligation of his contract, and to divest the other party of the right which has been vested in him by that contract. Sir, I am sure I need only state the proposition to shock the mind of the legal profession of the country, so thoroughly has it been imbued with the idea of the sanctity of the obligation of contracts by those who have taught it the beneficent maxims of constitutional law.

As for the rest, this bill provides that it shall be illegal to make a contract for dealing in gold and silver coin; or, to state it more exactly, it provides that, whatever executory contracts parties may make concerning the gold and silver coin of the country, they shall be discharged upon the performance of another and different duty—by the delivery of an equivalent number of dollars in these notes. Where, sir, does Congress get this power? Where is the grant to be found? One would suppose that a power like that—a power which involves the impairing of the obligations of such a vast class of contracts, which proposes to disturb vested rights to such an immense extent—would be worthy of a place in the express grants of the Constitution.

The gentleman from New York [Mr. Spaulding], in his argument yesterday, deduced this power from the general powers of the Government. He told us that Congress had power to lay and collect taxes; to raise and support armies; to provide and maintain a navy; and that all power necessary to effectuate these purposes was expressly given by the general grant of the Constitution. If I should admit his statement in the very language in which he has made it, am I not entitled to ask whether he has shown us any legitimate connection between making these notes a legal tender and the power to raise an army? Might I not ask whether the repudiation of the obligations of the Government to pay its interest is a legitimate means for providing and sustaining a navy? Whether impairing the obligations of contracts between private individuals throughout the country will, in any degree, assist the Government in its great duty of laying and collecting taxes? We had no demonstration of the necessity or propriety of these means to accomplish those ends.

The gentleman spoke quite at large in reference to the sovereign power of the Government. He told us that this power was not prohibited in the Constitution. He told us that in times of great emergency everything may be done except that which is prohibited; and he read an argument from the Attorney-General, which concludes, as it began, with the proposition that such a power is not prohibited to Congress. Sir, I repudiate this whole idea. I think it has no solid foundation in the Constitution. In all its external relations, standing among the nations of the earth, the Government of the United States is sovereign, and is invested with all the attributes of sovereignty; but in its relations to its own citizens, in its relations to the States, in its relations to its own constituents, it has no power except that which is granted. It has no original power; its powers are all delegated, and delegated by the terms of the Constitution itself. I repudiate the idea that all the sovereign power which rightfully resides in the nation must necessarily find expression in any department of the Government, whether it be national or State. I stand upon the provision of the Constitution, that all power which is not delegated to the Federal Government is reserved from it; and that all power which is not delegated to it, and thereby reserved from it, resides either in the States or the people. There are many powers which are denied by the Constitution to the States, and yet not delegated to the general Government. They find their proper repository in the people.

When I come to examine the powers of Congress, according to the principles of interpretation to which I adhere, I look to the grants of the Constitution. I find no grant of this power in direct terms, or, as I think, by fair implication. It is not an accidental omission; it was intentionally left out of the Constitution, because it was designed that the power should not reside in the Federal Government.

Prior to the adoption of the Constitution the States had nearly all—perhaps all—emitted paper money, and had made it a legal tender in the payment of debts. It was designed originally to forbid to the States the exercise of that power, and to delegate it to the Federal Government; and, accordingly, the first draft of the Constitution reported by the committee of revision contained a clause prohibiting this power to the States, and another clause granting to the Federal Government the right "to borrow money and emit bills on the credit of the United States." When that clause came up for discussion—as it appears from page 1343 of the third volume of the Madison Papers—

"MR. GOUVERNEUR MORRIS moved to strike out 'and emit bills on the credit of the United States.' He said, if the United States had credit, such bills would be unnecessary; if they had not, unjust and useless."

Mr. Madison thought it was advisable to leave in the Constitution the provision that Congress might *emit bills of credit,* and to deprive Congress of the power of making them a *legal tender,* thus removing

"the temptation to emit them with unjust views. And promissory notes, in that shape, may in some emergencies be best."

A very sharp debate followed upon the proposition to strike out from the Constitution the clause conferring that power:

"MR. ELLSWORTH thought this a favorable moment to shut and bar the door against paper money. The mischiefs of the various experiments which had been made were now fresh in the public mind, and had excited the disgust of all the respectable part of America. By withholding the power from the new Government, more friends of influence would be gained to it than by almost anything else. Paper money can in no case be necessary. Give the Government credit, and other resources will offer. The power may do harm, never good." . . . .

"MR. BUTLER remarked that paper was a legal tender in no country in Europe. He was urgent for disarming the Government of such a power." . . . .

"MR. READ thought the words, if not struck out, would be as alarming as the mark of the beast in Revelation."

And, on the motion to strike out those words from the Constitution, it was decided by a vote of nine States "aye," and two States "no."

And so thoroughly was that understood to be the meaning and policy of the Government that none of the early statesmen of the country, either those who had been present at the time of the making of the Constitution or those who followed so closely after as that they were familiar with those who did make it, even suggested that such a power existed.

Mr. Hamilton, certainly, a gentleman who was in favor of enlarging to the utmost the powers of the Government, in his very first report to Congress upon the subject of a national bank, takes a distinction between the emission of bills by the Government and the creation of a bank with power to emit its own bills. In that famous report on a national bank, in 1790, he uses this language:

"The emitting of paper money by the authority of the Government is wisely prohibited to the individual States by the national Constitution;

and the spirit of that prohibition ought not to be disregarded by the Government of the United States. Though paper emissions, under a general authority, might have some advantages not applicable, and be free from some disadvantages which are applicable to the like emissions by the States separately, yet they are of a nature so liable to abuse—and, it may even be affirmed, so certain of being abused—that the wisdom of the Government will be shown in never trusting itself with the use of so seducing and dangerous an expedient. In times of tranquillity it might have no ill consequence; it might even perhaps be managed in a way to be productive of good; but, in great and trying emergencies, there is almost a moral certainty of its becoming mischievous. The stamping of paper is an operation so much easier than the laying of taxes that a Government in the practice of paper emissions would rarely fail, in any such emergency, to indulge itself too far in the employment of that resource to avoid, as much as possible, one less auspicious to present popularity.''—''Hamilton's Works,'' Vol. 3, p. 124.

And Mr. Webster, who followed closely the principles of government and of finance laid down by Mr. Hamilton, sought occasion several times in his speeches in Congress to express his decided and firm convictions upon this subject. In his speech upon the renewal of the charter of the United States Bank, made in 1832, Mr. Webster says:

''Congress can alone coin money. Congress can alone fix the value of foreign coin. No State can coin money. No State can fix the value of foreign coin. No State, *not even Congress itself*, can make anything a tender but gold and silver in payment of debts.''—''Webster's Works,'' Vol. 2, page 81.

And again, sir, in 1836, when Mr. Webster was at the very height of his intellectual power, and when by the financial condition of the country he was led to apply all his power to develop the true meaning of the Constitution in this regard, and to devise legislation suited to the evils then existing, in his speech upon the specie circular, says:

''But if we understand by currency the *legal money* of the country, and that which constitutes a lawful tender for debts, and is the statute measure of value, then, undoubtedly, nothing is included but gold and silver. Most unquestionably there is no legal tender in this country under the authority of this Government, or any other, but gold and silver, either the coinage of our own mints, or foreign coins, at rates regulated by Congress. This is a constitutional principle, perfectly plain, and of the very highest importance. The States are expressly prohibited from making anything but gold and silver a tender in payment of debts; and although no such express prohibition is applied to Congress, yet, as Congress has no power granted to it, in this respect, but to coin money and to regulate the value of foreign coins, it clearly has no power to substitute paper, or anything else, for coin, as a tender in payment of debts and in discharge of contracts.''—''Webster's Works,'' Vol. 4, page 271.

RUNNING THE MACHINE

[Meeting of Lincoln's Cabinet, with Fessenden Grinding Out Greenbacks]

From the collection of the New York Historical Society

And Mr. Calhoun, in his speech on the bill authorizing the issue of treasury notes, in 1837, assumes, as indisputable, that Congress possesses no such power.—3 "Calhoun's Works," p. 102.

Sir, it seems to me that if the language of the Constitution and the weight of authority can settle any proposition, it is that Congress has not the power to do that which it is proposed shall be done by the provisions of this bill.

Now, sir, the argument which I have made in reference to the constitutional power of Congress does not depend in any degree upon the question whether or not these notes can maintain their par value in gold and silver. But it may give point to the argument to show the effect which will be produced by the provisions of the bill itself in that respect.

The bill fixes the values of these notes; they shall be equivalent to an equal number of dollars expressed in the twenty-year bonds of the United States, carrying six per cent. interest. What are these bonds worth to-day? Sir, I read in the New York papers that last Saturday they were selling at eighty-nine cents on the dollar. Thus you confiscate, wickedly and unnecessarily, one-tenth—even at the present rates—of all the indebtedness of the country. Sir, it is a monstrous proposition, which I hope will not be tolerated by this House.

But, Mr. Chairman, I go a step further. I doubt whether there is any power in the Federal Government to issue the notes described in this bill, whether they are made a legal tender or not. I have shown to you that the power to "emit bills of credit" was expressly withheld by the convention which framed the Constitution. Now, what is a bill of credit? Chief Justice Marshall, in the case of Craig against the State of Missouri (4 Peters's Reports), defines it. He says:

> "To emit bills of credit conveys to the mind the idea of issuing paper intended to circulate through the community as money, which paper is redeemable at a future day. This is the sense in which the terms have been always understood. The term has acquired an appropriate meaning; and "bills of credit" signify a paper medium intended to circulate between individuals, and between Government and individuals, for the ordinary purposes of society."

Judge Story, in his dissenting opinion in the case of the Bank of the Commonwealth of Kentucky, defines them in the same way. What are these notes? They are made, by the very language—it is their chief purpose—of the bill, lawful money. They are intended to circulate as currency. They come within the definition of "bills of credit."

But, even if I believed this bill to be constitutional in both aspects, I yet see enough in it to merit, as I think, the hearty condemnation of the House. It provides that these notes shall be redeemable only at the pleasure of the United States. The gentleman from New York [Mr. Spaulding] called them "demand notes." They have been so called throughout the country. They do not bear a single characteristic of a demand note. There is no time, from the hour when they shall pass into the hands of the holder, when he can by their terms demand that they shall be redeemed. There is no time when the faith of the Government is pledged to their payment. The holder may present them, and he is told that the time has not arrived at which, by the face of the bill, they are to be paid. They will inevitably depreciate. The wit of man has never discovered a means by which paper currency can be kept at par value, except by its speedy, cheap, certain convertibility into gold and silver. I need not cite gentlemen to history or to authorities—writers on political economy—to prove it. Unless convertible they have always depreciated; they always will depreciate; they ought to depreciate, because they are only valuable as the representatives of gold and silver; and, if they are not convertible into that of which they are the representative, they must necessarily lose their value. You send these notes out into the world stamped with irredeemability. You put on them the mark of Cain, and, like Cain, they will go forth to be vagabonds and fugitives on the earth. What then will be the consequence? It requires no prophet to tell what will be their history. The currency will be expanded; prices will be inflated; fixed values will depreciate; incomes will be diminished; the savings of the poor will vanish; the hoardings of the widow will melt away; bonds, mortgages, and notes, everything of fixed value will lose their value; everything of changeable value will be appreciated; the necessaries of life will rise in value; the Government will pay twofold—certainly largely more than it ought—for everything that it goes into the market to buy; gold and silver will be driven out of the country. What then? The day of reckoning must come. Contractions will follow. Private ruin and public bankruptcy, either with or without repudiation, will inevitably follow.

Can we not learn something from the early experience of our own country? Can we not learn something from the overthrow of the revolutionary government of France by this very over-issue of depreciated paper? Can we not learn something from those throes which the society of England endured during the long suspension of, and at its return to, specie currency in 1822? Can we not now rise to a wisdom of statesmanship which shall control the finanical necessities of the country without plunging it into that gulf from which there is, with honor and safety, no recovery?

Sir, I beg gentlemen to permit me to read, in closing what I have to say, one more lesson of wisdom from that statesman of New England [Daniel Webster], to whom I have had occasion to refer.

> "No nation had a better currency than the United States. There was no nation which had guarded its currency with more care, for the framers of the Constitution and those who had enacted the early statutes on the subject were *hard money men.* They had felt and duly appreciated the evils of a paper medium; they therefore sedulously guarded the currency of the United States from debasement. The legal currency of the United States was gold and silver coin. This was a subject in regard to which Congress had run into no folly. Gold and silver currency was the law of the land at home, the law of the world abroad; there could, in the present condition of the world, be no other currency."

Let gentlemen heed this lesson of wisdom. Let them, if need be, tax the energies and wealth of the country sufficiently to restore the credit of the Government. Let them borrow whatever money in addition may be necessary—borrow it to the full extent that may be necessary—and let us adhere rigidly, firmly, consistently, persistently, and to the end, to the principle of refusing to surrender that currency which the Constitution has given us, and in the maintenance of which this Government has never, as yet, for one moment wavered.

On February 3 Clement L. Vallandigham [O.] spoke against the bill.

I do not agree, Mr. Chairman, with the gentleman who opened this debate [Mr. Spaulding] that this bill is a war measure. Certainly, sir, it has been forced upon us by the war; but if peace were restored to-morrow these $100,000,000 of treasury notes would be just as essential to the public credit as they are to-day. The argument of "military necessity" has been carried quite far enough already, without being now urged in behalf of the proposition—so unconstitutional, disastrous, and unjust—to make paper money a legal tender in discharge of all debts. I support this measure—not, indeed, as reported—impossible—but as I would have it amended—because it is absolutely essential to even the ordinary credit of the Government, and because without it I see nothing but bankruptcy to the Government in the midst of immense aggregate wealth among the people. The credit of the country is the honor and strength and support of the country, and it must be maintained at all hazards, and no matter who is President or what party is in power. And I am not willing to hazard the entire credit and honor and good faith of the country, because the Administration may, perchance, use this recuperated credit to continue a war which I have not approved. "War is disunion," said Mr. Douglas; and bankruptcy is disunion, and, as a true Union man, I have opposed the first, as I shall labor now to avert the last.

Sir, disguise it as you may, this bill is but a forced loan from the people. It is an abuse and a stretch of power which no Government, except one either in the first throes of revolutionary madness and desperation, or in the last agonies of dissolution, or in the midst of the most imminent danger of either bankruptcy or conquest and overthrow, and no king or potentate, except a usurper, ever ventured to exert. If voluntarily submitted to, or by fear or power enforced, it will corrupt, derange, and debase the currency, and afflict the country with financial and commercial disaster and ruin, and shake the foundations of public and private credit for half a century to come. But we shall be fortunate if it does not precipitate a revolution, sooner or later, in our own midst.

But, independently of all this, tried by the plainest principles of finance, the commonest maxims of political economy, as exhibited and enforced in the experience of other nations, this bold but ill-advised and most hazardous experiment of forcing a paper currency upon the people, ought to be met by the representatives of the people with unanimous and emphatic condemnation. Otherwise, the experiment, if successful, will be followed by other enormous issues, till not a dollar of gold or silver will be seen again in your day or mine, and but little of ordinary bank paper. Exportation, hoarding, melting, and manufacture into articles of luxury of every kind will follow as the legitimate and inevitable consequence of your irredeemable Government paper currency. The golden age of America henceforth will belong only to the *Saturnia regna*[1] of poets and mythologists.

Nor is this all, nor the worst. An immense inflation or bloat in this wonderful paper money which our financial Midas by his touch is to convert into gold must come next. Cheap in material, easy of issue, worked by steam, signed by machinery, there will be no end to the legions of paper devils which shall

[1] "Reign of Saturn," *i. e.*, the "Golden Age."

pour forth from the loins of the Secretary. Sir, let the army rejoice; there will be no more "shoddy," for there will be no more rags out of which to manufacture it.

And now, sir, what must follow from all this? First, that which never has failed in times of bloated currency—high prices, extravagant speculation, enormous sudden fortunes, immense fictitious wealth, general insanity. These belong to all inordinate and excessive paper issues, and even to plethoras in the circulation of gold and silver, if such plethoras could occur. But the evil will not stop here. Every banker, every lender, every merchant, every business man, and every seller of real or personal estate, or anything else, compelled to receive in payment for whatever he lends or sells an irredeemable paper money, dependent for its value solely upon force, and without the smallest credit, and himself having no confidence in the Government, and no special good will to the borrower or buyer who forces him to take its paper, will demand a still higher price, by way of insurance, than if the currency were sound and safe, no matter how much inflated.

And now, sir, what is to be the result of all this? What else but the result from like causes in years past in foreign countries and in our own? It is written in the commercial convulsions and sufferings of France in 1720, and of England a century later, and of the United States in 1837. The collapse follows the inflation, and is terrible and disastrous just in proportion as the bubble has been magnificent. Your legal tender laws will avail nothing. They have been tried before; tried in this country and tried abroad; and have always failed in the end. The regent of France proclaimed them in Law's time, in 1717; and what followed? Let M. Thiers answer:

> "Violent and vexatious as the measures were to sustain the credit of the notes, they were insufficient to give them a value which they did not possess. *Dishonest debtors alone used them to pay their debts.* Coin was secretly used for daily purchases, and was concealed with care. Many accumulated it clandestinely. The greater part buried it in the earth, and the rich realizers used every artifice to transfer it to foreign countries. Another portion of our coin left France; and although the exportation of specie is not necessarily injurious, it was so at this time, since it left behind only a false paper currency and an imaginary capital."

But again, sir: this bill declares these notes to be "payable *at the pleasure of the United States.*" In other words, the debtor dictates terms to the creditor, and declares that a debt payable in cash down or on demand shall be paid at the pleasure of the debtor, or otherwise, in either case, shall be utterly extinguished. O most wonderful, righteous, and equitable Secretary!

Sir, there is no subject so delicate as credit. What is it? Confidence, trust, faith. In its very nature it is voluntary, and you can no more coerce credit than you can compel belief in a particular creed or religion, or love between man and woman. It withers before suspicion, and languishes and dies at the sight of force. Sir, in the reign of Henry VIII, Parliament passed "an act for the *abolishing of diversity of opinion* in certain articles concerning the Christian religion." How much worse or more abused, I ask, was that act than the bill before us? Good faith is the foundation of all credit; but this bill proposes, not bold and outright, but timid—I will not say cowardly—and indirect repudiation. More than this: it is an open confession of bankruptcy. If the Government has solid means, it needs no notes. If it has credit, why declare its notes lawful money and a legal tender, equal with gold? If it has neither means nor credit, it is exactly what is meant by a bankrupt.

Here, sir, is one of the Continental bills of November, 1776. It bears small resemblance to the delicate paper issues and exquisite engraving of the present day in the United States. It smacks a little of the poverty of "Dixie." Instead of the effigies of Lincoln, it bears on its face a rudely carved wood cut of the wild boar of the forest. It was bad money, sir; but issued in a noble cause. It is redolent of liberty; it smells of habeas corpus, free speech, a free press, free ballot, the right of petition, the consent of the governed, the right of the people to govern, public indictment, speedy public trial, trial by jury, and all the great rights of political and individual liberty for which martyrs have died and heroes contended for ages—although I am not quite sure, sir, that even now it is altogether without somewhat of the odor of rebellion lingering about it. But even this Continental bill purports to be payable, though not paid, in specie. It recites that "this bill entitles the bearer to receive four Spanish milled dollars, or the value thereof in gold and silver, according to a resolution of Congress, passed at Philadelphia, November 2, 1776," and it is issued in the name of "the United Colonies."

But though in the midst of a revolution, and struggling for liberty and life, and in the darkest hour of that sore trial—it was just previous to the victory at Trenton—it never occurred to the just men and patriots of that day to usurp the power to make this paper money a legal tender, and to force it, by this usurpation, into credit and circulation by the strong arm of the law; and to that extent—and it is great—the United States notes proposed by this bill are fifty-fold worse and more to be abhorred than Continental money. But this paper of 1776 bears no interest, is payable to bearer, payable in gold and silver, payable at no particular time, intended to circulate permanently and generally as money, and without a dollar of tax or revenue to support it. The men of that day relied on patriotism to keep their bills in credit; and yet we know that even then, in the purest and best times of the Republic, they sank in value till at the close of the war $1,000 in paper were worth but one dollar in specie. In short, sir, they so utterly depreciated that to this day, if a profane man would describe anything as totally and hopelessly worthless, he would say of it that it was "not" worth a Continental—*dollar.*"

Sir, what I beg to know is the object of this bill, if it be not to create an enormous and endless public debt, to be interwoven with every political, social, and business relation of life; to subjugate the States and the people perpetually to the Federal Government, and therefore never to be extinguished? The seven years of famine are upon us, and our modern Joseph is to buy in the property of the whole people, and lease it out to them again as tenants at a perpetual rent. Sir, I commend to him the ancient and significant Hebrew proverb: *Quum lateres duplicantur venit Moses*—when the bricks are doubled, Moses comes.

Mr. Vallandigham then proposed a substitute measure, the chief feature of which was the elimination of the legal tender provision of the original.

The bill was passed by Congress and approved by President Lincoln on February 25, 1862, with various amendments. The amount of issue was increased to $150,000,000; the notes were not to be receivable for customs duties nor for interest on Government securities; Government bonds were to be exempt from State taxation. The legal tender provision, which had been the chief cause of objection to the bill, was retained. Salmon P. Chase, Secretary of the Treasury, who was opposed to it, finally yielded to its retention on the score of military necessity.

CHAPTER X

NATIONAL BANKING SYSTEM

Salmon P. Chase, Secretary of the Treasury, Proposes a National Banking System to Supply Currency—John Sherman [O.] Introduces Bill for Same in the Senate—Debate: in Favor, Sen. Sherman; Opposed, Lazarus W. Powell [Ky.]—Bill Is Passed and Goes to the House—Debate: in Favor, Elbridge G. Spaulding [N. Y.], Reuben E. Fenton [N. Y.]; Opposed, Stephen Baker [N. Y.], Warren P. Noble [O.]—Bill Is Passed.

IN his annual report, of December, 1861, Salmon P. Chase, Secretary of the Treasury, deriving his idea from a free banking law of the State of New York, which had been in successful operation since 1838, had proposed an act authorizing the organization of banking associations to provide a currency (national banknotes) based on the combined credit of these organizations and of the Government. No action was taken upon it by Congress during the ensuing session, the issue of treasury notes ("greenbacks"), which was then authorized, being deemed sufficient to provide the Government with the needed funds. In his report of December 4, 1862, the Secretary renewed his proposition which the steady depreciation of the greenbacks in value, due to Union defeats which foreshadowed a long and doubtful war, rendered more acceptable now to Congress and the country. The provisions of the measure and the arguments in its favor were thus set forth:

THE NATIONAL BANKING SYSTEM

REPORT OF SECRETARY OF THE TREASURY CHASE

The central idea of the proposed measure is the establishment of one sound, uniform circulation, of equal value throughout the country, upon the foundation of national credit combined with private capital.

Such a currency, it is believed, can be secured through banking associations organized under national legislation.

It is proposed that these associations be entirely voluntary. Any persons, desirous of employing real capital in sufficient amounts, can unite together under proper articles, and, having contributed the requisite capital, can invest such part of it, not less than a fixed minimum, in United States bonds, and having deposited these bonds with the proper officer of the United States, can receive United States notes in such denominations as may be desired, and employ them as money in discounts and exchanges. The stockholders of any existing banks can, in like manner, organize under the act, and transfer, by such degrees as may be found convenient, the capital of the old to the use of the new associations. The notes thus put into circulation will be payable, until resumption, in United States notes, and, after resumption, in specie, by the association which issues them, on demand; and if not so paid will be redeemable at the treasury of the United States from the proceeds of the bonds pledged in security. In case any association shall fail in such redemption, the Treasurer of the United States will probably, under discretionary authority, pay the notes and cancel the public debt held as security.

It seems difficult to conceive of a note circulation which will combine higher local and general credit than this. After a few years no other circulation would be used, nor could the issues of the national circulation be easily increased beyond the legitimate demands of business. Every dollar of circulation would represent real capital, actually invested in national stocks, and the total amount issued could always be easily and quickly ascercertained from the books of the treasury. These circumstances, if they might not wholly remove the temptation to excessive issues, would certainly reduce it to the lowest point, while the form of the notes, the uniformity of devices, the signatures of national officers, and the imprint of the national seal, authenticating the declaration borne on each that it is secured by bonds which represent the faith and capital of the whole country, could not fail to make every note as good in any part of the world as the best known and best esteemed national securities.

The organization proposed, if sanctioned by Congress, would require within a very few years, for deposit as security for circulation, bonds of the United States to an amount not less than $250,000,000. It may well be expected, indeed, since the circulation, by uniformity in credit and value, and capacity of quick and cheap transportation, will be likely to be used more extensively than any hitherto issued, that the demand for bonds will overpass this limit. Should Congress see fit to restrict the privilege of deposit to the bonds known as five-twentieths, authorized by the act of last session, the demand would promptly absorb all of that description already issued, and make large room for more. A steady market for the bonds would thus be established and the negotiation of them greatly facilitated.

But it is not in immediate results that the value of this support would be only or chiefly seen. There are always holders who desire to sell securities of whatever kind. If buyers are few or uncertain, the market value must decline. But the plan proposed would create a constant demand, equaling and often exceeding the supply. Thus a steady uniformity in price would be maintained, and generally at a rate somewhat above those of bonds of equal credit, but not available to banking associations. It is not easy to appreciate the full benefits of such conditions to a government obliged to borrow.

Another advantage to be derived from such associations would be found in the convenient agencies which they would furnish for the deposit of public moneys.

The Secretary does not propose to interfere with the independent treasury. It may be advantageously retained, with the assistant treasurers already established in the most important cities, where the customs may be collected as now, in coin or treasury notes issued directly by the Government, but not furnished to banking associations.

But whatever the advantages of such arrangements in the commercial cities in relation to customs, it seems clear that the secured national circulation furnished to the banking associations should be received everywhere for all other dues than customs, and that these associations will constitute the best and safest depositaries of the revenues derived from such receipts. The convenience and utility to the Government of their employment in this capacity, and often, also, as agents for payments and as distributors of internal revenue stamps, need no demonstration.

Another and very important advantage of the proposed plan is that it will reconcile, as far as practicable, the interests of existing institutions with those of the whole people.

All changes, however important, should be introduced with caution, and proceeded in with careful regard to every affected interest. Rash innovation is not less dangerous than stupefied inaction. The time has come when a circulation of United States notes, in some form, must be employed. The people demand uniformity in currency, and claim at least part of the benefit of debt without interest, made into money, hitherto enjoyed exclusively by the banks. These demands are just, and must be respected. But there need be no sudden change; there need be no hurtful interference with existing interests. As yet the United States note circulation hardly fills the vacuum caused by the temporary withdrawal of coin; it does not, perhaps, fully meet the demand for increased circulation created by the increased number, variety, and activity of payments in money. There is opportunity, therefore, for the wise and beneficial regulation of its substitution for other circulation. The mode of substitution also may be judiciously adapted to actual circumstances. The plan suggested consults both purposes. It contemplates gradual withdrawal of bank note circulation, and proposes a United States note circulation, furnished to banking associations, in the advantages of which they may participate in full proportion to the care and responsibility assumed, and the services performed by them. The promptitude and zeal with which many of the existing institutions came to the financial support of the Government in the dark days which followed the outbreak of the rebellion are not forgotten. They ventured largely and boldly and patriotically on the side of the Union and the constitutional supremacy of the nation over States and citizens. It does not at all detract from the merit of the act that the losses which they feared, but unhesitatingly risked, were transmuted into unexpected gains. It is a solid recommendation of the suggested plan that it offers the opportunity to those and kindred institutions to reorganize, continue their business under the proposed act, and, with little loss, and much advantage, participate in maintaining the new and uniform national currency.

The proposed plan is recommended, finally, by the firm anchorage it will supply to the union of the States. Every banking association whose bonds are deposited in the treasury of the Union; every individual who holds a dollar of the circulation secured by such deposit; every merchant, every manufacturer, every farmer, every mechanic, interested in transactions dependent for success on the credit of that circulation, will feel as an injury every attempt to rend the national unity, with the permanence and stability of which all their interests are so closely and vitally connected. Had the system been possible, and had it actually existed two years ago, can it be doubted that the national interests and sentiments enlisted by it for the Union would have so strengthened the motives for adhesion derived from other sources that the wild treason of secession would have been impossible?

The Secretary does not yield to the fantasy that taxation is a blessing and debt a benefit; but it is the duty of public men to extract good from evil whenever it is possible. The burdens of taxation may be lightened and even made productive of incidental benefits by wise, and aggravated and made intolerable by unwise legislation. In like manner debt, by no means desirable in itself, may, when circumstances compel nations to incur its obligations, be made by discreet use less burdensome, and even instrumental in the promotion of public and private security and welfare.

The rebellion has brought a great debt upon us. It is proposed to use a part of it in such a way that the sense of its burden may be lost in the experience of incidental advantages. The issue of United States notes is such a use; but, if exclusive, is hazardous and temporary. The security by national bonds of similar notes furnished to banking associations is such a use, and is comparatively safe and permanent; and with this use may be connected for the present, and occasionally, as circumstances may require hereafter, the use of the ordinary United States notes in limited amounts.

No very early day will probably witness the reduction of the public debt to the amount required as a basis for secured circulation. Should no future wars arrest reduction and again demand expenditures beyond revenue, that day will however at length come. When it shall arrive the debt may be retained on low interest at that amount, or some other security for circulation may be devised, or possibly the vast supplies of our rich mines may render all circulation unadvisable except gold and the absolute representatives and equivalents, dollar for dollar, of gold in the treasury or on safe deposit elsewhere. But these considerations may be for another generation.

The Secretary forbears extended argument on the constitutionality of the suggested system. It is proposed as an auxiliary to the power to borrow money; as an agency of the power to collect and disburse taxes; and as an exercise of the power to regulate commerce, and of the power to regulate the value of coin. Of the first two sources of power nothing need be said. The argument relating to them was long since exhausted and is well known. Of the other two there is not room nor does it seem needful to say much. If Congress can prescribe the structure, equipment, and management of vessels to navigate rivers flowing between or through different States as a regulation of commerce, Congress may assuredly determine what currency shall be employed in the interchange of their commodities, which is the very essence of commerce. Statesmen who have agreed in little else have concurred in the opinion that the power to regulate coin is, in substance and effect, a power to regulate currency, and that the framers of the Constitution so intended. It may well enough be admitted that, while Congress confines its regulation to weight, fineness, shape, and device, banks and individuals may issue notes for currency in competition with coin. But it is difficult to conceive by what process of logic the unquestioned power to regulate coin can be separated from the power to maintain or restore its circulation, by excluding from currency all private or corporate substitutes which affect its value, whenever Congress shall see fit to exercise that power for that purpose.

The recommendations now submitted, of the limited issue of United States notes as a wise expedient for the present time, and as an occasional expedient in future times, and of the organization of banking associations to supply circulation secured by national bonds, and convertible always into United States notes, and after resumption of specie payments into coin, are prompted by no favor to excessive issues of any description of credit money.

On the contrary, it is the Secretary's firm belief that by no other path can the resumption of specie payments be so surely reached and so certainly maintained. United States notes receivable for bonds bearing a secure specie interest are next best to notes convertible into coin. The circulation of banking associations organized under a general act of Congress, secured by such bonds, can be most surely and safely maintained at the point of certain convertibility into coin. If, temporary, these associations redeem their issues with United States notes; resumption of specie payments will not thereby be delayed or endangered, but hastened and secured; for, just as soon as victory shall restore peace, the ample revenue, already secured by wise legislation, will enable the Government, through advantageous purchases of specie, to replace at once large amounts, and, at no distant day, the whole of this circulation, by coin without detriment to any interest, but, on the contrary, with great and manifest benefit to all interests.

The Secretary recommends, therefore, no mere paper money scheme, but, on the contrary, a series of measures looking to a safe and gradual return to gold and silver as the only permanent basis, standard, and measure of values recognized by the Constitution—between which and an irredeemable paper currency, as he believes, the choice is now to be made.

The National Banking System

Congress, February 9-20, 1863

On February 9, 1863, John Sherman [O.] brought forward in the Senate a bill from the Committee of Finance framed in accordance with the proposition of Secretary Chase. A discussion followed, chiefly upon the details of the bill.

Lazarus W. Powell [Ky.], however, attacked the measure in a fundamental point. Proposing an amendment requiring each banking association to keep in its vaults gold and silver coin to the amount of at least one-fourth of the issue of notes, he said:

This is to me a most singular bank bill. I have read it over hastily twice, and I have not observed the words "gold and silver coin" mentioned anywhere. I am clearly of the opinion that any bank note issued upon any other than a specie basis will be injurious to the country in which it is issued. Bank notes, in my judgment, to be a benefit to the community, should be redeemable at the counter at which they are issued, in coin. Any other issues in my judgment are destructive to the best interests of the country. The amendment I propose requires each one of these banks to keep in its vaults in coin at all times an amount equal to one-fourth of its issues. That is a very limited amount; but, when you take the United States bonds at their present value, it would not be more than sufficient to protect the note holder against loss in case the institution should wind up.

These issues are to be made upon United States bonds. The issue of notes is, I believe, to be within ten per cent. of the value of the bonds. These notes are to be issued on that basis. Now, suppose it should turn out—and I verily believe it will turn out whenever it is submitted to an intelligent court—that the legal tender clause of your note law will be declared unconstitutional, what will become of the security of the note holder? Your United States bond to-day, I suppose, is not worth over fifty or sixty dollars on the hundred. When I speak of dollars, I mean gold or silver dollars. If the legal tender note should be declared unconstitutional, this money will be in the hands of the people, and they will be driven to the United States bond for security, and it will be worth still less for the redemption of these notes, and at least forty per cent. of these notes would be found to be without any adequate fund out of which they could be redeemed, and consequently this worthless trash would be in the hands of the people throughout the country without any hope of redemption.

I am opposed to this bill in every form; but, if it is to be passed, I think it proper that we should give it at least a little stiffening. If the amendment that I propose should be adopted I think it would greatly benefit the bill, but I do not wish Senators to understand that even then I shall vote for it. It should be guarded and protected by such wholesome amendments as will secure the note holders against loss. As it is, the note holder will have but very little security. Of all bank issues, that, in my judgment, is the least secure which is issued upon a credit. You propose to issue bank notes here upon the credit of the United States, upon the bonds of the United States. That is to be the basis for the redemption of the notes, and for the security of the note holder. Your bonds to-day are at a very great discount. Where is the security of the note holder? Gentlemen may fall back on the individual liability clause that they have inserted, but that will be worth very little when you have to go all over the country hunting the persons who own stock in these banks, and perhaps two-thirds of them will be worth nothing except the stock they have in the banks, and, when that is gone, nine-tenths of them, perhaps, will have nothing which can be taken on execution.

It is clear to my mind that we should require these banks to keep some portion of coin in their vaults, at least, as security to the holders. All the States which have adopted this free banking system, as far as I know, require the banks to keep on hand a limited amount of specie, some twelve per cent., some thirty per cent., some more. Here, however, is a proposition for a series of banks, a gigantic scheme that absolutely does not require them to pay coin or keep any on hand at all. It is a system of banking that, in my judgment, with all intelligent bankers and merchants will fall still-born. I have conversed with some very intelligent merchants and business men from New York, Boston, and Philadelphia, about this *projet,* and I have yet to find the first one that does not condemn it.

Senator Sherman.—When this bill was drawn I did not

expect that my friend from Kentucky would vote for it; nor did I expect that he would vote for any bill which required the banks which might be organized under it to pay specie from this moment, because, as he knows, that would be futile. His amendment would require these banks to keep twenty-five per cent. of gold and silver in their vaults. The bill as reported provides that they shall keep twenty-five per cent. in lawful money of the United States in their vaults. If the courts shall decide, as the Senator says they will, that the paper money of the United States is worthless trash, illegal and unconstitutional, then the phrase "lawful money of the United States" would mean gold and silver; and the bill suits him now. If the courts shall decide that the paper money of the United States is not worth anything, is unconstitutional, is worthless trash, then the only lawful money left will be gold and silver coin; and the bill as it stands requires the banks to keep twenty-five per cent. of lawful money in their vaults.

But, Mr. President, while we are in war specie payments are naturally suspended. They always will be, as they always have been in every country involved in a great war. They were suspended in England during her wars with Napoleon. Would it not have been singular if some man had stood up in the British Parliament, when during a long war specie payments were suspended, and the Bank of England notes were made the basis of currency, and had denounced the Bank of England paper as worthless trash? It would have been considered a very remarkable thing; and yet that is done now. The United States money, to which the faith of the United States is pledged, to which the faith of every State in the Union is pledged, to which all the property of the United States is pledged, is here denounced, in the Senate of the United States, as worthless trash. And yet without this "worthless trash" we must submit to be overrun by armed confederates who are seeking to subvert the Government, and every man knows it. Every man knows—none better than the Sentaor from Kentucky—that without the issue of paper money it would be impossible to carry on the operations of the Government, and there would be nothing to prevent Jeff Davis from encamping within sight of New York City. It is by the use of just such money that armies are formed in the South.

None of the banks of the United States now pay gold and silver, nor can they; and therefore the amendment was moved, I think, not with much expectation that it would prevail, but to enable the Senator to announce as his opinion that the money of the United States, the notes issued by this Government, are worthless trash, unconstitutional and unlawful, and that therefore all the banks which might be founded upon it would be unlawful.

Sir, the very moment this war is over; the very moment our credit is good; the very moment the bonds of the United States are worth above par, that moment all these banks will be specie paying banks. My hope is that Congress will never authorize the issue of more than $400,000,000 of United States notes, and that these will be made the basis during the war of the currency of the country, and that by this bill the money of the people, through their banking associations organized all over the country, may be combined in support of the credit of the United States to make a safe and stable currency which will give us during time of war the best substitute possible for gold and silver. That, I believe, will be done; but the very moment our bonds are equivalent to par with gold and silver, as they will be when the war is over, that moment all these banks will be specie paying banks, and every one of them will then be required to keep the very amount of specie in their vaults that the Senator provides for; that is, twenty-five per cent. of the lawful money of the United States. There are but two species of lawful money; one gold or silver coin, and the other the United States greenbacks, as they are called. During the war the greenbacks are necessary to carry on the Government, and necessary as lawful money. They are made so by the Government.

Senator Powell.—It is singular to me that the Senator cannot discuss a legitimate matter of finance without lugging in "Jeff Davis" here as a kind of bugbear to somebody. I do not know what Mr. Jefferson Davis has to do with this matter.

I believe the legal tender clause of your note bill to be unconstitutional. I do not believe that, if a man has contracted to pay me $1,000, which meant $1,000 in gold or silver coin, this Congress can pass a law saying that I shall receive it in paper money, and paper money that is at as heavy a discount as this is.

The Senator says you cannot go on with the war without the issue of greenbacks. I think, and I have always thought, that it was an unwise policy to issue one of them. I know very well that in these times it would be impossible to get along with the sub-treasury law requiring all the receipts and disbursements of the public treasury to be coined. I would have repealed that much of the sub-treasury law, and I would have allowed the notes of solvent banks to be received and paid for the public dues; and then I would have gone into the market and borrowed money. Your bonds were selling at a premium, in gold and silver coin, too, before you commenced grinding out this paper money. You have ground out paper money until now your bonds are at a discount, payable in paper money that is itself at a very heavy discount, a discount of some forty per cent. and upward; forty-seven I believe to-day. This policy has already ruined the credit of the nation, or at least very much weakened it; destroyed it to a very great extent. In my judgment this has been caused by the unwise financial policy of the Government. I desire to keep up the credit of the Government, and I believe it cannot be kept up by the excessive issue of irredeemable paper money. That is my firm conviction. I wish to put, if I can do it, a little stiffening into the Senator's bill, and I intend at the proper time to move to strike out the clauses which require these notes to be redeemed by what he calls "lawful money," and to insert "gold and silver coin," believing as I do that no bank issue will ever be of use to any country that is not convertible into gold and silver.

I shall move further to amend the bill, if this money is to be thrown on the people, by striking out that provision which prevents it from being received for your customs. If we compel the people to take it in every direction, the Government itself should receive it. I think it is disreputable to a Government to issue and force on its people paper money that it will not take itself. I think that of itself is a clear indication that those who issue it have no confidence in it. If this money is issued and forced on the people, the Government should take it for all its public dues. It should treat the people as it does itself. It should not compel them to use a depreciated currency, while itself, for a large portion of its public dues, demands coin.

Senator Powell's amendments were defeated. The bill was passed on February 12 by a vote of 23 to 21. It went to the House, and was there taken up for discussion on February 19.

Elbridge G. Spaulding [N. Y.] spoke in favor of the measure.

On a full review of this proposed plan of a national currency, it will be seen that it is based on public and private faith; that it proposes to combine the interest of the nation with the rich individuals belonging to it. Only men of surplus capital can profitably engage in the business of banking. If speculators and adventurers, without positive capital, attempt to bank under this bill they will fail. Money lenders, and not money borrowers, can successfully organize and manage banking associations under the provisions of this act.

The Bank of England is a striking example of the combined power of public authority and private influence in sustaining the credit of Government. We may safely profit by this example. This bank has been the chief agent in sustaining the British Government in the long and exhausting wars in which she has been engaged. The Bank of England is the fiscal agent of the British Government, and, notwithstanding it is a bank of discount, deposit, and circulation, it has thus far received and disbursed the public moneys without the loss of a dollar of the money intrusted to it.

It is also well known that our Government never lost any of the money deposited in the first or second Bank of the United States. They were both fiscal agents of the Government. All the public money was received and disbursed by them with fidelity and usefulness to both parties. Sound and well-managed banks tend to increase public and private credit, and extend as well as to facilitate commerce with States and individuals. They stimulate industry, commodities are multiplied, agriculture, mining, and manufactures flourish; these constitute the true wealth, greatness, and prosperity of the country. If there had been established years ago a sound national bank of $200,000,000 capital, which had been in full operation as the fiscal and financial agent of the Government at the time of the breaking out of the present rebellion, what a mighty support it would have been in sustaining the Government at the present time! The independent treasury law unnecessarily isolated the Government from all the capitalists and the accumulated capital of the country. A sound national bank, upheld and supported by the combined credit of the Government and rich men residing in all the States of the Union, would have been a strong bond of union before the rebellion broke out, and a still stronger support to the Government in maintaining the army and navy to put it down.

Sir, the United States Government has thus far established no permanent system of national currency except that of gold and silver. Ever since the adoption of the Constitution there has been a conflict of opinion among the ablest statesmen of the country upon the question of a national currency. Jefferson opposed the creation of all banks, both State and national. Alexander Hamilton proposed a national bank during the struggle for American independence in 1780, but his suggestions were not then adopted. During Washington's Administration, in 1791, the first Bank of the United States was incorporated, mainly under the influence of Mr. Hamilton, which continued in operation until 1811, when its charter expired. No national bank was in existence during the second war with Great Britain. That war was carried on by loans and by the issue of treasury notes. In 1816 the second Bank of the United States was chartered, and continued in existence until 1836, when its charter again expired. All will remember the decided opposition of General Jackson to its recharter, and the fierce struggle that ensued between the friends and opponents of a United States bank. The friends of the bank were finally beaten when Jackson was reëlected President in the fall of 1832. The friends of a United States bank again rallied in 1840-41, but were again defeated by the veto of John Tyler. In 1846 the independent treasury law was finally adopted, by which it was established that the operations of the Government should thereafter be carried on wholly in gold and silver coin, and that this money of the Government should be kept separate from all banks and banking transactions. Thus the law continued up to the session of the present Congress.

No settled policy has as yet been established by which the Government has assumed permanent control over the national currency. State banks still go on issuing circulating notes, selling exchange, discounting promissory notes and bills, and receiving deposits, and the sub-treasury law is still unrepealed. A national currency, adequate to the operations of the Government in *peace* and *war,* has yet to be established. It seems that the present is a propitious time to enact this great measure as a permanent system, and that the duty of the Government in providing a national currency shall no longer be neglected.

In the absence of a national bank the State banks have been most liberal in making loans to the Government since the war began. There is in the present imperiled condition of the Union more distrust of the stability of the general Government than there is of the State governments. Some doubt exists, owing to divisions at the North, as to our final success in crushing the rebellion. Could you make it certain that the Union will be preserved, and the national jurisdiction maintained over all the thirty-four States and the $16,000,000,000 of taxable property therein, which is liable for our public debt, excluding therefrom the debt of the rebel government, said to be $900,000,000, the six per cent. bonds of the United States would not be five per cent. below par, while the six per cent. bonds of the State of New York are worth a premium of twenty-eight per cent. Capitalists are naturally timid, and will hesitate about entering into new projects until they can see the way clear. They desire to know that the Union is to be maintained and the Government perpetuated. Being fully assured of this, your bonds will be immediately above par, and there will be less difficulty in organizing banking associations and carrying this act into effect.

Sir, banking is eminently a practical business. To be successful, it must be based on accumulated capital, and conducted by practical men, who are intimately acquainted with the commerce and business of the country. Finance and financial questions must all be finally brought to a practical standard. However fine spun the theories of visionary men may be, they cannot now be relied on to provide money in the present exigency to pay the army and navy and other needy creditors of the Government. Our plan of finance must be simple, efficient, and practical. It consists of two parts, debts and taxation, namely:

1. Contracting debts for the supply of the army and navy, issuing legal tender notes, and borrowing money in some form on the faith of the Government.

2. Taxation on the entire property, commerce, and business of the country, amply sufficient to pay the principal and interest of all the debts which have been or may be contracted on the faith of the Government.

It will require a strong, stable government, wisely administered, to adjust and enforce the collection of so large an amount of taxes as will be required to pay the extraordinary war debt that must be contracted to crush the rebellion and restore peace and tranquillity over the whole Union.

Many of our friends express sanguine expectations of immediate relief from the passage of this national bank bill, and I should be much gratified to know hereafter that their expectations have been fully realized. But, sir, in my judgment, the Secretary of the Treasury must not place too much reliance upon this plan. It will not give much relief to the treasury for one, two, or three years. It will not to any considerable extent supersede the necessity for the issue of treasury notes. It will go into operation slowly. The Government, having heretofore failed to provide a national currency, the State banks in the older States have been organized, become deeply rooted, and firmly established. It will take a long time to supplant these banks. Every coercive or violent attempt to do so will do more harm than good. This new system will come in competition not only with existing institutions, but will encounter the prejudices of a large class of people who are hostile to banks, and especially hostile to a United States bank. It will be toward the close of the war, when the Government is firmly established and its authority respected in all the States, that it will be most valuable in providing a way for funding the public debt and establishing a permanent system of national currency. It is chiefly on this ground that I am induced to support the bill at this time. It is more for the benefits to be realized in the future than during the pending war that I am induced to give it my support.

Every day that the war is prolonged the debt is largely increased. The daily increasing debt of $2,500,000 must all be raised by taxation in some form, or the debt will not be paid. The Government is spending at a fearful rate the accumulations of former years of prosperity. Every dollar of debt contracted becomes a first mortgage upon the entire property and productive industry of the country. It affects the farmer, laborer, mechanic, manufacturer, merchant, banker, commission merchant, professional man, and retired capitalist. Every pound of tea, coffee, and sugar used is taxed to pay the expenses of the war, and the persons using these articles of daily consumption pay the tax in the increased price.

This war tax is already beginning to be noticed by the people; but as the war is procrastinated and the debt increased, the burden will be more deeply felt. While we are running along at forty miles an hour, under the pressure of irredeemable paper, necessarily issued and circulated to prosecute the war, the present taxation is easily paid, and there is a seeming prosperity; but I can assure gentlemen that a reckoning day will surely come. Look at the immense army in the field, their commissariat, supply vessels, supply trains, ambulance corps, sutlers, teamsters, hangers-on, idlers, and assistants of all kinds, extending over a line of military operations of more than four thousand miles, and you will be impressed with two important facts:

1. The enormous expenditures necessary to their present support, and the future bounties and pensions that must be paid.

2. The number of men that are withdrawn from industrial pursuits, and the consequent loss of productive industry which ought to be added to the wealth of the country.

All this immense army add nothing by their labor to the wealth of the country, and the expense of supporting such an army devolves upon those who do labor and those who have already acquired property. What a mighty drain this war is upon the productive energies and resources of the country! It is, indeed, an exhausting as well as bloody war. Whether it be successful or unsuccessful, vast consequences are involved. If terminated successfully within three years, the Union maintained and the Government perpetuated under the Constitution, the results to flow from such a triumph would amply compensate for all this expenditure of blood and treasure. If it terminates unsuccessfully, the Union divided and the rebel government maintained, the war debt must still be paid; but no man here is wise enough to predict what results will follow such a calamity.

Reuben E. Fenton [N. Y.] supported the bill only as a war measure.

In times of peace and prosperity, when the receipts of the treasury from various sources were more than adequate to meet the expenditures of the Government, I might, indeed, hesitate and even oppose any congressional action which would make innovation upon the systems of banking established by the people of the different States. But now, when that peace and security, which we fancied would endure forever, have been so wantonly disturbed, and the former sources of revenue constitute but a fraction to meet the immense demands, the conviction of the necessity of a change, so as to give the Government the control of the currency of the country, cannot be avoided. Indeed, it has been found necessary, in the course of this extraordinary contest, to strengthen and enlarge the powers of almost every department of the Government.

That the present money system is not adequate for the wants of the crisis, and cannot be trusted as the instrument to work out the great fiscal problem of national finance, is evident by the greatly depreciated state of the currency. I do not here lose sight of or undervalue the aid and advantage of the banks to the Government. To say that those connected with them have not again and again responded to the calls of the Government, by direct loan or by purchase of bonds, would be a denial of facts and ingratitude. But considering the monetary system the banks bring to us—theoretically based on the precious metals and a paper currency which financial regulations have allowed to represent them, issued by banking institutions scattered over the Republic, more than one thousand in number, created by differing local legislation, in some States with a limited circulation and in others unrestrained, in some States based on solid securities, in others with no pledge for public safety other than the integrity of their management—the wonder is that such a system should have subserved the wants of a great commercial country so well, even previous to our present public disorders. And but for the wise policy of the Government in authorizing issues of treasury notes, everywhere receivable for public and private dues, it must have failed in a serious degree to meet the demands of the Government or the people; Government loans could not have been negotiated, its pecuniary engagements could not have been met, and paper depreciation, with general financial ruin, would have involved both Government and people, and the misfortune would have been as great as would be disaster in the field.

Having so far survived impending perils, we are to consider this uniform currency scheme, as it is called, with the view to provide for the future exigencies of the Government and country. It is warmly recommended by the finance minister of the Government, with the concurrence, as it is understood, of all the members of the Administration, and approved by experienced financiers in every section of the country. It is to have uniform value—everywhere receivable for public dues—and it is believed, without deranging business interests, or adversely to any great extent affecting existing banking institutions, will ultimately become the circulating medium—the money—of the country. It is not the immediate practice of this system which will alone produce the promised results; but the prospect—the being, and is to be—assured by the constant change to and adoption of the system by bankers and capitalists, together with the receptacle it furnishes for the Government bonds. Abstract questions on political economy, the possible effect in diminishing the speculative value of gold, or in regulating the currency so as at all times to prevent inflation and consequent derangement of business, I do not propose to discuss. It is observable, however, that gold has been withdrawn from circulation; and individuals who may have been fearful of the stability of the present system of banking, or who have availed themselves of the opportunities afforded by the system of banking and Government dependence, have made it, instead of a circulating medium or basis for a circulating medium, one of the most lucrative and favorite objects of speculation.

Specie having been heretofore considered the immediate basis of issue and circulation of paper currency, with the present system, as the large Government expenditures shall continue and the public debt increase, may we not expect a still greater depreciation of currency, or greater speculative value to gold, inflation, and derangement, until bankruptcy and ruin confront us? There is another evil, however, with the present system which should not be overlooked, and which has largely contributed to the depreciation of the currency; for it seems to be sufficiently established that there is not an alarming excess of currency in the aggregate; nevertheless, some of the banking institutions have overissued. It is *this uncontrolled issue and circulation* of paper as currency by irresponsible banks that I refer to.

In only nine of the States out of the thirty-four has the principle of securing payment of circulation by the banks by State bonds been adopted. In some of the loyal States where this regulation has prevailed as a basis of issue and circulation the bonds of some of the States now in rebellion were included in the securities. The past few years, in 1837 and 1857 especially, bring to mind suspensions and failures, the result in part of unregulated bank expansions and contractions and a want of proper basis, often involving in ruin institutions and individuals of long standing and reputation.

In the State of Illinois alone the failures of banks numbered eighty-nine within the last two years, and their paper is reduced from one hundred per cent. to thirty-eight in some instances. The great loss resulting from these failures of course falls upon the people who loan to these banks to the amount of the notes they hold at the time of the failures. Of the $12,000,000 of bank circulation created by and in Illinois two or three years ago, the people have lost two or three millions directly, besides the indirect loss of as many millions more by derangement of business and ruin to private interests.

This system not being compulsory upon existing banks, it will not be regarded with the jealousy of a purely rival scheme, and an intelligent consideration of their own interests, the interests of the Government and the people, which, after all, are *one* interest, will lead them to modify any contemplated opposition; and, even if their individual profits and the present modes of business are somewhat injuriously affected, the same liberal and devoted patriotism in support of the public credit heretofore exhibited will insure their acquiescence in all public measures deemed necessary to preserve that credit.

It is generally known that the bank circulation of New York is based on pledge in part of State and United States securities. There are now on deposit for this purpose in the banking department of that State some $19,000,000 of State and $12,000,000 of United States Government securities. New York State stocks, from their known safety and partly from their use for banking purposes, have long commanded considerable premiums above par. And it is urged by our bankers that one oppressive effect of this national scheme will be to subject them to depreciation and loss on their State securities, as existing banks may be obliged—by unequal competition, if not by taxation, or favor with the people to this uniform national currency—to abandon their present system, and organize under the one we propose. In my opinion all the banking institutions in the country would find it to their advantage to gradually work into this system, thus establishing one reliable, uniform currency; and while there is no intervention or compulsion to effect this, and State banks would make the change a matter of interest and convenience, of course those not of a reliable and solid character would be supplanted by this national system.

It can hardly be doubted, with these figures before us, that the banking interests of New York are largely concerned in the adoption of such a system as will save this vast national debt, in the form of stocks and bonds and treasury notes, from depreciation, and therefore from loss or ruin on the securities they hold, equaling almost their entire aggregate bank capital.

Many question this desirable result from adopting the Government scheme. They are not convinced that the three hundred millions or more of public stocks eventually required will be soon enough absorbed to make an early market for the securities and thus keep up their value. Let me again say that it is the assurance of a general national system—furnishing a sale for a portion of our public stocks, the interwoven interest of the people with the Government in the use, stability, and ownership of the currency—that gives value and stability to our entire amount of public stocks. We should create confidence resulting from the pledge of national faith and security, and the whole people would become immediately interested in sustaining the credit of the Government. Were the plan *now* inaugurated, with prospect of becoming the permanent currency system of the country, sagacious capitalists would at once invest in these securities, well relying on the safety of the investment and the steady market value and demand for them.

The Government bonds are certainly among the safest and most desirable obligations that can be obtained for the security both of currency and loans. If confidence is not to be placed in such securities, then it is difficult to conceive of any obligations which could insure it. The whole capital of the nation is pledged for their redemption; and the honor, welfare, and very life of the Republic rest upon their being kept inviolate. Indeed, if it was possible for the Government to fail; if this fabric, erected by the wisdom and sacrifices of the fathers, is to perish, then, indeed, is not only "life, liberty, and the pursuit of happiness" a thing of the past, but property, in all its forms, and capital, invested in whatever security, unsafe and insecure. In the preservation of the Government rests the security of all property, and with its preservation, of which I have never for a moment had a doubt, the best class of securities are those which it is proposed to make the basis of this uniform national currency, and to which the confidence and faith of the people are invoked.

Considered in a financial and industrial point of view, our large expenditures and heavy national indebtedness may not after all prove so damaging or disastrous as many suppose. It certainly increases the activity and business of the nation. The destruction of the vast amount of property by the war is somewhat compensated by the increased energy, skill, and production of the people. The productions of industry and skill constitute largely a people's wealth, and the nation or people which have the greatest capacity and facilities for production, protected by reliable and uniform currency and finance systems, will eventually, with equal physical force and patriotic purpose, triumph over the other.

The destruction of Moscow excited the Russian people to an activity and energy that it had not before known, and what was lost by its destruction was regained by the incentive to active industry which was aroused. In our country the destruction of our vessels of war in the Norfolk navy yard gave place to thrice as many more in an incredibly short space of time. The timber standing in our forests, and the iron imbedded in the earth today, to-morrow are used in the construction of vessels of war, and next day ride proudly on the bosom of the sea, protecting our national rights and the integrity of our national cause.

The railroads, engines, and cars, the wagons, arms, clothing, subsistence, and all other supplies for our vast army, destroyed to-day, but quicken and increase the industry and skill of our people to replace them in a new and improved manner to-morrow; and when the season for seed time returns, notwithstanding the large drain of men for the service from agricultural as well as other pursuits, we find still more hands, or more skill and industry, seeking the plow and the other implements and appliances of husbandry. Moderate capital that was in slothful hands is now made active; and, even when peace, with its gentle influence, shall again return to our distracted country, these lessons and habits of increased industry and production, stimulated by the necessities of the period, will remain with the people, and aid in rapidly restoring the lost wealth, if they do not carry us in a few years beyond the point we should otherwise have attained.

On February 20 Stephen Baker [N. Y.] opposed the bill as unnecessary and as interfering with the State banks.

The management of our finances, by resorting only to temporary expedients, has been grossly and radically wrong. I believe from the very outbreak of the rebellion that our permanent securities could have been sold to a large amount, and that the necessity of such an enormous and profligate issue of treasury notes could have been obviated. At the beginning of the war I favored the issue of interest-bearing notes to keep them out of circulation; and I should have been extremely gratified by the organization of a permanent sinking fund for the ultimate redemption of our large and accumulating public debt.

Sir, I have a deep and abiding confidence in the speedy success of our arms, and that success will overcome all financial distress and all financial disarrangements; and that victories by sea and land will restore the credit of the Government to a high standard, so that its treasury may be amply replenished.

I believe, too, that with the success of the holy and righteous cause in which we are engaged of preserving the integrity of the Union and of restoring every part of this widespread land in complete obedience to the Constitution and laws of the country, we shall rapidly recuperate from that prostration which now overwhelms a large portion of the country, and quiet that discord which distracts the halls of Congress. I am firmly convinced, moreover, that, under an improved system of labor, the South will become as productive and prosperous as other portions of our country, and that, with redoubled energy, increased resources, and added wealth, we shall soon recover from all the disasters of this accursed rebellion and go on in a career of unmatched glory and renown.

Warren P. Noble [O.] opposed the bill on constitutional grounds.

In the first place, I do not believe it was ever intended by the framers of our Constitution to grant any such power to

Congress by that instrument. Let us examine and see how liberal and even strained must be the construction of its provisions in order to even claim that such was their intention. Here the speaker read the eighth section of the first article:

The Secretary of the Treasury, in advocating the adoption of the system, has found it difficult to decide just where the power to create a national banking system is to be found. He says that it is proposed as an auxiliary to the power to borrow money, as an agency of the power to collect and disburse taxes, and as an exercise of the power to regulate commerce, and of the power to regulate the value of coin. Thus it will be seen that he bases his claim of power upon four different and distinct clauses of the Constitution, separately and distinctly divided from each other.

How the system is to be or become auxiliary to the business of borrowing money on the credit of the Government, or the business of collecting taxes, it would, indeed, seem difficult to determine, and the Secretary has not seen proper to tell us. The Government may obtain money on loan from its own citizens, from banks, or from other Governments; and to the party who has money to loan the only questions are interest and security. Is the security satisfactory? And is it his interest to make the loan? Anything, then, that will enable the Government to give better or more satisfactory security and to pay better interest may be auxiliary to the business of borrowing money. On the subject of collecting and disbursing taxes it is difficult to see how this system can possibly have any beneficial connection whatever with the subject. There never has been any difficulty in disbursing money when the Government had it to disburse, even in its palmiest days of prosperity; and now, when it is deeply involved and every creditor will be anxious to receive his dues, there will be far less prospect of any difficulty in this respect. Collections are facilitated only by anything that will render the collector more prompt or the debtor more able and willing to pay; any other agency than this would seem to be superfluous. If it were possible by this agency to collect the taxes imposed by the late excise laws at less expense than is now incurred, then there might be some claim, but nothing of that kind is pretended.

The next two grounds on which the Secretary bases his claim of constitutionality seem to stand in about the same relation to the subject, namely, that it is an exercise of the power to *regulate* commerce and to regulate the value of coin. To regulate means to adjust or govern by certain uniform rules or restrictions; it does not mean to destroy or to create, but merely to govern by certain rules of law. To regulate commerce was never intended by the framers of the Constitution to carry with it or include the power to establish a paper-moneyed banking system merely because the currency created by such a system might thereafter be used in paying for the commodities that might be interchanged by such commerce. It seems to me that such a claim would be a little too far-fetched to be worthy of any very serious consideration.

To coin money and regulate the value thereof—of what? Of the coin thus made. Is it not strange that anyone should contend at this day that a paper currency could in any way affect the *real* value of coin? Yet this is one of the principal claims on which the constitutionality of this bill is based. Coin is, and ever must be, the standard of all *real value* the world over; and what our Constitution meant by giving the power to coin money was merely to fix by law the size, shape, quality of metal, weight, value, and devices that should characterize the different coins that might be authorized by the Government of the United States. This is a power that is possessed and exercised by all civilized nations; and when confined to its legitimate purpose is certainly a very necessary and salutary power, as without it there would most likely be no uniformity or fixed and certain value to the coin or currency of the country. Without it the different kinds of coin might be so numerous and so various in kinds and values as to render exchanges very troublesome and vexatious. But with its proper exercise, as, for instance, in the case of our own Government, by fixing the size, weight, quality of metal, and devices of the Federal dollar, both in gold and silver, and then by adjusting and measuring the value of all other coins by this, we have a system which renders exchanges easy and convenient.

These provisions of the Constitution, together with that other provision in section ten of the first article, by which it is provided "that no State shall coin money, emit bills of credit, or make anything but gold and silver coin a tender in payment of debts," satisfy me that it was never the intention of the framers of the Constitution to authorize anything to be made a legal tender in payment of debts, excepting only what I am pleased to denominate the good old constitutional currency of gold and silver. It would be strange, indeed, if it was the intention of the framers of the Constitution that the Federal Government should have the power to issue or authorize to be issued and put in circulation any other currency which might be made a legal tender in payment of debts by it, and yet that it should restrict the States from allowing the same money which it might thus provide or authorize to be received as a legal tender. No one can be convinced for a moment that it was the intention that the Federal Government should have power to create a currency which the States should not have the right to give as much credit to as might be given to it by the Federal Government. The proposition is preposterous, and will not bear the test of reason. If this had been the intention of the framers of the Constitution, instead of providing that nothing but gold and silver should be made a legal tender in payment of debts, they would have provided that nothing but gold and silver coin and such other currency as might be authorized by law of Congress should be received in payment of debts.

If it were true, as some suppose, that in order that the Government should be able to make its great expenditures it must first have an amount of currency equal to the whole amount to be expended, it would require all the money of both America and Europe to carry on this war. This Government has already expended, since the war commenced, more than double the whole amount of all the circulation the whole nation and all its people possess, including all its gold and silver, bank bills, and treasury notes; and the present prospect is that this is not the half of what will be expended before the war closes. There never was a greater delusion than to suppose that because the Government expends large sums it must have money or currency to an equal amount. What the Government must have to carry on the war is means, capital, munitions of war, and supplies; and these it can only obtain by draft upon its citizens and their property. The capital and wealth of the nation is but a very small part of it in the shape of currency. Two hundred and fifty or two hundred and seventy-five million dollars, at most, would include every dollar of the gold and silver of the whole nation, while the last census shows the amount of individual wealth of the nation to be over sixteen thousand million dollars. The Government must be a self-sustaining institution. When its expenses are large it can only sustain itself by drawing more from its subjects in the shape of taxes, either direct or indirect. There is no other mode; this is its legitimate and only resort, unless it be to its credit, by contracting debts which must eventually be paid in the same way, by tax upon the citizen.

When the war commenced the currency of the country was all founded upon a specie basis; nothing but gold and silver could be made a legal tender in payment of debts. The banking institutions of the several States received credit in proportion to the public confidence in their ability to pay specie *on demand* for all their issues. As long as this continued to be the scheme of our financial system, there could be no great danger of sudden and disastrous eruptions in the currency of the country. But as soon as the treasury note legal tender scheme was adopted, and a sudden increase or expansion of the amount of circulation accrued, what followed was inevitable—sudden and astonishing increase in the prices of goods; or it might be more properly styled sudden and astonishing depreciation of all the paper currency of the country, legal tender and all. It to-day requires $1.70 of this paper, backed by the Government with all its wealth, to buy a single dollar of gold. And, in common parlance, it is said gold has gone up; the truth is, paper has gone down, and is still going down.

Mr. Speaker, what is the effect this system is now having upon the country and its business? A single illustration may serve to throw some light upon the subject, and may not be improper. When our soldiers entered the field their wages were made by law thirteen dollars per month, under the then financial system. The supplies for their families might then be bought for about the following prices, namely: muslins, prints, checks, cotton cloths, and drillings, at from eight to twelve and a half cents per yard; now these same articles will cost them more than twice as high. Almost the same thing may be said in reference to boots, shoes, coffee, sugar, molasses, and almost everything in the shape of necessary supplies for their families. The average increase in price of all these things will not be less than the average depreciation in the value of paper money. That is, they will now pay no less than $1.70 for what would then have cost them one dollar. Yet it is often boastingly said that "the greenbacks came to help the soldier." He may well say, save me from such blessings; a few more such would render him bankrupt, and bring his wife and children, who are dependent upon his pay for support, to the brink of starvation. To make his monthly pay equal now to what it was when he entered the service, and prior to the adoption of the paper system, we should be compelled to add seventy per cent., or more, to his pay, which would make his monthly wages, instead of thirteen dollars, about twenty-two dollars and ten cents. And yet, in my humble judgment, the Government itself has lost more than it has gained by adopting this system.

Mr. Speaker, I object to converting our treasury building into a printing establishment, or making our Secretary a printer to grind out paper money. I doubt not the integrity and honesty of the present Secretary; but we do not know who is to be his successor, and that they would not make use of such power for political or other purposes. Such things have occurred in the past, as in the case of the famous financier, Baron Brock, minister of finance of Austria, who committed suicide when his heavy forgeries were discovered; and in our own country there are names that have figured prominently in our public affairs to our national disgrace. But the greatest danger is among that class of employees who are subordinate to the Secretary, and necessarily must have control of these various departments in the manufacture of the notes, who, possessing no responsibility, and often of questionable character for strict integrity, have it in their power to purloin and overissue to any amount, thus causing the most serious disasters to the public and to the circulation of our national currency.

In regard to the economy which I have heard put forth as an argument in favor of this proposed money-making establishment, I can merely refer to the established fact that it costs our Government a great deal more to manufacture anything and everything for its own wants than to be supplied by private contracts; and I have good reason to believe that parties deeply interested in this enterprise are confident of realizing their dearest wishes by having the Government purse to support them, which does not present a very plausible evidence of economy, but is evidence that it would result more for the benefit of a few individuals than for the public good.

Mr. Speaker, it looks to me as if this was only another of the many schemes brought forward during the present Administration which have so abundantly opened the door to fraud and plunder upon our bleeding treasury, already amounting to many million dollars.

The bill was passed by a vote of 78 to 64. It was approved by President Lincoln on February 25, 1863.

CHAPTER XI

Extension of National Bank Charters [1882]

William W. Crapo [Mass.] Introduces in the House a Bill to Extend National Bank Charters—Debate: in Favor, Mr. Crapo, Roswell P. Flower [N. Y.], Benjamin Wilson [W. Va.], Augustus A. Hardenbergh [N. J.], William D. Kelley [Pa.], Waldo Hutchins [N. Y.], Abram S. Hewitt [N. Y.], Benjamin Butterworth [O.], George C. Hazelton [Wis.]; Opposed, Richard P. Bland [Mo.], Roger Q. Mills [Tex.], Thomas R. Cobb [Ind.], Samuel J. Randall [Pa.], Aylett H. Buckner [Mo.], Charles N. Brumm [Pa.], Joseph H. Burrows [Mo.]; Bill Is Passed by House and Senate, and Approved by President Arthur.

ON February 7, 1882, William W. Crapo [Rep.], of Massachusetts, introduced in the House, from the majority of the Committee on Banking and Currency, a bill "to enable national banking associations to extend their corporate existence."

National Banks

House of Representatives, April 17–May 17, 1882

The bill came up for discussion on April 17. Richard P. Bland [Dem.], of Missouri, gave notice that he had introduced a bill which he would like to be discussed in the same connection. This bill provided for retiring the circulation of the national banks and, on the expiration of their charters, continuing these banks as banks of discount and deposit.

Mr. Crapo supported his measure.

The indifference or possibly the ignorance of some gentlemen in reference to the financial or business interests of the country is to my mind simply amazing. There are to-day in operation fifty more national banks than there were six months ago, and yet to-day the national bank note circulation is $1,400,000 less than it was six months ago. How far these figures are the result of a belief on the part of business men that Congress is indisposed to act upon this and kindred questions I shall not undertake to say. But they indicate the possibility of a contraction which the failure to act upon this bill will greatly increase.

I do not wish to be understood as asserting that if the bank charters are extended there will be no diminution of national bank circulation, because as that bank circulation becomes unprofitable the tendency is naturally for its withdrawal; but by the extension of the charters of the national banks it may be safely assumed that the withdrawal will be less rapid, less extensive, and less serious. The consideration of this bill brings up all the questions which the friends or opponents of the measure may desire to present, and enables a vote to be obtained upon all propositions designed to substitute treasury notes for national bank bills. Let us by action upon the bill inform the business men of the country what they may expect, and give them the opportunity to prepare for the situation.

Mr. Crapo yielded time successively to Roswell P. Flower [N. Y.], Benjamin Wilson [W. Va.], and Augustus A. Hardenbergh [W. Va.], Democrats, who supported the bill.

Mr. Flower.—The financial policy of the Government touches every home throughout the length and breadth of this Union. The slightest discussion of it is felt everywhere. As long as it is before us there is no confidence nor business enterprise; no investments are made; employment of labor ceases, and widespread distress ensues. We have again and again had instances of the same thing.

The contemplation of a resumption of specie payment from 1875 to 1879 reduced us almost to beggary. The settlement of the question restored confidence and led to our present prosperity. The refusal of the House last Monday to consider this matter has caused a large amount of money to be withdrawn from trade already. What the discussion of the banking system must bring is further uncertainty and a decrease of prosperity, and the longer it is put off the greater will be our distress. The banks can under the present law liquidate, divide their surplus, change their names, put greenbacks into the treasury to the amount of their outstanding notes, draw new notes, and go on as before. The consequence of such action is contraction of the currency and disturbance to business. No one can estimate the distress which will be occasioned, but everyone will feel as though there were disturbing forces at work forbidding him to increase his business and compelling him to proceed with caution. No one can tell how he will be affected, but everyone will regard with dismay the approach of each successive charter expiration and will fear and tremble at the mention of the 25th of February next, when two hundred and ninety-seven bank charters expire and fifty-three million greenbacks will be placed in the treasury for the redemption of their notes, or thirty-five millions more than the banks foolishly withdrew in 1881.

Business men are always sorry when Congress assembles and pleased when it adjourns. I sincerely trust that in this case at least they will not have cause to say the House has neglected their interests.

Mr. Wilson and Mr. Hardenbergh spoke in like tenor.

At the conclusion of Mr. Hardenbergh's speech Roger Q. Mills [Tex.] congratulated Mr. Crapo on "the splendid strategy he has displayed in getting the Republican heresy advocated by Democrats."

Thomas R. Cobb [Dem.], of Indiana, opposed the bill.

This proposition was substantially presented to the House two weeks ago and was then voted down. But the bankers have thrust it upon us again to consume the time of the House as against other important matters of legislation. This organized system of capital has ever since I have been a member of this House constantly been thrusting itself in here to control legislation for its benefit to the injury of the country. This morning we see its hand again. It was said when this question was up before that the national banking system was a Democratic measure. I deny it. I assert that it is opposed to the teachings of Democracy. There were scarcely half a dozen Democrats in Congress who voted for the present national bank law when it was passed.

It is said by the friends of the banks that if the bill pending in the House is not passed the banks will go into liquidation, and that in consequence the business interests of the country will be shocked and untold ruin will befall the country. This is done to alarm the House. It is not the first time we have heard the bankers sound the alarm on this floor. They did it when the bill to remonetize silver and the bill to stop the contraction of the greenbacks were pending in this House. They then predicted ruin to the country if these bills passed. They passed, however, and the country was blessed instead of being injured. But why this attempted alarm? The banks can reorganize under the law as now existing. There are but few, comparatively, of these banks whose charters expire before the 1st of December next; not enough of them to shock the financial interests of the country. Congress meets then, and can take action if necessary.

We are required to take this bill as prepared by the hands of the bankers without amendment, or we must defeat it. For one, I will never vote for the extension of the bank charters. I surely never will unless we are allowed to throw what I conceive to be necessary safeguards around the system. This system of banking is not satisfactory to the people. The agricultural, mechanical, and laboring classes are opposed to it. The great Northwest and South are opposed to it. But the capitalists of the East are in favor of it, and they will force the question on this House to the exclusion of all other business, however important that may be to the country.

Samuel J. Randall [Pa.].—The circulation of the national banks is based upon the debt of the United States, and as long as that debt exists that circulation can be maintained. It is proposed, however, that treasury notes shall be issued in lieu of such circulation. We cannot give to the treasury notes any other quality than that they shall be received by the Government in payment of public debts. It will hardly be contended that we can give to the treasury notes the quality of legal tender for the payment of all debts. Now, with all the advantages that pertain to the national bank circulation, there are gross abuses existing in connection therewith, and, if we are to be denied the opportunity of correcting those abuses, we must in self-defence resist the effort to continue these corporations in existence, so as to bring the national banks to their senses.

Owing to Democratic opposition consideration of the bill was postponed. It came up again on May 1.

Aylett H. Buckner [Dem.], of Missouri, of the minority of the Committee on Banking and Currency, opposed the bill.

I believe, sir, that this bill, if passed, will turn out to be a delusion and a cheat. The difficulty with the national banks is not that their charters are expiring, but it grows out of the fact that the debt upon which their circulation is based is bound to be paid at the rate of $100,000,000 a year for the next four years at least. Already the banks have decreased their circulation in the neighborhood of $1,000,000 since the 1st of January last, owing to the fact that the 3½ per cent. bonds held by the banks are being called in.

I say that the duty of this Congress to the country, and even to the banks, is, if possible, to find some constituent in place of the foundation being undermined by this determination of the people to pay these 3½ per cents. That is what they need, and not this legislation, or anything like it; for, sir, it will delude the people into the idea that everything is going on smoothly when there is danger and great danger ahead of us from the rapid contraction which will necessarily follow from the payment of this portion of the public debt.

William D. Kelley [Pa.].—Would not a reduction of the revenues of the Government to such an extent as to check the unwholesome rapidity with which our bonds are being called in leave a basis for the banks?

Mr. Buckner.—Unquestionably it would. But there is no more universal sentiment existing in this country than the determination of the people of the United States to pay off the national debt, without reference to the banks or anything else, as rapidly as the condition of the country will permit. [Applause.]

Waldo Hutchins [N. Y.].—The gentleman from Missouri [Mr. Buckner] and the other gentleman from Missouri [Mr. Bland] do not propose to give up the national banking system, but only desire to have a change from the national banking currency to the treasury notes of the Government. That question, however, should stand by itself, and we ought to reserve our opinion as to the best mode of reaching a desirable solution of it, for the present considering one thing at a time. My friend from Missouri says it is unnecessary to take action now. I want to say to him that in my opinion the action taken by the House heretofore renders it necessary that we should take action, and favorable action, without delay.

As every gentleman knows who has ever had anything to do with banking and currency, there is nothing so timid as capital. The business men of the country do not understand the situation of this matter; but there is an impression among them in the State of Missouri, as well as in the State of New York, that there is something wrong, and unless action is taken to provide for the extension of bank charters about expiring there will be trouble in the money market. And therefore the wheels of finance are being stopped. Men who were intending to go into operations that called for the expenditure of large sums of money have countermanded the order, waiting to see the action of this House, and there is not a gentleman here who, if he were called upon to enter into a new enterprise involving the expenditure of a large sum of money, not even my friend from Missouri [Mr. Buckner] but would refuse to enter into it till this question was settled.

I am sure this Congress has the ability, the sense, and the patriotism to arrive at last at a conclusion that will bring continued peace and prosperity to our whole country. [Applause.]

Mr. Hardenbergh.—If this were a question to-day before the House as to whether the national banking system should be created anew or not, then some of us might understand how to vote. But the national banking system goes on, because your banks can reorganize in a very day, and perpetuate their existence for twenty years. Therefore, by no discussion that you give to this bill, nor by any action of yours do you restrict its provisions or prevent the operations of the system throughout the country.

What, then, is the question before us? What is the difference between the two methods—the reorganization and the extension of the charters? The question is whether those banks shall liquidate or whether their existence shall be continued by your action upon this bill. If you force them to liquidate, you produce a contraction of over sixty millions of money that must be called away from the industrial interests of the country, and that just as we are going on conquering and to conquer in all our industrial pursuits.

The bank of which I am president has a capital of $250,000, a surplus of $225,000, loans out to the extent of $1,000,000 on call and on time. Now, if you refuse to-day, or before this Congress adjourns, to say the charter of that bank shall be extended it must immediately contract to recover the $225,000 of surplus to pay the stockholders. You force my bank into liquidation. Any five men can come forward and write their names for $50,000 each, and you have as perfect a monopoly as ever existed.

Roger Q. Mills [Tex.].—Will your bank have to go into liquidation unless this bill is passed?

Mr. Hardenbergh.—Certainly it will.

Mr. Mills.—Then I make the point of order that the gentleman cannot vote on this bill.

Mr. Hardenbergh.—I have this to say to the gentleman from

Texas [Mr. Mills]: if he thinks that the ownership of a thousand dollars of stock in the bank in which I happen to be president will control my action here he little understands me or the constituency I represent.

On May 16 Abram S. Hewitt [N. Y.] supported the bill.

As we are to have banks, the only question is whether they shall be national banks or State banks. We have tried the State banks. They were a failure. No one who has studied the history of the past would consent on any terms whatever to go back to the State banking system even when the most perfect, as in the State of New York, where we had the safety-fund system, which provided absolute security for the circulation.

Now, if we would not go back to the State banks and must have banks, we are driven to the conclusion they must be national banks. In regard to these national banks I think there is no controversy at this day except on one point. Even my friend from Missouri [Mr. Bland] in the substitute he has offered recognizes the propriety of their continuance as banks of discount and deposit. It is only, therefore, on the question of circulation that there is any criticism to be made upon the banks. Now, the circulating medium is in finance what the life-blood is to the human body. We must keep it in the best possible condition or disease is sure to occur and ruin and death, industrial death, to follow.

The system which we have is a national one. The currency is entirely supplied by the Government. It is at par everywhere, and no doubt exists in the mind of any human being, when he gets one of these bills, whether it be a Government note or a national bank note, that he can get for it in coin one hundred cents on the dollar.

I recognize facts as I find them. I would never by vote or act authorize or contribute to the issue of these legal-tender notes. I should be very glad if they could be retired. I do not think that this Government was created for the purpose of supplying circulation; on the contrary, I think the fathers and founders of the Constitution intended to prohibit the exercise of any such power.

I agree with Hamilton, whose superior as a financier has never lived, when he says, "to emit an unfounded paper as the sign of value ought not to continue a formal part of the Constitution, nor ever hereafter to be employed; being in its nature pregnant with abuses, and liable to be made the engine of imposition and fraud; holding out temptations equally pernicious to the integrity of government and to the morals of the people." (Hamilton's Works, II, 271.)

But we have Government paper money, and it now works well in practice. I know that principle is a good thing, but when you have a condition of things which works well it is dangerous to disturb it.

I am willing, no matter what the coming decision of the Supreme Court may be as to the legal-tender clause, that the $346,000,000 of Government notes now outstanding shall remain as a currency for the country until some better and more economical system shall be devised by the experience, not of Congress, but of men engaged in business.

How is the balance of the circulating medium provided? I assume that the $346,000,000 of Government notes will never come in for redemption. The balance is now provided by the national banks. The amount which the public receives fluctuates from day to day.

Now, somebody must provide for the redemption of these notes, and for their issue in accordance with the demands of business. Any banking system to be good, or, I should rather say, any circulating medium to be good, must have two elements. First, it must be surely redeemable in coin on demand; and, secondly, it must be issued daily in amounts sufficient to meet the legitimate requirements of business. That is precisely the condition we have now. The banks are ready, with adequate security, to wit, the security of the Government debt, to redeem every note that is presented. And, secondly, they are in condition, either out of the reserves which they have on hand, or out of the new bills which they can get for the deposit of additional Government bonds, to provide for whatever amount of currency the requirements of business may make necessary. And it is not conceivable that so far as business is concerned there should be a better state of things than this.

But I am met by the statement that this circulation is a source of profit; that the creation of circulation is a sovereign right, and that the profit belongs to the State, to the Government, to the people. Therefore if there be any profit in this circulation it ought to be taken by the Government, and the banks are not entitled to any of it.

Now, if the Government assumes this duty, if it has any such right, which I deny, if it assumes to itself this duty it must also assume the duty of redemption and of the expansion and contraction of the currency to meet the fluctuating demands of business. Now, I think I speak only the lesson of history when I say that redemption depending upon congressional action would be a delusion and a snare.

I think I may go further and say that not only would there be no certainty of redemption, but it is absolutely certain that there would come a time when in the absence of congressional action, or by congressional action, redemption would be made impossible. Therefore the first element of a sound circulation is absent, that is, if made dependent upon action of Congress.

Secondly, it would be impossible for Congress by any earthly contrivance to meet the demands which are made daily for a change in the amounts of the currency. We are not always in session; and when we are in session gentlemen about me know how exceedingly difficult it is to secure action upon any question, and much more upon questions so much in doubt and controversy as the currency question is. Therefore there could be no automatic action of expansion and contraction in the currency (which is the fundamental element in a good circulating medium) by the legislation of this body.

I shall be told that it would be possible to relieve Congress of this duty, and transfer it to a board who should decide from day to day, and from week to week, how the currency should be issued, and the methods by which it should be got into circulation. My answer to that is that we have had during the refunding operations and since the war an experience of the dangers of confiding power over the currency to public officers, however capable and however honest. The fact is that to put the control of the currency into individual hands is to put the whole property of the country at the mercy of the men who control the currency. The power is too great not only for human knowledge, but for human character. It is impossible to find any one man, or any half dozen men, who can comprehend the wants and business interests of a country like ours; and it is impossible to find men who can separate themselves absolutely from the interests which they themselves may hold, or which may be represented by their faith.

I have no personal knowledge of the alleged scandals in regard to refunding; I do not propose here to make any charges; but this I say, it is notorious that in the refunding operation particular banks, representing particular individuals, had practically a monopoly of that vast transaction, and that one bank in my own State cleared its capital stock five times over in the course of the refunding operations in two years.

That may have been all legitimate. The refunding operation was the grandest financial operation that has ever been made in the history of man.

But, sir, for one, I do not want what little I have laboriously gotten together to be placed at the mercy of any man. I should like to be able to manage my own property, and to keep or give in my own way what I have accumulated. I do not want a *deus ex machina* to administer the business of this country. There could be but one result of such a system, utter and absolute ruin. I therefore dismiss as impracticable the idea that any board composed of men can undertake this task which is beyond the reach of human capacity.

I come back to the fact that currency we must have, and that this currency will not be issued unless it be made profitable to the parties who issue it. Banks are not benevolent institutions. They are not governmental agencies except in a very narrow sense. They are organizations of men with capital for the purpose of carrying on a business which is not only lawful, but absolutely necessary to the community. They are not going to conduct this business without profit; it ought not to be asked of them. But, if the profits should ever become excessive, the taxing power resides in Congress. There is no difficulty at all in regulating the business and taking to the Government as we now do such portions of these profits as Congress may think belong legitimately to the treasury.

But more than that; when a business is free, and when there is no monopoly at all, excessive profits cannot long endure. Only show me that a bank is able to make more than I can make in my iron business. I should take my capital out of the iron business and put it in banks. There is no possibility that the profits of these institutions can for any considerable period of time, except in very abnormal circumstances, exceed those of legitimate business in other directions. The fact is that these banks, while they have been highly profitable at times, made their money very largely out of the refunding operation. That operation is done and ended; it will not be renewed in our day. On the contrary we should pay off the existing national debt, and, as I hope, never in our time should we have occasion to create another.

So that on the question of what the profits of these banks may be, it seems to me it must be conceded that as we must have agencies, and the banks are acceptable agencies to the business of the country, and as we can regulate their profits by law, and as they are still better regulated by free competition, nobody who is willing to get rid of his prejudices can make any fair criticism against the continuance of the present national banking system.

Now, we have been told that, while the circulation of the national banks is at present adequately secured, there will very shortly come a time when Government bonds will be retired, and there will be no such security for this circulation.

What, then, are we to do in regard to the circulation of the country? There my friend from Missouri comes in and says give us treasury notes in lieu of it. I have shown you, I think, conclusively that treasury notes would not answer the valid purposes of money. The banks that will close up their business unless they take out new charters under the operation of existing law will in the present year withdraw a very considerable amount of money.

The reason is that owing to the low rate of money all over the world it will not pay the banks to purchase such Government bonds as they can buy to replace the called bonds, and the result is they will take their money and retire the circulation.

A remedy was suggested by my colleague [Mr. Flower] which is the prompt passage of a refunding bill, so that these bonds may be replaced by the new 3 per cent. bonds which will be created by that refunding bill.

And I want to say to gentlemen on the other side of the House that the responsibility, the onus, in this business is on them. This side of the House in the last Congress, of which I had not the honor to be a member, did pass a refunding bill, which was vetoed. If the Republicans fail to make it possible for the banks to replace the bonds which will be withdrawn, followed by a withdrawal of circulation, then there will be a tide of indignation sweeping over this country which will carry their majority away, and put some other party in power which is ready to meet the necessities of the adverse condition in which the country will find itself.

Now, by extending these charters we actually give no new rights to the banks. They may reorganize and are organizing all the time under the bank act, taking out new charters for twenty years. I would prefer to allow them to run on; first, to avoid the expense of reorganization, and, secondly, to avoid the inconvenience of winding up their affairs and starting again; but more particularly to avoid the distribution of $128,000,000 of surplus profits which they hold on hand and which is the basis of business in this country to the extent at least of $1,000,000,000 per annum.

I will make some suggestions as to what kind of a currency might be substituted when the stock of Government bonds shall be sensibly diminished. I would still continue to require that $50,000 of the capital of each of the national banks should be invested in Government bonds, and this for reasons which will be obvious to every gentleman present.

I propose that the national banking system under the law as it now stands shall not be changed in any respect whatever except one. I would do all that as is done at present under the law, but I would no longer compel the banks to deposit Government bonds for the amount of the circulation issued to them.

What security would I substitute?

I would deliver to banks 90 per cent. in circulating notes on the amount of their capital. I would make the notes of the bank a first lien on the assets of the bank. Secondly, I would make the stockholders, as they now are, personally liable for 100 per cent. in addition to the capital of the bank, and make the notes of the bank a first lien upon this amount. Now, I have at least under this arrangement 200 per cent. behind the notes. Thirdly, I would compel the banks to put a redemption fund of 10 per cent. in coin into the hands of the Treasurer of the United States. Taking the present capital of the banks, $360,000,000, that would put $36,000,000 of coin as a redemption fund in the hands of the Treasurer. Lastly, I would make the banks as a whole guarantee the circulation of each individual bank.

Now, let us see what will happen. A bank breaks; its note is redeemable at the treasury of the United States in coin without a moment's delay. Next, I would recoup the amount paid out for redemption of these notes by immediate assessment on the banks and require them to make it good, and when the bank is wound up and the lien for circulation is collected I would refund the money to the banks for the assessment they might have paid.

I submit to this House whether it is conceivable that a circulation secured in that way would be irredeemable, or that there would be a particle of doubt about it from one end of the land to the other. But while it is so absolutely secure as to be bombproof and fire-proof it imposes no harder condition on the banks than does the present law, which requires the stockholders to be personally liable for an amount equal to the capital stock held by each.

Benjamin Butterworth [O.] supported the bill.

I would pay the greenbacks as we are pledged to do, and dissociate the Government from all banking operations, and remit the issuing of paper to the national banks, under charters so restricted, so limited, as to impose individual liability; and with the certain result that bad faith, corrupt management, reckless issue should entail the first and most disastrous calamity to the banks and bankers.

It is strange that there is no end to the folly that constantly repeats itself in shouting about the outrage of permitting the national banks to deposit one hundred thousand dollars in bonds and draw out ninety thousand dollars of what certain very clever but thoughtless persons insist on calling money. National bank notes represent credit. The national banker wants to loan the credit of the bank to such as may desire to utilize it in their business or pursuits. To facilitate this enterprise, and for the convenience of the bank and the borrower, certain printed evidences of credit known as bank notes are provided by the Government at the cost of the bank, and the bank is permitted, under certain restrictions, to loan these credit notes. The Government, however, for the protection of those who borrow those notes and those into whose hands they may come, says to the bank, "Before you can issue these notes of credit you must secure the noteholders against loss; you must deposit with the Government United States bonds to secure the redemption and payment of the notes"; not to secure their exchange for other notes or paper, but their payment, and payment means the delivery of gold or silver.

The Government does not give to the banker a cent of money, not a farthing. If it did deliver money to the banks there would be no need of providing for its redemption. Who ever heard of redeeming gold dollars or silver dollars? So, when gentlemen talk about depositing bonds with the Secretary of the Treasury and receiving so much money, they simply confuse and mislead and positively misstate the fact, through ignorance in many cases, and in a spirit of demagogy in other cases.

The whole system is simply a means of loaning credit to those who desire to borrow. Business demands such convenience, and the Government regulates its utilization so as to be most advantageous and safest to the borrower and holder of the legal evidence of the credit so loaned.

The statement that the Government or that the people are thus compelled to pay double interest, etc., and suffer hardships unnecessarily, is amusing, or would be if it was not pronounced with such seriousness as to befog and mislead. Will gentlemen devise some scheme, or suggest one, by which those who borrow money or credit will not have to pay interest? If they borrow gold they must pay interest. If they borrow greenbacks they must pay interest. The Government does not distribute treasury notes gratuitously nor loan without interest. The bonds would bear interest even if not deposited to secure the redemption of bank circulation.

Touching the proposition that the bonds should be paid in greenbacks, it is needless to discuss it. Those who deem it honest to make such payment, regardless of the value of the greenbacks, are laboring with a difficulty which has its seat in their moral nature; logic will not reach it.

Those who think it is consonant with the spirit of the contract contained in the bond to compel the surrender of that interest-bearing bond which on its face provides for payment in money, and the acceptance in payment thereof of a large number of non-interest-bearing promissory notes, have a moral and intellectual make-up which is, I am glad to say, exceptional in this country. The Government was in the throes of dissolution. She had issued her non-interest-bearing promissory notes, and our people had taken them. Great uncertainty existed as to whether she ever would or could redeem these promissory notes. They had ceased to be worth more than fifty cents on the dollar. The Government offered to take them up and issue time-interest-bearing bonds to such as would take them. Many patriotic citizens took them. Now some gentlemen solemnly propose that, the country being now out of danger, these men who accepted the bonds shall be called up and told that the Government is ready and willing to rescind the bargain, and in fact insists on taking up its interest-bearing bond and restoring the non-interest-bearing promissory notes; and not only that, but insists on calling it payment.

In an individual this would be plain swindling. In my judgment it would in the Government be something worse. Of course if the holder of our promises to pay, or whatever they may be called, are willing to take other paper which is par, there can be no objection. But until this Government is fouled with dishonor and debased beyond recovery we will not adopt a system of paying which does not in fact discharge the debt. Bankers do best and flourish most when trade and commerce are in their normal condition, when the law of supply and healthful demand regulate our manufacturing and producing industries. They find their prosperity in the general prosperity. Their reserves should be in coin. No paper partition of greenbacks should be permitted between the note holder and the coin dollar it represents.

But what will become of your national banks when the national debt is paid? Well, I am not of opinion that as much good to ourselves or to posterity will result from the hurried ex-

SUBSTANCE AND SHADOW

Cartoon by M. Woolf

tinguishment of the national debt as from its utilization to secure the redemption of our circulating paper currency. I would make it when reduced to, say, twelve hundred millions the security for our circulation, and also the basis of a postal-saving system, which would afford our people the means of safely investing their earnings and preparing a fund against age and the rainy day which comes to us all. As to the interest on the bonds, we collect the full amount from the banks in taxes imposed by the United States and by State and local taxation.

There may be a better system than the national bank system. But nobody to this hour has pointed it out. When it is presented we will make haste to adopt it. Time and experience have demonstrated that the old State and wild-cat system could only be restored with a view to rob the laborers and producers of the country. If the world's experience teaches anything, it is that the issue of paper money by the Government, in the discretion of Congress, would entail like disaster. No nation ever failed to abuse that power when once conceded to it. No nation ever redeemed its notes so issued. Ours has not to this hour, and I predict that it never will.

The idea of leaving the volume of the currency to be regulated by the wants of trade and the discretion of Congress excites alternately laughter and disgust. The very time Congress should stand firm and resist the panicky clamor for larger volume of currency it would bend like a reed. Congress wants to be right, but there is one thing that it wants still more, and that is to be popular. It wants to protect the best interest of the people, but it must have their votes; and it unfortunately occurs that that which is wisest and best is not always most popular at the time when action is to be had, and it occurs that we sometimes please the people least when we serve them best, and *vice versa.* Can you not trust the people, questions some Solon? Yes, certainly. So our fathers did, but they none the less provided a Constitution to prevent them from governing themselves too much under sudden impulse, under stress of adverse circumstances, when prejudice, passion, and excitement clouded or unhorsed the judgment—a Constitution to restrain us in hours of peril until wise and intelligent judgment could assert its sway.

We have few systems, few institutions on this earth that are unmixed good—few that are unmixed evils. National banks are not an exception. I am told that in urging the observance of good faith on the part of the Government in the payment of the greenbacks and the bonds, and the restriction of the volume of our paper currency, I am digging my political grave. So be it. If to insist upon preserving the national honor and maintaining the national faith is to be buried, so be it. I shall have some consolation in remembering that there is a resurrection for the just. If for insisting that the man who labors shall not be robbed by being paid in dishonest money; if for insisting that the wage man's dollar shall be worth a hundred cents throughout the year and everywhere; if for insisting that we shall not have under the influence of an inflated currency a few years of fatness, followed by a longer term of leanness and hunger; if to insist that our prosperity shall be real and not imaginary is to compass my political death, I will accept the reward of my stewardship with calmness and satisfaction. I would rather be retired by my people with the consciousness of having served them faithfully and been right than to be promoted by them amid acclamations of applause burdened with the knowledge that I had, to secure their favor, betrayed their interests.

I am asked if I would perpetuate the national debt; if I deem it a national blessing. I answer: A national debt is in a sense a burden. It may be so utilized as to become a blessing. I can readily see that if it was the basis and security of a wise postal-saving system, by which the mechanics, the artisans, the laborers, and such of the producing classes as would could find absolute security for the investment of their earnings, thus encouraging industry, sobriety, and economy among all classes, the debt, being transferred to this class, would prove indeed a blessing.

It would not only encourage the cultivation of the virtues to which I have referred, but it would induce all these people to feel and take a watchful and intelligent interest in their government; to study carefully its proper functions and labor to see that it is confined to them. They would be prompted by principle and interest alike to shield and protect the public faith and credit in the preservation of which each depositor would find his hope and safety. It is a question of the greatest good, and rather than return to the old scheme of organized plunder of the ante-war period, which robbed the toilers of this country every day in the year, I would without hesitation fund the bonds at 3 per cent., after the manner of the English consols, and make them the security of the noteholders of the country and the basis of the postal-saving system; the good resulting from such a course being so far paramount to any ill or inconvenience it would entail as not only to be defensible but to render it greatly to be desired.

The charge that I am for the bankers and gold bugs is one that a very moderate ability can make. Those who have such words on their tongues may not be malicious. Their trouble is usually congenital.

I have never eaten food that I have not earned in the sweat of my face.

I have three boys whose lines will not fall in more auspicious places. They, too, must eat their bread in the sweat of their faces. And in advocating a sound currency, and a just financial system and the preservation of the national faith and credit, I only desire to preserve to them the equal opportunity to labor with their fellows and that they shall be paid for that labor with dollars that are worth one hundred cents, with money the value of which does not depend upon the whim or caprice of a Congress or the fidelity of bank directors or conditions of war or peace, which shall be worth one hundred cents every day in the year and everywhere.

Charles N. Brumm [Pa.], a "Greenbacker," on the committee, opposed the bill.

Mr. Speaker, we live in a remarkable period, one in which there have been greater advances in arts and sciences, greater social, intellectual, and moral development than in any previous age. We are living in an age that has reduced time and space, brought mankind together from the remotest regions of the earth, and utilized and subordinated the elements to the use of man, thus enabling us to increase our productions and ease our burdens a hundred to a thousand fold.

We have advanced and progressed in everything except finance, *i. e.*, we have multiplied our commodities or resources a thousandfold, but have not advanced the system of distributing or interchanging these commodities or resources one jot. We are still adhering to the barbarous system of barter, namely, intrinsic value for value, varied only by a postponement of the delivery of the intrinsic value commodity by a promise to pay or deliver that commodity in future, and this promise made by individuals or corporations the creatures of the Government, instead of reserving to the sovereign the exercise and use of one of its most vital functions, and by controlling the currency or the circulating medium to exert practically a control of the interchange of every commodity that man creates or can utilize. We thus give to individuals the exercise of that sovereign power of government which enables them to control everything that money can buy. To this great question the tariff, transportation, and wages are but incidents, monopolies are subordinate, the social problem contingent, and the moral and intelligent status dependent.

In discussing this question I propose not only to separate bank functions from the Government, as suggested by my friend from Ohio [Mr. Butterworth], but also to separate all Government functions from banks. What does this bill contemplate?

I contend that it contemplates the continuation of the issuing function of the banks, the discount function, the deposit function, and the function of exchange and transmission of money.

There is no war at present upon any of these three functions, but simply upon the issuing of money. This is not a banking function; it is a right that belongs exclusively to the sovereign power of a government.

I say here frankly that the national banking system is the best banking system of any we have ever had, and while I say this I also say that the worst system we have ever had was the wild-cat State banking system.

Now, sir, the great trouble in the discussion of this question has been that gentlemen who urge the continuance of the issuing function of the national banks measure all their advantages and virtues by their comparison with the old rotten State banks. I say that is unfair. No man on this side of the House, that I know of at least, is in favor of the old State banking system. We only oppose at this time, so far as I know, the national banks in their issuing functions.

Now, to consider this question intelligently it becomes necessary for us to ask ourselves, first, what is money? I contend, sir, that money is a creature of law created only as a medium to facilitate the interchange of commodities, and therefore should not be a commodity itself, but only a representative of the value of commodities.

But to do this it must have one essential function or attribute, which can only be imparted to it by the highest power known to man, namely, the sovereign power of the nation; and that is the function of legal tender for the payment of all debts.

And this does not conflict with the rights of States to control contracts between individuals, as suggested by my colleague on the committee from Missouri [Mr. Buckner] for a legal tender, or the power of a legal tender, is simply this: when John owes money to Jake and John makes him a tender of that which the Government has said is a legal tender and Jake refuses to take it, then Jake cannot go into the courts established by authority of law and say that the State must take hold of John and put its hands into his pocket or levy upon his goods and take from him that which will pay the debt in kind. But if I make a contract to barter, trade, or swap one commodity for another, then the interchange must be made in kind; *e. g.*, if I agree to furnish labor for potatoes, when my labor is performed the legal-tender act will not prohibit the man who is to pay me for my labor from making a tender to me in the potatoes agreed upon.

The legal-tender act has nothing to do with it. It is only when I agree to do a certain thing or to sell a certain commodity for money that then I must carry out that contract in good faith, so that, when that money which the Government has established in its sovereign capacity is tendered, then I must either accept that money, or that tender will be a good plea in bar. That is the whole sum and substance of legal tender and its effect.

Gentlemen tell us that we must have money which will pass current in England and the rest of the world. I ask any man here to show me or tell me if he has ever seen the money of the world, whether he has ever seen or ever heard of money that will pass current and is a tender anywhere except within the jurisdiction of the sovereign that has issued it, be he prince, potentate, or fifty million freemen. There is no money of the world. Whenever you go within the border of England or any other nation you settle your balances there, not with money, even if it is your legal-tender eagle or dollar, whether gold or silver. They will not count them; they weigh them. They but take the faith of the Government from the stamp on it, as to its fineness, and in that way they will make their calculation and receive it, not as money, but as commodity, merchandise, or bullion.

Gold is not money; neither is money gold. Money is only that which is so created by law, whether made of gold, silver, nickel, copper, brass, iron, or paper. Gentlemen have a great deal to say about fiat money. Now, I ask you in all sincerity, and I want gentlemen to answer the question if they can, did any of you ever see a dollar of money that was not fiat money? I pause for a reply; and I challenge you to show me a dollar of money that is not fiat money. I care not whether it be made of gold or silver or nickel or copper, or whether it be made of paper. Why, sir, you may take your subsidiary coin, and how much of that has intrinsic value, and how much is fiat? Take the Bland dollar, which is worth in the market some twenty cents more than the trade dollar. One is a legal-tender dollar, while the other has a superabundance of commodity, but no legal tender; and yet it is worth twenty cents less. Take your copper and nickel coin; it does not contain near the commodity value of gold or silver, and yet to the extent that it is legal tender it will buy as much as any other money, and always serves the purpose contemplated within the jurisdiction of the government that utters it. What are your bank bills? Are they money? No. Take the act that has created them, take the bill itself and read it, and you will find that they are promises to pay money, and not money at all. When gentlemen talk about Continental paper money, French *assignats,* and Confederate scrip as repudiated and worthless money, they talk of that which never existed. There never was Continental paper money; there never was Confederate paper money. They were mere promises to pay money. The French *assignats* were never money; they were mere promises to pay land.

Gentlemen talk also of the standard of value; and my friend from Ohio who has just taken his seat said he wanted a standard of value, and that the standard of value he wanted shall be gold or silver, or both, because the value is there in the commodity before it is uttered; and also that that value was based or depended upon the amount of labor or the cost of production. I deny the whole proposition. The cost of labor and the cost of production have nothing to do with the value of any commodity. The question of value rests exclusively upon the matter of supply and demand.

Take an acre of ground on Broadway, New York; cost nothing to create; it's worth millions. Take an acre on a mountain top; cost the same; worth nothing. Build an ocean steamer on the mountain top; it costs more money and labor than to build it at the shipyard, yet it is worthless. Build it where there is a demand or use for it, and it is worth millions. All the gold on the ship was not worth as much to Robinson Crusoe as a needle. There was no demand for gold; there was use for a needle. Therefore, what nonsense it is for any gentleman to attempt to establish the proposition that you can fix a standard of value. The value of all things depends exclusively upon their usefulness. Take it upon your own proposition. Even if the value depends upon the price of production there can be no standard, for the price of production will depend upon the demand and supply. Value is ever shifting. It has no permanence. Specific gravity, distance, bulk, etc., can be fixed, but values are as shifting as the winds, and have no maximum nor minimum.

When, therefore, gentlemen talk of the standard of value they talk of that which cannot exist and which never existed. You may have a unit by which you may measure values, and that is the closest you can possibly come to it; and when you adopt that unit you may make it a dollar, or you may call it a pound, or you may call it a franc, or whatever you will, but it is still the unit established by the Government, and by that unit men may measure the value relatively of one article with another, and that is all the use there is in money so far as the question of value is concerned.

The question of supply and demand as to money is a question of judgment. There is no standard for that. There is nothing that you can fix it by. I contend that the best scale by which you can ascertain it is the price of money, namely, interest.

Money, if you allow the Government to issue it, will not hang for the want of supply, because the Government will be able to issue it in unlimited amounts if necessary; and therefore the question of supply and demand does not apply. Government can control the supply of money, and to a great extent the demand for money. At any rate it may control entirely the supply of money if you only let it exercise that function which it has a right to exercise and not limit it to any specific commodity, such as gold and silver.

I have said this is only a matter of judgment. The only difference between my friends and myself on that proposition is that they want to have the judgment of a part and I want to have the judgment of the whole. I want the judgment of fifty millions of freemen. They want the judgment of directly interested and soulless corporations, responsible to no God for their acts, responsible to no penal code, responsible to nothing but to the extent of their assets in a civil sense; while man, responsible to God, to his neighbor, to his family, penally and civilly, would be a better, a more disinterested judge than these corporations, whose existence and prosperity depend, not as my friend says, on their being able to see that there is a stability in the currency, but, as the experience of ages shows, on their being able to see that there is anything else but a stability in the volume of the currency. In that sense, having the avarice of humanity at least, they control it in their own interest, asking no questions as to what the effect of it will be on the rest of mankind. Therefore I again repeat that the question of volume shall be left to the people. They will be better able to take care of themselves than the banks will be to take care of them. Besides, when the bankers control the volume they keep it hovering between universal bankruptcy and the highest possible interest that can be squeezed out of business, for the lower the volume the higher the interest. Therefore the bankers always keep the volume as close to the brink of bankruptcy as possible, with the margin so small that the slightest flurry brings on a crisis; for, mark you, the banker makes more money with one dollar out at 6 per cent. than he does with two dollars out at 3 per cent.; besides he requires only half the capital, runs less risk, and requires less work. When interest is six cents on one dollar the purchasing power of those six cents is much greater than when the interest is six cents on two dollars.

I know it is often said, "Why, you contend that by the Government putting its fiat under the law upon a piece of paper that will make that paper worth a dollar"; and they tell us, "But you cannot legislate a value out of nothing"; they tell us, "You cannot make that dollar worth a dollar, because it is not issued upon value." Just at this point let me tell you, sir, that you are wrong. Value depends entirely upon utility; everything is valuable only according to its usefulness. Anything that is of no use is of no value; hence if by legislation we can grant a franchise, extend a privilege, create a function, prevent an evil, or establish anything that will do good or be of use, we are by such legislation creating value just to the extent of that usefulness; and here, if you will bear with me, I will illustrate to you the difference between this fiat dollar and that which you call the dollar, the bank note. I here first say that a bank note is never issued. No man can show me a bank note that ever was issued. Banks do not issue money. What do they do? They loan money out. They give their promissory note for the individual's promissory note, always taking care to pay the individual nothing for his promissory note, but demanding of the individual interest for the promissory note of the bank, and the result is there is not a dollar of bank money out to-day, and never was, that is not drawing interest by day and by night, on week days and Sundays, on holidays and work days; and labor has to make up that interest.

How is it with the Government issue? There never was a dollar of Government money put out that was not put out for value received. I want to repeat that, for I wish you to remember it. Governments do not loan money out; governments pay money out, and they pay it for value received.

Will gentlemen tell us that when this Government called its 75,000 boys in blue, and then its 300,000 more, and repeated it from call to call, and paid these soldiers in the greenback dollar, the Government did not get value received? When these men sacrificed their right arms or their legs, shed their blood, laid down their lives, that the nation might live, will gentlemen say that the Government did not get value received? And, if it did, those greenbacks still represent that value.

But, they say, how are you going to redeem it? Sir, if ever there was a holy redemption the redemption of the greenback by the sacrifice of the soldiers of this country was as holy a redemption as any since the advent of the Son of God? Do you ask me how it was redeemed from the hands of the soldier? Why, when that soldier sent his greenback home to his wife and little ones, and when that wife and those little ones ate the bread they bought with it from the baker, that greenback was redeemed in bread. And when the baker paid for his flour that greenback was redeemed again. So when you start money out right, you start it out for value received, and every time it passes from hand to hand it is redeemed. In that very passage it is its own redeemer, and when it comes back to the Government in the shape of taxes or dues it comes to its fountain source, as the rain which rises from the ocean gets back to the spring and trickles down the mountain and waters the valley and again finds its outlet into its mother ocean. So would we have the Government money, not based upon gold, not based upon silver, not based upon any one or two commodities, but by the Government's power of taxation based upon every commodity that the American people can create; based upon the whole wealth of the nation, based upon the entire credit, the honor, the integrity, the patriotism, and the intelligence of the American people; paid out for value, and, not like the bank note, loaned out on interest.

Dietrich C. Smith [Ill.].—I understand the gentleman to say that he wants all the currency of the country to be issued directly by the Government. I would like him to state who is to determine the limits of the amount of currency to be issued?

Mr. Brumm.—The difference between the banks determining the amount of currency and the Government determining the amount of it is that in one instance the banks are made the judge, and in the other fifty millions of freemen are made the judge. Now, if the gentleman wants something more specific——

Mr. Smith.—I do.

Mr. Brumm.—I will state that I believe with my friend from Ohio [Mr. Butterworth] that a postal system of deposits is a healthy one. I believe that by such a system of deposits we could absorb the plethora of money, and by that system the amount of circulation could be gauged, because it would gauge the rate of interest. I do not know but that the introduction of one of the functions of the Bank of England might be a good one in connection with the postal system of deposits. That is, that a commission established by the Government shall, upon due notice to the holders of the certificates of deposits, raise or lower the rates of interest just as money may become plethoric or scarce in the business of the country. The amount of circulation could be regulated in that way, for when money would be scarce the rate of interest could be lowered and men would draw their money from deposit, and when there was a plethora of money the rate of interest could be raised and men would put the money on deposit. In that way you would have an automatic system within the control of the Government by the people and for the people, not by the banks and for the banks. That is but one scheme, and there are others, but I cannot now take the time to state them all.

MR. SMITH.—I understand the gentleman to say that the treasury should be authorized to issue promises to pay for all debts of the Government.

MR. BRUMM.—No, sir; oh, no! I would never have the Government or anyone issue promises to pay, but would have them pay at once.

MR. SMITH.—Issue currency?

MR. BRUMM.—Yes, currency. Issue fiat dollars to pay the debts of the Government under its sovereign power and exclusive jurisdiction over the subject-matter, and not postpone the payment of its honest debts by issuing promises, especially when those promises are burdened with interest.

MR. HARDENBERGH.—Would they not be promises to pay?

MR. BRUMM.—No; they would be the same as coin. Your gold dollar and your silver dollar is not a promise to pay. You cannot go to the Government and ask it to redeem this half dollar [holding one in his hand] or a gold eagle. The Government would tell you that they had nothing to do with that; that you might pay it to the Government for a debt and that would be all. Even then, if it were worn or short in weight, the Government would not receive it for as much in value as it was worth when it was issued. It would not receive it as money at all, but would receive it according to weight as a commodity or bullion for recoinage only, while it will receive its paper dollar for full value at all times.

As my colleague on the Committee on Banking and Currency, the gentleman from Massachusetts [Mr. Crapo], says, the currency of the country should rest upon the prudence as well as upon the power of the Government.

That brings me back again to the original proposition. You must not issue too much money. We understand very well what inflation means, and we do not ask for anything of the kind. But we do ask that you keep the issuing function, even though it be gold, silver, fiat paper money, or Government promises to pay, under the exclusive control of the Government, and let it be regulated by any scheme or plan that will establish a proper bulk or quantity of currency.

MR. SMITH.—What part of the Government is to determine the amount to be issued?

MR. BRUMM.—I said that I would recommend the election of a commission, under control of Congress, or would have it under direct control of Congress. We might by act of Congress give the treasury unlimited power to issue fiat or full legal-tender paper money (which is the same thing) as long as money fetches more than 3 per cent. interest. Whenever it gets down to that point I would have it stop the issue; if it should go up again, then I would have it issue more. But you never need contract currency that is properly issued.

I agree with my friend from Ohio [Mr. Butterworth] that of all the evils of currency that of contraction and expansion is the greatest. The laborer is the last to feel the effects of inflation and the first to feel the effects of contraction. Therefore I would put it where there would be no amount issued that would ever need to be contracted, except by natural results, such as loss and destruction. If the Government keeps within the bounds of wisdom, as it can, and in my judgment will, as soon as the issuing function is forever taken from the banks, it never need contract the currency.

Gentlemen may tell us that during the war it would not have done to have issued an unlimited amount of paper currency. I answer no; but as the Government issued the currency it could draw it back by taxation and thus keep the volume at a healthy point at all times. During the war, when we had an immense army, the Government could do this. In time of peace I grant you the Government cannot do it easily; but in such a time there is no necessity for a superabundance of issue, and therefore of course there is no occasion for absorbing it by taxation. But in time of war the Government can set a limit upon the issue by the exercise of the power of taxation, drawing back the currency and keeping it at all times in a healthy condition.

MR. HARDENBERGH.—How are you going to get that money out, and how are you going to restrict or regulate the issue? Suppose you have an extravagant Congress or commission that issues more money than is required, so that people throughout the country refuse to take it. You then establish a gold basis, a silver basis, and what you call your treasury-note basis. Confidence is gone, and the people suffer.

MR. BRUMM.—No, I propose to establish nothing of the kind. We would get this money out just as the people want it by always paying and receiving for value. When there is a Government issue you cannot get more money out than the Government can receive value for. The amount of money in circulation is thus limited at all times. If after the debt is paid the amount of currency in circulation should not be sufficient, our friends from the South are asking us to educate their people. In the North, too, we have ignoramuses enough that ought to be educated, and I would recommend that the Government issue its fiat money and educate the people, if perchance there should be no other way of getting money in circulation. Internal improvements would be another method. Thus you enable the Government to be master of the situation at all times. Neither would there ever be a lack of confidence, for confidence is only lost when you make a lot of promises in shape of bank notes, etc., that you cannot redeem, whereas if you have cash legal-tender money based on the power and wisdom of the whole nation you have the very essence of confidence itself.

Mr. Hardenbergh.—I would like to ask my friend what volume of currency under his system he would issue? Would he pay every bond and obligation of the United States now out by this fiat money, as he calls it?

Mr. Brumm.—No, sir; not at once, but as fast as they mature and as rapidly as consistent with financial stability. I am unable to state the exact amount which would be proper for the volume of currency; and no other man in the world is able to do it. But I can do so just as well as the banker can. No man can tell beforehand the amount of currency required for a country like ours. Experience as the money is out will settle the question; and nothing else under the sun can.

The gentleman from Massachusetts [Mr. Crapo], my colleague on the committee, remarked in regard to the banks that "the necessities of their creation have not been forgotten." He also speaks of their past "patriotic services." What did the gentleman mean? Did he mean to corroborate my other colleague on the committee [Mr. Hardenbergh], who said that the bank note paid the soldier and carried us through the war? If he did, I deny the proposition. I say that no soldier ever received one dollar of national-bank-note money. I read from Judge Martin:

> There was not one national bank note issued until 1864.

Why, sir, Vicksburg had fallen then; Gettysburg, the turning point of the war, had been won. Our soldiers were marching triumphantly, crushing the shell of the late rebellion. Confidence had been restored; the danger of foreign intervention had passed; and the war was practically over. The battle had been fought and the victory won. Then these national banks came in and said: "Now we want you to let us control the currency."

MR. HARDENBERGH.—The Government forced them to do it.

MR. BRUMM.—The Government did not force them to do it. Wall street came here to Congress. In the language of the old commoner, Thad. Stevens, "a wail came up from the caverns of Wall street," and insisted upon an amendment in the Senate to the House bill reported by him as chairman of the Committee on Ways and Means, putting in a clause that repudiated the greenback and became the basis of the national-bank system. It was done at the bidding of Wall street. Yet gentlemen tell us that the banks were forced to take control of the currency. The Government did say to the State banks, "we will tax you 10 per cent. on your circulation"; but did that force anybody to establish national banks?

MR. HARDENBERGH.—Certainly it did.

MR. BRUMM.—No; it simply got rid of the wild-cat system of bank notes.

MR. HARDENBERGH.—Was not the primal evidence that Salmon P. Chase "wiped out" the State banks by putting the tax of 10 per cent. on their circulation and forcing the national banks to take bonds whether they wanted to do so or not?

MR. BRUMM.—I do not care what the primal idea of Mr. Chase or any other man was. The fact is the Government issued these treasury notes. He made the bankers receive these treasury notes; he made them receive the first $60,000,000 for debts, although it had not been put in the original act, but was rather left to his discretion.

MR. CRAPO.—My colleague on the committee seems to have forgotten that part of the history of the country when the Government had a large amount of 7.30 bonds[1] and when the question of funding the public debt was an intricate and doubtful one, and when the banks did come forward and aid the Government in the funding process, converting the 7.30 bonds into those of a lower rate of interest.

[1] Really notes bearing interest at 7.30 per cent., and payable in three years, which, by an act passed shortly after their issue, were made convertible into "five-twenty" bonds, that is, bonds payable after five years at the option of the Government, and peremptorily redeemable in twenty years. The "five-twenty" bonds bore six per cent. interest. [See Chapter IX.]

Mr. Brumm.—Yes, they did come and refund the debt; that is, they so refunded it that, instead of the Government owing the debt to the bondholders, to the contractors, and to the soldiers whose pay was far in arrears, they made it over to the bankers at 40 cents on the dollar. They came and helped to refund the debt, which was the cause of the crisis of 1873. They did come and aided the Government to do that which brought on the greatest calamity this nation ever had save alone the last rebellion. They did come and make the Government refund this debt by contracting the currency so rapidly that labor lay prostrate, and men, women, and children were starving throughout the length and breadth of the land.

While on this point, Mr. Speaker, let me say that gentlemen here are fond of throwing into the teeth of the "Greenbackers" the fact that we prophesied the Government never could resume specie payment under your refunding system. I insist that we were right when we said that, for, sir, you have not resumed to-day. Under your original refunding act and resumption policy you changed your policy. You were going to cut down every dollar of greenbacks. You had demonetized silver, and, when the greenback prophecy was proved to be only too true, you changed your policy and you remonetized silver, stopped the destruction of the greenback and made it a full legal tender except for the payment of the public debt.

What is the result to-day? You boast of resumption. I deny it. You have not resumption, and especially of specie payment on demand for national bank notes. To resume is to get back to where you started. This you have not done. You have a new idea of redeeming the national bank note by a redeemer for which we on this side of the House are denounced.[1]

After you call in the entire $350,000,000 bank notes and redeeem them in greenbacks, you may resume by taking a fixed sum, not less than $50, pay the expense, and run the risk of getting it to and from New York City, and then put it in a little bit of a hole in that city and have it redeemed. That is what you gentlemen boast of as your resumption policy.

Now, my colleague, the chairman of the Committee on Banking and Currency, says that banks are not large moneyed monopolies. For the purpose of showing the power of the national banks, I read a small extract from the secretary's report of the proceedings of the National Bankers' Association, held at Saratoga in 1879.

[1] Judge Brumm acted with the majority of the Democrats on financial questions. He was a protectionist, however, on the tariff question.

Bank managers are the most apathetic business people that I have ever come in contact with; an earthquake will hardly induce them to move out of their easy-chairs. They need not be suppliants. They want justice and not favors. Did they but realize their strength, and, acting together, exert it as do other great interests, they would have to ask but once, and any proper request would be granted. The banks represent the entire commerce of the country, the mining, the iron, the manufacturing, the agricultural, even the whisky and tobacco interests are dependent upon and are tributary to the banks, and the banks in turn to them. Suppose banks and bankers should stop discounting for any one of these interests for thirty or forty days; nay, suppose the banks should cease making discounts to all of these interests at the same time, would not chaos come again? The movable capital of the entire commercial public of the country is in the banks.

There are over 6,000 banks and bankers in the United States, wielding of capital and deposits over $3,000,000,000. They have only to move along the lines and retire from business and let the windy demagogues supply their place with money and credits, if they can. They will soon be told by the farmers that they want something besides words for their wheat, and so also will the manufacturers and other producers for their productions. Nothing is so timid as capital, nothing so easily scared as one million, unless it be two millions.

Here is an acknowledgment that two of the most dangerous elements to republican institutions are incident to your banks, namely, unlimited power and unmitigated cowardice.

Now, Mr. Speaker, I want to ask our national bank friends what redeeming feature has the national bank note that the greenback note has not? What advantage to the people of the country, to the business interests of the country, has the national bank note that the national treasury legal-tender note does not possess?

Do you say that it is current all over the Union? I say amen; but so is the greenback. Do you say it has the confidence of the people? I say amen, for that confidence is based on the people themselves, that confidence is based on the Government, and on its redeemer and savior, the greenback dollar. Do you say it will surely be redeemed? I again say amen; it will be redeemed, but by the greenback dollar.

And now let me ask another question. Let me ask the gentleman what advantage has the greenback that the national bank note has not got? We claim that it has a number of advantages that your national bank note has not got. In the first place, it saves the interest on the bond upon which the bank note is based, whatever that may be, great or small. In the second place, it saves the discount paid the broker or the banker; I have illustrated that heretofore; that is, the national bank note goes out for interest and interest must be paid; hence the

Government pays interest first on the bond, then the man who receives the discount pays interest on the bill, both of which are wiped out the moment you allow the Government to issue this money in the first instance. Then, sir, it does not bridge the chasm between the creditor and the debtor, as has been said by both my colleagues on the committee, the gentleman from Massachusetts [Mr. Crapo] and the gentleman from Illinois [Mr. Smith]. The national bank note does not bridge the chasm; it widens the chasm; because it makes the holder of the note pay double interest. It leaves the volume to the people and prevents the concentration of power in the hands of the few. I wish I had time to illustrate the damning and blighting effect of this concentration of power by the moneyed men of the country in the hands of perhaps a few dozen men practically in the city of New York. Any system of issuing banks fosters this centralization of power.

Again, there is a centralization of power in this that, whenever you take from the Government at large any of its functions, any of its rights, and give them to a portion of that Government, you take it from the aggregate and give it to a few, and they in their selfishness would always use it and utilize it to their own interest. Functions that are sovereign should be held sacred by the Government, and not delegated to the few under any circumstances. You change it from an interest-bearing to a non-interest-bearing debt; and, let me ask gentlemen who are so solicitous about the redemption of the greenback, is it not easier to redeem a debt, even if it is to be redeemed in kind, is it not easier to redeem a debt bearing no interest than it is to redeem a debt bearing interest? If you wipe out the interest of the bonds, cut them up into small denominations, make them legal tenders and serve the purposes of money; when the time comes for redemption the Government will be better able to redeem them if you do not charge interest than it will be if you compel it to pay interest for twenty-five or one hundred years.

Again, when you liquidate the Government debt by the issue of greenbacks you take the Government out of the money market. To-day the Government is one of the greatest if not the greatest competitor in the money market for loans. The Government is practically a bidder against any man who wants to borrow money. The Government is a borrower of money under a national-bank system and a competitor in the business market for the money of the country, whereas it ought to stand back and be a helpmeet, rather than to draw that money.

There will be no currency suspension as there was of the

national banks in 1873. The national currency will redeem the bonds. Do gentlemen ask me, do I want to repudiate? I say no; I say I want the debt paid, dollar for dollar, according to the contract; coin, since it says so; gold, if the Government makes it so; blood, if the necessity requires it. I want it paid according to the contract. But I say that the national treasury note will pay this bond without repudiating a dollar or a penny.

Senator Sherman said that some six hundred millions of the national debt was redeemed and paid in the national treasury note; not because the Government said it must be, but because the holder of the bond said: "I do not want your gold and silver; I would rather take the national treasury note, and let the Government take of its surplus at any time and call in so much of the debt as there is surplus." There will scarcely be one man that will say, "I want gold or silver." If they do say so, the Treasurer can easily tell them to go back up their cart and take the silver that is now in the treasury; and, as they take it out, it will come back in the twinkling of an eye, and then it can say, in the language of the barber, " 'Next;' back up your cart and we will give you your silver again"; and it can keep this up till the national debt is paid. I would not pay it off so quickly as to bring on any calamity. There must be wisdom as well as honesty, and the Government will act in a truly wise and judicious manner if you only give it a chance.

There will be no currency suspension. The Government need never be troubled about suspending specie payments under that system. The only reason that specie payments are in danger today is because under your banking system you allow the banks of the country districts to deposit their money in the city banks. They deposit all their surplus and the banks in the city loan it to stock speculators and gamblers. In the country they would rather put it out on call loans at 3 per cent. than on a permanent loan at 6 or 7, because their deposits are on call. In the city they keep it in a spasmodic condition, loaning it constantly to stock-jobbers and speculators, and hence, when in 1873 stocks fell and could not be sold, a demand was made suddenly upon the banks for this money, and then it was that banks suspended not only specie payments, and honoring their own notes, but closed their doors, and refused to honor the drafts and checks of their depositors; then it was that they suspended all payments, and the result was the crisis of 1873.

And then it was that the Government was compelled to bridge over the chasm by loaning these very banks $26,000,000 of legal-tender notes. Therefore, not only during the war did you rely upon your treasury notes, but in time of profound peace, in times of crises you have always called upon your savior to come to your relief in all emergencies.

But, again, the most important element of the system is in the fact that it will prevent the contraction and expansion of the currency. It will keep it on a permanent basis, not subject to the double fluctuations of gold and silver as commodities, and as coin, nor to the whim, caprice, and avarice of biased individuals or interested corporations. It will be on a permanent basis, for the money will never be issued beyond the amount that is wanted, and will be contracted only in a wholesome degree. Now, as to the merits of this bill and of the several amendments, I would ask what do gentlemen really expect to accomplish by the passage of this bill?

You come down now to the proposition that you must either have a perpetual national debt or the days of the national banks are numbered. Either one or the other of these horns of the dilemma you must take. You must either say that you want to mortgage our children and their prosperity indefinitely or that national banks must give up their issue. Now, since the days of the issuing function of national banks are numbered, and since you do not propose any substitute for it, let me ask if we had not better begin now to let them down easy, to let them down gradually? You say they have lived for nineteen years and that you want them to have twenty years more of existence. If you give that to them, then at the end of that time you must either give them twenty years more or else let the bottom drop out all of a sudden.

Now, I do not want anything of the kind. I am more generous toward the national banks than that. I want them to start now and prepare for the day of judgment. The time is at hand, and their days are numbered. I only ask them to prepare now, that they may meet their judgment when it comes upon them, and not inflict another crisis upon this country like that which they have heretofore inflicted.

I have submitted a compromise measure which does all that is contemplated by the Crapo bill except that it provides for the contingency of a crisis, in this, that as the national-bank notes are wiped out we shall substitute therefor the treasury notes—legal-tenders—just as they are to-day. Besides, this substitute fixes twelve months as the time for the final payment or liquidation of those national-bank notes that are lost or destroyed.

Gentlemen talk about giving banks, the right to issue money

because the Government cannot do it. How can bankers do it? To what extent can they do it? To the full extent of the national debt, less 10 per cent. Now, gentlemen, if you are honest in claiming that the Government should not issue money, but that creatures of the Government should issue it, I ask why do you not offer a proposition something like this, that any individual may go to the Secretary of the Treasury with a bond of not less than $100, and not exceeding, I would say, $20,000, and receive not bank notes, but individual notes, if you please? What objection is there to allowing an individual the same privilege which you allow to a corporation? What is the difference?

John Smith, a business man in my county, has $20,000. He wants to go into manufacturing business. He finds that it will take $18,000 to build his factory. He says: "Here is a banking corporation with $25,000 capital that can go to the United States Treasury and by depositing bonds get money for them to the full amount of the bonds, less 10 per cent., and shave the people with it. Why should I not do the same thing? I will go to the Secretary of the Treasury, and say to him: 'Here are $20,000 of Government bonds; give me $18,000 in notes.' I will take these notes home—not for the purpose of shaving my neighbors, not to draw sweat and blood from them by usury. I will use them in erecting my factory, in giving employment to my neighbors, in building up the industries of the country. I will not loan out this money to draw the blood from the man who wants to build a factory. I will build the factory myself. I only ask the Government to do for me what it is doing for the national banks." He says to the Secretary of the Treasury: "Give me money upon the same terms on which you give it to this soulless corporation." The Secretary says: "No, no; you are a creature of God; you are a being of flesh and bone and blood; a responsible creature; I cannot give you this money. Besides, you want this money to use it as a blessing to your neighbors; that is against our policy."

What does John Smith do? He goes home and gets several of his neighbors to join with him. Then say we will apply to the Secretary of the Treasury; and it will no longer be the application of John Smith; it will be the First National Bank of Hookstown. They go to the Secretary of the Treasury, and he says: "Oh, I see; you are not here as a responsible creature, a creature of God—a mortal man, with soul immortal; you are an immortal creature without a soul. Deposit your $25,000 of bonds, and I will give you $22,500 in money. You may then go home—not to erect factories, not to give employment to your neighbors, not to build railroads and other improvements, but to shave your fellow-citizens, to draw from them their life-blood.

Mr. Crapo.—Let me ask my colleague whether the greenback is a promise to pay?

Mr. Brumm.—The greenback on its face is a promise to pay. It is not the money I want, but it comes nearest to what I want and what I can get under the present circumstances. On its face it is a promise to pay, but by the act creating it it does not promise to pay. Under the act which created it, it is provided that it shall be receivable in payment of dues, and may be convertible into bonds. The bankers of Wall street are those who put this character upon the greenbacks. Under the act creating the greenback it is not redeemable either in gold or silver.

George C. Hazelton [Wis.].—Has not the Supreme Court decided that you can issue nothing except a promise to pay in gold or silver dollars, and that there is no such idea as a fiat dollar, or a paper dollar, under our Government? If so, how are you to get around it?

Mr. Brumm.—There never can be a dollar that is not a fiat dollar.

Mr. Hazelton.—Have they not so decided?

Mr. Brumm.—The Supreme Court have gone so far as to say that the Government treasury note is a legal tender, first; and here let me say that the first money that the Government issued or created was a paper dollar—a promise to pay, a treasury note. It issued treasury notes before it ever issued coin of any kind, or before it ever coined a silver dollar, or a gold dollar, or a copper coin. The next money coined was copper; the next was silver, and the last was that gold of which my friend from Missouri talks so much. The men who framed the Constitution knew what they intended to do, and they passed an act establishing a Government national bank, with a right to issue legal tenders to the Government, I grant you, not to individuals; and they then issued treasury notes—the very men who sat in the constitutional convention. Now, the Supreme Court has gone further; Chief Justice Chase deciding that our greenback note is a legal tender for every debt, public and private, except those reserved in the act.

The Supreme Court, lacking two of being full, when it was filled went further, went beyond and up to that point that my friend, Judge Buckner, is so much afraid of, that is, that they are legal tender for the payment of antecedent debts. We do not ask you to go that far. We are willing to stand by the first decision of the court. We do not ask you to go as far as Judge Strong went when he rendered the opinion of the court. We only ask you to make your notes legal tender, not to the Government alone, but to the individual as well.

Mr. Hazelton.—Suppose you had a piece of paper and the Government said "this is a dollar," would that be good money under your construction?

Mr. Brumm.—Yes, sir.

Mr. Hazelton.—That is all I want to know. The Supreme Court, in the legal-tender cases, decided that it would not be money.

Mr. Brumm.—I beg the gentleman's pardon; that question was not presented at that time. I say the Government has a right to make this a dollar, and it will be a dollar, if the Government so declares, regardless of its intrinsic value.

Mr. Hazelton.—Well, now, again on that same point, if the Government says this seat is a dollar, according to that construction it will be a dollar, won't it?

Mr. Brumm.—It would be a dollar, so far as it goes, but it could not be utilized.

Mr. Hazelton.—The Constitution only mentions gold and silver. It does not mention seats or old boots.

Mr. Brumm.—I am aware of that; nor shad. [Laughter.] The gentleman from Ohio [Mr. Butterworth] said he wants a dollar that is an honest dollar, that has a hundred cents to the dollar. Will the gentleman, or will anybody else, a friend of his, show me a dollar that has not a hundred cents? Did you ever see any? Did you ever know a dollar that had not a hundred cents in it and was not worth a dollar? When I ask you what is a dollar, what do you tell me? If you ask me, I say it is a hundred cents, or a unit fixed by the Government by which you may measure value. That is all you can say. You may make this dollar of gold, or part gold, and can put a certain kind and quantity of gold in it. And so you may of silver, of nickel, of copper, or of paper. That is all there is in that. The constitutional right of the Government is to coin money and regulate the value thereof, and to save itself, and to do all that is necessary and incident to the exercise of any sovereign power.

Now, then, as to seats and old boots, and shad. I have heard that thing spoken of before. They say, suppose you take a block of wood, and the Government puts its stamp on it and says, "This is a shad," and you throw it into the Potomac and a fisherman down the river fishes it up, and, when he looks, he reads, "by the authority of the United States this is a shad";

then says "but I do not believe anything of the kind; I would not want to eat it, and, of course, it is not a shad."

Let me illustrate. These questions are asked by the money changers, just as the tempter asked Jesus Christ when he said, "To whom shall we pay tribute?" Christ said, "Show me your token, your tribute money." The tempter showed him a token, a penny token, I believe. Christ said, "Whose superscription is that?" The tempter said, "Cæsar's superscription." Christ said, "Render unto Cæsar that which is Cæsar's and unto God that which is God's." And so I say to my friend, when you talk of the coining of money, it is a function of Cæsar, of the Government; therefore render unto that Government, that Cæsar, that which is Cæsar's. When you talk of making shad, that is a function of the Deity, and therefore render unto God that which is God's. When you talk of seats, boots, etc., they are functions of individuals; therefore render to the carpenter and shoemaker their functions. Do not attempt to rob God Almighty and the poor carpenter and shoemaker of their proper functions, simply for the purpose of justifying your attempt at robbing the Government of one of its most sacred functions.

The only reason that I can imagine why bankers oppose such a proposition as mine is that they are determined to have either national-bank notes or force us back into the old wild-cat State-bank notes, and for that reason will not allow us to issue any more legal-tender treasury notes. Yet I submit that unless some substitute be provided we cannot escape a contraction of the currency, which must necessarily bring about another crisis very soon; hence the only question is, shall that substitute be the pure legal-tender greenback or shall it be the thirty-eight species of State-bank vermin to poison our issue, or shall it be the Democratic mongrel treasury note, not a legal tender, as contemplated by the Bland-Buckner substitutes? And here let me say that I would rather vote for the Crapo bill a thousand times than vote for this Democratic wolf in sheep's clothing. Though the Crapo bill makes us bear the ills we have, the Buckner-Bland frauds drive us to others we know not of. By the Crapo bill we are at a stand-still; by the others we drift back to the State wild-cat system, and rivet it with multiplied horrors more firmly than ever upon our body-politic. Sir, you issue treasury notes now not a legal tender; you deny by implication the right of the Government to issue a full legal tender in time of peace; and thus you force the final withdrawal of the greenback, and substitute for it your half-breed apology. Then you throw yourself, soul and body, into the clutches of bankers, money-changers, and monopolists, and allow them to repudiate your issue by refusing to receive them in payment of commercial paper or any other debt, and by declaring that they are not current funds force them below par. And thus you make them repugnant to the people, and create a clamor against any national issue of money; and when the people are in that temper we will again fall an easy prey to the demands of the money-sharks for the restoration of State banks. Thus you cheat the people by making them believe that you are Simon Pure Greenbackers, and by diverting their attention from the true doctrine you become our most dangerous enemies.

In fighting a righteous cause it is an easy thing to subdue an open enemy, for then we can give blow for blow, but it is hard to fight guerilla skulkers and dodgers who steal into our camp under the guise of friendship and attempt to cut the legal-tender heart out of us; and then because we will not tamely submit to their butchery, and allow them to sail under false colors, they denounce us and say they are better Greenbackers than we are, and by thus robbing the livery of Greenbackism to serve the Democracy they put us on the defensive, and compel us to combat all the ridiculous heresies preached by these hypocrites.

Gold, silver, bank notes, and Democratic mongrels may do for financial dress parade, but in the heat and brunt of battle, and in every crisis, you must resort to the nation's credit. The bankers always urge the necessity of their assistance in time of peace and prosperity, but leave the nation to its fate in time of war. "A friend in need is a friend indeed." The money that could bear the terrible strain of the rebellion, spurned, mutilated, and crushed as it was by Wall Street, will always be strong enough to resist every shock or crisis in peace. Even now they are the support of the national-bank note. Wall Street and my friend Butterworth agree that during the war legal tenders were constitutional, that is, the legal-tender clause is only a war measure. But why? Because then Wall Street & Co. shrank and, coward-like, refused their aid. When this nation was struck by the leprosy of rebellion, we were too loathsome to be treated by these doctors of finance. When England and our other very friendly neighbors across the pond left us to our fate, and joined the enemy, these professors of monetary *materia medica* were the first to desert from our camp with their physic. When the martyred Lincoln called for seventy-five thousand men and then for three hundred thousand more, the youth and bloom of our country promptly responded with the best blood of our land. But when he called for the money to pay them to keep their wives and little ones from starving at home these currency scientists could make no sacrifice for such a holy cause. When defeat followed disaster foreign intervention was threatened, our armies driven back, our soldiers slaughtered by the thousands, and the darkest cloud of rebellion hung over us, there was no succor from Wall Street. When the loyal heart was bursting with anguish, its gaunt arm extended, begging for help, the mighty North with all its powers and resources lying prostrate at the feet of Wall Street, naked, hungry, sick, and sore, these frozen blood physicians refused all nourishment, not even encouragement or honest medical advice. They had nothing to offer but second-hand porous-plasters in shape of wild-cat bank bills. No sooner did the patient convalesce under the nourishment of the greenback when this ungrateful and unblushing quack again intrudes himself upon our forgetful and forgiving nation, and acknowledges that, while we are sick, weak, and in great distress, the best thing to strengthen and cure us is that greenback which produced a good and healthy circulation, and that during the war we were right in using the national legal-tender panacea, for then it seemed to agree with our constitution, and really saved our life and made us the greatest nation of the earth. But now that we are so strong and vigorous they don't think that our constitution will bear any more of this national legal-tender nourishment, that is, it is not good to be too healthy; our constitution requires that in time of peace we should have some financial poison to stagnate our circulation. Then you know we will be so fashionable, and like our royal English neighbors we can get an occasional financial fit or spasm, and sometimes faint away and get downright sick. Then these financial mountebanks will take the best care of us, for they are so well posted in the anatomy of finance, and the physiology of political economy, that they alone are fit to take charge of our system, especially our circulation, as they still believe in the old practice of phlebotomy, and therefore they will draw our blood until our commercial heart almost ceases to beat, when they must again resort to the greenback nourishment, even in time of peace, as they did during the financial plague of 1873.

Joseph H. Burrows [Mo.], a "Greenbacker," opposed the bill. His conclusion was as follows:

Gentlemen who profess to be anti-monopolists, who can see the evils of railway monopoly, of gas monopoly, of water monopoly, of shipping or manufacturing monopolies, shut their eyes at the command of the banker who exacts tribute from them under guise of doing them the favor to shave their notes or discount their paper credit, and obediently refuse to see the size or iniquitous character of the master monopoly of them all, the parent monopoly of all the rest, that of the money or currency monopoly of these national banks.

How dare you pass this bill? When its indefensible provisions, its ridiculous subserviency to the power of the "reserve fund" and the "other undivided profits" are exposed before your constituents, as they surely will be; when the appeal is taken from your action here to the people whom you by this bill propose to keep enslaved to the money-kings; when the faithful Greenbackers go to the hustings to expose to the people the full extent of this crime against their rights and best interests, as we surely will do; when, finally, want, oppression, monopoly, and enlightened public opinion combine to bring to justice or to scourge with stripes the men who chose to obey the money-kings rather than the people, you who vote for this bill will be praying for the mountains to fall on you and the waves of a political oblivion to hide you forever.

Upon no ground can the passage of this bill be defended with success. For no valid reason can a vote be asked for it.

It is one of the most wicked, defenseless, inexcusable, flagrant cases of a popular swindle that ever came before Congress, not excepting the land-grant, Crédit Mobilier, granite contract, river and harbor, whisky bill, or other swindles that have disgraced the Congressional legislation of the past or threaten it at the present moment. Here and now gentlemen must make their record and choose their fate. They know whether they will serve the people, who are opposed to this bill and to the national banking system, or whether they will obey the commands of the Shylock Radicals and Bourbon Democrats who conspire to pass this measure. The crisis has come, and the old dodge of Bourbons and Radicals talking against the national-bank swindle in their districts to get votes and voting with the political harlots who think they conceal their acts from their distant constituents can be played no longer with any hope of success.

In conclusion, I ask, in all candor and seriousness, why should we, how can we, and how dare we pass such a bill as this? Let the bank charters expire. Banking will not cease.

Over two-thirds of the banks and banking of the country is already done without these bank charters. Let the charters expire, and put all the banks on a level. Let the charters expire, and put the Government again in sole and exclusive possession of its rights. Let the charters expire, and put the vast revenue accumulations in the bank vaults into trade, commerce, business, and productive enterprises. Let the charters expire, and behold "the best banking system the world ever saw" thereby superseded by the best currency and most equitable financial system that man has ever devised. Let the charters expire, and forbid with the spirit of Andrew Jackson the rechartering of banks by the Government or by any authority which shall claim the right to empower them to issue currency! Let the charters expire, and the end of monopoly will be in full view! Let the charters expire, and let the people live freed from the national-bank incubus that now assumes to be their master.

Could we have a financial Peter the Hermit to thunder over the land his anathemas, and to preach a new crusade against these banks, his cry at this moment would be: The national banks must go! Let the charters expire!

Mr. Hardenbergh replied to the "Greenbackers."

Seven years ago I took my seat and with uplifted hand swore to support the Constitution of the United States and the laws made in accordance therewith. Since then my constituents have seen proper to retain me in the position I have occupied; and I come to it with a spirit to discharge simply what I believe to be its duties as a matter of right to my people, as well as in a spirit of justice and fairness to all, and in opposition to that miserable, wretched spirit of communism and socialism now extending itself throughout the land, which threatens capital in whatever shape or whatever amount or however it be invested with the most dire and dreadful consequences.

Why, sir, it was but two days ago, in my morning mail, came a letter signed by generous-hearted Peter Cooper, of New York, a man ninety-two years of age, a man who has been known, honored, and trusted by the American people; whose whole life has been one of benevolence, piety, and justice, but who in his declining years, when the shadows of the next world are gathering thick around him, and when his mind cannot be in the course of nature as clear and bright and strong as it was, indorses doctrines the most unwise in our financial history.

Enclosed with the letter was a pamphlet. Read it, representatives of the people, and you will see that, instead of strikes against labor, suggestions are made to men to save three months of their wages to buy Gatling-guns and, with three months of provisions, to crush out monopolies of whatever kind. And this, Mr. Speaker, in a representative government of the American people. Crush where you can monopolied power, but let it be done by proper process of law. Why, sir, what can there be behind all this crusade upon the national banks? Men are tender in their utterances about it as if they were afraid to speak their minds. I believe in educating the people and elevating them to a full knowledge of these great questions rather than pander to sentiments born of hasty and unreasoning prejudice. [Applause.] I have been advised by letters, time and often, to be careful of my public political aspirations as to what I may say upon the national banking system lest it may thwart them all. Sir, I will accept all the responsibility and will in face of all such opposition stand by what I conceive to be the principles of justice and right. [Applause.]

Now, sir, I have thought that in this war which has been waged against this national banking system there were other interests behind it. Can you conceive that a system that has been acceptable for twenty years to the American people should all of a sudden, within the last six months, especially since Congress has been in session, be found so imperfect that we have been called upon by a pressing public demand not only to denounce, but to degrade and crush it, and to refuse to extend their charters, merely because the system is in the interest of monopoly? There must be something else behind all this. The movement is not an honest one. It may be the tariff; it may be railroad monopolies; but there is something behind it. It is not a spontaneous movement. It has not the sanction of the American people, and never can and never will have this sanction.

You and I have been in our brief lifetime witnesses of great events in American history. We have seen how the swelling tide of public opinion has risen and surged from one end of the Republic to the other. We remember the days of Know-nothingism, when a man was compelled to announce where his great-grandfather was born, and when the tattered remnants of a political piety were flaunted upon the cross of an insulted Saviour. That was considered then as American patriotism, but buried and damned to-day and forever, as it will be by any republic on earth which seeks to create distinctions between its citizens or refuses to extend to the humblest citizen the broad shield of its common protection.

What next? Then came the mighty exigencies of war. What carried us through that war? It was not the greenbacks. My friend from Pennsylvania [Mr. Brumm] announces the greenback as the redeemer, the great redeemer of his country. Why, sir, the redeemer that I acknowledge is always at par, and can save you under any circumstances; but the redeemer of my friend rose and fell in its redemption power, and you never can tell whether you are saved or lost. [Laughter.]

A national bank is not a monopoly. By a law that was passed some few years ago the national banking act was made general; any seven citizens accumulating a capital of $50,000 could organize a national bank. All the monopoly features of it were taken away.

Capital is timid; it does not dare to defy public opinion; it must do what is right; it must conform to the action of Congress. The national banks must obey the national banking law. They must keep their reserves as required by law; they must pay their taxes.

Now, gentlemen, take one course of the two; refuse to extend these charters and divide this reserve, force contraction within one year of $128,000,000, tell the people you have done it, and, when hungry mouths and vacant hands come to you and ask you why, tell them behind it there is some railroad monopoly scare that forced you to make a war on the national banks.

No, gentlemen, you have high, you have awful, responsible duties to discharge. Do it not in fear of communism, not in fear of socialism, but do it as the representatives of Christian America which God gave to the nation for the salvation of a world. Then we shall agree in harmony in our actions here. Then we may go forth to the people feeling our duties are discharged, and it will be "a grander sight than fleets of mightiest admirals seen beneath the lifted clouds of battle; grander by far than the serried tramp of armed men marching by tens of thousands to the music of an unjust glory." [Applause.]

The bill was passed on May 19 by a vote of 125 to 67. After an extended discussion in the Senate it was passed with amendments on June 22 by a vote of 34 to 13. A joint conference was held, and an agreement reached, which was ratified by both Chambers on July 11. President Arthur approved the bill on July 18, 1882.

CHAPTER XII

Gold or Greenbacks?

[Payment of Bond Interest]

Debate in the House: in Favor of Gold, James G. Blaine [Me.]; in Favor of Greenbacks, Gen. Benjamin F. Butler [Mass.].

NEXT to reconstruction the problem of the currency was most discussed during Johnson's Administration. On this question a new alignment of Congress formed, in which the old party divisions of Republican and Democrat, Administration and Opposition, were broken. On the one side were those who supported national banks, insisted on payment in coin of interest on all Government bonds, and wished to retire treasury notes ("greenbacks") from circulation; on the other were those who wished to make treasury notes the main element of the currency, and to pay these as interest upon those bonds which did not specifically call for such payment in coin.

Men who had been bitter opponents upon reconstruction, such as Representatives Thaddeus Stevens [Pa.] and Thomas E. Noell [Mo.], joined together to uphold "greenback" currency. Outside of Congress ex-Senator George H. Pendleton [O.], and inside of it General Benjamin F. Butler [Mass.], a new Representative, were the leaders in opposition to the banking interests. James G. Blaine [Me.] was the protagonist of the bank supporters in the House.

Blaine and Butler met on November 26, 1867, in a culminating debate on the question of the kind of money to be paid as interest on Government bonds.

James G. Blaine

Payment of Bond Interest—In Gold or "Greenbacks"?

House of Representatives, November 26, 1867.

Mr. Blaine.—Within the past few months, Mr. Chairman, some erroneous and mischievous views have been put forward in regard to the nature of the public obligation imposed by the debt of the United States. Without stopping to notice the lesser lights of the new doctrine, and not caring to analyze the various forms of repudiation suggested from irresponsible sources throughout the country, I propose to review, as briefly as may be, the position contemporaneously assumed by two able and distinguished gentlemen—the one from the West, the other from the East—the one the late candidate of the Democratic party for the Vice-Presidency—(George Pendleton, of Ohio)—the other a prominent member of this House from one of the strongest Republican districts of the State of Massachusetts [Mr. Butler].

The position of these gentlemen I understand to be simply this: *that the principal of the United States bonds, known as the five-twenties, may be fairly and legally paid in paper currency by the Government after the expiration of five years from the date of issue.*

A brief review of the origin of the five-twenty bonds will demonstrate, I think, that this position is in contravention of the honor and good faith of the national Government; that it is hostile to the spirit and the letter of the law; that it contemptuously ignores the common understanding between borrower and lender at the time the loan was negotiated; and that finally, even if such mode of payment were honorable and practicable, it would prove disastrous to the financial interests of the Government and the general prosperity of the country.

The issue of the five-twenty bonds was originally authorized by the act of February 25, 1862, which provided for the large amount of $500,000,000. It was this series which was sold so successfully by Jay Cooke & Co. in 1863, and of which so great a proportion was subsequently purchased by foreign capitalists. It will be borne in mind that up to that time in all the loan bills passed by Congress not one word had ever been said in regard to gold payment either of bond or coupon; and yet it will be equally borne in mind that gold payment, both of the principal and interest of the public debt, had been the invariable rule from the foundation of the Government. No instance to the contrary can be found in our history. In the pithy language of

Nathaniel Macon, "our Government was a hard-money Government, founded by hard-money men, and its debts were hard-money debts."

And it will be still further borne in mind that when the bill authorizing the original issue of five-twenties was under discussion in Congress no man of any party, either in the Senate or the House, ever intimated that those bonds were to be paid in anything else than gold or silver. The issue of legal-tender notes of contemporaneous origin was regarded as a temporary expedient, forced upon us by the cruel necessities and demands of war, and it was universally conceded that the specie basis was to be resumed long before the bonds should mature for payment. And in order that the public creditor might have the amplest assurance *of the payment of both principal and interest in coin* it was specially enacted that all duties on imports should be paid in coin, and the amount thus raised was distinctly pledged, not only to the payment of the interest in coin, but to the formation of a sinking fund for the ultimate redemption of the principal in coin. This provision is so important that I quoted entire. After providing that the duties shall be paid in coin, the act devotes that coin to the following purposes:

"First. To the payment in coin of the interest on the bonds of the United States.

"Second. To the purchase or payment of one per cent. of the entire debt of the United States, to be made within each fiscal year after the 1st day of July, 1862, which is to be set apart as a sinking fund, and the interest of which shall be in like manner applied to the purchase or payment of the public debt, as the Secretary of the Treasury shall from time to time direct.

"Third. The residue thereof shall be paid into the Treasury of the United States."

Considerable carping and criticism have been expended on the second clause of this provision, mainly by those who seem desirous of wresting and distorting its plain and obvious meaning. Brushing aside all fine-spun construction and cunning fallacy, it is quite manifest that the sinking fund herein authorized was primarily to be formed from gold, and that it was only to be invested and reinvested in securities whose interest was equally pledged and guaranteed in gold; that this process was not to be confined to any specific number of years, but was limited only by the amount and the duration of the debt which was ultimately to be redeemed by the sinking fund thus constituted. The sinking fund was thus to receive an annual increment *in gold* amounting to the one-hundredth part of the entire debt of the Government; and this increment was to be invested only in securities which would yield *gold* interest for the further increment of the fund. It would be difficult to conceive how the language of an enactment could more distinctly recognize and provide for the ultimate coin payment of the entire bonded debt of the nation. And, instead of the Government having the right at this late day to change its gold obligation into one of paper, it seems to me that the public creditors could with far more consistency allege that the Government had not fully kept its faith with them in failing, as it has, to provide the sinking fund which was thus guaranteed at the outset as one of the special securities of the loan.

But we do not rest merely on the after construction of a statute to prove that the principal of the five-twenties is payable in coin. The declarations in Congress at the time the measure was under consideration were numerous, direct, and specific. Indeed, no other possible mode of payment was even hinted at, and Mr. Stevens, as chairman of the Ways and Means, was emphatic and repeated in his assertions to the effect that the bonds were *redeemable in gold.* He stated this fact no less than three times in his speech of February 6, 1862, giving it all the prominence and emphasis that iteration and reiteration could impart. He spoke of the "redemption in gold in twenty years" as one of the special inducements for capitalists to take the loan, and he gave, in every form that language could assume, the sanction of his influential position, and still more influential name, to the maintenance of the gold standard in the payment of the bonds.

It may astonish even the gentleman from Pennsylvania himself to be reminded that within less than three years from the date of these declarations he asserted on this floor—referring to the five-twenty bonds—that *"it is just as clear as anything is clear that the interest is payable in gold, but the principal in lawful money."* He made this startling statement in answer to a question addressed to him by my honorable friend from Ohio [Rufus P. Spalding]. Should this scheme of repudiation ever succeed it is but just to give the gentleman from Pennsylvania the honor of first proposing it. He announced it on this floor while yet the gentleman from Massachusetts was doing honorable service on the tented field, and while Mr. Pendleton was still adhering to those hard-money theories of which he was a conspicuous and eloquent defender during his service in this House.

While so many gentlemen in both branches of Congress were repeating that these bonds were redeemable in gold, it is a very significant circumstance, as already intimated, that no one ventured the opposite opinion. The universality of the understanding at that time is that which renders a different construction now so reprehensible. Mr. Pendleton was present in his seat during the whole discussion of the measure, and he was an active and frequent participant therein. Then was his time to have enunciated his scheme of greenback payment if he ever intended it in good faith. As a gentleman of candor, however, I am sure he will confess that he never dreamed of such an idea till long after the bonds were purchased by the people, and possibly not until some prospect of party vantage lured him to the adoption of a theory which is equally at war with the letter of the law and with sound principles of finance.

After the bill became a law Mr. Chase, the Secretary of the Treasury, proceeded to place the loan formally on the market, and following the uniform previous practice of the Government, and especially adopting the language used by Mr. Stevens, and other gentlemen in both branches of Congress, he officially proclaimed through the loan agents of the Government that the five-twenty bonds were *"a six per cent. loan, the interest and principal payable in coin."* And it was on this basis, with this understanding, with this public proclamation, that the people were asked to subscribe to the loan. They had the assurance of an unbroken practice on the part of the Government, rendered still more significant by the provision for a sinking fund in coin; they had the general assurance of both branches of Congress, especially expressed through the appropriate channels of the chairman of Finance in the Senate and the chairman of Ways and Means in the House, and further and finally enforced by a distinct declaration to that effect by the public advertisement proposing the loan to the people, issued by the authority and under the direction of the Secretary of the Treasury. If anything could constitute an honorable contract between borrower and lender—between Government and people—then was it a contract that the five-twenty bonds should be redeemed in coin.

The next loan bill passed by Congress was that of March 3, 1863, authorizing the borrowing of $900,000,000. This is commonly known as the ten-forty act, and it contains the special provision that both principal and interest shall be payable in coin. But this provision was never inserted by way of discrimination against the five-twenties, implying that they were to be paid in paper currency. The origin of the provision palpably discredits any such inference. It was moved as an amendment by Mr. Benjamin F. Thomas, of Massachusetts, and it was moved to meet and repel the first covert insinuation that any bond of the United States was redeemable in anything else than coin. The chairman of Ways and Means, in apparent forgetfulness of his declaration the preceding year, had for the first time intimated that the principal of United States bonds was payable in paper money, and the amendment of Mr. Thomas, as the discussion reported in the *Globe* clearly discloses, was intended as a sharp protest against this heresy of the gentleman from Pennsylvania, and as such it was adopted by the House by a majority so overwhelming that its opponents did not call for a division.

In this connection I desire the special attention of the House to one fact of conclusive import, and it is this: at the time this ten-forty loan bill was passed, March 3, 1863, only $25,000,000 of the five-twenty loan, authorized the year before, had been disposed of. It was in the succeeding summer and autumn of 1863, especially after the triumph of the Union arms at Vicksburg and Gettysburg, that those marvelous sales of $500,000,000 were effected through the Government agency of Jay Cooke & Co. And yet the gentleman from Massachusetts would have us believe that the people subscribed for a loan of $500,000,000 that was payable in five years in paper currency, when another loan, for a larger amount, to run forty years, absolutely payable in gold, was already authorized and about to be put on the market. Such a conclusion cannot be reconciled even with the common sanity, to say nothing of the proverbial shrewdness, of those who invested their money in the five-twenty loan. Why, sir, every one sees, every one knows, that not one dollar of the five-twenty loan could have been disposed of on the understanding that the bonds were redeemable in currency, when another loan for a longer and more favorable period, possibly at the same rate of interest, for the bill so allowed, and absolutely redeemable in gold, was already authorized by Congress, and immediately to be offered to the public.

The next loan bill in the order of time was the act of March 3, 1864, which was merely supplementary to the ten-forty bill, whose history I have just reviewed. It covered the amount of $200,000,000, and, like the bill to which it formed a supplement, it provided for both interest and principal to be paid in coin. Under this bill more than one hundred and seventy-five million dollars were negotiated, partly in ten-forties, and partly in five-twenties; by far the greater part in the former. But, as some five-twenties were negotiated under it, the gentleman from Massachusetts, even on the line of logic which he has sought to travel, will be compelled to acknowledge that they were payable in coin, and hence, according to his theory, some of the five-twenties are redeemable in coin and some in paper—a distinction which has never yet been proclaimed, and the equity of which would hardly be apparent to the holders of the same description of bonds—precisely identical in phrase, and differing only in the subordinate and immaterial circumstance of date.

The last loan bill to which I need specially refer is that of June 30, 1864, under the provisions of which the five-twenties bearing that date were issued. The seven-thirties, authorized by the same act, as well as by the subsequent acts of January 28 and March 3, 1865, were convertible into five-twenties of the same tenor and description with those whose issue was directly authorized; so that in reviewing the history of the loan bill of June 30, 1864, I shall in effect close the narrative of congressional proceedings in regard to five-twenty bonds. And the history of that bill shall be brief. It was discussed in its various provisions very elaborately in both branches of Congress. As reported from the Ways and Means Committee it was worded like all previous bonds, promising to pay so many dollars to the holder, without specifying that they were to be anything else than gold dollars, in which United States bonds had always been paid. Toward the close of the discussion James Brooks, of New York, then, as now, a member of this House, moved to insert an amendment providing especially that the bonds should be *"payable in coin."* Mr. Brooks was answered by Samuel Hooper, of Massachusetts, on behalf of the Ways and Means Committee, as follows:

"The bill of last year, the $900,000,000 bill, contained these words, but it was not deemed necessary or considered expedient to insert them in this bill. A letter from the Secretary of the Treasury gives his views upon this point:

"TREASURY DEPARTMENT, May 18, 1864.

"It has been the constant usage of the department to redeem all coupon and registered bonds, forming part of the funded or permanent debt of the United States, in coin, and this usage has not been deviated from during my administration of its affairs.

"All the treasury notes and other obligations forming part of the temporary loan are payable, and will be redeemed, in lawful money; that is, in United States notes, until after the resumption of specie payment, when they also will doubtless be redeemed in coin or equivalent notes.

"The five-twenty sixes, payable twenty years from date, though redeemable after five years, are considered as belonging to the funded or permanent debt, and so also are the twenty years sixes, into which the three years seven-thirty notes are convertible. These bonds, therefore, according to the usage of the Government, are payable in coin.

"The three years seven-thirty treasury notes are part of the temporary loan, and will be paid in United States notes, unless holders prefer conversion to payment.

"S. P. CHASE, *Secretary.*"

Mr. Brooks, apparently satisfied with this statement, withdrew his amendment, regarding the point as conclusively settled, I suppose, not only by the uniform practice of the Government, but by the special declaration of the Secretary of the Treasury, who immediately afterward proceeded on the basis of that letter to put the bonds on the market.

We thus find that the voice of Congress has been uniform and consistent in support of the principle of paying the bonded debt in gold. No vote in Congress, even implying the opposite theory, has ever been given; even the weighty influence and conceded ability of the distinguished gentleman from Pennsylvania failing to carry with him any support whatever when he made his surprising and unprecedented change on this question. But the public creditors did not rely solely on the declarations of leading men in Congress in regard to gold payment, nor did they rest wholly on the past practice and the good faith of the Government. They had, in addition to both these strong grounds of confidence and assurance, the more direct and implicit guaranty of the treasury department, the authorized agent of the Government, speaking *ex cathedra,* with the knowledge and assent of Congress.

I have already quoted Secretary Chase's significant declarations in his letters and his public proposals for loans, and I have now to quote one of his equally significant acts. At the close of 1862 the twenty-year loan of 1842, amounting to nearly three million dollars, fell due. Nothing was said in that loan about coin payment, and thus a grand opportunity was afforded to test the theory of paper payment. Circumstances all conspired to favor such a policy if it could be honorably adopted. Gold was at a high premium, and the Government was passing through the darkest and most doubtful hours of the whole struggle. Could there have been even a decent pretext to pay the debt in paper currency the temptation was surely great enough to resort to it, if not fully to justify it. But in the face of all the adverse circumstances; with gold very high and daily rising; with expenses enormous and daily increasing; with resources already embarrassed and daily growing more so, and with a military situation rendered well nigh desperate by months of almost unbroken disaster, Secretary Chase decided that the faith of the Government demanded that its funded debt, falling due no matter when and owned by no matter whom, must be paid in coin. *And it was paid in coin;* and no voice but the voice of approval was raised in either branch of Congress. The course of Secretary Chase was not only honorable to himself and the country, but it was in the highest degree wise merely from the standpoint of worldly wisdom; for it created such a profound confidence in the good faith of our Government that it aided us incalculably in the negotiation of all our great loans for the war. When the Government paid its debt to the uttermost farthing at such a time capitalists at once argued that there never could come a crisis when any evasion or denial of public obligation would be resorted to. It has been reserved for the gentleman from Massachusetts, and the gentleman from Ohio, and the gentleman from Pennsylvania, jointly and severally, to propose that our Government should adopt a policy in the calm sunshine and prosperity of peace which it scorned to resort to in the terrible storms and dark adversities of war.

The course of Secretary Chase in guaranteeing gold payment on all bonds of the United States was followed, indorsed, and repeated by his successors, Fessenden and McCulloch.

In view of the uniform declarations of the treasury department, made through official reports, through public proposals for loans, and through personal letters of assurance, all guaranteeing coin payment of the five-twenty bonds, I submit that the Government is bound thereto even if there were no other obligation expressed or implied. These official and unofficial promulgations from the treasury department were made with the full knowledge of Congress, and without the slightest expression of dissent on the part of Congress. It is too late for Congress to declare now that the Government is not bound by the stipulations which the treasury department proclaimed to all lenders of money—proclaimed with the full knowledge and the full assent of Congress. Had Congress not believed or intended that the five-twenty bonds were to be paid in coin the Secretary should not have been allowed with its evident assent to so advertise; and for Congress, after this permission and warrant so significantly given, to step forward at this late day and declare itself not bound by the conditions published by the Secretary is simply to place the United States Government in the position of a man playing a "confidence game" of the meanest description, in which the treasury department and Congress are the confederate knaves, and the whole mass of bondholders the unfortunate victims.

But now, Mr. Speaker, suppose, for the sake of argument, we admit that the Government may fairly and legally pay the five-twenty bonds in paper currency, what then? I ask the gentleman from Massachusetts to tell us, what then? It is easy, I know, to issue just as many greenbacks as will pay the maturing bonds, regardless of the effect upon the inflation of prices and the general derangement of business. Five hundred millions of the five-twenties are now payable, and according to the easy mode suggested all we have to do is to set the printing presses in motion, and "so long as rags and lampblack hold out" we need have no embarrassment about paying our national debt. But the ugly question recurs, what are you going to do with the greenbacks thus put afloat? Five hundred millions this year, and eleven hundred millions more on this theory of payment by the year 1872, so that within the period of four or five years we would only have added to our paper money the trifling inflation of $1,600,000,000. We should all have splendid times doubtless! Wheat under the new dispensation ought to bring twenty dollars a bushel, and boots would not be worth more than $200 a pair, and the farmers of our country would be as well off as Santa Anna's rabble of Mexican soldiers, who were allowed ten dollars a day for their services and charged eleven for their rations and clothing. This $1,600,000,000 of greenbacks, added to the amount already issued, would give us some $2,300,000,000 paper money, and I suppose the theory of the new doctrine would leave this vast mass permanently in circulation, for it would hardly be consistent to advocate the redemption of the greenbacks in gold after having repudiated and forsworn our obligation on the bonds.

But if it be intended to redeem the legal tenders in gold, what will have been the net gain to the Government in the whole transaction? If any gentleman will tell me, I shall be glad to learn how it will be easier to pay $1,600,000,000 in gold in the redemption of greenbacks than to pay the same amount in the redemption of five-twenty bonds? The policy advocated, it seems to me, has only two alternatives: the one to ruinously inflate the currency and leave it so reckless of results; the other to ruinously inflate the currency at the outset, only to render redemption in gold far more burdensome in the end.

I know it may be claimed that the means necessary to redeem the five-twenties in greenbacks may be realized by a new issue of currency bonds to be placed on the market. Of results in the future every gentleman has the right to his own opinion, and all may alike indulge in speculation. But it does seem to me that the Government would be placed in an awkward attitude when it should enter the money market to negotiate a loan the avails of which were to be devoted to breaking faith with those who already held its most sacred obligations! What possible security would the new class of creditors have that, when *their* debts matured, some new form of evasion would not be resorted to by which they in turn would be deprived of their just and honest dues? *Falsus in uno, falsus in omnibus* [1] would supply the ready form of protest against trusting a Government with a new loan when it had just ignored its plain obligation on an old one.

Payment of the five-twenty bonds in paper currency involves, therefore, a limitless issue of greenbacks, with attendant evils of gigantic magnitude and far-reaching consequence. And the worst evil of the whole is the delusion which calls this a payment at all. It is no payment in any proper sense, for it neither gives the creditor what he is entitled to, nor does it release the debtor from subsequent responsibility. You may get rid of the five-twenty by issuing the greenback, but how will you get rid of the greenback except by paying gold? The only escape from ultimate payment of gold is to declare that as a nation we permanently and finally renounce all idea of ever attaining a specie standard; that we launch ourselves upon an ocean of paper money, without shore or sounding, with no rudder to guide us and no compass to steer by. And this is precisely what is involved if we adopt this mischievous suggestion of "a new way to pay old debts." Our fate in attempting such a course may be easily read in the history of similar follies both in Europe and in our own country. Prostration of credit, financial disaster, widespread distress among all classes of the community, would form the closing scenes in our career of gratuitous folly and national dishonor. And from such an abyss of sorrow and humiliation it would be a painful and toilsome effort to regain as sound a position in our finances as we are asked voluntarily to abandon to-day.

The remedy for our financial troubles, Mr. Speaker, will not be found in a superabundance of depreciated paper currency. It lies in the opposite direction; and the sooner the nation finds itself on a specie basis the sooner will the public treasury be freed from embarrassment and private business relieved from

[1] "False in one thing, false in all things."

discouragement. Instead, therefore, of entering upon a reckless and boundless issue of legal tenders, with their consequent depression, if not destruction, of value, let us set resolutely to work and make those already in circulation equal to so many gold dollars. When that result shall be accomplished we can proceed to pay our five-twenties either in coin or paper, for the one would be the equivalent of the other. But to proceed deliberately on a scheme of depreciating our legal tenders, and then forcing the holders of Government bonds to accept them in payment, would resemble in point of honor the policy of a merchant who, with abundant resources and prosperous business, should devise a plan for throwing discredit on his own notes with the view of having them bought up at a discount ruinous to the holders and immensely profitable to his own knavish pocket. This comparison may faintly illustrate the wrongfulness of the policy, but not its consummate folly; for in the case of the Government, unlike the merchant, the stern necessity would recur of making good in the end, by the payment of hard coin, all the discount that might be gained by the temporary substitution of paper.

Discarding all such schemes as at once unworthy and unprofitable, let us direct our policy steadily, but not rashly, toward the resumption of specie payment. And when we have attained that end—easily attainable at no distant day if the proper policy be pursued—we can all unite on some honorable plan for the redemption of the five-twenty bonds, and the issuing instead thereof a new series of bonds which can be more favorably placed at a lower rate of interest. When we shall have reached the specie basis the value of United States securities will be so high in the money markets of the world that we can command our own terms. We can then call in our five-twenties according to the very letter and spirit of the bond, and adjust a new loan that will be eagerly sought for by capitalists, and will be free from those elements of discontent that in some measure surround the existing funded debt of the country.

As to the particular measures of legislation requisite to hasten the resumption of specie payment gentlemen equally entitled to respect may widely differ; but there is one line of policy conducive thereto on which we all ought to agree, and that is on a serious reduction of the Government expenses and a consequent lightening of the burdens of taxation. The interest-bearing debt of the United States, when permanently funded, will not exceed $2,100,000,000, imposing an annual interest of about $125,000,000. Our other expenses, including war, navy, the pension list, and the civil list, ought not to exceed $100,000,000; so that if we raise $250,000,000 from customs and internal revenue combined we should have $25,000,000 annual surplus to apply to the reduction of the public debt. But to attain this end we must mend our ways and practice an economy far more consistent and severe than any we have attempted in the past. Our military peace establishment must be reduced one half at least, and our naval appropriations correspondingly curtailed; and innumerable leaks and gaps and loose ends that have so long attended our Government expenditure must be taken up and stopped. If such a policy be pursued by Congress neither the principal of the debt nor the interest of the debt, nor the annual expenses of Government, will be burdensome to the people. We can raise $250,000,000 of revenue on the gold basis, and at the same time have a vast reduction in our taxes. And we can do this without repudiation in any form, either open or covert, avowed or indirect, but with every obligation of the Government fulfilled and discharged in its exact letter and in its generous spirit.

And this, Mr. Speaker, we shall do. Our national honor demands it; our national interest equally demands it. We have vindicated our claim to the highest heroism on a hundred bloody battlefields, and have stopped at no sacrifice of life needful to the maintenance of our national integrity. I am sure that in the peace which our arms have conquered we shall not dishonor ourselves by withholding from any public creditor a dollar that we promised to pay him, nor seek by cunning construction and clever afterthought to evade or escape the full responsibility of our national indebtedness. It will doubtless cost us a vast sum to pay that indebtedness, but it would cost us incalculably more not to pay it!

General Butler.—I hold that, by the letter, by the spirit, and by the justice of the contract, the five-twenties are payable in the lawful money of the United States.

Now, there are three grounds upon which the gentleman from Maine [Mr. Blaine] insists that this is not so. He says, first, by the letter of the law the five-twenties are payable in coin. Let us carefully examine that proposition. Up to the time of the issuing of the five-twenties no loan of the United States had ever been issued payable in anything else than coin. The gentleman says no loan had ever been issued in which anything was said as to what was the currency in which it was payable. Why? Because up to that time there was never any currency known to the Government of the United States other than coin. Therefore the seven-thirties of 1861 and the 1881 sixes of 1861, with all the debt prior to the war, were, in letter and in spirit, payable in coin. Because Congress in issuing them was dealing with a condition of things and a currency then existing, and therefore the 1881 sixes are payable, according to the fair spirit of the contract, in coin. Therefore I enunciate, as my first proposition, and one that I shall endeavor to enforce on the House and the country, that every dollar of indebtment of the United States which is contracted by the acts of Congress making it payable in coin shall be paid in coin although it takes the last dollar to pay it; but every debt contracted not payable in coin shall be paid in the lawful money of the United States, such as you paid your soldiers with and such as you furnish to your citizens; such as alone is now used as money of the Government, and upon which alone you impress the image and superscription of the Government as a guaranty that it shall hereafter be made good.

Now, then, when the argument is pressed upon me that in the loan bills passed previously to the five-twenty loan nothing was said as to the currency in which the bonds should be paid, I reply that there was but one currency at the time they were passed in which they could be contracted or payable. But that state of things changed on the 25th of February, 1862. The Congress of the United States had to provide means for carrying on the war; accordingly it passed a law, the first section of which provided for $150,000,000 of legal-tender notes, the language of which, as to their validity and effect, is in these words:

"And such notes, herein authorized, shall be receivable in payment of all taxes, internal duties, excises, debts, and demands of every kind, due to the United States, except duties on imports, and for all claims and demands against the United States of every kind whatsoever"—

Except what?

"except for interest upon bonds and notes, which shall be paid in coin; and shall also be lawful money and a legal tender in payment of all debts, public and private, within the United States, except duties on imports and interests as aforesaid."

These are the provisions of the first section of the act thus creating "a lawful money," payable and receivable for every debt, public or private, known to the law or known in the United States, except what? Except interest on the bonds and notes of the United States.

Now, what does the second section provide? It authorized

$500,000,000 of bonds, registered or coupon, payable at the option of the United States in five years, and in twenty years at all events. Payable how? Let me read again, so that I may not be mistaken:

"to an amount not exceeding $500,000,000, payable in twenty years from date, and bearing a rate of six per cent., payable semi-annually."

Not a word is here said as to the money in which these bonds shall be paid, either as to principal or interest. And why? Because the very section preceding had provided that the interest of all notes or bonds of the United States should be paid in coin, and had further enacted another lawful money which should be receivable in payment of all indebtment of the United States whatsoever, except duties on imports, and interest on the public debt. Is not the principal of the debt an indebtment other than interest?

There is the plain letter of the law. I need not discuss this point further. If there is any lawyer who, reading this law without taking into consideration anything except what stands on the statute-book, will tell me that this law enacts that the principal of the five-twenties is payable in coin, then "for him have I offended," and either he is or I am so stupid as not to be worthy of an argument.

But the gentleman does not leave his proposition upon this only. The next ground he puts it on is what this or that Congressman said or omitted to say in his speech as to the currency in which this loan should be paid. And the first evidence of the contract he puts forward is that the honorable member from Pennsylvania [Mr. Stevens]—not now in his seat—did not say, at the time the act was passed, that the principal was payable in currency. Well, the gentleman from Pennsylvania sets forth, in a letter recently written by him as a reason why he did not say it was payable in currency, that he did not think anybody but a fool would think it was not. That is not my language; it is his; that is the ground he puts it on; and when he comes in he and the gentleman from Maine can fight the battle out. I am quite certain that the old man sarcastic will take care of himself when he does get here without any aid from me; and therefore I pass from further consideration of this topic.

But it is said that various speeches were made on the one side and the other, which are cited to interpret this contract. I had supposed that there is no better settled rule of interpretation of either public or municipal law, or of the law of nations, than that nobody is bound by any portion of the negotiations or any portion of the declarations made either in regard to a treaty or a law prior to the enactment of the law or conclusion of the treaty, because the enactment settles the terms of the whole obligation, and you cannot go to the speech of this member or that member, in case of legislation, to find out what the legislation means, nor can you go to the protocols and negotiations prior to a treaty to find out what the treaty means. You must take it upon the letter, and I have never yet found any man bold enough—until my friend from Maine exhibited a degree of courage much superior to any bravery required to face Minie bullets in the field—bold enough to insist that the letter of the law did not authorize payment of the principal of the five-twenty bonds in lawful money of the United States.

The next class of arguments that the gentleman from Maine puts forward on this question is the proposals in the advertisements of those he terms the authorized agents of the United States who disposed of the loan. Allow me here to say that for contracting a national debt I know no other authorized agent of the nation but the Congress of the United States; I know no broker, whether he is in the treasury office or out of it, that has a right to fix the terms of the national debt for the United States. No man is authorized to pay a dollar of money unless appropriated by the Congress of the United States, and therefore no man can contract a dollar's debt unless authorized directly and distinctly by an act of the Congress of the United States. I agree that Mr. Jay Cooke advertised, after some sort, when endeavoring to sell it, that the principal of this loan was payable in coin; but in the same newspaper you find another of his advertisements, intended also to sell the loan, that "a national debt is a national blessing." Are we bound by contract to that? If, as the gentleman claims, we are bound by advertisements in the one case, we are bound as well in the other; and does my friend insist that Mr. Jay Cooke has bound the country to the proposition that a national debt is a national blessing to anybody except bankers? With that amendment I might agree to the declaration. When I called the attention of the country to this some little time ago Mr. Jay Cooke, for whom I have very high respect, wrote me that I was mistaken; that what he did advertise was that a national debt rightly managed was a national blessing. I am at issue with him upon that. I insist that a national debt managed any how, by anybody—the Angel Gabriel or Jay Cooke or any other body—is not a national blessing. [Laughter.] No management of a national debt can make it a national blessing. And yet, if we are bound by brokers' advertisements we are bound to the doctrine that it is a national blessing which we must enjoy and bequeath to our posterity forever!

The next evidence which the gentleman from Maine presents in support of his contract to pay the five-twenties in gold is the declarations of Secretaries of the Treasury. Now, no Secretary of the Treasury had a right to make any declarations on this subject which can be binding on the country. The gentleman does not claim that he had; he only says that Congress stood by and saw the Secretary make declarations and did not interfere. Once for all I protest against Congress being bound by what Secretaries do or do not do that Congress does not interfere with. If you once admit that doctrine you will involve Congress in difficulties which it will take a long time and great wisdom to unravel.

But no one of the Secretaries ever has said that the contract is that the principal of this loan is payable in coin; and if there has been disingenuousness on this subject it has not been on our part, but on the part of the Secretaries in their attempts to interpret this law so as to sell the loan. The first thing said about the probability that this debt would be paid in gold was in the answer of Secretary Chase to a letter sent him from abroad—Frankfort, I believe. It was said in that letter—I do not give the words, but the substance—"It is not understood here in Frankfort that these bonds are payable in gold. If it should be so understood they would bring a much higher price." Why was it not so understood? Because a foreign lawyer reading the act would never think of such a thing for a moment. The bonds were selling—for what? For forty cents on the dollar, and that at a time when the Confederate loan was at a premium in Europe.

Now, I will not think so meanly of this country as to believe it could be supposed these bonds were payable in gold, and then were at this discount even in Europe, which was against us. And I will not think so meanly of this nation as to believe that there could have been any question in the minds of the people of Europe as to our being able to pay more than thirty per cent. of our debt in gold if such had been our plain contract and obligation. No, sir; the bankers in Europe of that day were simply betting as to whether we should pay our paper money in gold; they were betting on that proposition when they were buying our bonds at from sixty to seventy per cent. discount. They knew that every other government that had issued paper money had depreciated it, and the question was whether we, who set out here so differently from other governments, would in the end depreciate our paper money.

This letter was sent over here as a stock-jobbing proposition to Mr. Chase. How did he answer it? Through his assistant secretary. The answer all will remember. "The Government of the United States has always paid all its obligations in gold, and it is to be presumed that it always will." It was an evasive answer—an answer tending to mislead; whether intended so to do I do not know or say.

What was the next act and declaration of a Secretary of the Treasury? Mr. Fessenden is cited. I have a bone to pick with Mr. Fessenden upon this subject. I am very glad he has been brought in here, for I should have felt some delicacy in saying a word about him, as he is a member of the other House, had not his friend from Maine [Mr. Blaine] brought him upon this floor in his capacity of Secretary of the Treasury. I can therefore deal with the Secretary of the Treasury as roughly as I please, without infringing upon the courtesy due to a Senator of the United States. Mr. Fessenden, as Secretary of the Treasury, was called upon to say whether the three-year loan treasury notes, issued in 1861, when there was nothing but gold to pay with, and for which gold was paid by the people to the Government, were payable in coin or in currency. He decided that these gold-bought and gold-contracted notes were payable in currency; and the whole of that issue, put forth at a time when there was nothing but gold as currency, for which the faith of the country was pledged, under the decision of Mr. Fessenden, had to be received by the people (who paid for it in gold) in paper, or they were compelled to convert it into such bonds as the Government chose to give them.

Mr. Blaine.—The decision in regard to the payment of the first series of seven-thirty notes was made on the 18th of May, 1862, by Salmon P. Chase, Secretary of the Treasury, in these words:

> "The three-year seven-thirty treasury notes are part of the temporary loan, and will be paid in treasury notes, unless the holders prefer to exchange them," &c.

That was three months before Mr. Fessenden went into the treasury. He found the question *res adjudicata.* The gentleman is all wrong in charging this upon Mr. Fessenden. There is not the remotest foundation for his assertion.

Mr. Butler.—The House will judge whether I was wrong,

without the *dictum* of my friend from Maine [Mr. Blaine]. I did not say that Salmon P. Chase was not guilty of the same thing; I only said that William P. Fessenden was guilty of it; that is the distinction. [Laughter.] If Salmon P. Chase had broken the faith of this Government—if he had said that, although the Government had received gold in the hour of its necessity, immediately after the first battle of Bull Run, the darkest day the Government ever saw, and had pledged gold in return—for then we paid gold to meet all our obligations—if Salmon P. Chase, on the 18th of May, 1864, when called upon to say whether we should pay gold for the gold we had received, broke the faith of the Government, if he was one of those repudiators and scoundrels and knaves we hear of so glibly when we attempt to discuss this question of finance, why did not and why should not Secretary Fessenden overrule him when he became Secretary of the Treasury? If so great a wrong was *res adjudicata,* it was *res* very badly *adjudicata,* and should have been forthwith set right.

My friend does not pretend that Mr. Fessenden altered this; and when we, who believe in maintaining the faith of the nation, but not in oppressing the people with taxation, are attacked on all hands by hard words and strong inferences, and when, to get us down, we are yoked up with everybody who happens to have bad political sentiments, I would ask who was the first repudiator? The gentleman chooses to cite Mr. Chase as the promisor of this bad note. Be it so; I am dealing only with the indorser, William Pitt Fessenden. He indorsed it and acted upon it. By his decision the seven-thirty notes of 1861, issued when there was no other currency, were caused to be paid in greenbacks, and the gold-paying public creditor was obliged, for his gold paid to the Government, either to take his pay in greenbacks or convert his Government notes into bonds; and that whole loan was thus redeemed. And on what ground was this so great a wrong on the public creditors perpetrated? It was said by the Secretary that this three-year seven-thirty gold loan was a temporary loan only. Oh, then, it is right to cheat the temporary creditors of the Government, the hand-to-mouth men, who loan their hard coin for a few days to save the Government; but the long-bond creditors of the Government you must not cheat; you must let them cheat you. Is not that the proposition? Is there any escape from it? Is not that the Maine doctrine of finance, if you please? [Laughter.] My friend here from Maine [Mr. Blaine], following in the footsteps of the Secretary of the Treasury from Maine, holds it to be in the last degree wrong if we do not pay principal and interest of our debt in gold. He invokes us, in the name of national honor, national faith, and everything else that is sacred, to save the long-bond creditor, who bought our bonds for currency, while the short creditor, who paid for his notes in coin, has lost his gold by the action of the Secretary of the Treasury from Maine. We have had many things good from Maine—among others a "Maine law"—and now we have got Maine finance. I repudiate the last, and I am afraid my State has repudiated the other [Laughter.]

The next authority adduced by the gentleman in support of his contract to pay gold for the five-twenties bonds is Secretary McCulloch. Well, if this House proposes to be bound by the financial theories of Secretary McCulloch I should hardly wish to argue this question further. But even Secretary McCulloch does not undertake to say that there is a contract to pay gold for these bonds. When asked by a foreign banker, "What is the contract as to the payment of the principal of the five-twenties?" what does the Secretary reply? Does he say that the contract is to pay in gold? Oh, no; he says that all the Government obligations that have fallen due have been paid in gold (he forgot that temporary loan), and that it is the policy of the Government to pay all its obligations in gold. I agree with him; such is the policy of the Government. But that is not the question. The question is, what has the Government contracted to do, and what is it able to do? I wish that we could pay this enormous debt in gold, or in anything else, so that we could relieve the people from taxation. You will find running all through this letter of Secretary McCulloch an evasion of this question. What is the contract by law?

When the $900,000,000 loan, commonly known as the ten-forty loan, was issued, what did the Secretary of the Treasury do? Of the six per cent. five-twenty loan (which the gentleman from Maine contends was payable in gold) he says only some $25,000,000 of the $500,000,000 authorized had been issued; yet he makes the Secretary of the Treasury guilty of the absurdity of attempting to put on the market $900,000,000 of the five per cent. ten-forty loan as a competing loan, expecting to get that taken up, when he could not get his five-twenty six per cent. gold-payable loan in principal and interest taken up. Why did he do this? If both loans were payable in gold he must have been entirely demented. But no; the ten-forty five per cent. loan was payable, principal and interest, in gold by its terms; and this same Secretary of the Treasury, through his brokers advertised this ten-forty loan as the only one the principal and interest of which were payable in gold. And nobody objected in this House. I was not here then; but where was the eloquent voice of my friend from Maine protesting against selling this five per cent. loan upon an advertisement that it was the only loan payable, principal and interest, in gold? Why did he allow the public creditors to think that the only loan payable in gold was the five per cent. loan; that the six per cent. loan was not payable in gold? This only illustrates the fact that, in interpreting public law, we must not deal with what members of Congress do individually, but we must be bound by the statute.

MR. BLAINE.—Does the gentleman mean to say that the Government agents advertised that the ten-forty loan was the only loan payable in gold?

MR. BUTLER.—Yes, sir; I do. Certain Government agents, called the New York *Tribune,* the New York *Times,* or the New York *Evening Post,* contained that advertisement, and if the gentleman will go there he will find it.

MR. BLAINE.—Authorized by whom?

MR. BUTLER.—Authorized by the Secretary of the Treasury, so headed. It was a little difficult at that time to find out who the negotiators were. That was the advertisement. You can find it. If I had known this question was to arise at this time I would have had the advertisement to present to the House.

MR. BLAINE.—I gave the gentleman notice some days ago that I should speak on this subject.

MR. BUTLER.—True. But, while I presumed the gentleman would speak on this subject, it never entered my conception that he would make such a speech as he has. [Laughter.]

If the gentleman will tell me why it is that we are to construe this law differently from any other law I will be obliged to him. If he will inform this House why the people of this country should tax themselves to the amount of many millions ($400,000,000 is the difference this day and this hour), whether these five-twenties are payable in gold, as gold stood yesterday, or in greenbacks.

The only answer suggested is, why agitate this now. These loans are not payable now, and therefore we may wait until the twenty years are out, when we all believe greenbacks and gold will be correlative terms. I believe so, too, in twenty years; but in the meantime the interest on these five-twenties is sinking this country, the labor, the manufacture, and the commerce of this country, to a degree that even its vitality and its strength will hardly be able to meet it.

What is the rate of interest on the five-twenties? Six per cent. in gold, payable semi-annually, gold being at 140 to 145, equal to 150 and upward. That makes nine per cent.; they are exempt from State and municipal taxation, which makes from two to three per cent. more. So on these almost two thousand million of interest bonds the people of this country are paying at this day and at this hour, either by remission of taxes or otherwise, in the currency of the country, from eleven to twelve per cent. What is the consequence? They could stagger under this burden of taxes if needed to pay the soldiers; they could deal with this burden of taxes if it even were to be thrown into the sea; but the difficulty is that paying this high rate of interest on these five-twenties of from eleven to twelve per cent. causes capitalists to withdraw from legitimate business and keep their money in these bonds. See how it operates. I have my money in five-twenty bonds at eleven per cent., and I am told that I am to have gold at the end of the twenty years for the principal besides. You cannot tempt me, then, to go into any enterprise which shall not promise me more than eleven to twelve per cent. I must have much more before I will take my money out of Government securities and put it at the risk of business. And it is this high rate of Government interest which is crushing the life out of the industrial pursuits of the people. There can be no mistake about this. Look at the market reports of Cincinnati, one of the great marts of the West. No money can be got there for less than fifteen to eighteen per cent. Why? Because our capitalists get from eleven to twelve per cent, on five-twenties, and they are encouraged to hold on to their bonds and keep their money out of the business of the country; because the gentleman from Maine tells them that the Government will pay the principal in gold, although they paid but forty cents on the dollar for them when they bought them. This is the reason why this five-twenty loan is crushing our people, and why we must get rid of it at all hazards consistent with national honor and national faith, and no man asks that to be broken.

But I am told if we undertake to pay any portion of this debt in greenbacks we shall depreciate greenbacks so that they will be worthless; that there will be an inflation of prices. The gentleman from Maine riots in imagination over the picture of the payment of $200 for a pair of boots if we issue any more legal-tender notes, that is to say, notes not bearing interest.

Speaking of greenbacks, I am reminded of one thing to which I meant to have adverted: of the nation's being bound by the advertisements by which its bonds were sold. My friend says we did not notify capitalists that we would claim the right to pay these five-twenty bonds in any other way than in coin. Why we put it upon $150,000,000 of United States notes, and thus advertised everybody we did not mean to pay them in gold. This notice was put on the back of every greenback. Let me read from one:

"This note is a legal tender for all debts, public or private, except duties on imports and interest on the public debt."

There is "*inclusio unius, exclusio alterius*" for the gentleman.

MR. BLAINE.—If the gentleman will allow me I hold the two notes in my hand, one of which contains precisely the words the gentleman has just read. But does the gentleman say that this is the lawful money authorized by the act of February 25, 1862?

MR. BUTLER.—Yes, sir.

MR. BLAINE.—I deny it.

MR. BUTLER.—Now, then, let us see. I will compare this indorsement on the note with the law which I have before me. The second section of the law reads thus:

"Shall be receivable in payment of all taxes, internal duties, excises, debts and demands of every kind due to the United States, except duties on imports, and of all claims and demands against the United States of every kind whatsoever, except interest on the public debt and customs."

MR. BLAINE.—Will the gentleman allow me to make a statement?

MR. BUTLER.—Yes, sir.

MR. BLAINE.—The act of February 25, 1862, was the first legal-tender act. It is true, the notes were made a legal tender for all debts public and private, but they were also convertible into five-twenty bonds. Now, the gentleman places himself on the ground that whatever was by contemporaneous construction lawful money the Government was bound to pay. I assert that the law for the issue of the five-twenties of 1862 was embraced in the same act which authorized the issue of $150,000,000 of legal-tender notes which were themselves convertible into five-twenties. Now, if the gentleman will stick to his own words, then the Government can only pay off these five-twenties by issuing a like amount of these same legal-tender notes, on the back of which are printed these words:

"This is a legal tender for all debts, public and private, except duties on imports and interest on the public debt, and is exchangeable for United States six per cent. twenty-year bonds, redeemable at the pleasure of the Government after five years."

Therefore, if, as the gentleman contends, these bonds are redeemable at the treasury in the kind of money which was declared a legal tender when they were issued, they must be paid in this kind of notes. In that case the treasury of the United States would be receiving five-twenty bonds at one door and issuing the legal tenders at another, and then again issuing the bonds and taking back the legal tenders, and so they would go round and round the circle.

MR. BUTLER.—And you do not think that desirable. [Laughter.]

MR. BLAINE.—Does the gentleman think it desirable to have a revolving wheel at which one class of men shall stand in a row for the redemption of their bonds, and another for a reissue of the same? Is that the gentleman's idea of finance? The gentleman adheres to the exact letter of the law.

MR. BUTLER.—The difference between my friend and myself is this: I was putting advertisement against advertisement.

MR. BLAINE.—And I law against law.

MR. BUTLER.—There is no law of this exact form, and it is not the exact form of the law or of the advertisement. I was only putting advertisement against advertisement. I will answer the gentleman, if I have time, that I do think it is desirable to have a currency, and if Congress agrees with me we will have a currency before we get through exactly like what the gentleman describes, so that when a man wants money he can give the treasury his Government bond and get it, and when he gets through using his money he can go back again and get his bond. That is exactly the thing I want, and I hope to get it if I live long enough.

MR. BLAINE.—And issue $2,000,000,000 of legal tenders.

MR. BUTLER.—I have not said I wanted $2,000,000,000 of greenbacks issued. I want only so much as will be absorbed in the needs of the business of the United States.

But this episode takes me a little way out of my course. I was upon the question whether there would be depreciation, whether there would be inflation if more legal tenders were issued to supply the wants of the country for currency, when I turned aside for a moment to speak to the question of advertisements on the back of the greenbacks.

The common idea is that there will be inflation when you

issue paper money. It is drawn from the old idea of bank circulation. A bank issued its notes without any basis except the gold basis. That gold basis was sometimes one to four. Let me illustrate: suppose there were four hundred millions of bank paper in circulation on one hundred millions of gold as a basis, then I agree it would be an inflation to issue another one hundred millions, making the relation of the paper dollar to the gold dollar as one to five. But what is a greenback? Have gentlemen considered? A dollar greenback as it stands to-day is one twenty-five hundred millionth part of the debt of the United States, secured by a mortgage upon every dollar of public or private property in the United States. Is it not that, under my theory or anybody else's theory of finance? Now, suppose we issue five hundred millions of greenbacks, and pay up five hundred millions of the interest-bearing debt of the United States, what is a greenback then? Why, it is still one twenty-five hundred millionth part of the national debt of the United States, appreciated, and not depreciated, by the amount of interest which we have saved by buying up five hundred millions of the interest-bearing debt. The way to test it would be this: suppose we could issue the whole amount and pay all interest-bearing debt at once, then the one hundred and fifty millions of customs which we have to pay for interest without getting ahead in payment of our debt at all could be directed to redeeming the greenbacks. There is a limitation on this power of issuing greenbacks, and only one, and that limitation my friend does not seem to understand. It is this: these greenbacks are non-interest-bearing notes, and therefore they can only be issued in such quantities without depreciation in fact as will be absorbed by the community to the degree that they are required for business purposes. They may be issued to the degree they will be absorbed as currency. I think that the country can bear to-day some two hundred millions more of them, not issued primarily and arbitrarily for the purpose of paying off the interest-bearing debt, but issued for the purpose of providing a currency for the country which should not be so contracted as to bring ruin, as now, upon the business interests of the country. When you have issued two hundred millions more of these greenbacks and paid your interest-bearing debt with them, have you altered their relation to property, to each other, or to gold? Are they appreciated or depreciated? Appreciated, in fact, because you save the interest on the two hundred millions which you have paid off with them; depreciated if you issue more than will be absorbed as currency, because business men do not want non-interest-bearing notes on hand; and if they are not needed as currency they will sell them at a discount for some property that will pay interest.

Now, then, sir, let me state, for the benefit of my friend, my proposition of finance, and the House can contrast it with any other that may be better, and there will be found better I doubt not. There are now some two thousand five hundred millions of debt. Some two thousand millions of it stand in the shape of interest-bearing debt. There are nineteen different kinds of that description of debt bearing different rates of interest and times of payment. There are some five hundred millions, more or less, in various forms of non-interest-bearing debt, gold certificates, legal-tender notes, and others. Now, my proposition is that, in the first place, we should substitute greenbacks for the national bank currency, releasing to the banks the bonds which we hold as security for that national bank currency. It can be done without shock to the business of the country.

I agree, sir, that any proposition of legislation is vicious which tends in any considerable degree to interfere with the industrial pursuits of the people, but I propose we should enact in some proper form that the Secretary of the Treasury should each month retain in the treasury all the national bank bills which have been collected by the collectors of the internal revenue, or which have come through other means into the treasury of the United States, and at the same time should issue to the banks, if they desire to receive them, or to issue in payment of the interest-bearing notes which are payable in currency an equal amount of legal tenders. In a very few months, four or five, the national bank notes would be withdrawn from circulation and their place supplied with greenbacks without any shock to the business of the country, and, *pari passu*,[1] the bonds of the banks held as security for these notes could be restored to them. This proposition, sir, if carried out would put into circulation some three hundred million dollars more of national legal-tender notes without increasing that circulation, and release the country from the payment of between twenty and thirty million dollars in currency which is now paid to the national banks on these bonds, and the place of their bills would be taken by the non-interest-bearing notes of the United States without any shock to the business of the country.

What objections are urged to this proposition? The first

[1] "With equal step."

is that it would be a breach of faith with the banks. I would like some gentleman to put his finger upon any act of Congress by which we pledged ourselves for a single day longer than the good pleasure and discretion of the Congress of the United States thought best to allow this bank currency to exist. What effect would it have upon the banks? Those dependent wholly upon their circulation, which are not in fact banks of loans and deposits, would wind up, and their managers would seek some other and equally honest employment. Banks that are needed would still be banks of loan and discount, but not of circulation.

It is said that the banks furnish now the best currency this country ever saw, because it is the same in New Orleans, Boston, New York, and Chicago. But what is the currency? It is the notes of the bank. What makes them equal all over this country? It is the indorsement of the United States. So that we have come into this very remarkable position, that when a bank breaks its currency is better than when it was solvent, and sells at a slight premium. Therefore, as the United States is primarily responsible for all the circulation, we ought to supply the currency to the people and receive the profit of doing it.

But it is said that the banks really cost the United States nothing. One of the ablest bankers of them all, Mr. Jay Cooke, has undertaken to tell us that the banks pay in taxes a large amount, and therefore in equity we ought not to disturb them. Sir, if Mr. Jay Cooke or any one else will tell me of any business in this country that is not taxed and does not pay a large amount of taxes, then I will agree that the banks are not favored. Take for example a manufacturer. Take a single case, only two years ago, in the State of Massachusetts, of a manufacturing corporation of $750,000 capital and of $1,500,000 annual product of manufactured goods. It exactly divided profits with the United States. Its stockholders received two dividends of five per cent. each on $750,000, and it paid five per cent. tax on the entire amount of production, $1,500,000; so that they in fact took the United States into partnership, only the United States got all the profits, but the stockholders bore all the loss. Now, if there is any greater or more onerous burden of taxes on the banks than that, I have yet to learn where it is.

Again, it is said that this banking system is a better one than we ever had. For some purposes so it is. And it is said, further, that if we do not encourage it we shall go back to the old State bank system. No, Mr. Chairman, never, never! The day of State banks has gone by. They were always, in my poor judgment, unconstitutional; but they got themselves fastened on to the country, and there was never power enough, until the necessities of the country required a new system of finance, to break off their hold. We have rid the country of them, and the Congress of the United States, ay, and the good judgment of the people, will never permit that system again to be imposed upon the country.

What is the next proposition? Why, it is said we must not interfere with the national banks because they patriotically helped us during the war. Upon that I take issue with each and every advocate of the banks. On the contrary, they helped themselves, not us. It is said they lent money to the Government. How did they do it? Let me state the way a national bank got itself into existence in New England during the war, when gold was 200, and five-twenties were at par, in currency, or nearly that. A company of men got together $300,000 in national bank bills, and went to the register of the treasury with gold at 200 and bought United States five-twenty bonds at par. They stepped into the office of the Comptroller of the Currency and asked to be established as a national bank, and received from him $270,000 in currency, without interest, upon pledging these bonds of the United States they had just bought with their $300,000 of the same kind of money. Now, let us balance the books, and how does the account stand? Why, the United States Government receives $30,000 in national bank bills more from the banks than it gave them in bills; in other words, it borrowed of the bank $30,000 in currency, for which, in fact, it paid $18,000 a year in gold interest, equal to $36,000 in currency, for the use of this $30,000. Let me repeat. The difference between what the United States received and paid out was only $30,000, and for the use of that the Government pay on the bonds deposited by the company, bought with the same kind of money, $18,000 a year interest in gold, equal to $36,000 in currency.

But the thing did not stop there. The gentlemen were shrewd financiers; their bank was a good one; they went to the Secretary of the Treasury and said, "Let our bank be made a public depository." Very well; it was a good bank; the managers were good men; there was no objection to the bank. It was made a public depository, and thereupon the commissaries, the quartermasters, the medical director and purveyor, and the paymasters were all directed to deposit their public funds in this bank. Very soon the bank found that they had a line of steady deposits belonging to the Government of about a million dollars, and that the $270,000 they had received from the

Comptroller of the Currency would substantially carry on their daily business, and as the Government gives three days on all its drafts if the bank was pressed it was easy enough to go on the street if they had good security. They took the million of Government money so deposited with them and loaned it to the Government for the Government's own bonds, and received therefor $60,000 more interest in gold for the loan to the Government of its own money, which in currency was equal to $120,000. So that when we come finally to balance the books the Government is paying $156,000 a year for the loan of $30,000. And this is the system which is to be fastened forever on the country as a means of furnishing a circulating medium!

This, only using round numbers for the purpose of illustration, is an actual and not a feigned occurrence. You will see it was a perfectly safe operation for the banks, though not a very profitable one for the Government, because they held ample security for the Government deposits in its own bonds. But the difficulty is the Government was paying interest all the while on its own deposits; and this state of facts is only rendered possible by this system of supplying the banks with circulation by the Government without interest.

The next reason advanced why we should not interfere with these banks, if I understand it, is that we are told by very high authority this system will become the banking system of the world; having inaugurated it, we are so much in love with it that all the nations will pattern after it. Let the rest of the world try it for a few years when we have done with it, and then, if the rest of the nations adopt it, we can return to it, but not till then.

Sir, am I slandering these institutions? Are they not making money at a rate which is beyond all precedent. Let me state another case, which might be an actual case, and perhaps I could call the name of the man. A very shrewd man takes his $100,000 and goes to the treasury and obtains bonds; he then gets a banking charter, and receives his bills amounting to $90,000; then he buys with those same bills $90,000 worth of bonds, and comes home and sits in his office, and that is his bank, and his money is all in circulation. Says he: Why should I trouble myself to lend my money to the farmers around me on sixty-day notes when I can lend it at from ten to twelve per cent. on long twenty-year Government bonds, and Mr. Blaine says I am to be paid in gold for them; that is as good banking as I want to do; the bills never come home; they are going all over the West and South, and I am getting $22,800 interest on my original $100,000; what do I want more? I am comfortable and happy; I think this "banking system is the wisest one the world ever saw, and that it ought to be adopted all the world over."

But let us take the banks' own exhibit of themselves. I hold in my hand the abstract of reports of national banking associations for the 1st of October last. Let us see their condition. They have $419,000,000 of capital stock paid in; they have been in operation on an average of less than four years; they have divided from twelve to twenty per cent., about twelve in New England and from fifteen to twenty per cent. where money is scarcer and the rate of interest ranks higher. In addition to these dividends, take their own statement: "surplus fund, $66,000,000; undivided profits, $33,000,000"; showing that they have got, after all these dividends, near twenty-five per cent. surplus of that capital stock laid away. What other business, taxed or untaxed, if any untaxed business can be found in this country, will allow a yearly dividend of from fifteen to twenty-five per cent. and a surplus accumulation in four years of twenty-five per cent. on the capital? And from whom and from where do these profits come? They come ultimately from where all taxation, all profits, all productions must come, the labor of the country and nowhere else; and we are asked here to perpetuate a system which takes these immense profits from the labor of the country and puts them into the hands of capitalists without a pretence of adequate benefit received by the people.

Why, sir, it is an axiom in finance, if there are any axioms in finance, that any business which is safe should have small profits, and business that is hazardous should have large profits; but here the state of things is reversed; the banking business, which, if well conducted, is the safest business on earth, and which heretofore has always been content with small profits, is now the most profitable of all businesses, and has the largest returns without any risks.

Every member of this House can argue these propositions for himself better than I can argue them for him. It is my part only to suggest the topics upon the question of currency. I insist, as my first proposition, that there should be this change in bank circulation, and by that means we would diminish our interest-bearing debt $300,000,000 by redeeming it with the greenbacks we should thus issue.

We have to-day in circulation in various forms in round numbers $759,000,000. A portion of it, I agree, is locked up in banks; fifteen per cent. in the country, and twenty-five per cent. in the city banks as their currency for the redemption of their bills; a procedure the wisdom of which I have yet to be taught, because the United States is the final indorser and payer of all their bills. I do not see how it makes it any safer to lock up fifteen to twenty-five per cent. of the indorser's notes for their redemption; and I desire some of the able bankers in this House to explain to me what good result is hoped for from this smothering of a portion of the national currency, which the banks take care, however, shall be interest-bearing to them.

I will suggest a reason why that requirement was placed in the statute book. There was a lingering idea in law of the old specie basis, and of getting an equivalent in its place. Legislators seem to have forgotten that we had wandered away from the specie basis; that they were putting in its place but the notes of the United States to redeem notes of the United States. If we can release, therefore, the whole circulation of about seven hundred million dollars, perhaps that will relieve the present contraction in the currency.

We are told that we must preserve the national banks, because if we do not there will be nobody to circulate our money. Let us examine that a moment. If money will not circulate it is because nobody wants money. My anxiety is to provide the people with money that they do want and will circulate, not with money they do not want. I have never yet seen any man who has refused the notes of the United States when the Government has paid them out. When I find such a man, I will agree to charter a bank for the purpose of forcing them upon him, and not until then.

The truth is that at the present hour the country is suffering from the want of those very notes. We have nominally some seven hundred and fifty millions of currency, but actually only about five hundred and fifty millions in circulation. Mr. Chase reported the circulation of this country before the war, including gold, to be about four hundred and seventy-seven million dollars. Now we have only $550,000,000 in actual circulation, though we are doing more than three times the business calling for the use of cash that we were doing before the war. During the ten years from 1847 to 1857 the deposits and circulation of the banks averaged about thirteen dollars per man. Now, on account of our doing so much more of our business for cash, the deposits and circulation of the banks are about twenty-four dollars per man. And, if you take into consideration the currency furnished by the United States, the $300,000,000 of greenbacks, or about that sum, you will find that it is about thirty-four dollars per man, reckoning thirty-six million people in the United States. This shows that we require in our business three times, or certainly two and a half times, as much cash as before the war. Everybody knows this to be fact.

How was it before the war with the Eastern manufacturer? He sent to New Orleans and bought his cotton, giving drafts for six or eight months. The merchant in New Orleans came East and bought the manufactured goods, giving his notes for from six months to a year; and all the cash that was wanted was enough to settle up the balances.

And now, when we send out for cotton we must send out greenbacks, because of the change in the mode of doing business; and we have a currency that stands at par there, and for what they want from us they must send the greenbacks. Everyone knows that the business of this country is done twice or thrice as much in cash as it was before the war; and therefore I think this country will bear from eight hundred to a thousand million dollars of circulation without redundancy as soon as business revives, and that will make it revive. But my friends say "that may be too much." Perhaps it may be; but it is very easy, it seems to me, for us to have that amount of circulation without redundancy; and as each legal-tender note is, as we have seen, a part of the debt secured by mortgage of the whole property of the United States, without depreciation.

Our debt now is $2,500,000,000, about $2,200,000,000 of it interest-bearing. Suppose we issue our legal-tender greenbacks, as I will call them for convenience, and buy up or redeem our interest-bearing debt that is due to the amount of $1,000,000,000. Then our debt stands, $1,000,000,000 of non-interest-bearing debt and $1,500,000,000 of interest-bearing debt. Now, if that $1,000,000,000 of circulation is too much, *i. e.*, more than is needed for currency, I agree with the gentleman from Maine that it will be depreciated. But what is too much? Too much is more than will be absorbed as currency in the business of the country. That is to say, if because of an over-issue by the Government there is an accumulation of non-interest-bearing notes, greenbacks, in the hands of any man, they are not productive, and he will dispose of them at a discount, if he can do no better, for something that is productive. The only question as to redundancy, therefore, is whether the notes in his hands are worth more for use in his business as currency than they would be to him if invested in a loan to the Government. Now, then, I propose that for $300,000,000 of this non-interest-bearing debt we shall issue an interest-bearing loan at once which shall be that exact loan which my friend from Maine yesterday thought would be so absurd—a loan bearing a low rate of interest and convertible and reconvertible into greenbacks at the pleasure of the holder at any day and at any hour.

Let us see how such a loan would operate. A man has more money than he wants to use. He with such a loan can go to a public depository, leave his money and take his bond. Then when he wants his money again he goes to the depository, leaves his bond and takes his money for his bond, principal and interest; that is to say, when the non-interest-bearing note of the United States is worth less to a business man than his bond he will exchange it for this bond; when the notes as currency are worth more to him to use in business or speculation than the investment he will return the bond and take the currency. Thus, without any banks to push out the circulation just when it is not wanted or draw it back just when it is wanted, as the practice now is, we shall have an automatic financial system, self-regulating, or rather regulated by the great law of supply and demand, the best of all regulators. When money is wanted by the business community up to the amount of notes issued by the United States, it will be at once got; when it is not wanted, it will be returned to the Government, which being a borrower for a long series of years to come will be glad to take it. There can be no redundancy, because every man will know exactly where to place these non-interest-bearing notes when he has got through with them as money. When money is wanted at the West to move your crops in the fall you take it from the treasury and move the crops; when you get through with the money you take it back to the treasury and get the bonds, in the same manner as when you have got through with your wagons you put them back in your barns for use next year. Thus the whole monetary system of the country will go on without redundancy and without shock and without inflation.

More than that, sir, as I believe I demonstrated yesterday, it will be impossible to have inflation, because this currency being convertible and reconvertible from time to time, and being always an integral part of the public debt, it will never change its relative value to the property of the people of the United States. Why, sir, what is the measure of the value of your house? If it is worth $10,000 it is ten thousand twenty-five hundred millionth parts of the public debt; and it will remain so until a portion of that debt is paid, when it will be appreciated, or until the public debt is expanded, when it will be depreciated. It will remain of exactly the same relative value however much the form of the public debt be changed, but will always be more valuable as the public debt grows more valuable, *i. e.,* as it diminishes.

Now, sir, if I am right, and if the country will bear this thousand millions of non-interest-bearing notes as currency—and if it will not, the good judgment of the Ways and Means Committee and the Committee on Banking and Currency will settle that for us on full examination, so that I certainly may use that sum for illustration in so far as it will bear it—so far will it diminish the interest-bearing debt. You will, therefore, bring the interest-bearing debt down to $1,500,000,000, where it can easily be managed. It is said you must not pay these five-twenties in greenbacks? Why, sir, you will never need to pay them in greenbacks.

What shall you do, then? You should issue a loan on long time, at a low rate of interest, thirty or fifty years, with the proceeds of which to redeem them or to be exchanged for them. For, sir, I am not for this generation paying all this debt. I think we had done our share when we contracted it. [Laughter.] We ought to leave it to our children to do theirs by paying it. I see gentlemen smile. But, sir, in all solemnity, when we contracted this we contracted it with the loss of the best blood of the nation and the loss of the best lives we had; in suffering, in sorrow, in labor, in woe, amid horrors unnumbered, to save this great experiment of government, republican in form and freedom for all, for them and for our posterity forever, and they owe us some debt of gratitude for that so great a boon; and should we who bore all the suffering and agony bear also all the taxation consequent upon this great work?

I say, then, let us change these $1,500,000,000 of interest-bearing debt into a long loan—a taxable loan, taxable by State and municipal authorities. But some friend of mine may say that if we make the loan taxable by States the States will tax the loan out of existence; that there may be some State hostile to the general Government which will tax the loan out of existence. I beg his pardon; such hostile taxation will only tax the loan out of that State, and deprive the citizens of that State of a profitable and desirable investment, which will be taken up by citizens of other States where it is not so taxed.

There are some disadvantages in a taxable loan worthy of examination. Let us consider them. It is said that no government ever allowed another subordinate government to tax its loans. True, but there never was before any government, like ours, having a complex government of States and a national Government over all and the people the same in both and each.

It is said that what States get by taxing the loan to carry on their municipal governments the general Government loses. But is this so? The people have to pay the taxes to sustain both State and national governments. So what the people lose as citizens of the United States because of taxation of the loan they gain as citizens of the State by taxation; for the people at last pay all, lose all, and suffer all. If it be said that there will be inequality of taxation it is answered again that unjust taxation, too burdensome, will only drive the loan out of such State, so that in practice there can be no inequality.

Another objection is that you cannot sell a taxable loan at so high a price. Why not? Because it will depreciate because of taxation. It will depreciate, however, exactly according to the amount levied upon it by taxation. Be it so. Who gets the benefit of that taxation? Why, sir, the people. All that it depreciates because of taxation, being received back from the taxes, will relieve the people from so much taxation. If in some States the loan is taxed more than in others there will not be any unequality, because such excess of taxation will only send that form of investment out of that municipality.

There is another objection to a taxable loan, namely: that it is a form of investment easily to be concealed from taxation. But it cannot any more easily be concealed as an investment than can notes, bonds, or money in all shapes. Let me ask you what is the operation to-day of your five-twenty non-taxable loan. A capitalist has money which he is using in his business, and he sees the assessor coming round. He goes into market and puts his money into Government bonds. The assessor calls, the man has no taxable property, the assessor passes by, and the next day the artful dodger sells his bonds for the money, and goes on speculating. He saves the taxation, and next year he repeats the operation.

These are, I understand, some of the objections to taxable loans. But it has also its advantages. In the first place it puts the wealth of the country and the labor of the country upon an equal footing as to taxation. It compels the surplus wealth as well as the industry of the country to be taxed.

Another advantage of a taxable loan is that it relieves the public debt from an apparent injustice. And it is of no consequence how small the injustice is, for the people feel an unjust burden, however light, more than a just burden, however heavy.

Still another advantage is claimed for a taxable loan. It

has been held by many financiers—I do not claim to be enough of a financier to give an opinion as to the merit of the claim, but each gentleman will settle the question for himself—that it is a great advantage to borrow money abroad, in the various markets of the world, at low rates of interest. Therefore we find our canal and railroad companies and all great enterprises attempting to place their bonds in Europe. If that is good financiering, what is the objection to our national loans going abroad, provided we get back the money for them? The principal objection has been found to be that, whenever there is war or rumor of war abroad, a financial panic is created there, our bonds come home for realization and interfere with our money relations and unsettle our business. But, if our bonds were taxable for State or municipal purposes, they would not of course be taxable abroad, and would then stand from ten to fifteen per cent. higher there—perhaps twenty or twenty-five per cent. higher—no man can tell, until the theory is reduced to practice, how much higher than at home; and the holder abroad, having to consent to so great a sacrifice before he could realize on them, would not be very likely to send them home upon us, which is the greatest danger now to our finances whenever there is the slightest financial trouble in Europe.

Such a taxable loan held abroad would be kept there steadily. If, however, any great trouble should happen in Europe so that the bonds would be sent home at all hazards, they would come at such low rates as to be economically and readily bought up here, and our people could afford to take them even with the burden of tax upon them.

Therefore, I have no doubt that a loan of $1,500,000,000 for thirty or fifty years could be placed to-morrow at five per cent. if taxable, with which to get the money to redeem the five-twenties or in which to exchange them, and thus save millions of taxation. I should prefer, so far as I am advised, until I hear further debate, that such bond should be a taxable one of five per cent., or three and sixty-five hundredths sterling, if untaxable. Either would sell, in my opinion, to-morrow at as high rates in the markets of Europe as does our five-twenty loan now, while they would not interfere with the ability of this country to pay its debts or keep our loan down both at home and abroad. Our loan does not now sell at a discount because anybody doubts the ability or willingness of this country to pay every dollar it has contracted.

A Member.—Nor its willingness?

Mr. Butler.—Nor its willingness. Nobody doubts that.

I am obliged to my friend for the suggestion. I think I can convince the House that nobody doubts its willingness. What are our gold certificates—$14,000,000 of them—only promises of the United States to pay in gold on demand? And yet they are at a little premium over gold, both at home and abroad, because they are more convenient to handle. If anybody feared the willingness of the United States Government to pay according to its promise or doubted its ability, why should not these gold certificates go below par? It is because all people understand that, when we promise to pay in gold by a contract—which my friend from Maine [Mr. Blaine] does not need to argue is a gold contract, or the legal intent of which my older friend from Pennsylvania [Mr. Stevens] does not need to explain to us hereafter—when it is on the face of the certificate, "payable in gold on demand," then that promise is above par. This pledge of the Government causes that note to stand better than gold in the markets of the world to-day.

Nay, more, our ten-forty, five per cent. bonds, having six years only more to run before the Government has the option of paying them, and therefore hardly to be considered as a funded debt, are selling now within one or two per cent. of some of the five-twenty six per cent. loans, payable in gold according to the argument of my friend from Maine. What makes the difference? On five-twenties there is one per cent. interest due more than on the other. Why do they come so near to each other in price? It is because no man can read the statute book and doubt that the one is payable in gold and the other in lawful money of the United States. Therefore I repeat that in the markets of the world there is no doubt, as there is none in any man's mind, of the willingness or the ability of the United States Government to perform its contract. But the doubt is as to what is the contract—whether it is a contract of Jews and sharpers or it is a contract of the Congress of the United States.

But I am met right here again with the proposition. Why stir this now? Since I began my speech half a dozen gentlemen, some friendly and some unfriendly, have tipped me on the shoulder and said, "Now, Mr. Butler, what is the use of making a fuss about this now? Why not let these bonds run twenty years and by that time gold and greenbacks will be the same? Why disturb the matter? What are you getting up this row for?" [Laughter.]

A Member.—A sensible question. [Laughter.]

Mr. Butler.—Yes, very sensible, and I am going to answer

it in a sensible manner; and the answer is this, that these five-twenty bonds are on eleven to twelve per cent. interest, and they will double oftener than once in eight years; and if we let them go on for twenty years the people will have to pay them twice over in interest, and then owe them still. That is the answer. Is there not good sense in that, now? [Laughter.] The reason why I am anxious about this now is that it is our urgent, pressing duty, not to be shunned or avoided, to relieve the people from the burden of this great weight of taxation.

Let me restate it so that nobody will forget it. At the rate of interest we are paying these bonds double once in six years; at six per cent. they double once in eleven years, and with the tax making eight per cent. they will double once in about eight years. Set down the figures and when you find out let me know how the figures read.

Rufus P. Spalding [O.].—The gentleman is mistaken.

Mr. Butler.—When do you say they will double at eight per cent.?

Mr. Spalding.—Once in about twelve years.

Mr. Butler.—Six per cent. in gold, with the tax off, is equal to eight per cent. semi-annually at compound interest, and it will not double under twelve years! I do not know anything about figures in Ohio, but figures in Massachusetts do not bring out that result. [Laughter.]

Mr. Spalding.—We have had enough of that sort of wit.

Mr. Butler.—I presume you have had enough, sir.

Mr. Price.—Will the gentleman yield to me just a moment?

Mr. Butler.—Certainly.

Mr. Price.—I presume the gentleman from Massachusetts means to be correct.

Mr. Butler.—Yes, I try to be, exactly.

Mr. Price.—And to place upon record facts in reference to those things about which he talks.

Mr. Butler.—Yes, sir.

Hiram Price [Ia.].—The gentleman said a moment ago that the difference between ten-forties and five-twenties was one per cent. I was satisfied in my own mind that was a mistake and on referring to the document I find that on the 20th of November five-twenties were 108 and ten-forties 102 ⅜.

Mr. Butler.—Has the gentleman read quotations of the lowest five-twenties and the highest ten-forties?

Mr. Price.—I read those of 1862; I have not read the list.

Mr. Butler.—Ah! that will not do, if you please, those of 1865 are lower. [Laughter.]

Mr. Price.—Well, I will give them all if the gentleman wishes it.

The Chairman.—Does the gentleman from Massachusetts yield further to the gentleman from Iowa?

Mr. Butler.—Oh, certainly; I yield to everybody in this discussion.

Mr. Price.—I do not wish to encroach on the gentleman's time.

Mr. Butler.—It is no encroachment.

Mr. Price.—The statement made was evidently incorrect, I presume unintentionally so, and I thought it best to put the gentleman right.

Mr. Butler.—Now, will the gentleman take one or two things into this calculation and then I will stand corrected. He read from the quotation in the newspapers. Will he tell me how long before the coupons of the five-twenties are payable and how much interest is due, whether they are "flat," to use the language of the broker's board, and how long before the coupons of the ten-forties are payable? If he will make the calculation he will find this statement to be correct, and I am ready to meet him anywhere upon it; he will find that between the lowest class of five-twenties and the highest class of ten-forties there is less than two per cent. difference.

Mr. Price.—Does the gentleman want an answer to that?

Mr. Butler.—Certainly.

Mr. Price.—I need not say to the gentleman, I presume, nor to any gentleman in this House, that the coupons of the bonds that I have quoted were paid the 1st day of this month, and consequently there is only the balance of this month's interest due on them, and therefore they are "flat." Everybody knows about the ten-forties. The interest was paid on the five-twenties that I have quoted on the 1st of November. Before that they were selling at 113 and a fraction, and as high as 114. With the coupons cut off the 1st day of the month they are selling at 108, according to the quotations of the board on the 26th instant (yesterday), and ten-forties from 102⅛ to 102⅜. I give you the largest quotations for ten-forties, and the benefit of the doubt if there is any.

Mr. Butler.—I am always glad to be corrected, but I must still maintain my position. I may be wrong, but I must insist on the position until I am better advised than I have been yet. Is the discussion of this grave question to be decided by an accidental difference yesterday of one or two cents upon this class of securities?

Isaac Newton once said he occupied himself in his great studies by picking up pebbles on the shore of the great ocean of truth; but I have never heard that he selected the very smallest ones.

I was about saying, when I was interrupted, that the objection has been made that we shall never return to specie payments under this system. Let us be definite. What do gentlemen mean by "returning to specie payments"? Do they mean returning to the state of finances that existed before the war? That is, when this Government collected its dues in gold, and paid its debts in gold; and when people had a currency based on gold, but which never could be redeemed in gold? If they mean to return to that state of things I respectfully submit that for the present it is impossible.

It is impossible for this reason: we had a specie-paying Government from the time the sub-treasury law went into operation down to the war, that is, the Government collected all its dues in gold, and paid all its debts in gold; and all the money needed for governmental purposes collected and paid out was from about thirty to sixty million dollars from year to year, before 1860 running up at one time, I believe, to seventy-odd million. I am now using amounts bearing almost exactly correct relation to each other by way of illustration, and I hope no gentleman will hunt up an old newspaper to show that I am not right within two or three dollars. During the same period there was from about ninety to two hundred and ten million dollars of specie in the country. In other words, it took for governmental purposes alone about one-third of all the specie in the country. We all remember that whenever there was any hitch in governmental operations so that gold accumulated in the sub-treasury it disordered all our monetary affairs and produced financial crises.

In 1857, when some ten million gold had thus accumulated, it was deemed so disturbing an element in the commerce of the country that Mr. Cobb, then Secretary of the Treasury, paid thirty per cent. advance for the bonds of the United States in order to relieve the money market by putting out the accumulated gold in the treasury.

It took then one-third of all the gold in the country to carry on the Government business, and we could hardly get around at that. We now have from two hundred to two hundred and twenty-five million dollars of gold only, so far as is known, in the country. The Government is using every year for its operations some three hundred and fifty million dollars. If the

Government could not get around without disturbing the finances in collecting its dues and paying its debts in gold before the war, using only one-third of all the gold in the country, how can it now get on with its operations, requiring $350,000,000 to be taken out of $225,000,000, which is all the gold now in the country, not allowing anybody else to use a dollar? It is therefore entirely impracticable for the Government to carry on its great operations of $350,000,000 upon a gold basis, wholly irrespective of the question of the credit of the Government or its ability to command all the gold in the country. It might indeed carry on its operations partly in gold and partly in paper, but that is not a return to specie payments by the Government. But it is as utterly impossible at the present time for the Government to carry on its operations on a gold basis, in the manner in which it did before the war, as it is to make three hundred and fifty go into two hundred and twenty-five and have a remainder over, which, I take it, is impossible by any figures out of the State of Ohio. [Laughter.]

In my judgment, all talk about returning to specie payments in July, 1868, or any other period in the immediate future, is illusory and vain. How are we to get back to specie payments? In the first place, by reducing your taxation, stimulating your industry, raising your productiveness, bringing down the expenditure of the Government, specially the first and great expenditure and burden over all others—the taxation for the purpose of paying your doubly exorbitant interest on the public debt as now constituted.

Reduce your interest-paying debt as you may to some one billion five hundred million dollars, and then fund this at five per cent. at highest, even with taxation. This will call for $75,000,000 as interest of the public debt annually; or fund it at three and sixty-five one-hundredths per cent. sterling if untaxable, as you may, and that will make only some fifty-five millions as interest, and there will then be some $60,000,000 to $85,000,000 of gold coming in at your custom houses to help pay the expenses of the Government, after paying up the interest on the debt.

Then enforce faithfully and justly the collection of a judicious taxation on but two articles of luxury, whisky and tobacco, and you may release every other interest from taxation, and the land shall blossom as the rose, and the hum of productive industry give sweet harmony to the delighted ear.

Leaving financial matters as they now stand, you never can go back to specie payments. Get back to specie payments!

How is it proposed to be done by the Secretary of the Treasury? Why, in order to do that he asked Congress to aid him—to sell our bonds in Europe; and he came before Congress asking authority to deposit gold in Europe to pay the interest there, so that he might sell more bonds there. When he sells those bonds in Europe, what does he get for them? Seventy cents or thereabouts on the dollar. What is specie payment? Paying one hundred cents. How is he going to be able to pay one hundred cents on what we owe now? By making new debts at seventy cents? I would like somebody skilled in figures to cipher out that problem.

But the matter does not stop there. If the Secretary of the Treasury got even gold for his bonds he would have something to show. But what are those bonds sold for? They are sold abroad to meet the balance of trade. What does that mean? It means to pay the balances owing for broadcloth that we wear, for brandy that we drink, for cigars that we smoke. What would be thought of a financier who should insist he was getting solvent selling his notes at seventy cents on the dollar in order to buy broadcloth, brandy, and cigars? Who would insist such a one was a good financier? Yet this is the exact system upon which the finances of this country are being carried on to-day.

You may consult upon your tariff bills till you are blind; your Committees of Ways and Means may fix up schemes of protection for home manufactures till they are weary, but they will afford no protection to American industry. Why? The bankers and merchants of Europe never expect Government loans there to be paid. Most of the governments of Europe have irredeemable loans, the interest of which only is ever to be paid. Now, with the rate of interest two per cent. at Antwerp, two per cent. at London, one and three-fourths per cent. at Frankfort, two and one-fourth per cent. at Paris, our bonds are eagerly snapped up; foreign agents come over here to get them. With the discount of thirty per cent. on our bonds bearing six per cent. gold interest, they can always undersell us, and vitiate any tariff that we choose to pass. We are thus dealing with them in manufacturing at home with thirty per cent. against us. Nay, more; suppose there are two manufacturing establishments, one in this country and one in England, the two establishments equally well managed, both manufacturing the same article and making exactly the same profit; the English manufatcurer can make a ten per cent. dividend, while our manufacturer is losing money. Why? Because the capital of the English manufacturer costs him but two per cent., while with our high rate of interest, reduced by our Government rate on the five-twentieths, the American manufacturer's capital costs him twelve per cent.—a difference of ten per cent., which should be a sufficient dividend for any well-conducted business that was not a national bank.

Under such circumstances we cannot compete with the foreign manufacturer. It is useless for my friends from New England and my friends from Pennsylvania to ask for a tariff on their manufactures; it is useless for my friends from the West to ask for a tariff on their wool so long as this great difference in money is against us. Why, my friends from the West thought that, if they could only get a tariff on wool, wool would go up, command a fair price, and the farmer should get pay for his labor. They got all the tariff they asked, and I am glad they did. But the more tariff they got, the more wool went down. Am I not right? Was wool ever so cheap as it has been this year, since we have put a duty on it? Why? Because of this difference between this country and abroad in the rate of money, our taxation and the discount on our bonds entirely neutralizing any tariff for the protection of the East or the protection of the West.

There are some things we must do. They are the pressing duties of the hour. First, we must stop this contraction of the currency now going on. It has been contracted at least $100,000,000 in the last year. Some men say only $48,000,000, or $4,000,000 a month. But $77,000,000 of compound-interest notes must be reckoned in, and the contraction of the currency will in fact be found to be more than $100,000,000. Secondly, we must have the gold hoarded in the treasury of the United States sold at public auction at stated periods of time, so all may know when, except of course enough, with the receipts from customs to meet the interest on the gold-bearing debt. Thirdly, we must repeal the immense number of discretionary powers with which the exigencies of the war caused us to clothe the Secretary of the Treasury. The treasury of the United States should not be left in the power of any one man. It is of no consequence who that may be. Whenever the Secretary of the Treasury has discretionary powers he may exalt this man's property and decrease that of another; he may issue this loan and take in another. He holds the business of the country in the hollow of his hand. I by no means mean to make any charges of corruption or favoritism against anybody. Following his views of finance, the present Secretary of the Treasury has done his duty. But I say it is a dangerous power, one given in consideration of the exigencies of the war. The war now being over, the Congress of the United States, to whom the Constitution has wisely trusted the finances of the Government, should enact a positive law, not to be swerved from by the Secretary of the Treasury upon any pretence whatever, declaring exactly what shall and what shall not be done with the finances of the country. These three measures are of pressing necessity and imperative for prompt relief. When they are carried out, when the gold is sold and bonds paid with the proceeds so as to relieve greenbacks and send them back into circulation, when this discretionary power which may or may not be exercised improperly is taken away, and when the banks are brought back to their position of banks of loan and discount, then the country will be relieved. Then after full and fair discussion you will see exactly the amount which our country will absorb in non-interest-bearing notes of the United States, and fix that amount. Then consolidate the nineteen different kinds of loans and securities we have now into one long taxable loan of the United States that shall be a consolidated funded security known by all the people, exact in its terms, plain in its contracts, and unoppressive in its rate of interest. Then shall the country resume its onward march of prosperity.

George F. Miller [Pa.].—I should like to put this question to the gentleman from Massachusetts: taking for granted that by a legal construction of the statutes allowing the issue of five-twenty bonds the principal was payable in lawful money, which, of course, would include greenbacks, yet if the Secretary of the Treasury, believing that the principal as well as the interest was payable in coin, and he and others who had charge of disposing of them represented to the public that such bonds (principal and interest) were payable in gold, and thus inducing capitalists and others to vest their money in such securities at a time the country was in peril and funds were needed to carry on the war to put down rebellion, would it not be bad faith in Congress now to refuse to sanction the payment in coin?

Mr. Butler.—The question is fairly put, and deserves a fair and candid answer. The answer I make to it in the first place is this: That the Secretary of the Treasury did not believe these bonds were payable in gold, had no right to give any such assurance, and no man had the right to rely on such terms. Secondly, that we here, as the Government of the United States, are standing as trustees between the people of the United States, the debtor, and the bondholder, the creditor, and we have no right to administer that trust upon any equitable considerations not clearly arising out of the terms of the contract, or upon any chivalric notions of honor, but exactly according to the words and spirit of the contract creating the obligation. We have no more right than a guardian would have to pay what he supposes might be an equitable debt of his ward, or an executor to exercise his notions of honor by paying out the funds of his trust against the protest of the creditors of the estate or the legatees.

Mr. Miller.—One question more. Is there any other obligation upon the United States but that of an equitable one? The United States being a sovereign cannot be sued.

Mr. Butler.—The United States Government is bound by its laws to the same extent as the humblest individual; and it makes no difference as to its obligations that there is no court in which to enforce its contracts except this highest court, the Congress of the United States.

CHAPTER XIII

Contraction of the Currency

Report of Hugh McCulloch, Secretary of the Treasury, on Contraction of the Currency, Payment in Gold of Bond Interest, Etc.—Gen. Robert C. Schenck [O.] Introduces in the House Bill to Prevent Further Reduction of the Currency by Retiring United States Notes; It Is Opposed by James G. Blaine [Me.], Gen. James A. Garfield [O.], *et al.;* Passed—Debate in the Senate: in Favor, John Sherman [O.], William M. Stewart [Nev.], John B. Henderson [Mo.], Oliver P. Morton [Ind.], Timothy O. Howe [Wis.]; Opposed, Justin S. Morrill [Vt.], Henry W. Corbett [Ore.], William P. Fessenden [Me.], George F. Edmunds [Vt.], John Conness [Cal.]; Bill Is Passed with Amendments; House Refuses to Concur, and Bill Is Passed by Both Chambers without Amendments; It Becomes a Law Without Signature of the President.

THE report of Hugh McCulloch, Secretary of the Treasury, which accompanied President Johnson's message of December, 1867, is one of the most notable documents in the economic literature not only of the United States, but of the world. It deals with the principles not only of money, but also of taxation, in profound yet luminous fashion.

It was, in particular, a defence of the Secretary's persistent policy of contracting the currency on every opportunity afforded him under the law, and, connected with this, of paying in gold the interest of all Government bonds, whether or not such payment had been specifically promised in the law authorizing their issue.

McCulloch's Report

[abridged]

During the month of September, 1865, the army having been reduced nearly to a peace footing, it became apparent that the internal revenues and the receipts from customs would be sufficient to pay all the expenses of the Government and the interest on the public debt, so that thenceforward the efforts of the Secretary were to be turned from borrowing to funding. Besides the United States notes in circulation, there were nearly $1,300,000,000 of debts in the form of interest-bearing notes, temporary loans, and certificates of indebtedness, a portion of which were maturing daily, and all of which, with the exception of the temporary loans (which, being in the nature of loans on call, might or might not be continued, according to the will of the holders), must be converted into bonds or paid in money before the 16th of October, 1868. The country had passed through a war unexampled in its expensiveness and sacrifice of lives; it was afflicted with a redundant and depreciated currency; prices of property and the cost of living had advanced correspondingly with the increase of the circulating medium; men, estimating their means by a false standard of value, had become reckless and extravagant in their expenditures and habits; business, in the absence of a staple basis, was unsteady and speculative, and great financial troubles, the usual result of expensive wars, seemed to be almost inevitable.

It was under such circumstances that the work of funding the rapidly maturing obligations of the Government and restoring the specie standard was to be commenced. While the latter object could not be brought about until the former had been accomplished, it was highly important that the necessity of an early return to specie payments should never be lost sight of. At the same time it seemed to the Secretary that a return to the true measure of value, however desirable, was not of sufficient importance to justify the adoption of such measures as might prevent funding, and injuriously affect those branches of industry from which revenue was to be derived, much less such measures as might, by exciting alarm, precipitate the disaster which so many anticipated and feared. Thus the condition of the country and the treasury determined the policy of the Secretary, which has been to convert the interest-bearing notes, temporary loans, etc., into gold-bearing bonds, and to contract the paper circulation by the redemption of United States notes. For the last two years this policy has been steadily but carefully pursued, and the result upon the whole has been satisfactory to the Secretary, and, as he believes, to a large majority of the people.

There is not, in the opinion of the Secretary, any insuperable difficulty in the way of an early and a permanent restoration of the specie standard. It may not be safe to fix the exact time, but, with favorable crops next year, and with no legislation unfavorable to contraction at this session, it ought not to be delayed beyond the 1st of January or, at the furthest, the 1st of July, 1869. Nothing will be gained, however, by a forced resumption. When the country is in a condition to maintain specie payments they will be restored as a necessary consequence. To such a condition of national prosperity as will insure a permanent restoration of the specie standard the following measures are, in the opinion of the Secretary, important, if not indispensable:

First. The funding or payment of the balance of interest-bearing notes, and a continued contraction of the paper currency.

Second. The maintenance of the public faith in regard to the funded debt.

Third. The restoration of the Southern States to their proper relations to the Federal Government.

If this opinion be correct the question of permanent specie payments, involving, as it does, the prosperity of the country, underlies the great questions of currency, taxation, and reconstruction, which are now engaging the attention of the people, and cannot fail to receive the earnest and deliberate attention of Congress.

To this policy of contraction the action of the Secretary has been conformed, and the effect of it has been so salutary, and the continuation of it would be so obviously wise, that he would not consider it necessary to say one word in its favor were there not indications that, under the teachings of the advocates of a large and consequently a depreciated currency, such views are being inculcated as, if not corrected, may lead to its abandonment.

Money is simply a medium of exchange and measure of value. As a medium it facilitates exchanges, and by doing this necessarily stimulates production. It does not follow, however, that exchanges are facilitated and production stimulated in proportion to its increase. It is a measure of value, but it does not necessarily create values. It is an indispensable agent in trade between individuals, and in commerce between nations; the great incentive to enterprise and labor in the wide range of human energy and skill; but, great as is its power, and essential as it is to the progress of the race in civilization and refinement, there are limits beyond which its volume cannot be extended without a diminution of its usefulness. A certain amount is required for facilitating exchanges and determining values. The exact amount required cannot of course be accurately determined, but the excess or deficiency of money in a country is always pretty accurately indicated by the condition of its industry and trade. In all countries there is just as much money needed as will encourage enterprise, give employment to labor, and furnish the means for a ready exchange of property, and no more. Whenever the amount in circulation exceeds the amount required for these purposes, the fact will become apparent by a decline of industry, an advance of prices, and a tendency to speculation. Especially will this be the case when an irredeemable currency becomes the standard of value by being made a legal tender. Coin, being the circulating medium of the world, flows from one country to another in obedience to the law of trade, which prevents it from becoming anywhere, for any considerable period, excessive in amount; when this law is not interfered with by legislation, the evils of an excessive currency are corrected by the law itself. An increase of money beyond what is needed for the purposes above named, according to all experience, not only inflates prices, but diminishes labor; and coin, as a consequence, flows from the country in which the excess exists to some other where labor is more active and prices are lower: to flow back again when the loss by one country and the gain by another produce the natural results upon industry and production. Thus coin is not only the regulator of commerce but the great stimulator of industry and enterprise.

The same may be said of a convertible paper currency, which, by being convertible, will not for any considerable period be excessive; but it is rarely if ever true of an inconvertible currency, which is necessarily local, and would not be likely to be inconvertible if it were not excessive, and by being excessive and inconvertible is fluctuating and uncertain in value. The only possible exception to this rule would be found in the limitation of the amount in circulation to what might be absolutely required in the payment and disbursement of the public revenues. No matter what laws may be enacted to give credit and value to it, an irredeemable currency must, unless limited as above stated, always be a depreciated currency. The attempt to give value to paper promises by making them lawful money is not original with the United States. The experiment has been tried by other nations, and generally with the same injurious if not disastrous results. Indeed, with rare exceptions, nations that have commenced the direct issue of paper money have continued to issue it until prevented by its utter worthlessness. There may be no danger that this will be true of the United States; but there will always be ground for apprehension as long as an irredeemable and depreciated currency is not regarded as an evil—an evil to be tolerated only so long as may be necessary to retire it without great derangement of legitimate business. Inconvertible and depreciated lawful money is an agreeable but demoralizing deception. It is agreeable because it is plentiful, and because it deludes by the creation of apparent wealth. It is demoralizing by familiarizing the public mind with dishonored obligations. The prices of most kinds of property in the United States advanced near three fold during the war, but this advance was mainly the result of the increase of the circulating medium, and in reality only indicated its depreciation. The purchasing power of the money in circulation was diminished in the ratio that its volume was increased. The farmer, for example, received three dollars a bushel for his wheat, but, except for the payment of debts, these three dollars were of no more value to him than one dollar was before the suspension of specie payments.

The same was true of other kinds of property and other labor. The advance, except so far as it was the result of an increased demand, was apparent only and unreal. The same cause is sustaining prices at the present time, and will continue to do so as long as the cause exists, but the advantages resulting from it are merely imaginary, while the evils are positive and actual. No sane man supposes that his own wealth, or the wealth of the nation, is increased by the depreciation of the standard by which it is measured. If the paper circulation of the United States should be doubled during the next year, and the prices of property should be likewise doubled, would it be imagined that the real value of property would be thus advanced? Or, if the paper currency should, during the same period, be reduced fifty per cent., and prices of property should decline correspondingly, would it follow that the real value of property would thus decline? In the one case the value of the currency would be reduced in proportion to its increase in amount; in the other the currency would be increased in value as it was diminished in amount. The increase or decrease of prices would, if no counteracting causes intervened, be the natural result of the increase or decrease of the measure of value, while real values remained unchanged.

The United States notes were made a legal tender and lawful money because it was thought that this character was necessary to secure their currency. By reference to the first debates of Congress upon the subject it will be noticed that those who advocated their issue justified themselves on the ground of necessity. No one who spoke in favor of the measure favored it upon principle or hesitated to express his apprehensions that evil consequences might result from it. But the Government was in peril, the emergency was pressing, necessity seemed to sanction a departure from sound principles of finance, if not from the letter of the Constitution, and an inconvertible currency became the lawful money of the country. While the action of Congress, in authorizing the issue of these notes, seemed necessary at the time, and was undoubtedly approved by a large majority of the people, there can now, in the light of experience, be no question that the apprehensions of those who advocated the measure as a necessity were well founded. Had they not been made a legal tender, the amount in circulation would not have been excessive, and the national debt would doubtless have been hundreds of millions of dollars less than it is. The issue would have been stayed before a very large amount had been put in circulation, not because the notes would have been really more depreciated by not being made lawful money, but because their depreciation would have been manifest. By being made lawful money they became the legalized measure of value—a substitute for the precious metals—which, as a consequence, were at once demonetized and converted into articles of traffic. Made by statute a legal tender, they were of course popular with those who had debts to pay or property to sell; costing nothing, and yet seemingly adding to the value of property, supplying the means for speculation and for creating an artificial and a delusive prosperity, it is an evidence of the wisdom of Congress that the issue was stopped before the notes had become ruinously depreciated and the business of the country involved in inextricable difficulties.

But although the issue of these notes was limited, and we thus escaped the disasters which would have overwhelmed the country without such limitation, it can hardly be doubted that the resort to them was a misfortune. If this means of raising money had not been adopted bonds would have undoubtedly been sold at a heavy discount, but the fact that they were thus sold, without debasing the currency, would have induced greater economy in the use of the proceeds, while the discount on the bonds would scarcely have exceeded the actual depreciation of the notes below the coin standard. As long as notes could be issued and bonds could be sold at a premium or at par, for what the statute made money, there was a constant temptation to liberal if not unnecessary expenditures. Had the specie standard been maintained and bonds been sold at a discount for real money there would have been an economy in all the branches of the public service which unfortunately was not witnessed, and the country would have escaped the evils resulting from a disregard of the great international law, which no nation can violate with impunity, the one that makes gold and silver the only true measure of value. The financial evils under which the country has been suffering for some years past, to say nothing of the dangers which loom up in the future, are in a great degree to be traced to the direct issues by the Government of an inconvertible currency with the legal attributes of money.

Upon the demoralizing influences of an inconvertible Government currency it is not necessary to enlarge. They are forced upon our attention by every day's observation, and we cannot be blind to them if we would. The Government is virtually repudiating its own obligations by failing to redeem its notes according to their tenor. These notes are payable to bearer on demand in dollars, and not one of them is being so paid. It is not to be expected that a people will be more honest than the Government under which they live, and while the Government of the United States refuses to pay its notes according to their tenor, or at least as long as it fails to make proper effort to do so, it practically teaches to the people the doctrine of repudiation.

If the views thus presented are correct, there can be no question that there is still an excess of paper money in the United States, and that the legal-tender notes are an obstacle, and unless reduced in amount must continue to be an obstacle to a return to a stable currency.

In opposition to these views it is urged by many intelligent persons that as the credit system has been very much curtailed since 1861, and sales are made chiefly for cash, a much larger amount of currency is required than formerly for the convenient transaction of business; that there is in fact no excess of money in the United States, but that on the contrary an increase is required to move the crops, encourage enterprise, and give activity to trade. As an evidence of the correctness of this opinion, reference is made to the "tightness of the money market" in the commercial cities, and the scarcity of money in the agricultural districts.

It is undoubtedly true that the effect of a curtailment of credits would have been to increase the legitimate demand for currency, if no other means had intervened to counteract the effect of it. But such means have intervened. In all the cities and towns throughout the country, checks upon credits in banks, and bill of exchange, have largely taken the place of bank notes. Not a fiftieth part of the business of the large cities is transacted by the actual use of money, and what is true in regard to the business of the chief cities is measurably true in regard to that of towns and villages throughout the country. Everywhere bank credits and bills of exchange perform the offices of currency to a much greater extent than in former years. Except in dealings with the Government, for retail trade, for the payment of labor and taxes, for traveling expenses, the purchase of products at first hand, and for the bankers' reserve, money is hardly a necessity. The increased use of bank checks and bills of exchange counterbalances the increased demand for money resulting from the curtailment of mercantile credits. That money is in demand, and is commanding full rates of interest, is true, but this does not indicate a scarcity of it. The rates of interest in England and France have rarely been as low as within the last four months, and yet for commercial or manufacturing purposes money has not often been so difficult to be obtained. The speculative reaction or overproduction of manufactures, together with apprehensions of political troubles, have caused business to be sluggish and unprofitable, and made capitalists cautious and timid. Thus, in those countries, money was never more plentiful, and yet apparently never more scarce. Its apparent scarcity in the United States is attributable to high prices, to its uncertain value, and to its inactivity.

Money by no means becomes abundant by an increase or scarce by a diminution of its volume. The reverse is more likely to be true, especially when, as is generally the case, high prices are speculative prices, and prevent activity in exchanges. Money is in demand at the present time, not so much to move crops as to hold them—not to bring them at reasonable prices within the reach of consumers, but to withhold them from market until a large advance of prices can be established. Let the great staples of the country come forward and be sold at market prices, at such prices as, while the producer is fairly remunerated, will increase consumption and exports—let capitalists be assured that progress toward a stable basis is to be uninterrupted—and money, now considered scarce, will be found to be abundant. The actual legitimate business of the country is not larger than it was in 1860, when three hundred millions of coin and bank notes were an ample circulating medium, and when an addition of fifty millions would have made it excessive. Throughout a considerable portion of the best grain-growing sections of the United States there has been during the past year great complaint of a scarcity of money, and yet no single article of agricultural product, except wool, was to be sold there for which there was not a purchaser at more than remunerating, if not exorbitant, prices. There was no lack of money in these sections, but a lack of products to exchange for it. The hard times complained of were the consequence of short crops, and not of deficient circulation. To the farmer, who had little to sell and much to buy, an increase of the circulation would have been an injury; a curtailment of it a benefit. And yet by men in such circumstances the policy of contraction has met with a condemnation second only to that which it has received at the hands of speculators in stocks.

Next to the stock board of the commercial metropolis, the opposition to the policy of contraction has been most decided in those sections where, by reason of short crops, the people have been less prosperous than heretofore. Unfortunately, in the same sections, the harvest has been again unsatisfactory, and the demand not only for a cessation of contraction but for an increase of paper money may thus be more pressing than ever. This demand, no matter from what quarter it comes or by what interest sustained, should, in the opinion of the Secretary, be inflexibly resisted by Congress. To increase the volume of paper money for the purpose of giving relief to the country would be to foster the cause in order to cure the disease. To stay the process of contraction this year will but prepare the way for an increase of circulation the next. Whenever the policy of reducing the paper circulation of the country, with the view of a return to specie payments, shall be abandoned, it is to be apprehended that the demand for an increase will be irresistible, and that the country will plunge into bankruptcy. The specie standard must be sooner or later restored. Whether this shall be accomplished by elevating the currency by lessening its volume, or after lessening its value by increasing its volume, it is for Congress to determine. That this question will be determined promptly and wisely the Secretary is not permitted to doubt. Some progress has been made in the right direction during the past year, but there is still in the United States a plethora of paper money. If this is not so, how happens it that coin commands a premium of some forty per cent. over legal-tender notes?—that a high tariff has proved powerless to prevent excessive importations?—that capitalists hesitate in regard to the uses to which they shall put their surplus means?—that business is speculative and uncertain?—that expenses of living are driving thousands into crime and making dishonesty excusable, while honorable men of limited means are indignantly and justly complaining that they cannot live on incomes that formerly gave them a handsome support? Money may be inactive, but it is not scarce. Its inactivity is in fact the result of its uncertain value. With a circulation that is to-day at a discounty of thirty per cent., and which may by a change of policy be increased to sixty per cent. within the next year, with what safety can men engage in enterprises which look into the future, and which are needed to develop the slumbering resources of the country? Let the paper dollar truly represent the dollar in coin. Let men of capital and enterprise feel that the currency has come, or is steadily coming to the "hard-pan" of specie, and there will be a stimulus given to enterprise and labor which will banish all complaints of a scarcity of money.

If, then, it be admitted that the paper circulation is excessive, the question arises why should not the contraction be applied to the notes of the national banks instead of the United States notes, and thus a large saving of interest to the Government be effected? This question has already been answered inferentially, but its importance requires that it shall receive more definite consideration.

Prior to 1863 the banking institutions of the country, with the exception of the Bank of the United States, were created by the States, and were subject to State authority alone. They were State institutions, over which the general Government exercised no control. The right of the States to create and to manage them had been so long conceded that no interference with them by Congress, and no decision of the courts adverse to the constitutionality of their issues were apprehended.

Soon after the commencement of war it became manifest that a system of internal taxation must be adopted for the support of the Government and the maintenance of its credit, and that this would involve the necessity of a national currency of uniform value and undoubted solvency. To meet this necessity (United States notes being then regarded as only a temporary expedient) the national banking system was created, not to destroy the State banks nor injuriously to affect their business, but to furnish through their agency and that of new institutions which might be organized under it a permanent national bank note circulation. Had it been supposed that the object of those who advocated the measure was to bring the State banks under the control of the Federal Government for the purpose of destroying them, or that such would be its effect, it would never have been adopted. No such object was avowed or intended by its friends, and no such effect was anticipated by the banks.

With that spirit of patriotism which was so marked a characteristic of the people of the North during the war, the stockholders of the State banks relinquished, at the request of the Government, the greater privileges possessed by them under State laws, and in connection with the new banks organized under the law became efficient aids in negotiating the public loans and sustaining the public credit. To all banking systems under which circulating notes are issued there are grave objections, and if there were none in existence in the United States the Secretary would hesitate to recommend or to indorse even the most perfect that has been devised.

The question now to be considered, however, is not whether banks of issue should be created, but whether the national banking system should be sustained. In the present condition of the country, and in view of the relations that the national banks sustain to the Government (ignoring in this connection the question of good faith), the Secretary has no difficulty in coming to the conclusion that they should be sustained. They are so interwoven with all branches of business, and are so directly connected with the credit of the Government, that they could not be destroyed without precipitating upon the country financial troubles which it is now in no condition to meet. At some more propitious period, when the Union shall have been fully restored, and all the States shall have attained that substantial prosperity which their great resources and the energy of their people must sooner or later secure for them, it may perhaps be wise for Congress to consider whether the national banking system may not be dispensed with. The present is not a favorable time to consider this question. The condition of our political and financial affairs is too critical to justify any action that would compel the national banks, or any considerable number of them, to call in their loans and put their bonds upon the market for the purpose of providing the means of retiring their circulation. Conservative legislation is now indispensable. The public mind is too sensitive, business is too unsteady, and the political future is too uncertain to warrant any financial experiments. Fortunately none are required. The national banking system has accomplished all and more than was anticipated by its advocates. It has furnished a circulation, depreciated it is true, like the United States notes, but solvent beyond question, and current throughout the Union. It has prevented bank note panics and saved note holders from losses. It has aided in regulating domestic exchanges, and furnished the Government with valuable financial agents. Had it not been adopted

State banks would have continued, as long as they were tolerated, to furnish the country with bank notes.

Who can estimate the extent of the injury which the people and the Government would have sustained if State institutions, without any other restrictions than were enforced by State laws, had been permitted during the war to occupy the field? All having suspended specie payments, and thereby been relieved from the necessity of furnished evidence of solvency, banks unwisely or dishonestly managed would have stood on a level with those which were managed wisely and honestly. While the latter would have found it difficult to keep their issues within reasonable limits, stimulated as they would have been to issue freely, by the necessities of the Government and the increasing demand for money, which is always the result of an increased supply, the former would have poured out their irredeemable promises until distrust created panic and panic disaster. That the national banking system, with its limited and secured circulation, and its restricted provisions, by superseding the State systems, has prevented a financial crisis there can be but little doubt. For this it is entitled to credit; and for this and for other reasons suggested it should be sustained until a better system shall be devised, or the country is in a condition to dispense with banks of issue altogether.

The arguments in favor of compelling the banks to retire their notes, and yielding the field to the notes of the Government, are based upon the supposition that if $300,000,000 of United States notes were substituted for the $300,000,000 of national bank notes now in circulation the Government would save some eighteen million dollars in interest which is now a gratuity to the banks. That there would be no such saving, nor any saving, by the proposed substitution is clearly shown by the Comptroller of the Currency in his accompanying report, to which the attention of Congress is especially asked. If an account were opened with the banks, and they were charged with the interest on $300,000,000, and the losses sustained through those that have failed, and credited with the interest on the United States notes held by them as a permanent reserve, the taxes paid by them to the Government and the States, and with a commission covering only what has been saved in transferring and disbursing public money, it would be ascertained that the banks were not debtors to the United States. It is not necessary, however, for the Secretary to dwell on this point, as his main objection to the substitution would not be removed if a saving of interest would be effected by it. Regarding, as he does, the issue of the United States notes in the first instance as having been a misfortune, and their continuance as a circulating medium, unless the volume shall be steadily reduced, as fraught with mischief, the Secretary can conceive of no circumstances that would justify a further issue.

These depreciated but legal-tender notes, notwithstanding the reduction that has taken place, still stand in the way of a return to specie payments; a substitution of them for bank notes would be regarded by him and by the country as a declaration that resumption had been indefinitely postponed. If those now outstanding shall be retired at the rate of only $4,000,000 per month, the amount in actual circulation will soon be so reduced that they may not seriously retard the restoration of the true measure of value. If, on the contrary, under any pretence, or for any purpose whatever, their volume should be increased, especially if they should be made the sole paper circulation of the country, a false measure of value will be continued, speculation will be stimulated, industry will decline, and the great risk be incurred that financial health will only be obtained by a revulsion, the effect of which upon the material interests and credit of the country no one can estimate. Such a revulsion the Secretary is most anxious to prevent; and he therefore cannot approve the proposition of substituting the notes of the United States for those of the national banks, but recommends that the policy of contraction be continued.

The apprehension that this policy will embarrass healthy trade is in his judgment unfounded. Legitimate business has not suffered by the curtailment which has taken place within the last two years, nor will it permanently suffer by such a contraction, prudently enforced, as may be necessary to bring the precious metals again into circulation. What business requires is a stable currency. What enterprise demands is the assurance that it shall not be balked of its just rewards by an unreliable measure of value. It is frequently urged by those who admit that the currency is redundant that the country is not now in a condition to bear further contraction; that its growth will soon render contraction unnecessary; that business, if left to itself, will rapidly increase to such an extent as to require the $388,000,000 of United States notes and fractional currency, and the $300,000,000 of bank notes, now outstanding, for its proper and needful accommodation. Nothing can be more fallacious than this unfortunately popular idea. An irredeemable currency is a financial disease which retards growth instead of encouraging it; which stimulates speculation but diminishes labor.

A healthy growth is to be secured by the removal of the disease, and not by postponing the proper treatment of it in the expectation that the vigorous constitution of the patient will eventually overcome it.

The next subject to be considered, in connection with the permanent resumption of specie payments, is the maintenance of the public faith, which involves the necessity of wise and stable revenue laws, impartially and rigorously enforced; economy in the public expenditures; and a recognition of the obligation of the Government to pay its bonds in accordance with the understanding under which they were issued.

Nothing but absolute insolvency will save from the infamy of repudiation a nation that does not pay its debts according to the understanding at the time they were contracted; and when a nation voluntarily violates this understanding it will soon be unable, from the very effect of its own example, to enforce its revenue laws; and its expenditures will only be checked by its inability to collect. How much of the demoralization which exists in the revenue service of the United States is attributable to the failure of the Government to redeem the legal-tender notes according to their tenor would be an interesting subject of inquiry, but hardly appropriate in a communication like this.

Now, to what is the United States pledged in regard to the public debt? Is it not that it shall be paid according to the understanding between the Government and the subscribers to its loans at the time the subscriptions were solicited and obtained? And can there be any question in regard to the nature of this understanding? Was it not that, while the interest-bearing notes should be converted into bonds or paid in lawful money, the bonds should be paid, principal as well as interest, in coin? Was not this the understanding of the Congress which passed the loan bills and of the people who furnished the money? Did any member of the House or of the Senate, prior to 1864, in the exhaustive discussions of these bills, ever intimate that the bonds to be issued in accordance with their provisions might be paid, when redeemable, in a depreciated currency? Was there a single subscriber to the five-twenty bonds, or to the seven and three-tenth notes, which by their terms were convertible into bonds, who did not believe, and who was not given to understand by the agents of the Government, that both the principal and interest of these bonds were payable in coin? Does anyone suppose that the people of the United States, self-sacrificing as they were in the support of the Government, would have sold their stocks, their lands, the products of their farms, of their factories and their shops, and invested the proceeds in five-twenty bonds and seven and three-tenth notes, convertible into such bonds, if they had understood that these bonds were to be redeemed after five years from their respective dates in a currency of the value of which they could form no reliable estimate? Would the Secretary of the Treasury, or would Congress, when the fate of the nation was trembling in the balance, and when a failure to raise money for the support of the Federal army would have been success to the rebellion and ruin to the Union cause, have dared to attempt the experiment of raising money on bonds redeemable at the pleasure of the Government, after five years, in a currency the convertible value of which might not depend upon the solvency of the Government but upon the amount in circulation? No such understanding existed, and fortunately no such experiment was tried. The bonds were negotiated with the definite understanding that they were payable in coin, and the seven and three-tenth notes with an equally definite understanding that they were convertible at the option of the holder into bonds of a similar character or payable in lawful money. The contracts were made in good faith on both sides, a part of them when the Government was in imminent peril and needed money to preserve its existence, the balance when its necessities were scarcely less urgent for the payment of its just obligations to contractors and to the gallant men by whom the nation had been saved. Good faith and public honor, which to a nation are of priceless worth, require that these contracts should be complied with in the spirit in which they were made. The holders of our bonds at home and abroad who understand the character of the people of the United States and the greatness of the national resources ought not to need an assurance that they will be so complied with.

The acts of March 3, 1863, and March 3, 1864, are the only acts which state expressly that the bonds to be issued under them shall be payable in coin; and this provision in these acts, if not accidental, attracted no attention at the time, either in Congress or with the public. Under the former act $75,000,000 of twenty-year six per cent. bonds (part of those known as bonds of 1881) were issued, and under the latter act nearly two hundred millions of five per cent. bonds, known as ten-forties; and the fact that these six per cent. bonds have had no higher reputation than other bonds of the same class, and that the five per cent. bonds never were a popular security, and have in the market until very recently scarcely possessed a value corresponding with the six per cent. five-twenties, shows conclusively that dealers in Government securities, and the people generally, have not regarded this provision as placing them on a different footing as to the kind of money in which they are to be paid from the bonds issued under acts containing no such provisions.

There was nothing in the condition of the country when these acts were passed that required an unusual provision in order that the loans authorized by them might be successfully negotiated; on the contrary, the national credit was better then than at periods when other loan bills were passed; nor was there any intimation by any member of Congress, nor was it ever thought by the officers of the Treasury Department that the bonds authorized by them were of a different character from those issued under other acts. It is unreasonable to suppose that it was the intention of Congress that the bonds authorized by the acts of February 25, 1862, and June 30, 1864, might be paid in legal-tender notes while those authorized by the acts of March 3, 1863, and March 3, 1864, could be paid only in coin. The various issues of bonds, constituting the national funded debt, stand upon the same footing, and all should be paid in coin, if any are so paid.

National debts are subject to the moral law of the nations. Whenever there is no expression to the contrary, coin payments in such obligations are honorably implied. The policy of the Government of the United States in regard to the payment of its debts has been uniform and consistent. Prior to February 25, 1862, there was in the United States no lawful money but specie, consequently its treasury notes, and its bonds previously issued, were payable in the same currency. Subsequently all interest-bearing notes were made payable in lawful money, but no change was made in the form of the obligation of the bonds. Thus the seven and three-tenth notes issued after that date, the five per cent. notes, and the compound-interest notes were made payable in lawful money, while the bonds, not being so made payable, have ever been recognized by Congress, by the Treasury Department, and by the people, as payable only in coin. These different classes of securities were negotiated with this distinct understanding—an understanding which is as binding upon the honor of the nation as if it were explicitly stated in the statute.

It is true that the bonds, and notes convertible into bonds, issued after the passage of the first legal-tender act were paid for in a depreciated currency, and were therefore, in fact, sold at a discount; but it is not denied that they were sold fairly, and that everyone had ample opportunity to subscribe for them. Agencies were established and subscriptions solicited in every part of the country; and liberal subscriptions were regarded as evidence of loyalty. That they were paid for in a depreciated currency was not the fault of the subscribers. They were sold at the highest price that could be obtained for them—not chiefly to the capitalists of the cities, but to men of moderate means throughout the country, who subscribed for them, not for speculation, but to aid the Government in its struggles with a gigantic rebellion; and it is a significant fact that, with rare exceptions, the complaints that they were sold at a discount come from those who, doubtful of the result of the conflict, declined to invest in them. How would the Government of the United States stand before the world—how would it stand in the estimation of its own people, if it should decline to pay, according to agreement, the money it borrowed when its very existence was in peril, and without which it could not have prosecuted the war, on the ground that the lenders took advantage of its necessities and purchased its securities at less than their value?

But if the honor of the nation were not involved in the question the inquiry arises, In what shall the bonds be paid if not in coin? Some five hundred and fifteen millions of five-twenty bonds are now redeemable according to their tenor. No one, certainly, would propose that some of them shall be called in and paid in a currency now worth seventy cents on the dollar while the rest shall remain unredeemed until the currency shall be more depreciated by additions to its volume or appreciated by contraction. The holders of these bonds stand on the same footing; if any are to be paid before maturity in a depreciated currency the whole should be so paid, and in a currency of equal value. But the Government has no United States notes in the treasury, and as the annual receipts are not likely hereafter to be much in excess of the expenditures, and as a new loan to raise money for the purpose of violating an agreement under which a previous loan was negotiated would be impracticable, there would be no way in which the bonds now redeemable could be paid as has been proposed except by putting the printing presses again at work and issuing more promises which must themselves eventually be paid in coin, converted into coin bonds, or repudiated. This process of making money seems an easy one, but our own experience and the experience of every other nation that has tried it prove it to be neither judicious nor profitable.

As the paper circulation of the country is already redundant it would be lessened in value by every addition to it, and by the distrust thus created its depreciation would doubtless be in a greater ratio even than the additions would bear to the volume to which they would be added. It is not too much to say that an additional issue of $500,000,000 of United States notes would reduce the $700,000,000 of paper money now in circulation to one-half their present value; so that a legal-tender note or a national bank note, now worth seventy per cent. in coin, would not be worth more than thirty-five per cent., even if the apprehension of further issues did not place it on a par with Confederate notes at the collapse of the rebellion. The bonds would of course decline in value with the currency in which they would be payable. Can anyone seriously propose thus to depreciate, if not to render valueless, the money and securities of the people? Can anyone, knowing the effect which such an issue would have upon the Government bonds, upon the currency now afloat, upon business, upon credit, upon the public morals, seriously advocate such a measure, not as a matter of necessity, but to anticipate the payment of debts due many years hence? The statement of the proposition exposes its wickedness. When fairly considered it cannot fail to be stamped with universal condemnation. It is a proposition that the people of the United States, who own four-fifths of the national obligations, shall, by their own deliberate act, rob and ruin themselves, and at the same time cover the nation with inexpressible and ineffaceable disgrace.

In opposition to all such expedients for payment of, or rather for getting rid of, the public debt is the upright, world-honored *economical* policy of paying every obligation of the Government according to the understanding with which it was created—the policy of appreciating the paper dollar until it shall represent a dollar in coin, of giving stability to business and assurance to enterprise, and wiping from the country the reproach that rests upon it by reason of the low price of its securities in the great marts of the world. That this is the policy which will be sustained by the people and their representatives the Secretary has the fullest confidence. There may hereafter be nations which, ignoring their honorary obligations, may look only to their own statutes for the measure of their liabilities. If there shall be such nations the Republic of the United States will not be found among them. It has essentially suffered by the actual repudiation of some of the States and the virtual repudiation of others; it is still suffering from the same cause, although more than a quarter of a century has elapsed since this stigma was fixed upon American credit. It is suffering also from the fact that Massachusetts and California alone, of all the States, have continued to pay the interest on their bonds in coin. But, although it has suffered, and is still suffering, from the bad faith or false economy of some of its members, its own financial honor is unsullied. It has committed the mistake of making its inconvertible promises a legal tender, but it has never taken advantage of its own legislation to lessen in the hands of the holders the value of its securities or violate its engagements by covert repudiation. In the darkest hours of the rebellion it faltered not in the observance of its contracts. Shall it falter now when its ability to pay to the uttermost farthing, even without oppressive taxation, cannot be questioned?

There is a general sentiment among taxpayers that the exemption of Government bonds from local taxation is not exactly right, and that it ought to be in some way avoided in future issues. The Secretary has no hesitation in admitting that he is in sympathy with this sentiment. The difficulty in the way, however, as has been suggested, arises from the fact that if bonds hereafter to be issued were to be subject to local taxation very few would be held where taxes are high, and there would be a constant tendency to a concentration of them in States and counties and cities where taxes are low, or in foreign countries, where they would escape taxation altogether. It is a matter of great importance that the Government bonds should be a desirable investment in all parts of the country, and it is obvious that the States should be in some manner compensated for the right now denied of taxing them as other kinds of property are taxed.

After giving the subject careful consideration the Secretary can suggest no better way of doing it than by an issue of bonds to be known as the Consolidated Debt of the United States, bearing six per cent. interest, and having twenty years to run, into which all other obligations of the Government shall as rapidly as possible be converted; one-sixth part of the interest at each semi-annual payment to be reserved by the Government and paid over to the States, according to their population. By this means, all the bonds, wherever held, would be taxed alike, and a general distribution of them be secured.

The manufacturers of the country and those who had incurred pecuniary obligations were greatly alarmed at the persistent policy of Secretary McCulloch in contracting the currency, which, they claimed, lowered the price of goods as measured by money, and raised the price of money as measured by goods. Even the creditor class were opposed to too great a contraction, since this might throw their debtors into bankruptcy.

Accordingly petitions poured into Congress, asking that the hand of the Secretary of the Treasury be stayed, and during the first days of the session numerous bills were introduced to this effect. One of these, introduced in the House on December 5 by Robert C. Schenck [O.], was to the effect that "further reduction of the currency by retiring and canceling United States notes is prohibited." This was unanimously approved by the Committee on Ways and Means, and was passed on December 7 by 127 yeas to 32 nays. Among those who opposed the bill, as postponing the resumption of specie payments, were such prominent Republicans as James G. Blaine [Me.], and James A. Garfield [O.]. Samuel J. Randall [Pa.], who was rising in prominence as a Democratic leader, also voted in the negative.

The bill came up for discussion in the Senate on January 9, 1868.

Reduction of the Currency

Senate, January 9–15, 1868

John Sherman [O.], chairman of the Committee on Finance, supported the bill. He stated his reasons for doing so, as follows:

First. It will satisfy the public mind that no further contraction will be made when industry is in a measure paralyzed. We hear the complaint from all parts of the country, from all branches of industry, from every State in the Union that industry for some reason is paralyzed and that trade and enterprise are not so well rewarded as they were. Many, perhaps erroneously, attribute all this to the contraction of the currency—a contraction that I believe is unexampled in the history of any nation. One hundred and forty million dollars have been withdrawn out of $737,000,000 in less than two years. It may be wise, it may be beneficial, but still it has been so rapid as to excite a stringency that is causing complaint, and I think the people have a right to be relieved from that.

Second. This bill will restore to the legislature their power over the currency, a power too important to be delegated to any single officer of the Government.

Third. This will strongly impress upon Congress the imperative duty of acting wisely upon financial measures, for the responsibility will then rest entirely upon Congress and will not be shared with them by the Secretary of the Treasury.

Fourth. It will encourage business men to continue old and embark in new enterprises, when they are assured that no change will be made in the measure of value without the open and deliberate consent of their representatives. I have entire confidence that Congress will, in due time, provide such measures as will enable our people to pursue the industries of peace with all the energy and success with which they conducted war. Now, it is our duty to relieve them from perhaps a groundless terror; but, whether groundless or not, it is one that checks and paralyzes all classes and kinds of industry.

Justin S. Morrill [Vt.] opposed the bill as deferring the day of specie payments, and enhancing the price of gold measured in "greenbacks."

Henry W. Corbett [Ore.] opposed the bill as raising the price of commodities.

The present amount of currency in the country and the large amount that has been afloat the past few years have raised the price of every kind of product to such an extent that it is impossible for us to export anything from the country. We are using and consuming within ourselves our products. Flour has advanced to such an enormous price by reason of the inflation of the currency that it is impossible to ship it out of the country and compete abroad with the foreign product of that article. The inflation of the currency is acting as a protective tariff to foreign countries to produce this article, so important to our Western States, so that foreigners are furnishing flour and grain to England and other countries instead of our producing it ourselves and exporting it to them in place of the gold and United States bonds that we have been sending out of the country. We have sent within the past five or six years about six hundred million dollars of gold and United States stocks. Let this continue for one or two years longer, and by this inflated policy all our United States stocks will have been sent out of the country, and we shall be paying a tribute of gold interest to foreigners, and we shall also have sent all our gold out of the country, and we shall perhaps be prevented from resuming specie payments for the next fifteen or twenty years. It is alarming when you see $3,000,000 of gold a week going out of the country, and only $1,000,000 coming in.

The state of financial affairs is alarming to me, and it looks to me as though we had better leave the matter entirely to the Secretary of the Treasury to govern the financial policy as he has heretofore done, wisely, in my opinion, and for the best interests of the country. He is not going to adopt a policy that will cripple the Government or cripple the industrial interests of the country.

William P. Fessenden [Me.] opposed the bill. He agreed with Senator Sherman that Congress should control the currency, but said that it was now doing so, the Secretary of the Treasury having kept within the limits assigned him by the national legislature. The present agitation against reducing the currency was created by people who entertain different views from those held by Congress when it set those limits. These agitators were men "who have multifarious schemes for having a currency in the country irredeemable, mere rags, after the necessity has ceased." If Congress succumbed to this demand it would be a notification to the country that it had abandoned its policy of restoring, as soon as possible, the finances to a sound specie basis.

I believe that all the trouble we have arises from something that is unavoidable. The country is in an anomalous condition in regard to the currency. This arose out of a matter that we could not avoid—the enormous expenditures of the war. We have got to a point where our currency is disordered; we want to get back to a safe position, and as soon as we can. Now, my idea is that only time will accomplish it. Such a position as we are in we cannot get out of without suffering to the country in its business affairs, and the more you legislate to postpone that suffering, the more you legislate with schemes of one kind and another to tide over this time and tide over that time and the other, the more difficult, in my judgment, will it be to meet the crisis at last.

William M. Stewart [Nev.].—The financial troubles we are now laboring under are owing, in the first place, to the overestimates of the Secretary of the Treasury imposing burdens on the people heavier than they could bear, and in the next place to corruption in office causing a failure to collect the revenue. If Congress is to blame for these over-estimates and for this corruption in office, which has abstracted from the treasury, according to the estimate of some, $200,000,000 a year—if Congress is responsible for these two things, the one a great mistake and the other a great crime, it is time that the President of the United States held us up to scorn and contempt, and it is time that the people hurled us from power.

Now, I am anxious to know where the responsibility rests for these things. Being anxious to know these things, I am willing to pass this or any other bill which shall indicate that Congress does not feel full confidence in the Secretary of the Treasury, for disguise it as you will this bill amounts to nothing more nor less than a reflection upon the Secretary of the Treasury.

Senator Sherman denied that further contraction of the currency was a step toward resumption of specie payments, since

you cannot approach specie payments by contraction except through a distress and a destruction of all the business interests of the country that our people will not submit to. You cannot approach specie payments by contraction alone, though you must contract somewhat. Whenever money is easy it is right enough to contract, but when money is tight the contraction must cease.

So it is in England. When times become very tight the Bank of England is authorized by law to issue an increased circulation, and sometimes the very authority to increase destroys the necessity for it; and I have no doubt that if we could devise a way by which at times the currency might be increased temporarily it would be a wise provision. After the war between Napoleon and Great Britain by act of Parliament the time for resuming specie payments was extended four different times. They approached gradually the period fixed for specie payments; hard times came on; appeals were made to Parliament, and they extended the time one year, and again a year, and then a year more, and not until 1823, an interval of seven years, did they resume specie payments. The period was extended from time to time according to the condition of the trade of the country.

George F. Edmunds [Vt.].—Allow me to ask my friend whether on the passage of the last act the bank and the speculators were not just as much opposed to coming to specie payments as they were the first time?

Senator Sherman.—There is always a class of the community opposed to the resumption of specie payments. The debtors are always opposed to the resumption of specie payments and the creditors are always in favor of it.

Senator Fessenden.—Is it the intention of the Committee on Finance, with the view they take of the subject, again to assert the policy of contraction before Congress adjourns?

Senator Sherman.—The Senator from Maine knows very well that I cannot answer that question until the committee act.

Senator Fessenden.—I think the committee have acted, because they have reported what looks like the policy suggested by the Senator, of gradually increasing the currency when you want paper and reducing when you do not.

John B. Henderson [Mo.] compared the method by which the currency had been inflated to the getting of a canal boat through locks to a higher level.

Our public debt was created with a circulating medium rising one thousand million dollars. A large portion of the bonds were floated and sold at par. We did not want to sell them beneath par, but we floated them on a circulation of from one thousand million to twelve thousand million dollars. We passed laws declaring that we would not carry on the war with gold or the representative of gold, but we would adopt what we called a legal tender, and compel the creditors of the Government to take it. The soldier was paid in it. We had agreed to pay the soldier in coin, I suppose, if we agreed to pay anybody in coin. We agreed to pay him in what was known as the dollar prior to 1862. We paid him off, however, in the dollar fixed by the acts of 1862, 1863, and 1864. In order to keep our bonds at par we floated them up just as we would put a canal boat through locks. We run into the first lock, and we must have water enough to raise it to the second lock. We found a difficulty in floating our bonds. We wanted to get up into the second lock. We first issued $150,000,000 of greenbacks. That was not satisfactory. We issued $150,000,000 more, and then $100,000,000, making $400,000,000, or rather authorized it, and

THE POLITICAL MOUNTEBANK [GRANT]

Gold for Bondholders, Greenbacks for Soldiers and Sailors

From the collection of the New York Historical Society

issued very nearly that amount. We were not satisfied with that. We issued hundreds of millions of six per cent. compound-interest notes. We were not satisfied with that. We issued what we called, not United States notes, because those are the greenbacks, but we issued what were called treasury notes, bearing interest. All these went into the circulation. A great many of our bonds were bought by individuals at from forty to fifty cents on the dollar in gold. The debt was contracted with this bloated state of affairs.

Now, the very moment the war is over everybody looks to a resumption of specie payments. I want to come to it, too. We have now to bring our canal boat down the locks, and gentlemen will not permit us to let the water in the lock, but we must butt it down and destroy the boat. Sir, we went up by taking time and letting the water into the lock. Now let us come down in the same way, and thereby preserve the boat. If we undertake to come down otherwise we shall destroy the vessel.

Senator Edmunds.—We shall not come down by letting water into the lock. We must pour it out.

Senator Henderson.—I may not understand canal boating as well as my friend; but I undertake to say it would be well to leave the water in the lock and not draw it out before the boat comes upon it.

I may be allowed, perhaps, another illustration. It seems to me that to undertake to drive the country in this state of affairs to a resumption of specie payments by contraction is about as reasonable as it would be for a physician who should call upon a poor patient who had been laboring for some considerable length of time under *delirium tremens* to recommend that his liquor be stopped instantly.

Oliver P. Morton [Ind.] refuted the idea of Senator Stewart that the passage of the bill would be a reflection upon Secretary McCulloch.

We have a right to curtail the discretionary power of any officer without reflecting upon that officer. The Secretary of the Treasury is wise in financial matters, but he is not wiser than all the business men of this country, and they protest almost with one voice against having the further administration of the currency left absolutely in the hands of one man.

Timothy O. Howe [Wis.] supported the bill, because it released the people of the present tax-burdened generation from a system whereby the money paid into the treasury was there destroyed instead of being returned to them to be used in the business of the country until such time as better conditions would enable it to be destroyed, thereby reducing the public debt.

He admitted that his knowledge of finance was limited.

Sir, the only master of finance under whom I ever studied was Wilkins Micawber, Esq.[1] [Laughter.] Mr. Micawber had a remarkable facility for contracting debts. That facility has characterized the United States for the past few years. Mr. Micawber had but a limited faculty for paying debts. That is another characteristic that I have noticed in the United States for several years past. Mr. Micawber was an honorable man, an honorable debtor. So I hope the United States will turn out to be, as so far it has appeared to be. When Mr. Micawber met his creditor, without any of the coin of the realm in his pocket, he met him like a man and gave him his I O U, and discharged the debt! The United States has practiced upon the same principle so far. We were obliged to contract debts that we could not discharge in anything like money. We had got to employ something that was not money, somebody's credit, and we did as Micawber did—we gave our creditors our I O U. We gave them our notes of hand; and every note that every one of you holds in his pocket, and I hope your pockets are full [laughter], is a certificate of the United States that you have advanced the amount of that note to the United States Government over and above the proportion that was required of you under the tax laws of the country. But Mr. Micawber lacked one facility, for circulating his paper, which the Government possessed. His creditors were perfectly willing to take his notes because they could get nothing else. Our creditors were willing to take our notes for the same reason. But Mr. Micawber could not enable his creditors to circulate his notes as money. We did effect that. We enabled our creditors, whom we compelled to take our notes, to pass them to their creditors and use them as money.

Mr. President, I thought the United States were acting upon a sound principle; I thought the course they took was the only course open to them; but it will be borne in mind that when they first commenced the issuing of this paper the amount was controlled by one idea, and that was that they never would is-

[1] A character in "David Copperfield," by Charles Dickens.

sue a dollar of legal-tender notes when they could borrow the notes; in other words, that all the notes they issued should be convertible into interest-paying bonds. If the country were ready at any time to loan the Government the means to meet its engagements at a fair rate of interest the Government was willing to borrow; but when the country could not loan at a fair rate of interest the country would do like Micawber and issue its notes. That was a fair principle, and if we had kept sight of it until this time I do not think our finances would be in so embarrassed a condition as they are to-day. But unfortunately, to use the figure recently employed by the Senator from Missouri, although we did commence by floating the bonded debt of the country on to the country, we did not stop floating when we had reached the highest lock, so to speak. We kept on issuing these notes after the country preferred not to take them and after the country wished to loan them to the Government, when we might have borrowed them at a rate of interest which we agreed it was fair to pay. Hence, and from this cause you see to-day that it takes from one hundred and eight to one hundred and twelve dollars of the national notes which do not bear interest to buy one hundred dollars of the national notes which do bear interest. I do not think that is fair. If this law which you now propose to suspend had authorized every man holding these notes to turn them into the interest-paying bonds of the Government I think it would have been a just and honest thing; but that of itself would be a destructive measure while you have another statute upon your books which restricts by an iron rule the amount of paper circulation which can come from your banks.

The Senator from Ohio said that he thought the Secretary of the Treasury ought not to be authorized to restrict or to control the amount of circulation. I agree with him, but I think that Congress ought no more to be authorized to do it than the Secretary of the Treasury. Neither of them should do it. The law, in my judgment, ought to fix the condition upon which the first dollar of paper should be issued; but having fixed those conditions, having determined in its wisdom upon what conditions it was safe to let one dollar of paper be issued, every man who should comply with those conditions should have the same right to issue a dollar. This restriction upon the amount of bank circulation or of paper circulation, therefore, is open to two objections. First, I have this objection to urge: that I think there is no body of men in the United States of equal intelligence but what is just as competent to determine the amount of money which the country wants to use at any particular time as the Congress of the United States; and the same number of business men, as my friend from Missouri [Mr. Henderson] suggests, are much more competent to determine it. We know less about it. We are not capitalists; at least I can speak with the utmost confidence for one [laughter]; and we have no necessary connection with capital; we are not engaged in the business of the country; and we are the last men, in my judgment, to know just how much money the business of the country wants. Men who have money to loan, men who have money to operate with, know, it is their business to know, to keep run of the course of business, and know when it is safer to buy property with their money or safer to loan it at the current rates of interest.

Senator Edmunds.—How is it with men who have to borrow to pay their debts with?

John Conness [Cal.].—To which side?

Senator Howe.—To the party who has to borrow. I heard a remark once from a neighbor of mine, a very sensible one, and I subscribed to the truth of it at once, and I believe in the truth of it to-day. He said it had been more than fifty dollars damage to him being poor. [Laughter.] But, Mr. President, I do not believe it is the business of the legislature of the nation to provide for men who are poor and have to borrow money. I think, being one of the class myself, it is the business of men who have to borrow money to go to men who have money to lend and borrow it like men and pay for it if they agree to do so, and when they agree to do so and the nation cannot by law provide for their necessities.

Mr. President, I said when your first treasury-note bill was pending here what I repeat to-day, that, in my judgment, there never ought to have been a note issued by the Government promising to pay specie on demand, because we knew the Government could not pay specie on demand; and I say now that there ought not to be a piece of paper circulated under the protection of law by anybody, either by the Government or a bank, which is not convertible into something that the world recognizes as money, whatever that is. The Government cannot do it without bearing the brand of a bankrupt on its brow. I cannot do it without subjecting myself to the same penalty; and a bank cannot do it. I have said that we were justified in using this paper while the war was upon us; but I believe with the Senator from Maine that that necessity has passed by, and we must get rid of this paper as soon as we can; but it must not be taxed out of the pockets of the people and burned; and it must not be taken from the circulation of the country unless you allow the capital of the country the option of putting something in its place.

Senator Fessenden.—How is the debt to be paid without taxation?

Senator Howe.—You can never pay anything except by taxation, but you cannot collect taxes when you have taken the whole circulation of the country out of the country. If you will destroy this kind of paper you must put something in its place if the business of the country and the exigencies of the country demand it; and we cannot tell, I say, how much is demanded. But take off the restriction upon the issuing of bank paper, take off the restriction from the circulation of your bank notes, determine the conditions upon which, as I said, the first dollar may be issued, and let every man issue who will comply with those conditions; place your banking circulation on the footing that it was before the war commenced and before the Government entered into the business of banking, and then you can go on and allow these notes to be funded into the interest-paying bonds of the Government—just the principle upon which the first issues of these notes were authorized. But that will subject us to one disagreeable thing—the people will have to pay interest on these new bonds.

Gentlemen tell us that the country can carry three, four, or five hundred millions of this paper and we save the interest. Sir, we pay the interest three times over in the increased price put upon every commodity the country deals in; in other words, in the depreciation of paper or in the appreciation—I think that is about as correct an expression—of that which is the true representative of values, the coin of the country. While you have that system of finance which makes gold a merchantable article the price of gold is not regulated by the law of supply and demand. The price of gold is regulated by those men there in Wall street, New York, who buy and sell their millions and millions every day without seeing a dollar of it; and, while it is a merchantable commodity and stands as the representative of all other commodities, when gold goes up under the manipulations of these gentlemen everything else goes up. So they have in their hands the price of every commodity.

Further discussion of the bill dealt chiefly with amendments proposed thereto. It was passed with amendments on January 15, 1868, by 33 yeas to 4 nays.

The House disagreed to the amendments, and a joint conference committee of the two Chambers was appointed, which reported on January 22 that the Senate should recede from its amendments. This was concurred in by both Chambers. President Johnson refused to sign the bill, and it automatically became a law ten days after its passage.

By this act the minimum limit of legal tender notes was fixed at $356,000,000—the amount extant at the time.

CHAPTER XIV

Resumption of Specie Payments

Oliver P. Morton [Ind.] Introduces Bill in Senate for Resumption of Specie Payments without Contraction of the Currency—His Speech—Bill Referred to Committee on Finance—John Sherman [O.] Reports the Committee's Bill—His Speech—Bill Is Not Acted Upon—President Grant Advocates Resumption of Specie Payments—John Sherman [O.] Moves Resolution in the Senate for Resumption of Specie Payments and Establishment of a Uniform Currency—Thomas W. Ferry [Mich.] Moves a Substitute Declaring for Increase of Currency, Free Banking, and against Discrimination against "Greenbacks"—Debate on the Two Resolutions: Senator Ferry, General John B. Gordon [Ga.], George S. Boutwell [Mass.]; No Action—President Grant Repeats His Recommendation—John Sherman [O.] Introduces Bill in the Senate to Resume Specie Payments on January 1, 1879—Debate: Senator Sherman, Allen G. Thurman [O.], Carl Schurz [Mo.], Lewis V. Bogy [Mo.], Thomas F. Bayard [Del.]; Bill Is Passed by Senate and House, and Approved by President Grant—Samuel S. Cox [N. Y.] Introduces in the House Bill to Repeal Date Set for Resumption; Passed in House, Committed in Senate—General Thomas Ewing [O.] Introduces in the House a Bill to Repeal the Resumption Act—Debate: in Favor of Repeal, General Ewing; Opposed, General James A. Garfield [O.]; Bill Is Passed; It Is Committed by the Senate, and (Next Session) Passed; House Fails to Take Further Action.

ON the opening day of the session of 1868-9 Charles Sumner [Mass.] introduced in the Senate a bill for the resumption of special payments; it was shelved in committee.

On December 14, 1868, Oliver P. Morton [Ind.] introduced in the Senate a bill that sales of gold should be stopped at once, and the surplus gold accruing in the treasury be applied to the redemption of United States notes; that after July 1, 1871, the treasury should redeem in coin United States notes presented to it for such purpose; that after January 1, 1872, the national banks should similarly redeem their notes out of a reserve collected therefor; that after January 1, 1872, United States notes should cease to be legal tender except for Government dues; and that thirty-year Government bonds, payable principal and interest in gold, be issued to carry into execution the redemption at the treasury.

On December 16 Senator Morton spoke upon the bill. He first replied to objections against the resumption of specie payments at the time.

"It is said by many that the currency is redundant, and that we cannot return to specie payments until contraction has taken place."

He denied that currency was redundant for the business of the country; this, he said, had adapted itself to the large increase of currency, using it instead of the bills of exchange and promissory notes which were common before the war, when the local bank currency of one part of the country was not acceptable in another. About $100,000,000, he calculated, was employed in this way; $50,000,000 more was needed for the increase of business since 1860. He concluded that the currency was not more redundant now than then, when the banks were paying specie.

Again, it is said that the Government cannot return to specie payments until after we have checked the flow of our gold to Europe by largely reducing our importations of foreign goods. This is a clear case of putting the disease for the remedy. Gold, like every other commodity, is governed by the great commercial law of demand and supply. It goes where it is needed, and leaves the country where it is not in demand. In this country there is now but one demand for gold, which is to pay duties on imports.

In whatever country paper money has been made a legal tender it has invariably driven gold and silver from the circulation, and in great part from the country. Thus it is that Canada is now flooded with American silver. Thus it is that American gold has gone to Europe in a steady stream for five years.

We cannot retain our gold at home except by making a demand for it. The holders of it are not patriotic enough to keep it here for nothing. If we would reduce the importation of foreign goods we must withhold the gold with which they are purchased. And this we cannot do except by making it more profitable to keep it at home than to send it abroad. Until we create this home demand the annual product of our mines in chief part will go to England, France, and Germany to swell the rich volume of their currency.

Again, it is said that specie payments cannot be brought about by special legislation, but can be produced only by the operation of general causes, such as the increase of the tariff, the increase of population and development of the resources of the country, whereby the general credit of the Government will be improved. It is alleged that we can only raise the value of our currency by raising the value of our bonds in the market; that as we bring up the price of our bonds we shall thereby bring up the value of greenbacks; that we can only improve the value of the currency by improving the general credit of the Government, as shown by the value of our stocks, and to this end the surplus gold in the treasury and that which is to accrue should be applied to the purchase of our bonds in the market, to be canceled, thus diminishing the number of them and improving the value of the balance.

This view of the question I hold to be a total misconception. I do not believe that the existence of our bonded debt has anything to do with the depreciation of our currency. I believe our currency would be depreciated as it is if the Government did not owe a single bond or if all our bonds were at par. Why is our currency depreciated? And why would it be depreciated if the Government did not owe a single bond? Because the greenback note is a promise by the Government to pay so many dollars on demand, which it does not pay. The promise is daily broken, and has long been dishonored. The note draws no interest, and the Government has fixed no time when it will pay it. Under such circumstances the note must be depreciated. The solvency or ultimate ability of the promisor never kept overdue paper at par, and never will. To do that something more is required than the ultimate wealth or ability of the promisor. There must be certainty in the payment and time of payment, and if the time of payment be deferred compensation must be made by the payment of interest. One of the wealthiest men in the Northwest, now dead, who left some five million dollars to be divided among his heirs, had an unfortunate habit of refusing to pay his small debts. Instead of paying he would give his notes for them, refuse to pay the notes at maturity, suffer himself to be sued, then hire a lawyer to fight the cases. The result was that his paper was hawked about the streets at sixty or seventy cents on the dollar, while, perhaps, that of his near neighbor, who kept a small store and was only worth $10,000, but who was prompt in the payment of his debts, could be sold at a very small discount.

In overcoming the depreciation of the currency we have to overcome the difference in value between the greenback currency and the like amount of gold, and not the difference between two thousand millions of bonded debt and two thousand millions in gold. Even if the credit of the Government was so greatly impaired as that her bonds were not worth twenty-five cents on the dollar, still it would not be impossible to make the currency good and keep it at par. If the Government did not owe a single bond the value of our currency could not be improved, except by making arrangements to redeem it; and if the Government does make arrangements to redeem it the existence of the bonded debt will not prevent the improvement in its value. If we should take the surplus gold in the treasury and that which is to accrue and use it in the purchase of bonds in the market, to be canceled as purchased, we should inevitably further depreciate the value of the greenbacks. The explanation of this effect is simple. By taking the gold, which is the only means by which the greenbacks can be redeemed, and applying it to the purchase of bonds, it puts the redemption of the greenbacks out of the power of the Government, and proclaims to the world that it does not intend to return to specie payments.

The proposal to improve our currency by taking our surplus gold and investing it in bonds would be regarded by capitalists as absurd. The gold thus paid out would not enter into the circulation, but would sink back into an article of merchandise to be gambled for, as it now is in Wall street. What would the world think of the morality of such an operation? We have $356,000,000 of the public debt overdue and drawing no interest, and we take the only means of paying this debt and apply it to the purchase, at a discount, of our bonds, which will not be due under fourteen years. What would be said of the integrity of the man who should refuse to pay his debts which are due, leaving his creditors to suffer great loss, and should employ his money to buy up at a heavy shave his debts that will not be due under ten or fifteen years? Plain people would call such a man rascal and swindler, and would speak of the Government in the same terms under the same circumstances. The pretence that it was done to improve the value of the currency would deceive nobody. Such a plan of returning to specie payments is worthy of the circumlocution office, and should be labeled "How not to do it."[1]

The greenback currency is a part of the public debt, for the redemption of which the faith of the nation is solemnly pledged. The redemption of this pledge is not only demanded by every principle of national honor, but is imperatively demanded by the interests of the people, collectively and individually. The currency of a country lies at the foundation of its daily business and vitally affects the interest of every class and condition of people, and if the Government, overlooking its honor and its duty, should take the only means by which it can be improved and apply it to the purchase of bonds which will not be due for many years it would merit and receive the indignation and contempt of honest men everywhere.

But it is said that if the Government reserves and holds the surplus gold in the treasury, to be applied to the redemption of the greenback currency at some future time, to be fixed by law, it will suffer great loss in the interest on the gold thus held in reserve. In one point of view this objection is well taken. But what else can we do? Is not a difficulty to be encountered by every debtor who collects and holds the money wherewith to finally pay his debts? If a man owe $1,000 can he pay it in any other way than by collecting the money for that purpose and holding it until he gets enough to meet his debt? The Government owes a debt which can only be paid in gold, and it must, if it intends to pay it, collect the necessary amount in gold. If the debt was of that nature that the gold could be paid out on it as soon as collected, of course it should be done; but the debt is not of that nature. If the Government should pay out the gold as fast as it is received in the redemption of the greenback currency it would fail to bring the remainder of the currency up to par, and the gold thus paid out would not enter into the circulation, but would sink back into an article of merchandise such as it now is. The redemption of the greenback currency should not begin until the Government is prepared to redeem all that may be presented, for this would at once bring the whole body of the currency to par, and the gold paid out would go into the circulation and take the place of the paper money redeemed. But if paid out by piecemeal in advance it would not go into circulation or bring up the balance of the currency to par. But what will be the actual loss of the interest on the gold held in reserve compared with the loss sustained by

[1] Readers of "Little Dorrit," by Charles Dickens, will understand this allusion.

the great mass of the people in their labor, trade, and property, to be suffered by the continuance of the present condition of the currency? Scarcely as one dollar is to a hundred. The losses by the failure to employ labor; by the stagnation of business; by the paralysis of trade; by the delay in general progress and development, brought about by depreciated, fluctuating, and deceptive currency, when estimated in dollars, would form a vast sum, compared with which the loss of interest on the reserved gold would be a mere bagatelle.

But, if we do not obtain the gold to redeem the greenback currency in the manner proposed, in what other way or at what time shall it be obtained? Shall the Government go into Wall street and buy it like the importers or the gamblers? Or shall we sell new bonds in Europe at seventy or seventy-two cents on the dollar and obtain it in that way? Will it be easier to begin the process at the end of five years, the nation suffering in the meantime all the evils and losses of depreciation? Shall the nation stand shivering for years on the banks of this Jordan and then make the plunge when the waters are deeper, swifter, and colder than now? Such is not the part of wisdom or patriotic statesmanship.

If an individual fails to pay his debts payment may be enforced by the law against his property, but against the Government there is no such remedy. What would be mere neglect or failure, therefore, on the part of an individual would be repudiation by a Government.

If the greenback note is to be regarded as an obligation for the payment of which the faith of the Government is pledged the continued failure of the Government to make any provision for its redemption cannot be regarded in any other light than repudiation. When the first of these notes were issued it was provided that they might be funded into the five-twenty bonds, but that provision was shortly after repealed, and they now stand in the nature of a forced loan, drawing no interest, and, for all that appears, are to be left to perish in the hands of the people.

If when the five-twenty bonds fall due the Government should fail to pay them, or to make any satisfactory provision for funding them into a new bond, the cry of repudiation would at once be raised; and yet it cannot be shown that the legal and moral obligation to pay those bonds at maturity is greater than that resting on the Government to make prompt provision for the redemption of the greenback currency. The legal obligation is no greater, and the moral obligation hardly so strong;

for the greenback notes are in fact the people's bonds, the bonds of the million, in which are invested the laborer's toil and the meager profits of the humble occupations in life, which, more than any others, demand the fostering and protecting care of the Government.

But, while it is true that the discount on our bonds has little, if anything, to do with the depreciation of our currency, it is also true that the depreciation of the currency has much to do with the discount on the bonds. I do not believe that our bonds will ever reach par, or approach it nearly, until the currency is made good.

The legal-tender currency of a country bears an intimate and, perhaps, a mysterious relation to every form of credit and security, both public and private, and if it be depreciated inevitably drags them down to its own level. The legal-tender currency is at par in contemplation of law and in the payment of debts, though it may not be worth six cents on the dollar. It is the "par" and measure of price and value recognized in all the ordinary business of the country. The prices of property and all articles of trade are not given at so much in gold, but in greenbacks, and the legal-tender value of the greenbacks is so identified in the public mind with the measurement in price of every species of property, merchandise, and labor that it assimilates to itself as well the price of securities, even though by their terms they may be made expressly payable in gold.

As the value of our legal-tender currency goes up the price of our bonds will go up with it; and what is true of Government securities is equally true of the great mass of American securities, public and private.

Another obstacle to the adoption of any plan for returning to specie payments is the cry that the right way to resume is to resume at once. I have labored to find that this means anything but the indefinite postponement of resumption. Everyone must comprehend that the Government cannot redeem the greenback currency without first collecting the gold to do it with; that it cannot return to specie payments by contraction without taking time to contract, with all its attending calamities; that, in short, there is no process by which it can be done, however ruinous, that does not involve time. If the Government should pay out the $70,000,000 surplus gold now in the treasury in the redemption of an equal amount of greenbacks the whole country would know that it was not prepared to redeem any more. The gold paid out would not pass into circulation, but sink back into an article of merchandise, the balance of the greenback currency be but little improved, and the net result of the operation would simply be the contraction of the currency to the extent of $70,000,000 and the indefinite postponement of the redemption of the balance.

But the great obstacle to the return to specie payments, and the one which we will have the greatest difficulty in overcoming, is the interest against it. The premium upon gold, and the advantages it gives to certain classes over others were unavoidable in the beginning, but should not be allowed to continue a single day longer than is necessary. The present condition of things produces great inequalities among the people, which if longer continued will give rise to heartburnings and tend to demoralize the public sentiment in relation to our national obligations.

To illustrate: A is the owner of $10,000 five-twenty bonds, from which he derives an income of $600 in gold. This gold, when converted, will realize $800 in currency, and upon his bonds he pays no tax whatever. B is the owner of $10,000 in six per cent. railroad bonds, from which he derives an income of $600 in currency, and upon these bonds he pays at least two per cent. for State and county purposes, which will reduce his income to $400, just one-half the amount of A's. B may, perhaps, not feel very comfortable over this state of things, and will be led to inquire into the cause of this gross inequality. He will be told that so far as it arises from taxation it is unavoidable, as the States cannot tax Government securities; but so far as it arises from the condition of the currency speedy relief may be afforded by the Government if it will. Equal rights are the gift of God to all men, and equal conditions in society, equal facilities for acquiring wealth, equal rewards for labor, and the equal support of public burdens should be given by every Government to its people so far as it may be possible.

To the man who lent his money to the Government to carry on the war for the suppression of the rebellion I am grateful. Whatever may have been his motives he was a public benefactor, and entitled to the thanks of the nation. With him the Government must keep faith, whatever that faith may be; for good faith covers a nation like a clear and refreshing atmosphere, which imparts health and vigor to men and through which all nature seems beautiful and bright. But when faith is broken, it is as if the air were filled with noxious vapors, which obscure the sight, impair the health, and end in darkness, disease, and death. But while our creditors should receive all that they are entitled to in law and equity it is not bad faith to improve the condition of the balance of the people and bring them up as nearly as possible to the same prosperous level. The exemption from taxation is a legitimate advantage, as it results from the nature of their securities; but the additional profit of a premium on their gold was accidental in the beginning, and if continued for their benefit, and beyond the necessity which created it, would become fraudulent to the rest of the nation.

The credit of the Government of the United States was never so good as it is now. Its resources never developed so rapidly as now, were never so well understood as now, and the faith of the people in the destiny of our country is greater than ever before. While there are very few men in the country who doubt the ability of the Government to pay off the whole debt, I have never met with one who doubted its ability to redeem or pay off the legal-tender notes. In regard to the redemption of these notes it has never been a question of ability but of purpose, and to say that these notes cannot be paid until the general credit of the Government is improved by the expenditure of some hundreds of millions in the purchase of bonds that will not be due for years is to fly into the face of common sense and insult the intelligence of the people.

The policy of the Secretary of the Treasury [Hugh McCulloch] travels in a circle which invariably brings him back to contraction. He proposes nothing for redemption, and offers only that policy which he says has been emphatically condemned by Congress and as emphatically by the country. Contraction is the "Sangrado policy," of bleeding the country nearly to death to cure it of a disease which demands tonics and building up. The withdrawal of even $100,000,000 of the circulation would produce great stringency in the money market, innumerable bankruptcies, and most likely result in panic and crash from which the country would not recover for years, and during which the power of the Government to fund the debt and redeem the balance of the greenback currency would be paralyzed. To contract the currency to the extent of funding all the greenbacks would be financial suicide—would precipitate a disaster to the trade, industry, and prosperity of the country for which there is no example in history. We must not return to specie payments in that way. We must descend the mountain by easy slopes and gentle curves, though it may take much longer, rather than spring from the top of the precipice to be dashed to pieces at the bottom.

But it is broadly intimated by the Secretary that the Supreme Court will decide the laws making the greenbacks a legal tender in payment of debts to be unconstitutional, and therefore void. If the deed is to be done let it be by the court, and not by Congress. But it would have to be a very clear case that would justify the court in making a decision fraught with such terrible calamities to the country. If there be doubts hanging about the question they should be cast in favor of the legislation of Congress and the preservation of the vast interests that are dependent on the maintenance of the law. The Supreme Court, having jurisdiction over questions involving vast political, commercial, and social interests, should be something more than the rigid expounder of statutes or the collator of precedents, and should view such questions as statesmen as well as lawyers.

It was Lord Mansfield who plucked up by the roots the hoary abuses of the law, however deeply imbedded in ancient authorities, and who, in the construction of statutes and settlement of great questions, decided them in accordance with the progress of the times and the new conditions of society, and thus rendered himself immortal in the history of jurisprudence.

The speaker concluded by justifying the details of his bill. His speech may be considered as a reply to the theory of Hugh McCulloch, the Secretary of the Treasury, that the reduction of the currency was a necessary step to the resumption of specie payments. [See chapter XIII.]

Senator Morton's bill was referred to the Committee on Finance, which reported instead a bill framed chiefly by John Sherman [O.], chairman. Senator Sherman brought the bill forward on January 18, 1869. Its provisions appear in his speech.

The object we have in view is to appreciate our currency to the standard of gold as rapidly as the public interest will allow. Our present currency or "lawful" money consists of notes of the United States, and these are a legal tender in payment of all debts. Based upon them, and of equal value with them, is a subsidiary currency of notes of national banks, and these are redeemable in United States notes, and are receivable in payment of taxes. We have also a form of demand notes, convertible at the will of the holder into lawful money, called three per cent. certificates. We have also a fractional paper currency which is convertible into lawful money on demand. These four species of notes compose the paper currency of the country, and the amount of each is stated as follows:

United States notes	$356,021,073
National bank notes	299,806,565
Three per cent. certificates	55,865,000
Fractional currency	34,215,715
In all	$745,908,353

All this currency is by law at par. By law it is either made the standard of value or may at pleasure be converted into the standard of value. It is the legal measure of all commodities and of all debts, except for duties on imported goods and interest of the public debt. But in truth and in fact it is not at par in the standard money of the world. One dollar of it has only the same purchasing power as seventy-four cents in gold. Gold, which is real money, not the representative of money, but money itself, of intrinsic value, recognized as such by every man in all civilized countries and in all ages of the world—gold is demonetized by the law, cannot be collected in the courts, and, like cotton or wheat, is treated as a commodity whose value is measured by what we call "lawful money."

Now, it seems to me that the first step in our investigation should be to abandon the attempt to reason from a false standard. We must, to begin with, recognize the immutable law of currency; and that is, there is but one par, and that par is gold. Since the earliest records of humanity gold and silver have been employed as the equivalent for effecting exchanges. From Solon to our day innumerable attempts have been made to substitute something else as money, but in spite of all gold and silver have maintained their exclusive dominion as the money of mankind.

The gold in the shield of Achilles, the shekels that bought the field at Machpelah, the pieces of silver the price of the blood of our Saviour, will be current coin when the completed history of nations now rising into greatness will be folded away among the records of time.

No nation can permanently adopt a standard of value that will not be controlled and regulated by the standard of gold. No degree of isolation, no expedient of legislation can save any nation which maintains any intercourse with foreign nations from the operation of this supreme law. Like the tides of the ocean or the movements of the planets, it is beyond our jurisdiction. This higher law of the standard of values will sooner or later govern and regulate all prices, even of commodities that do not enter into foreign exchanges. It is utterly idle for a commercial people like the United States, with a foreign commerce of $800,000,000 annually, with citizens trading in every port of the world, and receiving annually four hundred thousand immigrants, to escape from the operation of this primary law of trade. Different nations have tried various expedients to evade it, and have always failed. For centuries gold and silver coins were clipped and alloyed, but it only took more of them to buy a certain commodity. In modern times paper money or credit has been substituted for real money. Laws compelled the people to take them as money. As long as this money did not exceed the amount of real money in the country it operated well. It promoted exchanges and gave great activity to enterprises, and its nominal value was the same as its real value. But when the paper money was increased or the gold exported, the paper money depreciated; it had less purchasable power, prices rose, and either the paper money became demonetized, was rejected and repudiated, or the false standard was advanced in value to the gold standard.

During our brief national history we have made several efforts to substitute paper money for real money. Continental money was a revolutionary effort to coin paper into money. General Spinner [Treasurer of the United States] has had occasion recently to inform some Rip Van Winkle, who wished Continental money redeemed in lawful money, that provision had been made to redeem it at the rate of one dollar in coin for one hundred dollars Continental money, but even this poor privilege expired in 1793.

During the war of 1812 the United States undertook to treat State bank bills as lawful money. They soon became depreciated, and, when the war was over and it became necessary to appreciate them to the gold standard, notes, banks, and debtors were swept into general bankruptcy, and the people commenced again upon the solid basis of gold and silver coin.

So, during our Civil War, both the United States and the rebels undertook to make paper not merely the representative of money, but real money. The paper money of the rebels followed the course of Continental money and French *assignats*. Ours, carefully limited in amount, supported by heavy taxes and by great resources, is still called lawful money; but, after all, its value is daily measured by the gold standard. It is only the substitute of money to be paid at a future day, and is not real money.

Even silver, long the standard of value among civilized nations, is now demonetized in some of them from the impossibility of maintaining a double standard. It was found by experience that the market value of these two precious metals varied as the production of one or the other increased in amount, thus creating confusion and compelling alterations in the coinage. The result is that silver in Great Britain and the United States is a legal tender for but small amounts, while gold is the universal standard of value. Even the stamp fixed by a government in the process of coining does not make it money or change its value. It only certifies to its weight and fineness as a matter of convenience and not as an addition of value. Indeed the mechanical process of coining has frequently reduced the market value of the gold by making it necessary to receive it when exported.

Let us, then, recognize as an axiom that nothing but coin is the real money before we undertake to deal with our currency. And Senators may think I consume too much time in dealing with an apparent truism, but it will be found that the denial of this truism, both in Congress and among the people, is the cause of most of the confusion in the public mind as to our currency. It affects our minds as it affected the Englishman in 1810. When told that the Bank of England note was depreciated he said: "Is not this pound note worth twenty shillings, and you tell me it is only worth sixteen?" Or like the reason of the learned priests in the time of Galileo, who saw the sun moving around the four corners of the earth and knew that Galileo was an imposter. So we call our paper money par, and having made a god with our own hands compare all other gods by it. We must, then, abandon the false standard, set up again the true standard, and compare again our money, our productions, our wealth, and our resources by the true standard, or we will allow ourselves to be led by false premises into the most erroneous conclusions.

And yet this does not impugn the wisdom of a paper currency founded upon the credit of a nation, or of it being made in times of great public danger a legal tender in payment of debts. Such paper money has exercised a powerful influence in ancient as well as modern history. It saved Rome in her fierce conflict with Hannibal. It enabled Great Britain to maintain her wars against Napoleon. Without paper money, and, as I believe, without making it a legal tender, we could not have mustered and maintained our immense armies during the recent war. Gold was banished by the war. The quantity was too small for the vast expenditure required by the war. We had then no legal paper representative of value. The State bank notes were wisely excluded from national circulation. We then cautiously issued our legal-tender notes, carefully limiting their amount, and only increasing the amount when we could not borrow them back at a reasonable rate of interest. We called them lawful money, and as a measure of the highest necessity compelled our citizens to receive them as such, but after all they were only a forced substitute for money, the promise to pay money, and not real money. Though they were made the legal standard of value their own value was daily fixed in gold in the open market in New York. We watched their depreciation as the dark days of the war came on, and tried to arrest it. We utterly failed. The effort was patriotic, but it was impossible. England did the same in her wars. She passed laws forbidding the purchase and sale or exportation of gold, but, like ours, her efforts were abortive. I am not ashamed to confess my part in all the efforts made during the war to maintain our paper money as the true standard of value, and I confess it was impossible.

A distinction between the standard of value and the actual agent of exchange must always be kept in view. One must be gold and the other ought to be paper money convertible into gold.

Such paper currency, with proper measures to meet panics or extreme drains of specie, is proven by all experience to be the best possible currency that has yet been devised by man. An unmixed coin currency cannot exist in a commercial country, for necessity will compel, merchants will devise, and the people will use some representative of money whether it be banker's bills of exchange, certificates of deposit, or bank or Government paper money. And one unbending, unrelaxing rule that compels payment in coin at all times, during panics, distress, or war, as well as in peace, will periodically produce disaster and bankruptcy. The requisites of a good currency are:

1. That it be a paper currency.
2. That it be amply secured either by the credit of a nation or by unquestioned collaterals.
3. That except in extreme cases of panic it be convertible into coin.
4. That provisions be made for a suspension of the right to demand coin during such panics.

And the only legislative questions that can arise on these points are whether the paper money should be issued by the nation or by corporators, and what relief shall be provided in case of a necessary suspension of specie payments. As to the first question, both England and the United States have settled upon a bank currency secured by the public credit. As to the second, they have tried various devices, as the raising of the rate of interest, a temporary suspension of payments, making the paper a legal tender; but all these expedients are merely temporary to bridge over a war, a panic, a period of starvation, or an unnatural adverse balance of trade. They are remedies in sickness to be discarded the moment that health comes again. Whatever theorists may suggest, however sugar-coated the remedy may be, there is but one test of a healthy paper currency, and that is its convertibility into gold coin.

If, then, gold only is the true standard of money, why shall we not commence our financial measures by restoring it to its place as a legal standard of money? Why not allow our citizens to base their future contracts on gold? Why not enforce these contracts in the courts as legal and valid? There are difficulties in applying a new standard to existing contracts made upon a different standard; but this difficulty does not apply to future contracts. We wish to restore specie payments, and yet we forbid all men from dealing in specie. Such contracts are put upon the same legal footing as gaming contracts. It would seem that if we are at all sincere in wishing specie payments we should not only promote specie contracts, but should encourage them.

Contracts, to a vast amount, are now from necessity made upon the gold basis. All our foreign commerce, exports and imports, amounting annually to over eight hundred million dollars, are based upon gold. The price of all public securities is fixed by the gold standard of London and Frankfort. The sale of all imported goods by the importer to the jobber is by the gold standard. The daily transactions in gold in New York often amount to $100,000,000. On the Pacific slope gold is the only standard of value. We could not alter this if we would. Why not recognize the fact, legalize these contracts, and conform our measures to the gradual adjustment of existing contracts, including paper money, to the standard of gold.

And, sir, let us also recognize the general principle that it is wiser and more in accordance with the spirit of our Government to leave this adjustment to the voluntary contracts of the people rather than undertake it by arbitrary rules of law. If our people are left free they can do this without injury to debtor or creditor, without confiscation of property, and without any change in the intrinsic value of property.

For these reasons the Committee on Finance regard the first

section of this bill, which legalizes gold contracts, as an indispensable preliminary to any plan for appreciating our currency to gold. This section has twice received the sanction of the Senate, and its primary importance has generally been admitted in popular discussions.

Not only ought specie contracts to be allowed, but they ought to be encouraged. Every such contract smooths the way to a general resumption. If they become general gold now hoarded will be let loose. This will produce an expansion of the currency.

It is only by restoring gold contracts that you can safely avail yourself of all the multiplied uses of paper money. Then, and not until then, you can issue paper money based upon gold. The gold now lying idle in the treasury may then be utilized, made to produce an interest by the issue of coin notes based upon it, and thus enter into actual circulation and gradually be made to perform all the uses of money now performed by a depreciated currency. This is the basis of the fourth section of the bill, which utilizes the gold by the issue of gold notes based upon it, and their application to the purchase of bonds and the reduction of interest.

And the right to make contracts in gold may now safely and properly be extended to banks organized under the national banking system. Upon a deposit of bonds existing banks or new banks may be authorized to issue gold notes equal to sixty-five per cent. of the value of United States bonds deposited to secure their circulation. Their payment will be in coin, but in all other respects they may be subject to the general provisions and limitations of the banking act. Many of the banks, especially in commercial cities, will gladly avail themselves of such a provision to withdraw their present circulation and substitute gold notes convertible on demand into coin. With such a provision and on such a basis the system may be free, and thus all the embarrassing questions about the inequality of the distribution of banking circulation will be avoided. A right conferred upon all, without limit as to amount and upon regulations applicable to all, would at once secure to the South and West new banking facilities, and would rapidly tend to substitute coin or its equivalent for legal tender notes, and without the severe process of contraction. The objection made, that this would create two currencies of unequal values, applies as well to the present state of the currency, for we have now two currencies of unequal value—gold and legal tenders.

If we are sincere in wishing specie payments we must not

only multiply the demands for coin; we must encourage coin contracts, issue coin notes both by the United States and by the banks, and thus without contraction dispense with the use of the inferior and depreciated currency.

The superior value of coin notes, their use in commercial cities, their convenience in the gold-producing States will soon give them higher credit, and secure them in every part of the country. I am confident that under such a system the national banks will, if allowed, and before specie payments are resumed, substitute coin notes for their present circulation, and that, too, without diminishing the aggregate of circulation. Many of them have now reserves and profits enough to make the requisite deposit of additional bonds; and the gold certificates now issued from the treasury might be used for their coin reserves without creating new demands for coin.

There is but one other consideration I wish to urge in favor of the sections of this bill relating to gold contracts and gold notes, and that grows out of the doubt that rests upon the validity of the legal-tender act. We must not forget that currency contracts depend not upon the agreement of parties, but entirely upon the validity of that act. This has always been doubted, and is now contested before the Supreme Court. It may be that the Supreme Court will deny the validity of the legal-tender act, or limit its operation to existing contracts made since its passage. It may subject currency contracts to enforcement in coin. Is it not wiser to bridge over this uncertainty by authorizing the adjustment of this matter between the creditor and debtor?

Again, sir, the law as it now stands is productive of gross injustice. You require nearly one-half of your taxes to be paid in gold, and yet you will not enforce a contract by which the merchant buys the gold for you. Cargoes of tea, coffee, and merchandise can only be bought in gold, and yet if property is delivered upon a promise to pay gold it cannot be enforced. Gross and palpable injustice may be done in a multitude of transactions necessarily based upon gold by appealing to the legal-tender act. I conclude, then, this branch of the subject by the earnest opinion that it was a good policy three years ago, and it is good policy now, to allow all parties to stipulate the time when, the amount, and the medium of payment, subject to the general laws of fraud, usury, and force. Free trade in domestic productions, liberty to contract and be contracted with, has never been restrained before. Let us restore these rights; and, having also provided a paper representative of the coin in the treasury of the United States and a bank currency convertible into gold and founded upon the highest securities, let us now deal with the much more difficult question—the appreciation of the present currency to the standard of gold.

If this question affected alone the Government of the United States we might resume specie payments very soon; sooner even than the Senator from Massachusetts [Mr. Sumner] proposes.[1] By funding a portion of the United States notes, by requiring the banks to maintain their full reserves in legal tenders, by withdrawing the three per cent. certificates, and by the use of the gold in the treasury, we could resume at once.

And if the burden of resumption fell alone upon the national banks the task would be an easy one. Their securities, deposited with the Treasurer of the United States, are now nearly equal in gold to the amount of their circulation. A call under the banking act of ten per cent. additional security could be easily met by the great body of them, and thus enable them to resume whenever the United States is prepared to resume. Their profits in the past have been large. Those not now strong enough to perform the great object of their organization, namely, to furnish a uniform currency convertible into gold, may well give way to other banks ready to take their places.

But redemption by the banks means redemption by all their debtors; by the merchants, manufacturers, and traders of the country. And we are therefore compelled to deal with this question, not as affects the United States and the banks merely, but as it affects all the people of the United States. How will the appreciation of the currency affect their interests? Suppose it accomplished, how will it affect different individuals? A person entirely out of debt but possessed of property of productive value would not be affected by the change. His property would be of less nominal value, but it would be of the same intrinsic value. Its producing capacity is undiminished. It will buy the same food, clothing, and necessaries of life. The relative value of commodities to each other is not affected by the currency used, but by supply and demand.

If the currency is depreciated it will take more of it to purchase the article. If it is appreciated it will take less; but the appreciation or depreciation of the currency does not affect the price of other commodities in their relation to each other. This can only be affected by the demand for them, by the supply of them, and ultimately by the cost of producing them.

So a man without property and not in debt, but who de-

[1] July 4, 1869.

pends upon his labor for his support, is not in the end affected merely by an appreciation in the currency. His wages may be less, but what he receives of the appreciated currency has the same purchasing power as the higher wages received before. The change does affect him for a time, for land and labor are the last commodities to feel a change in the currency. The immediate effect of a depreciation in the currency is injurious to him, for his food and clothing rise more quickly than his labor, but appreciation of the currency is immediately beneficial to him for the reason that his labor does not fall in price so quickly as food and clothing. The value of labor, however, may be disastrously affected by the mode of appreciation. If it is brought about by a sudden contraction the result will be a suspension of work, of enterprises, and consequently a reduction in the price of labor.

Persons of fixed salaries and incomes are benefited by an appreciation of the currency to the full extent of the appreciation. Their incomes have increased purchasing power, and they are enabled to extend their purchases, supply new wants, and add to their capital. The opposite effect during the war, when the currency was being depreciated, carried distress and want and poverty into many comfortable homes. It fell with severe effect upon preachers and widows and old men, who saw the purchasing power of their annuities melt away, and a condition of independence changed to poverty and want. They will, by an appreciation of the currency, be restored to their own again.

Merchants, dealers, traders, and bankers will be affected by an appreciation of the currency precisely as their debts and credits bear to each other. If they owe more than they can promptly collect on debts due to them they must lose to the full extent of the appreciation, and they must make this loss good by a sale of a part of their property at reduced prices or by contracting new debts to be paid in an appreciated currency. As a general rule, any appreciation of the currency is injurious to all these classes, for they are generally in debt, and even where enough is due them to pay with yet the delay in payment or the failure of their debtors almost always embarrasses them. Commercial and banking usage compels promptness, so that a merchant or a banker, however prudent he may be, is often compelled to sacrifice his assets to meet a sudden appreciation of the currency.

But the distress caused by an appreciation of the currency falls mainly on the debtor class; others suffer only by reason of their inability to pay. What do specie payments mean to a debtor? They mean the payment of $135 where he has agreed to pay $100, or, which is the same thing, the payment of $100 where he has agreed to pay seventy-four dollars. Where he has purchased property and paid one-fourth of it, it means the loss of the property; it means the addition of one-fourth to all currency debts in the United States. A measure to require a debtor now to pay his debt in gold or currency equivalent to gold requires him to pay one hundred and thirty-five bushels of wheat when he agreed to pay one hundred, and if this appreciation is extended through a period of three years it requires him to pay an interest of twelve per cent. in addition to the rate he has agreed to pay. When we consider the enormous indebtedness of a new country like ours, where capital is scarce, and where credit has been substituted in the place of capital, it presents a difficulty that may well cause us to pause. We may see that the chasm must be crossed, but it will make us wary of our footsteps. Good faith and public policy demand that we appreciate our currency to gold, but in the process we must be careful that bankruptcy, distress, and want do not fall upon our fellow-citizens who have based their obligations upon your broken promises. The debtors of this country include the active, enterprising, energetic men in all the various employments of life. It is a serious proposition to change their contracts so as in effect to require them to pay one-third more than they agreed to pay. They have not paused in their business to study questions of political economy. They have based their operations upon this money, which you have declared to be lawful money. You may change its relative value, but in doing so you should give them a reasonable opportunity to change their contracts so as to adapt them to the new standards of value you may prescribe for them.

The question then remains, what mode of appreciation of the value of greenbacks will operate the least injuriously to all the varied business interests of our constituents? and upon this point your committee, after the most careful consideration, came to the conclusion that the only and best plan was to allow them to be funded at the pleasure of the holder into interest-bearing bonds of the United States.

In designating the bond we have selected that now familiar to the people, the ten-forty bond. The market value of this bond is now but slightly above that of the legal tenders, so that the process of appreciation of the notes will be slow and will only advance with the improving credit of the country. It is a bond bearing as low a rate of interest as we are likely to negotiate, and yet of such intrinsic value that we may hope to see it at par with gold within a short period. It enables us after ten years to take advantage of the money market to still further reduce the interest. Its credit is supported by a permanent appropriation from an ample fund sufficient without further act of Congress to pay off every dollar of the debt in twenty-five years.

Again, sir, this provision of the bill is right when tested by the moral sense. When for sufficient reasons we cannot pay the note in coin we are bound to give to the holder our note with interest. Such from the beginning was the policy of the Government. When the notes were first issued under the act of February 25, 1862, they were convertible at will into bonds. We, with a questionable device, by the act of March 3, 1863, took away that right, and should now restore it. During the war a greenback would purchase an equal amount of bonds of any character offered in the market. It paid at par for the five-twenties, the ten-forties, and the seven-thirties. It is now less valuable than these bonds only because it is dishonored paper, which though due is unpaid, and is only valuable as a forced currency, which you compel your citizens to take in payment of their debts, but refuse to take for your own bonds except at a discount. You give the bond the benefit of the improving credit of the country, but you deny this to the note. The simplest and plainest rule of equity requires you if you cannot pay this note to give in exchange for it a bond bearing interest.

Such, sir, are the general provisions of this bill. It seeks to substitute gradually, by the voluntary action of the people, coin contracts, coin notes, and convertible bank bills for currency contracts and irredeemable and inconvertible paper money. It seeks to secure to the public creditor the prompt payment of his interest in coin, and to the people the like payment in coin of the depreciated notes held by them. If the process is too slow it is because the danger of a more rapid process is too great.

It now remains for me very briefly to state why other propositions submitted to the committee have not been approved. Your patience will not allow me to examine any of the multitude of suggestions that have been made in the public prints, though many of them are worthy of careful study. I will only allude to some propositions that have been referred to the committee. The suggestion of the President to pay the interest for sixteen years if the creditor would surrender the principal has already been disposed of. The plan of the Secretary of the Treasury to contract the currency until we reach the specie basis has already been incidentally referred to. The proposition of the Senator from Massachusetts [Mr. Sumner], though not formally referred to the committee, yet having the sanction of his great name, was carefully considered, and so much of it as was approved was embodied in the bill reported; but its principal feature, the repeal of the legal-tender act after the 1st of July next, is far too sudden, and will, if I am correct in the views already expressed, be disastrous to the great body of the active business men of the country.

The plan of the Senator from Indiana [Mr. Morton], supported by an able speech, was carefully considered by the committee. It rests upon two leading ideas:

1. The accumulation of gold in the treasury; and

2. The fixing a specific day for the resumption of specie payments.

Now, in most of his speech I heartily concur. All that he says of the necessity of resuming specie payments, of the effect of contraction, and the unjust discrimination that now exists between the noteholder and the bondholder—all this meets my hearty assent. It is the remedy he suggests we have to deal with. Would not the effect of his measure be that the Government would hoard the gold and the people the greenbacks, and thus make the contraction he fears? What more profitable investment could any man make than to take this dollar, now having a purchasable power of seventy-four cents in gold, locking it in his safe with a certainty that in two years it must be worth one dollar in gold or an annual advance of seventeen and a half per cent.? Would not every bank sharply contract its currency and hoard greenbacks as the best investment it could make? What prudent man would dare build a house or factory, a railroad, or a barn, with the certain fact before him that the greenbacks he puts into his improvement will be worth thirty-five per cent. more in two years than his improvement then is worth? Why not hold his money for two years until his building will cost him one-third less? When the day comes every man, as the sailors say, will be close-reefed; all enterprise will be suspended; every bank will have contracted its currency to the lowest limit, and the debtor, compelled to meet in coin a debt contracted in currency, will find the coin hoarded in the treasury, no representative of coin in circulation, his property shrunk not only to the extent of the appreciation of the currency, but still more by the artificial scarcity made by the hoarders of gold.

All the historical precedents show that fixing the day for resumption inevitably led to a contraction of the currency by the banks, so that when the day came the actual scarcity of currency prevented a demand for coin. We, therefore, think that the general objects sought for by the Senator from Indiana [Mr. Morton] can be better attained by legalizing specie contracts; by utilizing the coin in the treasury; by the gradual substitution of coin, United States notes, and bank bills for the present currency, rather than accumulating gold and fixing a day for resumption.

The bill was discussed at various times during the session, but no action was taken upon it.

FINE-ASS COMMITTEE

Sketch by Thomas Nast

In his second inaugural address on March 4, 1873, President Grant referred to the financial panic of that year, saying that, although it had materially lessened Government revenues, it might prove a "blessing in disguise" by inciting Congress to take steps against its recurrence, and to seize the opportunity afforded by it to hasten the resumption of specie payments.

Resumption of Specie Payments

Second Inaugural Address of President Grant

My own judgment is that, however much individuals may have suffered, one long step has been taken toward specie payments; that we can never have permanent prosperity until a specie basis is reached; and that a specie basis cannot be reached and maintained until our exports, exclusive of gold, pay for our imports, interest due abroad, and other specie obligations, or so nearly so as to leave an appreciable accumulation of the precious metals in the country from the products of our mines.

The development of the mines of precious metals during the past year, and the prospective development of them for years to come, are gratifying in their results. Could but one-half of the gold extracted from the mines be retained at home our advance toward specie payments would be rapid.

To increase our exports, sufficient currency is required to keep all the industries of the country employed. Without this, national as well as individual bankruptcy must ensue. Undue inflation, on the other hand, while it might give temporary relief, would only lead to inflation of prices, the impossibility of competing in our own markets for the products of home skill and labor, and repeated renewals of present experiences. Elasticity to our circulating medium, therefore, and just enough of it to transact the legitimate business of the country and to keep all industries employed, is what is most to be desired. The exact medium is specie, the recognized medium of exchange the world over. That obtained, we shall have a currency of an exact degree of elasticity. If there be too much of it for the legitimate purposes of trade and commerce, it will flow out of the country. If too little, the reverse will result. To hold what we have, and to appreciate our currency to that standard, is the problem deserving of the most serious consideration of Congress.

The experience of the present panic has proven that the currency of the country, based as it is upon the credit of the country, is the best that has ever been devised. Usually in times of such trials currency has become worthless, or so much depreciated in value as to inflate the values of all the necessaries of life as compared with the currency. Everyone holding it has been anxious to dispose of it on any terms. Now we witness the reverse. Holders of currency hoard it as they did gold in former experiences of a like nature.

It is patent to the most casual observer that much more currency, or money, is required to transact the legitimate trade of the country during the fall and winter months, when the vast crops are being removed, than during the balance of the year. With our present system the amount in the country remains the same throughout the entire year, resulting in an accumulation of all the surplus capital of the country in a few centers when not employed in the moving of crops; tempted there by the offer of interest on call loans. Interest being paid, this surplus capital must earn this interest paid, with a profit. Being subject to "call," it cannot be loaned—only in part at best—to the merchant or manufacturer for a fixed term. Hence, no matter how much currency there might be in the country it would be absorbed, prices keeping pace with the volume, and panics, stringency, and disasters would ever be recurring with the autumn.

Elasticity in our monetary system, therefore, is the object to be obtained first, and next to that, as far as possible, a prevention of the use of other people's money in stock and other species of speculation. To prevent the latter, it seems to me that one great step would be taken by prohibiting the national banks from paying interest on deposits, by requiring them to hold their reserves in their own vaults, and by forcing them into resumption, though it would be only in legal-tender notes. For this purpose I would suggest the establishment of clearing-houses for your consideration.

To secure the former many plans have been suggested, most if not all of which look to me more like inflation, on the one hand, or compelling the Government, on the other, to pay interest without corresponding benefits upon the surplus funds of the country during the seasons when otherwise unemployed.

I submit for your consideration whether this difficulty might not be overcome by authorizing the Secretary of the Treasury to issue, at any time, to national banks of issue, any amount of their own notes below a fixed percentage of their issue—say 40 per cent.—upon the banks depositing with the Treasurer of the United States an amount of Government bonds equal to the amount of notes demanded; the banks to forfeit to the Government, say, 4 per cent. of the interest accruing on the bonds so pledged, during the time they remain with the Treasurer, as security for the increased circulation; the bonds so pledged to be redeemable by the banks at their pleasure, either in whole or in part, by returning their own bills for cancellation to an amount equal to the face of the bonds withdrawn.

I would further suggest for your consideration the propriety of authorizing national banks to diminish their standing issue at pleasure, by returning for cancellation their own bills and withdrawing so many United States bonds as are pledged for the bills returned.

In view of the great actual contraction that has taken place in the currency, and the comparative contraction continuously

STAND BACK!

"I am not a believer in any artificial method of making paper money equal to coin."—President Grant's Veto of the Inflation Bill.

Cartoon by C. S. Reinhart

going on, due to the increase of population, increase of manufactories, and all the industries, I do not believe there is too much of it now for the dullest period of the year. Indeed, if clearing-houses should be established, thus forcing redemption, it is a question for your consideration whether banking should not be made free, retaining all the safeguards now required to secure bill holders.

In any modification of the present laws regulating national banks, as a further step toward preparing for resumption of specie payments, I invite your attention to a consideration of the propriety of exacting from them the retention, as a part of their reserve, of either the whole or a part of the gold interest accruing upon the bonds pledged as security for their issue.

I have not reflected enough on the bearing this might have in producing a scarcity of coin with which to pay duties on imports to give it my positive recommendation. But your attention is invited to the subject.

During the last four years the currency has been contracted, directly, by the withdrawal of 3 per cent. certificates, compound-interest notes and 7-30 bonds, outstanding on the 4th of March, 1869 (all of which took the place of legal tenders in the bank reserves), to the extent of $63,000,000.

During the same period there has been a much larger comparative contraction of the currency. The population of the country has largely increased. More than 25,000 miles of railroad have been built, requiring the active use of capital to operate them. Millions of acres of land have been opened, requiring capital to move the products. Manufactories have multiplied beyond all precedent in the same period of time, requiring capital weekly for the payment of wages and for the purchase of material; and probably the largest of all comparative contraction arises from the organizing of free labor in the South. Now every laborer there receives his wages, and for want of savings banks the greater part of such wages is carried in the pocket, or hoarded until required for use.

These suggestions are thrown out for your consideration without any recommendation that they shall be adopted literally, but hoping that the best method may be arrived at to secure such an elasticity of the currency as will keep employed all the industries of the country, and prevent such an inflation as will put off indefinitely the resumption of specie payments; an object so devoutly to be wished for by all, and none more earnestly than the class of people most directly interested—those who "earn their bread by the sweat of their brow." The decisions of Congress on this subject will have the hearty support of the Executive.

The Currency

Senate, December 10, 1873–January 22, 1874

On December 10, 1873, John Sherman [O.] introduced in the Senate a resolution that the committee report a bill for the early resumption of specie payments, and for the supply of "a currency of uniform value, always redeemable in gold or its equivalent, and so adjusted as to meet the changing wants of trade and of commerce."

On December 15 Thomas W. Ferry [Mich.] moved a substitute to the resolution to the effect that the bill submitted be one to

"restore commercial confidence and give stability and elasticity to the circulating medium, by making banking free to all, by pro-

THE RAG BABY

Sketch by Thomas Nast

viding for an increase of currency of $100,000,000 (including the $44,000,000 reserve), by making the whole currency of Government issue and lawful money by the issue of currency bonds bearing 3.65 per cent. interest."

The issue of the "greenbacks," said Senator Ferry, was of the nature of a forced loan, justified only as a war measure. Therefore the holders of these notes ought in justice to be protected, and not be discriminated against in favor of holders of other forms of currency.

Congress had made such discrimination in repealing, on March 3, 1863, the permission to convert greenbacks into bonds at the option of the holder.

From that time forth the greenbacks have been at a discount as compared with the bonds, and must continue so until Congress shall take measures either to allow their conversion into interest-bearing bonds or compel their redemption in coin.

As the matter stands now, we have $356,000,000 of this legal-tender issue afloat, circulating as money, without any power in the holders to get the promised coin, or to exchange them for bonds. They are dishonored promises to pay, or, as my friend from Vermont [Justin S. Morrill] the other day styled them, "engraved falsehoods." This state of things has continued for ten years, and is likely to continue for ten years to come unless Congress takes measures to wipe away the dishonor.

On January 20, 1874, General John B. Gordon [Ga.] spoke upon the two resolutions, with special reference to the agricultural interests of the country, particularly the South.

Let the apologists of our unfortunate financial system—unfortunate as manipulated—explain the recent panic as they may, or fail, as they will, to find any satisfactory explanation, it is still true that the recent commercial convulsion, which has changed in a day opulence to ashes, and, what is of infinitely greater moment, has deprived the laborer of his daily toil and his daily bread, is no inexplicable financial catastrophe. It is but the crowning effect of a system which can be perfected, but which is far from perfect at present.

I wish I had the time to analyze all the objections which I think lie against the present system. I think it would be easy to prove that, by the very operation of the law which lies at the bottom of the system, it does induce at seasons undue flow of money to New York and to the great centers.

That these accumulations do encourage speculations, and speculations create panics.

I think it would be easy to show that its very rigidity of volume, its non-elasticity, its insufficiency make it the subject of control by heavy capitalists, and thereby place at the mercy of Wall street the profits on the legitimate industries of the country.

That it prevents competition, and thereby insures a high rate of interest, which is death to the debtor and to the producing sections.

That it brings of necessity the treasury into competition with Wall street in the sale of gold, and thus makes it not only a speculator in its own promises, but an absorber of the currency already insufficient for the people.

It changes, in a word, the Government into a gigantic banking establishment which, in violation of every principle of equity, and unmindful of its effects upon the morals of the people, demands payment in one currency, while it makes payment in another.

It thus sets an example whose pernicious influence is fast debauching the people and changing the nation into a nation of speculators and gamblers.

Mr. President, these are evils which I think exist in this system, and evils which can be easily, and I hope will be, remedied by the legislation of this Congress.

I come now to the most important question, the question of remedies. Senator Sherman proposes a speedy return to specie payments. This, sir, is a remedy hoary with age; but, as I shall show, hoary with failure also.

In all that I have to say on this subject I trust I shall not be understood as opposing specie payment when consistent with the best interests of the producing classes of this country; but I do wish to be understood as taking issue, broad and emphatic, with the position that a speedy return to specie payment under our circumstances, or any forced return at any date which this Congress could set, will relieve the country is practicable, just, or expedient.

First, can it relieve the country? The honorable Senator from Michigan [Mr. Ferry], in his able remarks on this question, referred to the well-known fact that specie payment never had prevented disaster when it existed; and it is true. In 1837 the suspension of specie payment followed, and did not precede, the commercial difficulties of the country. Suspension was the consequence, not the cause, of the disaster. Our whole commercial fabric was shaken from turret to foundation before a solitary bank in the United States suspended. The honorable Senator from Indiana [Mr. Morton] showed clearly the additional fact that a return to specie payment had never been successfully resorted to to relieve commercial disaster. Absolutely the reverse is true. Suspension has been the remedy. It has been so in this country; it was so in England and everywhere.

Senators seem to have forgotten the good old adage that an ounce of prevention is better than a pound of cure; but the force of their logic would lead us to conclude that an ounce of cure was better than a pound of prevention. For if existing, established specie payments could not prevent a coming disaster, how —will Senators tell us how—can a prospective resumption cure an existing disaster? I leave to the ingenuity of Senators to reconcile such incongruous logic and bring it to the apprehension of the Senate.

I am unable, Mr. President, to see the wisdom of insisting on a program which, as has been shown, has never prevented disaster when it existed, has never cured disaster when resorted to, and which cannot relieve the country, and is neither practicable, just, nor expedient.

Is it practicable? Can we return to specie payments within any short period? The honorable Senator from Vermont [Justin S. Morrill] said in his remarks that it was not a question of the ability of the Government to redeem its currency in gold, but a question of will; and he facetiously added that "we might pardon the inability to pay, but who could defend the lack of will?" The honorable Senator will pardon me for suggesting that if a day were now set by this Congress upon which the treasury of the United States should begin the redemption of its greenbacks, and proclamations made thereof, in an incredibly short time thereafter the speculators on Wall street would control every dollar of gold in that treasury, or that is likely to be in the treasury within any given time.

Mr. President, this is not a question of whether Mr. A. or Mr. B. shall receive at the treasury five dollars for his five-dollar greenback when it is presented, but it is the infinitely greater question of whether the tens of thousands of holders of greenbacks all over this country shall be subjected to irretrievable loss by having the Government undertake to redeem when it cannot redeem, and thereby leave the millions of greenbacks dishonored in the pockets of those persons who fail to secure redemption.

But, if forced resumption were practicable, would it be just? If my surroundings were those of the honorable Senators from Vermont, Massachusetts, and New York, if the people who sent me here were creditors, as are their constituents, instead of debtors, then I, too, might look upon this proposed change in our financial status with some degree of philosophic complacency.

But, sir, the people of the South and of the West are debtors; and their obligations were formed, mark you, when gold was at 110 to 150; and now to force them to pay in a currency equal to gold would be simply to increase their debts by the amount of 10 to 50 per cent.

But, if it were both practicable and just, would it be expedient, would it be consistent with the best interests of the producers, to return to specie payments within any limited space of time? This is the great question, after all. I apprehend that there are but two roads with a government currency to specie payments. One is by contracting the currency, as proposed here, to within a certain relation to the specie which you may hold in the treasury, which would bring bankruptcy to the country; the other by giving vitality to production, which can only be done by giving facilities for production. To give facilities for production we must give money at low interest in order that our exports, our trade, internal and foreign, may be built up, and that we may enhance individual as well as national wealth.

Which of these two roads shall we take? That is the question on which the Senate is to vote. Shall we contract, or shall we give to the country more currency? Here the battle is joined; here the roads diverge. I ask which shall we take? To my mind, supported, as I think I am, by experience and history, the latter is the shortest, surest, easiest, and best. We cannot pay gold for greenbacks until we get gold; we cannot get gold until we bring it back to this country; we cannot bring it back to this country until our exports and our sales bring it to us. We cannot increase our sales until we increase our productions; we cannot increase our productions until we increase our facilities for production, by giving to the producers money at low interest—not an inflated or redundant currency, as Senators would term it—but a sufficiency of low-rate money.

Sir, I want no inflation, which means a volume unduly swollen beyond all the legitimate wants of the country; but I make bold to say that when a people are burdened with debt, when every enterprise languishes, when every industry is prostrate, when widespread blight is upon us, even inflation, which, like the stimulant to the enfeebled pulse, may give new life and vigor, is better than insufficiency. I repeat, I want no inflation. Do you inflate the sick man starving for food by furnishing to him the nutriment which shall bring blood to his veins, flesh to his bones, and vigor to his whole system? Inflation is one thing; sufficiency is a very different thing.

But Senators talk of the idea of increasing the currency at all as a subject of alarm. Mr. President, are the teachings of history and our own experience to go for naught in solving this important and complex problem? Have Senators forgotten what history and our own experience have taught us upon this point? Let me repeat that mere theory should be silent when facts and history talk. Why, sir, look at Scotland, within the short space of twenty-five years nearly quadrupling her wealth after doubling her currency. Look at France, with her currency more than doubled, I believe, or quite doubled during the war. Notwithstanding her devastation she has been able, by quickening her enterprises and her industry, to pay her indemnity of one thousand millions in gold to Germany, to keep her interest at 6 per cent. per annum, to make her paper money receivable for all dues to government and individuals alike, and now confronts us with the overwhelming argument of this increased volume at par with gold. These are stubborn facts, Mr. President. Look at England, too, again and again, in times like these, by an act of government, suspending specie payment and authorizing an increase of the currency, even at the cost of the suspension of the most solemn enactments of the British Parliament. What was the effect there? Are the effects here to belie the effects everywhere else in the universe? What were the effects there? They were absolutely magical, as I intend to show. Panic subsided immediately; failures abated; commercial confidence was restored; and, what is a most significant fact, gold flowed into the country.

The relief which this expansion gave to England was not even delayed until the money reached the hands of the people; the very expectation of the money's coming gave relief; and I make the prediction here to-day that if this Senate and the other wing of the Capitol should announce by a vote that they intended to give more money to the people, and give it flexibility, the very hour that the electric telegraph bore the intelligence to the country, that very hour would relief be practically inaugurated, and it would bring millions of hidden greenbacks from the safes of the hoarders. I have no question about it. History does not belie itself. The people of England are not unlike the people of this country. The same disasters which were cured there by certain remedies can be cured here by the same remedies, and in no other way.

But now I wish to examine the effect of the opposite course—the course so eloquently pleaded for by the speedy resumptionists. I have shown what was the effect of expansion; now what was the effect of contraction? They tried that in England, too. At a later day, when commercial disaster approached, they did contract and they did resume; but did they cure the panic? Did they bring relief to the country? Nay, sir; hear again the facts:

> It is clear at least that it did not in the more recent instance succeed, by the diminution of notes, in curing the evil which it aimed to remedy.—Mr. Thornton, M.P.

Now, sir, I believe it is conceded that no portion of English history furnishes a parallel in prosperity to the twenty years of suspension of specie payment; but I am not going into that question. I think our own experience teaches precisely the same lesson. Why, sir, at the South during the war, with one dollar of gold worth sixty dollars of Southern money, there was less of financial distress in the country than there is to-day. And what was the truth at the North? Prosperity reigned everywhere, notwithstanding your young men were in the army. Do you tell me that it was the mere semblance of prosperity; that it was a mushroom growth of wealth? Nay, sir; it remains there still, in your improved lands, in your railroads, in your bonds, in your banks, and your brown-stone fronts.

But what was the effect of the opposite course of contraction in this country? At the end of the war there were about $900,000,000 in all of currency, seven-thirties, and compound-interest notes—so estimated. The Secretary of the Treasury began a course, which has been much applauded by the specie resumptionists, of contraction, of calling in the seven-thirties and the compound-interest notes; and then, as was stated on this floor a few days ago, within two months contracting $16,000,000. What was the effect? Interest became high, agriculture began to languish, and disaster has followed.

Now, Mr. President, in view of all these facts is it wise to refuse to the people the currency which experience and history and reason demand should be furnished? To give currency to industry is a course, the wisdom of which is suggested by reason, sustained by experience, and demonstrated by history.

But, again, this contraction, which was inaugurated by the former Secretary of the Treasury, was inaugurated at the most inopportune time. It was just when the South was being restored to the Union, without a dollar of currency, without a bank, with more than $5,000,000,000 of her property gone down forever in revolution; and with four millions of her newly emancipated population all paupers. It was therefore a time for more currency rather than less.

Before taking leave of this subject of specie payment, permit me to say that I was impressed by the remark of the honorable Senator from Indiana [Mr. Morton] in his opening speech on this subject. He said that he was not so much of a hard-money man as he once was. When, a few years ago, business engagements turned my attention to the investigation of this subject, I set out, as he did, with the idea that gold and silver were the only basis for currency—the only basis of a credit. I was born into that idea. It strengthened with my boyhood, and grew stronger with all of my political associations. But upon investigation, upon mature reflection, I have found the position less and less tenable, less and less supported by the experience and financial history of all countries. That specie is a good basis no one denies. That it is the only basis I do emphatically deny. That it is even the best basis which this Government can find I think will be seriously questioned before the country is much older. Why, sir, the suggestion that our houses, and our lands, and our crops, and our cattle upon a thousand hills would lose any portion of their value, or that their value would be less ascertainable if gold were banished from this country, occurs to me as the most irrational of propositions. All the gold of the universe could not pay for the property of the people of the United States; and if it were brought here and molded into a monument it would stand in one corner of this chamber, and would not then make a respectable monument to the absurdity of such a dogma. If every dollar of gold now in the treasury or in the pockets of individuals in the United States were banished from this country, and every gold and silver mine upon the continent were obliterated by Jehovah's fiat, or sunk by an earthquake, it would not make one farthing's difference in the productive value or the prosperity of this country, provided in lieu thereof we had a currency universally recognized; a currency universally receivable by Government and individuals alike; a currency founded upon the good faith and the stability and the revenues of the Government itself. Why, sir, some of the most beggarly countries in the world are countries where there is nothing but specie payment. Look at Spain, and Portugal, and Mexico. While some of the eras of great prosperity, as I have shown, in many of the leading countries of the world have been eras of the suspension of specie payment.

Mr. President, it seems to me difficult to determine which is the more irrational, the laws of old Sparta that forbade gold coming into the country, or of modern Spain that forbade gold going out of it; but, more irrational than either is the effort of the United States to bring gold in and keep gold in the country by stifling industry, which is the surest way to keep gold out of it.

A sufficient supply of circulation of cheap money—cheap money which insures productions and enterprise; enterprise and productions which insure exports and domestic traffic—these are the links of natural consequence in which the blessedness of commerce lies. These are the links of natural consequence which lead to specie payments, too. Show me a country without cheap money—and I mean by cheap money, cheap interest for money—and I will show you a country where agriculture languishes. Cheap money is the one thing needful for the agricultural and productive interests of this country; and let the debt-burdened West and the debt-burdened South heed it. Cheap interest is what we want. If you will show me a country that pays, as we do in the South, from 15 to 26 per cent. per annum for its currency, I will show you a country where prosperity is dead or dying, and every industrial interest prostrate. High interest is *high* evidence of *low* prosperity. It is at the same time the evidence and the cause of the destruction of the prosperity of any community.

Eli Saulsbury [Del.].—I ask the Senator if that high rate of interest did not occur under, and if it was not the result of, the very system which he is advocating?

Senator Gordon.—When I inform the Senator that the South has a little over two dollars of these greenbacks for each man [1] he will understand very readily how insufficient that amount is for the demands of the industries of the South, and why money must of consequence command these exorbitant rates of interest. I will inform the Senator in advance that I am not advocating greenbacks under the present system, but under a system which I shall indicate directly, and which I hope this Senate will adopt.

Now, sir, talking of the South, I trust the Senate will bear with me one moment while I discuss very briefly the high rate of interest and its effect upon the cotton culture, as well as the rate at the West and its effect upon the grain-growing. I affirm whereof I do know when I assert that the South is poorer to-day than she was the day Lee surrendered at Appomattox Court-house. Her lands, which after the surrender commanded from ten to thirty dollars per acre in the cotton belt, can be bought

[1] In fact, $2.98.

to-day at from two to five dollars per acre; and the cotton planters are so hopelessly involved that, unless this Congress gives them speedy and permanent relief, nothing but utter ruin and bankruptcy await them in the near future. Burdened with debt, each succeeding year, with its oppressive interest, adds to the burden.

The ruling bank interest is from 1 to 1½ per cent. per month, and has been ever since the war, and that discounted from the face of the note and compounded every thirty or sixty days; so that at the end of the year it amounts to from 24 to 27 per cent. I ask Senators what industry on the face of the earth can survive such a rate of interest? Did any ever do it in any country, however blessed of Heaven? Sir, this rate of interest has so impoverished us, that if the old laws of imprisonment for debt were in force, and I owned the debts, I could turn the jail keys within six months upon seven-tenths of the cotton growers of Georgia.

Am I asked why we borrow money at this exorbitant rate of interest? I will answer that question when I am told how our people, without a dollar, without a bank, without mules to plow, without food to feed the laborer, could begin their enterprises without borrowing; and each year's interest has not only eaten up the profit, but has brought the planter deeper and deeper into debt, and subjected him year after year to the necessity of additional loans and increasing loans.

But, Mr. President, we are told that as a means of relief we must diversify our labor. No man is more impressed with the importance and the necessity of diversity of labor than I am; but I shall appreciate that advice, so kindly given and so kindly meant, much more if Senators will also tell me how the people, without any money, with interest already at from 18 to 25 per cent., are to live, much less inaugurate new enterprises. Give us the means, give us a sufficiency of circulation to make interest cheap, and we will diversify our labor. Give us the means, and we will seize upon all the advantages which nature has given us. Give us the means, and we will soon wake up from our mountains, from their long sleep, our coal and iron, those twin sons of Hercules, whose stalwart arms will assist to lift us from our low estate. Give us the means, and we will improve our water powers, until the murmurs of discontent shall be lost in the chorus of the water wheel and the music of the spindles—until our very atmosphere shall revel and thrill and tremble with the triumphs of our industry. Give us the means. This is what we ask of Congress. Give us a financial system which shall secure to us money at rates which rule in England and France.

It is a truth, which the national legislature would do well to note, that cotton has been grown in the cotton belt since the war at a loss. This cannot continue, of course. We can cease to make cotton and learn to make the grain and the meat which we now purchase from our brother farmers in the West; but we cannot continue to make cotton, which loses us money every year. The four million bales must soon give place to the three millions, the three to the two, and the two to one. Already a convention of the farmers of Georgia have, by formal resolution, declared that they will not plant during the next year more than one-third of their crop in cotton; and the planters of Alabama have determined the same thing, I believe, as well as the planters of other States. Sir, it is time that this great industry were rid of its burdens.

Do you tell me that it is a local interest, and therefore cannot be considered in the discussion of a great question like this?

Mr. President, no industry that gives food, or clothing, or employment to the people, that adds to our exports or to the revenues of the Government, however insignificant it may be, is unworthy of the attention of the proudest statesman and the lordliest intellect in this Chamber or in this Union.

Is it a local industry which employs in its production four millions of people and in its manufacture over twenty-five millions, whose yearly wages amount to over $37,000,000?

Is it a local interest which gives motion to over $133,000,000 of the machinery of the United States?

Is it a local interest which furnishes the mills of the East with employment and the farms of the West with a market?

Is it a local interest which, according to a late Secretary of the Treasury, prevented commercial disaster to the whole country at the end of the war, and now, to use his own language, "maintains its supremacy as an article of export"?

Is it a local interest which, like the ligament which bound together the twins of Siam, so unites the sections of this country that you cannot separate it without bringing disaster to all?

It is time, I repeat, that the national legislature looked to this interest; at least that the national legislature should relieve it of its burdens of high money. Do this, or England will drive this—your heaviest export—from every market of the world. Already by her wise policy she has become an exporter of cotton. In the years 1862, 1865, 1867, 1871, and 1872 England absolutely exported an average of two hundred and fifty million pounds of cotton. Already she gives her money at low interest, and by her enterprise, by her appropriations of a thousand millions of money poured into the lap of India, she has almost driven us from the markets of the world; and now she stretches out her hands to Turkey, to India, to Prussia, to Austria, to Italy, to Brazil, to Peru, to Portugal, to Spain, to Egypt, and to Africa, and even Morocco and Greece are held in reserve for a last final assault upon the cultivation of cotton in America.

Sir, it is high time that the agriculture of both the South and the West were relieved of 25 per cent. money. It is high time that the agricultural interest, which is the foundation of all other interests, should have some special attention of this Government. Both the South and the West are prostrate. With money to the farmer at 18 and 25 per cent., with cotton below the cost of production at such a per cent. for money, with grain unable to pay its freights to market, with a financial system which places the productions of the country at the mercy of speculators, which in the striking language of the gifted Frenchman, Le Play, is "the art of oppressing the people," is it any wonder that this interest has at last awakened to a sense of its danger, and has combined for its protection?

Why should it not combine? Has not every other interest combined? Is not the money power of the country combined, and did it not dictate the financial policy of 1862, which has brought such disaster to the producer, and does it not now even at this very hour while I speak, by its delegations from Boston, from New York, and elsewhere, block the doors of this Chamber to influence the vote of this body? Labor combines, and receives at the hands of Government an eight-hour law. The fisheries combined, and received from the Government a bounty. Manufacturers combine, and receive a high protective tariff. The ironmongers combine, and, unlike the farmer's pigs which must be fed from his own crib, they have their iron pigs fattened at the Government crib. Railroads combine, and by Government bounties and Government grants they scale the mountains and link with bands of steel our eastern and western oceans. But, sir, this great interest, which lies at the foundation of all other interests; this interest, without which no other interest can survive; this interest, which numbers among its subjects near 25,000,000 of the 40,000,000 of the population of this country; this interest, which bears on its Atlantean shoulders the wealth, the commerce, the manufactures, and the very civilization of the country, has to-day less influence in shaping the legislation of the country than the fishers of salty codfish on the shores of New England. Sir, it is time, I repeat, that this were changed; it is time that agriculture was heard.

I hope we shall give to the people more money. I hope we shall give to the money elasticity by the issue of convertible and reconvertible bonds, and I hope we shall do so without delay.

If we require the Secretary of the Treasury to prepare bonds, bearing say 3 per cent. interest, in which greenbacks may be invested, and require that these bonds shall be reconvertible at the option of the holder, we shall give at once the elasticity to the currency which is essential to move it beyond the control of speculators. If we will then require the greenbacks, which are converted by the voluntary action of the people into these bonds, to be immediately reinvested by the Secretary of the Treasury in 6 per cent. bonds, we shall increase the volume of circulating medium, and, at the same time, rapidly reduce the public debt. These bonds, sir, would take, in large transactions, the place of currency, and if made available to the banks as reserves would turn loose the greenbacks now locked up in the bank vaults, and the reinvestment of the greenbacks so received by the Government for the 3 per cent. bonds would keep these greenbacks in circulation also. Again, sir, the great desideratum to the agriculture of the country, to wit, cheap interest, would be secured. The Government rate would become the ruling rate. It would give to us money at little above the Government rate.

It would make the money so elastic that it could no longer be made to subserve the purpose of heavy combinations to depress or inflate the prices of productions.

It would make panics impossible.

It would reduce rapidly the public debt.

It would, in a word, if we will but take one additional step, which I desire to see taken, solve the financial problem of America, and give to American agriculture and American enterprise an "Independence Day" which would be celebrated for all time to come.

The other step to which I refer is to strike from the laws the words "except duties on imports," and make Government money receivable for all dues to Government and to individuals alike. Do you desire to see the currency at par with gold? You will not see it as long as the Government dishonors its own currency, by making it a legal tender to the citizen, and refusing it for dues to itself. I should be glad for any Senator to answer how Government money can be kept at par with gold while the Government itself repudiates its own money? Sir, to this serious mistake—not to use the juster phrase, crime, against the people—are directly traceable all the depreciations of the currency, all the speculations in gold, all the "corners" to control the price of gold, and much of the disaster which has followed. The day we take this step the demand for gold will cease. It will be no longer needed for purposes of domestic trade or by Government. Relieve the merchants of the necessity of buying gold to pay duties, and that day the occupation of the Wall street gold kings, like Othello's, is gone. Gold being no longer needed for individual purposes, or by Government save to pay interest, would cease to be in demand, and the whole coin of the country would be upon the market without buyers. It must of necessity therefore fall to par, and if we continue this course would remain so forever. The amount of coin needed to pay interest would be largely supplied by the mines and receipts from abroad. If more were needed, let it be purchased abroad and not here. Free the farmers from the merciless claws of the speculators and the burden of high interest, and their exports will soon take care of foreign balances?

Mr. President, the day we take the step I have indicated, that day we shall proclaim a new Declaration of Independence—a declaration of the independence of our industries from the effects of our own money changers and "combiners," and of foreign intermeddlers with our currency. Let a dollar mean a dollar and not a promise to pay a dollar.

Equal rights to all demand a currency which gives equal benefits to all. From out of the black pall of smoke from the burning grain on the Western prairies and the desolation of agriculture all over the land the murmurs of discontent are already ominous. In their right to regulate wrong by the ballot the producers, despising party lines and party associations, will, sooner or later, rid the country of a system which, by its discriminations, but perpetuates their bondage to poverty.

On January 22 George S. Boutwell [Mass.] made an extended speech on the resolutions. He said in part:

I am of opinion that the process of holding the currency inflexible and allowing the business of the country to grow up to the volume of currency is a natural, in a certain degree an insensible, process, which does not interfere appreciably with the general prosperity. I believe that the country has never from the beginning of the Government enjoyed five years of such undisturbed prosperity as it has enjoyed during the last five years.

And if it be true, as the Senator from Georgia has asserted, that there is an absence of prosperity in the South, I apprehend, from the observations I have been able to make, that it is due to circumstances entirely independent of the policy of the Government. I call the Senator to witness that the cities of Charlotte in North Carolina, Columbia and Charleston in South Carolina, Jacksonville in Florida, Savannah, Macon, and Atlanta in Georgia, Chattanooga and Knoxville in Tennessee, are all more prosperous now than they were at any period before the war—that in all these cities there has been an increase of population, an increase of business, and an increase of wealth for the purposes of business.

Senator Gordon.—That is true., but it does not answer my question. My question was as to the producing classes in the country, not as to the growth of cities.

Senator Boutwell.—Cities are the outgrowth, the evidences of general prosperity. They exist only in the sunshine of general prosperity; and when you have demonstrated that a city is prosperous, increasing in numbers and wealth through months and years, you have established incontrovertibly the fact that that city is situated in a prosperous community.

There are two classes of people in the South. There are men who before the war were large landholders, and the possessors of immense estates in personal property and slaves. The fortunes of war divested them of all property except the land. They now hesitate to sell the land. Taxes are high, and they are unable to procure the capital for the economical and successful culture of their fields, and they are day by day growing poorer. Naturally they ask for some relief. There is also in the South a class of people, both black and white, a large and constantly increasing class of laborers who, either upon lands that they lease or upon lands that they have bought, are producing to the acre larger products than were realized under the old system. The aggregate products of the South demonstrate incontestably the fact that the South is prosperous as a whole.

Senator Gordon.—The increased production of cotton is not due to any great facilities that have been furnished to the production of cotton, but it is due entirely to the fact that new fields, new areas, higher latitudes, heretofore appropriated only to the growth of grain and grasses, are now used for the cultivation of cotton, and the cotton lands proper have so depreciated in value that they are no longer regarded as security for debt.

Senator Boutwell.—The statement made by the Senator

from Georgia is undoubtedly true. It is, if I do not misunderstand him, the process that was going on before the war. When lands were impoverished the owners abandoned them and sought new fields. That is what the owners of lands are doing now. But the general fact remains undisturbed that the South is a prosperous section of the country as compared with any previous condition of its history.

Before I pass from this branch of the subject, I wish to call the attention of the Senate to a remark made by the Senator from Georgia, which he submitted as a means of relieving the distresses which he imagined were afflicting his section. He demanded with emphasis and with repetition, "cheap money," "cheap money." If he meant by that demand to secure additional circulation of paper money for the purpose of cheapening it, I advise him to recall what must be to some extent his own experience in the South during the war. If we are not misinformed, the South then had cheap money, an abundance of it; so cheap that a householder would go to market in the morning with a basketful of currency and carry home his dinner in his waistcoat pocket. [Laughter.]

Senator Gordon.—I did not mean cheap money as the Senator understands it. I meant cheap interest upon money—money leant cheaply.

Senator Boutwell.—That is what I supposed the Senator might say in reply; otherwise I should have commenced this part of my speech at the other end. [Laughter.] If an increase of paper money diminished the rate of interest, then there would be one view of this subject which I could take with some degree of complacency. The theory on which an increase of paper money is demanded is that it stimulates business, inspires activity, opens new avenues for enterprise. Who does not see that the very process alleged to be beneficial upon which we are invited to accept the theory of inflation demonstrates conclusively that by the operation of those processes the price of interest must continually advance? But I ask gentlemen to consider further. Suppose a man wishes to deal in flour, and he can buy one hundred barrels of flour, as a stock in business, for $800. He wishes to borrow the money, and he can borrow the money for 8 per cent.; and with that capital invested in one hundred barrels of flour he can proceed with his business, at an annual interest cost of sixty-four dollars. Suppose the country enters upon a system of inflation, and the volume of paper currency is increased 50 per cent., and by an inevitable law prices advance 50 per cent., so that in order to buy one hundred barrels of flour he must have $1,200 of money. Everybody else is in the same condition. At what rate must his interest be in order that he can avail himself of capital to pursue his business as he would have pursued it under the old system? Twelve hundred dollars must be hired for sixty-four dollars in order to place him in the same condition that he would have been without inflation—that is, 5 1-3 per cent. The reverse, then, is the truth. The rate of interest increases when you inflate the currency. The interest on the capital required to do a particular business is not only greater from the fact that additional capital is required, but it is greater from the fact that every dollar of the capital so required demands and will obtain a higher rate of interest. Therefore the operator, whether he be a farmer owing for his farm, a manufacturer or a merchant who depends upon borrowed capital to enable him to conduct his business, is impoverished by each and both of these processes.

Senator Ferry.—I would ask the Senator how he accounts for the fact that during the summer months, when there is a redundancy of currency in New York, the rate of interest is much below the rate in the winter, when there is a scarcity of currency. Why, sir, currency goes begging in New York during the summer when there is that redundancy, and during the winter money can hardly be obtained there, which is the fact to-day.

Senator Boutwell.—Mr. President, one of the difficulties in dealing with every financial and economical question is that there are many influences at work the effect of which cannot be measured; and therefore it is that what is called statistical information is so untrustworthy. The inquiry made by the Senator from Michigan leads me to reflect upon one of those influences, operating temporarily in the city of New York.

Money accumulates in the city of New York by natural and artificial processes during the month of July; but the operators, the merchants, the speculators are taking recreation, and they are giving very little attention to the price of money. But when the 1st of August comes, and these men return to their stores and their banking houses, speculation begins; the prices of stocks advance; fortunes are made; the rates of interest increase; when, finally, in the month of September or October, there is an active demand for money to keep the margins good on the stocks that have been bought by irresponsible people and a demand also by responsible merchants for money to move the crops. Then and thus the borrowers are ground between the upper and nether millstone. This is the process that takes place every year, and is a satisfactory explanation of the phenomenon stated by the Senator from Michigan.

The Senator from Missouri [Carl Schurz] said he had been endeavoring to satisfy me that the true way to prevent inflation was to go for contraction, and that those of us (if I am allowed to say "us" in this connection) who think that the strong point is to stand on the present policy of the country and resist contraction on the one hand and inflation on the other are really in the interest of the inflationists. Further, that the strongest position we could occupy was to step off from this platform, to abandon this citadel, intrenched as we are in the settled policy of the country, and enter upon a contest outside; and then, in case we should be defeated by the inflationists, try to regain our position and hold to the old policy of the country. I am not sure that this may not be military strategy. There is certainly a great example in that direction. There was a student at West Point by the name of Charles Derby, known to the literary world as "John Phœnix." While a student there, it is said that a professor demonstrated, according to his ideas of demonstration, that a city or a citadel closely besieged could not hold out more than sixty days. That being demonstrated, he turned to the class, addressing them as a whole, but expecting answers of course by individuals, and said, "Young gentlemen, what would you do if you were commanding a force in a citadel subject to close siege?" "Well," said Derby, "upon the proposition that you have demonstrated, I would march out of the citadel, and let the enemy in, then I would besiege it closely, and in sixty days I would take it and reoccupy it." [Laughter.]

We have a citadel, and we had better keep in it. If we are driven out, we shall then only be in the position which the Senator from Missouri advises us voluntarily to accept. If those who are in favor of contraction and those who are in favor of the present condition of things, that is, a permanent volume of $356,000,000, are together unequal in the contest with those who demand an addition to the currency, I do not see how, even with the oration of my friend the Senator from Missouri, those who are in favor of contraction alone will be able to maintain their position.

There is but one remedy for the existing condition of things, and but one means by which we can ward off the evils which menace us—the remedy is taxation. I do not say on what, either of persons, classes, or property; but taxation there must be, or else the evils of an inflated currency, or the disgrace of borrowing money to pay the current expenses of our Government, will fall upon the people. Moreover, a loan does not redeem our pledge to maintain the sinking fund. The inflation of the currency, which is one way, and a poor way, of borrowing money, does not redeem our plighted faith to the world. When we have exhausted every resource in the matter of economy, as it is our duty to exhaust every resource, then, as between taxation and borrowing, as between burdens and disgrace, I will put burdens on the people; but I will not consent to disgrace them.

The bill was not acted upon during the session.

Resumption of Specie Payments

Sixth Annual Message of President Grant

In his sixth annual message of December 7, 1874, President Grant referred to the industrial and financial depression that was still continuing throughout the country. Nevertheless he said that capital was abundant and at moderate rates when the security was good, and labor's wages, measured by the cost of necessities, were cheap. Land, too, was abundant and rich, producing more than the country required for its needs.

With these facts in view, it seems to me that wise statesmanship, at this session of Congress, would dictate legislation, ignoring the past, directing in proper channels these great elements of prosperity to any people. Debt—debt abroad—is the only element that can, with always a sound currency, enter into our affairs to cause any continued depression in the industries and prosperity of our people. A great conflict for national existence made necessary, for temporary purposes, the raising of large sums of money from whatever source attainable. It made it necessary to devise a system of national currency which it proved to be impossible to keep on a par with the recognized currency of the civilized world. This begot a spirit of speculation involving an extravagance and luxury not required for the happiness or prosperity of a people, and involving, both directly and indirectly, foreign indebtedness. The currency, being of fluctuating value, and therefore unsafe to hold for legitimate transactions requiring money, became a subject of speculation in itself. These two causes, however, have involved us in a foreign indebtedness, contracted in good faith by borrower and lender, which should be paid in coin, according to the bond agreed upon when the debt was contracted—gold or its equivalent. The good faith of the Government cannot be violated toward creditors without national disgrace.

Our commerce should be encouraged; American shipbuilding and carrying capacity increased; foreign markets sought for products of the soil and manufactories, to the end that we may be able to pay these debts. But, in my judgment, the first step toward accomplishing this object is to secure a currency of fixed, stable value; a currency good wherever civilization reigns; one which, if it becomes superabundant with one people, will find a market with some other; a currency which has as its basis the labor necessary to produce it, which will give to it its value. Gold and silver are now the recognized medium of exchange the civilized world over; and to this we should return with the least practicable delay. In view of the pledges of the American Congress when our present legal-tender system was adopted, and debt contracted, there should be no unnecessary delay in fixing by legislation a method by which we will return to specie. It is easy to conceive that the debtor and speculative classes may think it of value to them to make so-called money abundant until they can throw a portion of their burdens upon others. But even these, I believe, would be disappointed in the result if a course should be pursued which will keep in doubt the value of the legal-tender medium of exchange. A revival of productive industry is needed by all classes—by none more than the holders of property, of whatever sort, with debts to liquidate from realization upon its sale. But, admitting that these two classes of citizens are to be benefited by expansion, would it be honest to give it? Would not the general loss be too great to justify such relief? Would it not be just as honest and prudent to authorize each debtor to issue his own legal-tenders to the extent of his liabilities? Than to do this would it not be safer, for fear of overissues by unscrupulous creditors, to say that all debt obligations are obliterated in the United States, and now we commence anew, each possessing all he has at the time free from incumbrance? These propositions are too absurd to be entertained for a moment by thinking or honest people. Yet every delay in preparation for final resumption partakes of this dishonesty, and is only less in degree as the hope is held out that a convenient season will at last arrive for the good work of redeeming our pledges to commence. It will never come, in my opinion, except by positive action by Congress, or by national disasters which will destroy, for a time at least, the credit of the individual and the state at large. A sound currency might be reached by total bankruptcy and discredit of the integrity of the nation and of individuals. I believe it is in the power of Congress, at this session, to devise such legislation as will renew confidence, revive all the industries, start us on a career of prosperity to last for many years, and to save the credit of the nation and of the people.

A nation dealing in a currency below that of specie in value labors under two great disadvantages: First, having no use for the world's acknowledged medium of exchange, gold and silver, these are driven out of the country; second, the medium of exchange in use being of a fluctuating value—for after all it is only worth just what it will purchase of gold and silver; metals having an intrinsic value just in proportion to the honest labor it takes to produce them—a larger margin must be allowed for profit by the manufacturer and producer. It is months from the date of production to the date of realization. Interest upon capital must be charged, and risk of fluctuation in the value of that which is to be received in payment added. Hence high prices, acting as a protection to the foreign producer, who receives nothing in exchange for the products of his skill and labor except a currency good at a stable value the world over.

It seems to me that nothing is clearer than that the greater part of the burden of existing prostration, for the want of a sound financial system, falls upon the workingman, who must, after all, produce the wealth, and the salaried man who superintends and conducts business. The burden falls upon them in two ways: by the deprivation of employment, and by the decreased purchasing power of their salaries. It is the duty of Congress to devise the method of correcting the evils which are acknowledged to exist, and not mine. But I will venture to suggest two or three things which seem to me as absolutely necessary to a return to specie payments, the first great requisite in a return to prosperity. The legal-tender clause to the law authorizing the issue of currency by the national Government should be repealed, to take effect as to all contracts entered into after a day fixed in the repealing act; not to apply, however, to payments of salaries by Government or for other expenditures now provided by law to be paid in currency in the interval pending between repeal and final resumption. Provision should be made by which the Secretary of the Treasury can obtain gold as it may become necessary from time to time from the date when specie redemption commences. To this might and should be added a revenue sufficiently in excess of expenses to insure an accumulation of gold in the treasury to sustain permanent redemption.

With resumption, free banking may be authorized with safety, giving the same full protection to bill holders which they have under existing laws. Indeed, I would regard free banking as essential. It would give proper elasticity to the currency. As more currency should be required for the transaction of legitimate business new banks would be started, and in turn banks would wind up their business when it was found that there was a superabundance of currency. The experience and judgment of the people can best decide just how much currency is required for the transaction of the business of the country. It is unsafe to leave the settlement of this question to Congress, the Secretary of the Treasury, or the Executive. Congress should make the regulation under which banks may exist, but should not make banking a monopoly by limiting the amount of redeemable paper currency that shall be authorized.

Resumption of Specie Payments

Senate, December 21-22, 1874

On December 21, 1874, John Sherman [O.] introduced a bill in the Senate, from the Finance Committee, providing for the resumption of specie payments on a new plan. In a speech on the following day he urged its immediate consideration. At this there was some demur.

Allen G. Thurman [O.] declared that his colleague had allowed his financial measures to be discussed through all the long previous session, until the Senate and the country were sick of them. Senator Sherman's purpose in this had been that the intelligent minds of the country might express their opinions on the measures. But now he introduced a new measure, which had not, like the old, been recommended by the President nor considered by the country, and proposed to push it through before the people had time to express an opinion on it. He hoped that it would lie over until after the holidays.

Senator Sherman, on the contrary, thought that "it would be a happy Christmas gift to the people of the United States if we could give them some bill that would assure the business men of the country that stable times were coming.''

Cárl Schurz [Mo.] pleaded for more time for considering the bill. He himself wished to study it with special reference to ''whether, under present circumstances, we can issue silver and keep it in circulation, or whether the circumstances surrounding us to-day, or liable to surround us to-morrow, are not such as will make it probable that silver put out will be melted into bullion and sent abroad.''

By a vote of 39 to 18 it was decided to take up the bill. Senator Sherman explained its provisions.

The first section of the bill provides for the resumption of specie payments on the fractional currency. It so happens that at this particular period of time the state of the money market, the state of the demand for silver bullion, and more especially the recent action of the German Empire, which has demonetized silver and thus cheapened that product, enables us now, without any loss of revenue, without any sacrifice, to enter the market for the purchase of bullion and resume specie payments on our fractional currency. The market price of bullion to-day will justify the Government of the United States, without any sacrifice, at a price about equivalent to our fractional currency, to purchase silver bullion in the money markets of the world, mostly of our own production, perhaps entirely of our own production. This bill simply directs that the Secretary of the Treasury shall purchase this bullion and shall coin silver coin and substitute that in the place of fractional currency. To that extent it is a resumption of specie payments upon the silver standard for the fractional currency. This section is recommended not only by the Secretary of the Treasury and the President of the United States, but I believe will meet the general concurrence of every member of the Senate. The mints of the United States are now prepared, immediately upon the passage of this bill, to resume the coinage of silver coins of all the legal denominations.

The second section rescinds the charge now made for converting gold bullion into coin. This removes the inducement to send the bullion to Great Britain, where no charge is made for this conversion. The annual loss of revenue would be only $85,000. Gold when coined into

American money would naturally tend to remain in this country, and so aid the return to specie payments.

The third section of the bill contains only two or three affirmative propositions. The first is that after the passage of this act banking shall be free. Perhaps there is no idea stronger in the minds of the American people than a feeling of hostility against a monopoly—a privilege that one man or set of men can enjoy which is denied to another man or set of men. Under the law as it now stands banking is substantially free in the Southern and some of the Western States; but banking is not free in the great commercial States, in the older States, where wealth has accumulated for ages. This may be a mere sentimental point, but it is well enough to meet it; and by the operation of this bill banking is made free, so that there will be no difficulty hereafter for any corporation organized as a national bank either to increase its circulation or for banks to be organized under the provisions of existing law to issue circulating notes to any extent within the limits and upon the terms and provisions of the banking law. This section, therefore, by making banking free, provides for an enlargement of the currency in case the business of the community demands it, and in case any bank in the United States may think it advisable or profitable to issue circulating medium in the form of bank notes under the conditions and limitations of the banking law. Coupled with that is a provision, an undertaking, on the part of the United States that as banks are organized or as circulating notes are issued, either by old or new banks, the Government of the United States undertakes to retire 80 per cent. of that amount of United States notes. In other words, it proposes to redeem the United States notes to the extent of 80 per cent. on the amount of bank notes that may be issued; and here is the first controverted question that arises on this bill and the first that is settled. It may be asked if we provide for the issue of circulating notes to banks, why not provide for the retirement of an equal amount of United States notes? The answer is that under the provisions of the banking act by the law as it now stands a bank cannot be organized and maintained in existence unless the reserve which is in that bank, or required for that bank in the ordinary course of business either on its deposits or circulation, is at least equal to 20 per cent. of the amount of its circulating notes, so that it was believed, according to the judgment of the best business men of the country, and I may say, with the Comptroller of the Currency, that the retirement of 80 per cent.

of the amount of bank notes is fully equivalent to keeping the amount of circulating medium in actual circulation on the same footing, so that this provision of the bill neither provides for a contraction nor expansion of the currency, but leaves the amount to be regulated by the business wants of the community, so that when notes are issued to a bank 80 per cent. of the amount in United States notes is redeemed, and this process continues until United States notes are reduced to three hundred millions.

SENATOR SCHURZ.—Will the Senator permit me to ask him a question in reference to this section? When the 80 per cent. of greenbacks are retired will they be destroyed and never issued again?

SENATOR SHERMAN.—I will speak of that in a moment.

The third section fixes January 1, 1879, as the date for completely returning to specie payments.

It has always been a question in the minds of many people as to whether it is wise to fix a day for specie payments. That matter was discussed at the last session of Congress by many Senators, and the general opinion seemed to be that if we would provide the means by which specie payments would be resumed it might not be necessary to fix the day; but, on the other hand, it is important to have our laws in regard to the currency fix a probable time, or a certain time, when everybody may know that his contracts will be measured by the coin standard. We also know that by the example of other nations which have found themselves in the condition in which we are now placed, and by some of the States when specie payments were suspended, that they have adopted a specific day for the resumption of specie payments.

This bill also provides ample means to prepare for and to maintain resumption. I may say the whole credit and money of the United States are placed by this bill under the direction of the proper executive officers, not only to prepare for but to maintain resumption, and no man can doubt that if this bill stands the law of the land from this time until the 1st day of January, 1879, specie payments will be resumed, and that our United States notes will be converted at the will of the holder into gold and silver coin.

Mr. President, these are all the provisions contained in this bill. They are simple and easily understood, and every Senator can pass his judgment upon them readily.

Now I desire to approach a class of questions that are not embraced in this bill. Many such, and I could name fifty, are not included in this bill; and I may say this: that if there should be a successful effort by the Senate of the United States to ingraft any of this multitude of doubtful or contested questions upon the face of this bill it would inevitably tend to its defeat. I am free to say that if I were called upon to frame a bill to accomplish the purpose declared in the title of this bill I would have provided some means of gradual redemption between this and the time fixed for final specie payments. All of these means are open to objection. There have been three different plans proposed to prepare for specie payments, and only three. They are all grouped in three classes. One is what is called the contraction plan. The simplest and most direct way to specie payments is undoubtedly the gradual withdrawal of United States notes or the contraction of the currency. Now, we know very well the feeling with which that idea is regarded not only in this Senate, but all through the country. It is believed to operate as a disturbing element in all the business relations of life; to add to the burden of the debtor by making scarce that article in which he is bound to pay his debts; and there has been an honest, sincere opposition to this theory of contraction. Therefore, although it may be the simplest and the best way to reach specie payments, it is entirely omitted from this bill. The second plan, that I have favored myself often, and would favor now if I had my own way and had no opinion to consult but my own, is the plan of converting United States notes into a bond that would gradually appreciate our notes to par in gold. That has always been a favorite idea of mine. There is nothing of that kind in this bill except those provisions which authorize the Secretary of the Treasury to issue bonds to retire the greenbacks as bank notes are issued; and it also authorizes the Secretary of the Treasury to issue bonds to provide for and to maintain resumption. I therefore have been compelled to surrender my ideas on this bill in order to accomplish a good object without using these means that have been held objectionable by many Senators.

The third plan of resumption has been favored very extensively in this country, which is the plan of a graduated scale for resumption in coin or bullion; what I call the English plan. That is, that we provide now for the redemption at a fixed rate or scale of rates of so much gold for a specific sum of United States notes. At present rates we would give about $90 of gold for $100 of greenbacks, and then provide for a graduated scale by which we would approach specie payment constantly, and reach it at a fixed day. This may be called a gradual redemption. This, also, is objectionable to many persons, from the idea that it compels us to enter the money markets of the world to discount our own paper. It is an ideal objection, but a very strong objection; an objection that has force with a great many people. We have undertaken to redeem these notes in coin, and it is at least a question of doubtful ethics whether we ought to enter into the markets of the world and buy our own notes at a discount. Although that plan has been adopted in England and successfully carried into execution, yet there is a strong objection to it in this country, and therefore that mode is abandoned. Either of these plans I could readily support; but they have met and will meet with such opposition that we cannot hope to carry them or ingraft them in this bill without defeating it. We have then fallen back on these gradual steps: first, to retire the fractional currency; second, to reduce United States notes as bank notes are increased; and then to rest our plan of redemption upon the declaration made on the faith of the United States that at the time fixed by the bill we will resume the payment of the United States notes in coin at par. That is the whole of this bill.

Not only are all these plans of gradual redemption omitted from the bill, but there are also many troublesome questions omitted from the bill, among the rest the one suggested by the Senator from Missouri [Mr. Schurz]. If we undertake to define precisely what shall be done four years hence on the resumption of specie payments, to say whether the legal-tender act shall then be repealed, or whether it shall be repealed before or not, we enter upon a very difficult field, and will undoubtedly divide the Senate and divide the country. Is it not better to postpone until the time comes to meet them these questions which must then arise, rather than to engage in an attempt to settle them now, four years in advance?

Senator Schurz.—The question I asked the Senator does not relate to a time four years ahead, but it refers to the immediate operation of the bill.

Senator Sherman.—I will answer that question. I did not intend to avoid it. The Senator sees the force of the argument that we ought not to put in this bill anything about the reissue of notes or the character of those notes when reissued after redemption shall come.

Senator Schurz.—Does the Senator say that I see the force of that argument?

SENATOR SHERMAN.—I think the Senator ought to see it.

SENATOR SCHURZ.—Ah! Very well.

SENATOR SHERMAN.—I hope the Senator does. If he was himself preparing a bill to resume he would probably take some other plan, but he may very well leave a difficult question to the time when that question commences to operate. We declare the time when specie payments shall be resumed in order to give fair notice, so that market values for the future may be adjusted and so that people will prepare themselves for resumption. Our people may then base their transactions upon that solemn declaration made by Congress.

SENATOR SCHURZ.—I think that the Senator from Ohio has probably not understood my question. What I meant to ask was whether whenever any greenbacks were retired by the Secretary of the Treasury, or as the bill styles it are redeemed in consideration of so many thousands of dollars of bank notes having been issued, the greenbacks so retired shall be canceled and destroyed never to be reissued again. The Senator will remember very well that we had a protracted struggle about a similar question once, and that the framing of a law gave rise to much controversy on that identical point. Now, what I am after is to understand whether the provisions of this bill will in their practical operation work in the direction of specie payments or not, and for that it is a very essential question whether the greenbacks so retired shall be destroyed never to be reissued again, or whether they shall be held as a reserve, as the forty-four millions were, certainly to be put into the market again.

SENATOR SHERMAN.—I say frankly that we do not propose to decide that question in this bill. I have no doubt that, when the time arrives when the question becomes material, it will be met. Undoubtedly until the reduction of the United States notes to $300,000,000 they cannot be reissued. The process must go on *pari passu* until the amount of legal-tender notes is reduced to $300,000,000. Before that time will probably arrive in the course of human affairs, at least one or two Congresses will have met and disappeared, and we may leave to the future these questions that tend to divide us and distract us, rather than undertake to thrust them into this bill and thus divide us and prevent us from doing something in the direction at which we aim.

SENATOR SCHURZ.—I want to be satisfied on that point. The Senator then admits that the bill is open to the construction that the Secretary of the Treasury may gather up the 80 per cent. as a reserve and reissue the notes again, and that it is the intent of those who made the bill that it shall be open?

SENATOR SHERMAN.—I made no such admission. I leave

that question to be decided upon the law as it stands. The case that is put of what I regarded as an illegal issue of notes probably may never arise, and certainly it cannot arise for a considerable period of time.

SENATOR SCHURZ.—I do not want to annoy the Senator at all; but I put it to him whether we should pass a bill on a subject like this, so delicate and so important, the meaning of which is so obscure that the champion of the bill has to admit himself that its construction will be left to the courts of the United States?

SENATOR SHERMAN.—In supporting a bill of this kind, I do not meet all possible questions that may arise in its construction, and no human mind could do it. I know this, and upon this rock I stand: that this bill has provisions in it which tend to accomplish the purpose which the Senator and I have so diligently sought, and I will not seek to obstruct the passage of this bill or defeat it by thrusting into it doubtful questions of law or public policy which may tend to the defeat of the bill. I take this bill not as the bill that I should propose myself, a bill which itself surrenders many of my convictions as to the means to be employed to accomplish the particular purpose designed, but I take it because I see that every provision in it tends to the object that the Senator and I seek, and I will not weaken it by putting in questions of grammar or construction which may tend to weaken and destroy it.

SENATOR SCHURZ.—I think I shall not want to annoy the Senator or obstruct the bill, but I submit that we are not interpreting financial legislation here, but that we are making financial legislation, and we want to make it as clear as it possibly can be made. The Senator knows from his own experience that, if the least loophole is left, he cannot foretell what the treasury will do; whether it will not under the pressure of public opinion some time or other issue twenty or thirty or forty millions again of that which was accumulated, as he says redeemed, but possibly accumulated only as reserve. The thing was done before, and it may be done again. He knows very well also that that may defeat the whole scheme of returning to specie payments.

SENATOR SHERMAN.—Now, sir, the great weakness of our currency is that we have undertaken to pay our notes in coin and do not fulfill our promise. No man denies that obligation. It is so written upon the statute-book now six years old. But from the fact that we have not said when we will do it, at what time we will do it, the question is still open to rest upon the construction which each Senator and member may give to the words "as early as practicable"; an indefinite phrase at least, and one that applies to all future ages. The object of this bill is to fix a time within which the honor of the United States is pledged to redeem these notes in coin; and that pledge, if made by Congress (and I trust it may be made by the whole of Congress—all parties—and by the whole people) will be redeemed. It is true a subsequent Congress may repeal it, and anything we can do may be repealed by a subsequent Congress. All we can do is in our time to pledge the faith of the United States to do this in the future, and if the people in their power and might, through agents hereafter elected, violate this promise there is no power in our Government to prevent it. We only know that they probably will not do it; that a pledge thus specific, made as to a definite day and time, with ample powers given to an executive officer to execute it, will be maintained.

I desire to say to the Senator one word more, that this pledge is made knowing the full extent of the obligation imposed by this law, and I believe that every Senator who votes for this bill is personally pledged and all his influence is pledged, all his political influence is pledged to maintain that declaration just as our fathers felt themselves bound by their lives, their fortunes, and their sacred honor to maintain the pledges they made in the Declaration of American Independence.

SENATOR THURMAN.—The first two sections, so far as my opinion is concerned, are perfectly right; but they do very little toward the resumption of specie payments, for when you shall have paid the fractional currency in silver you will have paid it in something that is no more valuable than the greenbacks in which it is now redeemable. And when you shall have done away with the coinage charge, as provided in the second section, you will have done a little, it is true, toward increasing the amount of gold coinage and that is all—an almost infinitesimal step toward specie payments. Therefore, if there is anything in this bill that looks toward specie payments, it must be in the third section. Now let us look at that.

After hearing the statement by the chairman of the committee of the omissions from the bill, it is very difficult to find what there is in it. We know that there is a great deal of omission, but the least possible amount of commission that ever I have seen in a great public measure. Let us see what this section proposes to do. It proposes that there shall be free banking, and then for every $100 of bank notes that shall be issued there shall be redeemed $80 of legal-tenders, and that that process shall go on until the amount of legal-tenders outstanding shall be three hundred millions and no more. If that were all there was in this section, and it were fairly and distinctly stated that the legal-tenders thus redeemed were not to be reissued but were to be canceled, one could very well understand what the section is, and it would only be a question of time when the effect of the section would be to reduce the legal-tenders to $300,000,000; but that is not all that is in the section by any means. It goes further, and provides that, after the 1st day of January, 1879, there shall be full and complete resumption of specie payments by the Government on the legal-tenders, and that means full and complete resumption by the banks, because the banks by their charters are bound to redeem either in legal-tenders or in coin; and, if legal-tenders are redeemed by the Government in coin, it is equivalent to declaring that the banks shall also redeem in coin. Therefore, this bill provides that from and after the 1st of January, 1879, four years hence, there shall be complete resumption of specie payments in the United States. Put that provision in the bill, coupled with the other provision for retiring 80 per cent. of greenbacks for every additional dollar of national-bank issue under this bill, and see how they work.

Does my friend, the chairman of this committee, believe that there will be in the next four years $100,000,000 of additional national-bank currency issued? What warrant has he to believe any such thing as that? But without the issue of $100,000,000 more national-bank currency he cannot retire $80,000,000 of greenbacks and bring them down to $300,000,000. Pray how much increase has there been in national-bank currency under the law which you passed last session? About $1,400,000. You will have no increased banking under this bill, if you pass it, until business begins to revive; and when will business begin to revive? All that is necessary is for a man to open his eyes and read the history of his country to know when it will revive.

At intervals of about twenty years we have one of those things called a panic, followed by stagnation in business, the result of overtrading, overproduction, of extravagance of all sorts and descriptions, extravagance in individuals, extravagance in corporations, extravagance in governments large and small, until at last the bubble bursts, and then comes a season of retrenchment, of economy; and how long does that last? How long is it before debts are liquidated and a surplus is accumulated, so that there begins to be an upward tide in the business of the country? Never has it been less than four years in the United States.

My colleague says that this bill will have one great and good effect: it will let the country know what is to be our policy, and then business will go on steadily, because people will know what they have to expect. Yet my colleague says to the people—this bill, which is to inform you what is to be the policy of the Government, does not inform you whether these $80,000,000 of retired greenbacks are to be poured out again at the pleasure of a Secretary of the Treasury! Why, sir, if this bill were to have operation, if there were issued $100,000,000 of national-bank notes and then you retired $80,000,000 of greenbacks, it would become the most material thing in the world for the capitalists and business men of the country to know whether these greenbacks were to be reissued again; for, if they be reissued, the effect would be an inflation of the currency of $100,000,000. If they are to be canceled, then the inflation is only $20,000,000, and may not be even so much as that on account of the reserve that the banks are required to keep against their deposits; but if they are to be reissued then there is unmitigated inflation to the amount of $100,000,000, and the business men of the country are told by the chairman of the Committee on Finance: "I will not give you any light on this subject at all; I will not tell you; I will not even express my own opinion, whether or not you are to go on doing your business without knowing at all whether there is to be an inflation of $100,000,000 in the next four years or whether there is to be an inflation of only $20,000,000, or no inflation at all." That will not do, sir. Pass the bill in its present shape, and instead of settling you will unsettle, instead of fixing you will unfix, the minds of the people.

I felt this morning a little like complaining that our Republican friends should mature such a measure as this, if they did do it as the newspapers say in secret caucus, without allowing their fellows of the Senate on this side of the chamber to know anything about it; but that is a most venial offence, if offence it was, a most trifling thing compared to this studied ambiguity of the bill and keeping from the people the knowledge whether it means inflation or whether it does not.

I think my colleague is entirely right in saying that this is a bill from which all questions that have divided the financial people of this country and the parties of the country and the different sections of the different parties, have been carefully omitted. But there is one thing upon which my colleague places great reliance, and that is the declaration that we will resume at the time named. Sir, I do not believe that a mere verbal declaration will satisfy the country or produce much effect. I have heard my colleague stand in his place here and with an eloquence that I admired, and felt proud of, speak of how this Government had failed to redeem its pledge in regard to these very greenbacks; how it had repealed the law, which was contemporary with them, that made them convertible into bonds of the United States; how it had broken that pledge. And now, after he has held up to the country these broken pledges of the Government, it will not do for him to say to the business men of the country "you can shape your business in perfect safety and rely on the pledge of the Government that from the 1st of January, 1879, we will have a specie currency." That will not do. That is entirely too small a foundation on which to build any such superstructure as the resumption of specie payments.

Therefore I propose to add a section to the bill:

Section 4. That from and after June 30, 1875, one-twentieth part of the customs duties shall be payable in United States legal-tender notes, or in national bank notes, and after June 30, 1876, one-tenth, and after June 30, 1877, one-fifth part thereof may be so paid.

Lewis Bogy [Mo.].—I desire to move an amendment to his amendment:

On and after the 1st day of July, 1875, duties on imports may be paid in legal-tender notes or coin, at the option of the importer.

I am opposed to contraction. I believe that, if contraction is adopted as the policy to effect the object of resumption, it will paralyze the country so completely as to defeat the object intended to be accomplished. Under the existing circumstances, with the system of finance inaugurated by the Republican party, —which system they were determined should be enforced—I believe that, instead of contraction being adopted as the means to accomplish resumption, an increase of currency is needed, at least in the West, so as to stimulate industry and commerce and relieve the debtor class. Therefore, under the law, which has given birth to legal-tender paper and to national-bank notes, I favor an augmentation of the currency; never, however, admitting that paper money is equal to gold or silver; and paper money never can be equal to gold and silver unless it observes one law, and that law must be obeyed at all hazards and under all circumstances, and without any doubt attending it, and is its convertibility into coin on demand. Whenever paper money is conveniently convertible into coin at all places, it is then for all purposes of commerce infinitely more convenient and better than coin; but it is only as a representative of coin, and because it can be converted into gold or silver. But under the law as it is now our paper money is not convertible, and we use no coin at all excepting for one purpose, and that is to pay duties on importations. Hence this paper money, good or bad, is the only means of exchange for the entire country. It being the only means of exchange, I believe that the way to get to specie payments is by issuing a reasonable amount of this paper money, so as to establish a healthy prosperity throughout the country.

Now, sir, to make paper money equal to coin, it must at all times be convertible. The fundamental law of its existence is its convertibility under all circumstances and with great facility. When the greenbacks were originally issued, they were convertible into 6 per cent. bonds. The object was to give them a positive value. Those bonds were coin bonds. If you could convert legal-tender notes into bonds payable in coin, you were giving to that paper money a value very nearly equal to specie. That law, in my estimation, was a wise one, but it was soon repealed.

Legal-tender notes were issued also upon another condition, that they should be received by the Government in payment of all debts, of every nature and description whatsoever; not only that they should be legal-tenders as between A and B in ordinary transactions, but they were to be such for debts due to the Government. It is so printed upon the back of every one of them. Although that was the promise to the ear it was not carried out to the hope, because in point of fact no individual in the nation owes the Government any money except two classes of persons, the importers and the defaulters, and these latter do not pay in greenbacks or anything else. The Government does not credit anybody. It pays in cash or in paper money for all that it buys, and there is in point of fact no debt due the Government excepting as already stated.

Yet by the very contract this debt due by importers is excepted. This excepts everything, and the legal-tender notes stand exactly in the attitude of a note issued by an individual payable in goods that may be in his store, excepting, however, brown sheetings, while keeping in said store nothing but brown sheetings. On its face it is a very handsome note, payable on presentation in merchandise at his store. Although it is a promise, the exception defeats the very promise. So in this case. What has been the result? From the very beginning the demand for gold to pay duties has been so great as continually to depreciate the legal-tenders. This demand during the period of a year exceeds the supply of gold. The demand for gold has been two hundred millions; it is now one hundred and sixty-three millions; and according to the report of the Secretary of the Treasury the amount of coin in the United States is only $166,000,000, so that the demand for coin at this day to pay duties is virtually equal to the whole amount of gold that is in the country.

The result is therefore a very high premium on coin, and it amounts now to 10, 11, or 12 per cent.; and yet we have been heretofore so habituated to large premiums that we have got to think that 10 per cent. premium is a very small thing; but in point of fact it is destructive to the prosperity of the people. It is an enormous premium, and no commercial people can prosper when all the money that is used in the exchanges of commerce is at a discount of 10 or 12 per cent.

Now, sir, in order to resume specie payments, the first step is to give value to this paper. Contraction would give it value beyond all doubt, but in giving it value you would produce great distress and ruin over the land. But, if you will give to your paper money a value without diminishing its amount, you will have taken a great step toward resumption; and so soon as you make paper by legislation equal to gold, as it is more convenient in all the commercial transactions of the world than specie, gold will not be wanted.

If the legal-tenders are made receivable for duties, you at once give to them a positive value. You at once take away the only demand for gold. At the present day gold is not used for any purpose whatever in this country except to pay duties on imports. It is to-day an article of commerce as much so as iron or lead or dry goods or sugar or coffee. It is not used at the present time as a medium of exchange. It remains a measure of value, because it is so recognized by the entire commerce of the world. But as a means of exchange it is not used only as an article of commerce, and is sold from day to day in Wall street; and for what purpose? Only for one: to enable importers to pay duties amounting to from five to eight hundred thousand dollars a day. Do away with the demand, and what will be the result? There being no demand for gold, as the national-bank notes are redeemable in legal-tenders, and these are not yet redeemable in gold, the effect would be that the gold of this country, amounting to $160,000,000, would at once flow into the channels of trade, and you would really have an expansion of coin of that large amount. The $160,000,000 now used as an article of merchandise would immediately go into the channels of business. It could not be used for any other purpose.

SENATOR THURMAN.—I should be inclined to favor the amendment of the Senator from Missouri but for one thing, to which I wish to call his attention; and that is the pledge of Congress that so much of the customs duties as shall be necessary are pledged for the payment of interest on the public debt and the creation of a sinking fund, and that interest is payable in gold. I have made my calculation in my amendment so as to leave an ample amount to meet that pledge; but the amendment of the Senator from Missouri would destroy the pledge altogether.

I wish to say further, in reference to that, that the bill as reported and now before us disregards that pledge quite as much and more, a great deal, than can be said of my amendment, for mine does not disregard it at all. This bill allows the Secretary of the Treasury to use all the gold that may be received from customs duties to carry out the purpose of the bill, and in fact disregards the pledge totally.

SENATOR BOGY.—The law of 1862 requires all duties to be paid in gold; not a part, not nineteen-twentieths, but the whole twenty-twentieths. The object of the law beyond a doubt was to create a gold fund to pay the interest upon the gold bonds. But what is really the essence of that contract? The contract is that we shall pay this character of debt, both interest and principal, in coin.

Now, Mr. President, I leave it to the intelligence of the Senate and the country, if we continue, as we shall be sure to continue, to pay our bonds as they fall due in coin, and if we continue, as we are certain to continue, to pay the interest every six months also in coin, will the credit of the nation be at all affected whether we raise this money by one means or another? I deny the proposition that a nation of the high character and standing of this need pledge any special source of revenue to maintain its credit at home or abroad, although it is customary for nations having doubtful credit to pledge certain sources of revenue by way of mortgage. The character of the nation, the means, the ability, the standing, everything that belongs to this people, is pledge enough to the world to maintain our credit, and there is no necessity for this additional security. Again, if you look at the law of 1862, which provided that the duties upon imports should be paid in gold, there is no pledge that this gold shall be used alone for that purpose. It is true it was a part of the legislation of that day, and I have no doubt that the object was to give to us at that time a credit which the exigencies of the day required. But that awful day has gone by, and there is to-day no reason why we should be subjected to the necessity of maintaining a mortgage upon any of our means of revenue for the purpose of sustaining our credit. Our credit is good enough, and I believe is too good, for the interests of all classes of people.

As a question of finance, not as a matter of national honor, our credit is too good. The nation makes nothing because the bonds are worth 115 or 117. There is no profit to the people, but only to a few speculators. We as a people make nothing by it, and a large portion of that profit inures to the benefit of foreigners and not to the benefit of our own people; and, when to them, to a very small portion, the most of whom hold but a nominal citizenship and are to be found in the large cities.

But, sir, the answer, if I am correct in my argument, is that, if by receiving legal-tenders in payment of duty you appreciate them and make them equal to gold, there will be no necessity for having gold to pay interest upon the bonds. The interest is not paid by shipments of gold abroad. The Secretary of the Treasury, representing the United States, does not send every six months a load of gold to London or to Berlin to pay this interest. It is done through a system of exchange. He buys in New York or somewhere else the amount necessary to pay this interest abroad. It is not therefore paid by the shipment of gold. It is true that according to the laws of commerce if we are indebted abroad the balance has got to be paid in gold, but the mere payment of the interest is done through and by exchange. And if the legal-tenders are as good as gold, having been appreciated by receiving them for duties, you will not need gold to procure this exchange.

There is a remarkable case in point. On the termination of the French war with Germany an indemnity was exacted of five thousand million francs—a thousand million dollars —which had to be paid in a very short space of time. The German Government required every dollar of it in coin, and declined to receive any of the national securities of France. This exceeded the amount of coin in France by some four hundred million francs. Yet the obligation was met, and one large installment was anticipated, and every dollar of the indemnity was paid in coin. What did France do? It authorized the Bank of France to issue paper money, and three thousand million francs were issued, being six hundred million dollars, and this paper money was made a legal tender and receivable for all debts of every nature and description whatsoever. What has been the result? The prosperity of France continued, her manufactures were kept in a healthful condition, the circulation needed for commerce was not diminished, only it was changed from gold to paper, and gradually and rapidly, too, the gold came back to France in accordance with those great laws of trade which are just as fixed and certain as the laws of mathematics. The Bank of France reduced and canceled its circulation as the gold increased; and now, although they have not yet resumed, for a year or more resumption has in point of fact practically taken place. To-day the paper money in France is worth as much as gold. There is in point of fact no difference; and why? Because the government of France at once created a legitimate demand for that paper money, made it a legal tender between individuals, and made it a legal tender from individuals to the Government for everything whatsoever, and in a very short time the whole Government had righted itself financially, while we have been here floundering in the mud and mire for a great many years.

Thomas F. Bayard [Del.].—I do not desire to banish from this country the last trace of gold payments to the treasury. It is plain that if we are to resume specie payment there must be a fund of gold accumulated wherewith to resume, and this is nothing but a measure to abolish the only nucleus left by law for such accumulation and make a return to specie payments an impossibility while such a policy controls the Government. I hope this amendment offered by the Sentaor from Missouri will not be adopted, nor even that offered by my friend from Ohio.

Sooner or later, a sound public sentiment, born perhaps of the sufferings of the people, will demand that an honest measure of value shall be restored to the dealings of our citizens. That must come sooner or later, and I shall never be satisfied with the legislation of the country until it has produced that effect. Any measure tending to it shall find my vote recorded in its favor, and any measure hostile to it will find in me an opponent.

I want to vote in favor of a simple, straightforward, business measure, and I want to know the effect of what I vote for, and I do not choose to vote for a bill with two faces, and I do not choose to vote for a bill concerning which the gentleman having it in charge will not answer, if he can, plain questions as to the meaning of his own words used in the bill, but chooses to say, "You may make your own construction, you may put what amendment you please on the bill, and then put what construction you please on your amendments; but I do not choose to answer you as to what this bill is intended to do, or what is to be done with this currency which we have redeemed, or tell you how long it shall be redeemed, or whether the Secretary of the Treasury shall issue it the day after he has redeemed it, whether he shall accumulate it until it reaches $50,000,000 and then issue it again, or what he shall do with it."

Now, Mr. President, it seems to have been decreed in party caucus that this bill shall be passed to-night. To attempt to prevent it would simply be a question of physical endurance, of great personal inconvenience, and one that I am not disposed in this case to court for myself or others. My present feeling about it is that I would rather not vote at all upon the subject. I think that this subject has not been treated worthily in this debate and by this measure, and that the people of this country will say it has not been treated worthily by this debate and by this measure. There is no need for the passage of this bill this day, nor for two weeks to come, as a measure of relief. Its effect cannot be instantaneous. I do not think it is in the power of any man or party instantly to relieve the country from the financial embarrassments and pressure which are now upon it. Time must work relief. Wise laws will greatly assist and hasten the returning tide of prosperity, which, when it shall come back, should rest upon a sound basis. That, I think, is all that even wise laws can justly be expected to do. You cannot suddenly make a nation prosperous nor cure the ills of extravagant, corrupt, and reckless administration. Excess and improvidence must bear their punishment. All you can do is to set your administration upon a path of economy and honesty, that gradually prosperity may grow again.

The amendments to the bill were rejected, and it was passed by a vote of 32 to 14.

The bill was passed by the House on January 7 by a vote of 136 to 98.

It was approved by President Grant on January 14, 1875.

The rise of the silver question in 1875-7 caused a new aspect to be given to that of resumption of specie payments, and the Democrats made determined efforts to secure the repeal of the resumption act.

On August 5, 1876, Samuel S. Cox [N. Y.], chairman of the Committee on Banking and Currency, introduced in the House a bill providing for a repeal of the date set for resumption of specie payments in the act of January 14, 1875. The bill was adopted by a vote of 106 to 86, "hard money" Democrats, such as Abram S. Hewitt [N. Y.], voting in the negative. It was referred to committee in the Senate, and not acted on during the session.

In the presidential campaign of 1876 the question of "hard" money and "soft" money was a leading issue.

THE ELASTIC DEMOCRATIC [DEFORMED] TIGER

They Pull Together so Very Nicely

Caricature by Thomas Nast of Tilden and Hendricks, in "Harper's Weekly"

General Rutherford B. Hayes [O.] and William A. Wheeler [N. Y.], Republican candidates, were both in favor of "hard" money, while the Democratic candidates, Samuel J. Tilden [N. Y.] and Thomas A. Hendricks [Ind.] held opposing views on the subject.

Repeal of the Resumption Act

House of Representatives, October 31–November 22, 1877

On October 31, 1877, General Thomas Ewing [O.] brought forward in the House, from the Committee on Banking and Currency, a bill to repeal the third section of the resumption act, which had repealed the restrictions on national banking, had provided for the retirement of 80 per cent. of the increased national bank circulation, and had fixed January 1, 1879, as the date for the final redemption of legal tenders.

Various amendments were offered to the bill by both

Democrats and Republicans, which ranged in their effect from one extreme view on the currency to another.

On November 16 General James A. Garfield [O.] spoke against repeal.

We are engaged in a debate which has lasted in the Anglo-Saxon world for more than two centuries, and hardly any phase of it to which we have listened in the course of the last week is

BY REPEALING THEY RESUME—BY RESUMING THEY REPEAL

Extremes Have Met, and Now You Can't Tell Which Is Which

Cartoon by Thomas Nast in "Harper's Weekly"

new. Hardly a proposition has been heard on either side which was not made one hundred and eighty years ago in England, and almost a hundred years ago in the United States. So singularly does history repeat itself.

That man makes a vital mistake who judges of truth in relation to financial affairs from the changing phases of public opinion. He might as well stand on the shore of the Bay of Fundy and from the ebb and flow of a single tide attempt to determine the general level of the sea as to stand on this floor and from the current of public opinion in any one debate judge of the general level of the public mind. It is only when long spaces along the shore of the sea are taken into the account that the grand level is found, from which all heights and depths are measured. And it is only when long spaces of time are considered that we find at last that level of public opinion which we call the general judgment of mankind. From the turbulent ebb and flow of the public opinion of to-day I appeal to that settled judgment of mankind on the subject-matter of this debate.[1]

If one thing was settled above all other questions of financial

[1] General Garfield again used this figure, and with great effect, in his notable speech in the Republican National Convention of 1880 nominating John Sherman for President.

policy in the American mind in 1860, it was this, that the only sound, safe, trustworthy standard of value was coin of a standard weight and fineness, or a paper currency convertible into coin at the will of the holder. That was and had been for several generations the almost unanimous opinion of the American people. It is true there was here and there a theorist, dreaming of the philosopher's stone, dreaming of a time when paper money, which he worshiped as a kind of fetish, would be crowned as a god; but those dreamers were so few in number that they made no ripple on the current of public thought, and their theories formed no part of public opinion, and the opinion of 1860-'61 was the aggregated result of the opinions of all the foremost Americans who have left their record upon this subject.

Every President who has left a record on the subject has spoken without qualification in favor of the doctrine I have announced. No man ever sat in the chair of the Secretary of the Treasury of the United States who if he has spoken at all on the subject has not left on record an opinion equally strong, from Hamilton down to the days of the distinguished father of my colleague [Mr. Ewing] and to the present moment.

What happened to cause a departure from this general level of public opinion? War, the imperious necessities of war, led the men of 1861-'62 to depart from the doctrine of the Fathers; but they did not depart from it as a matter of choice, but compelled by overmastering necessity. Every man in the Senate and House of 1862 who voted for the greenback law announced that he did it with the greatest possible reluctance and with the gravest apprehension for the result. Every man who spoke on the subject from Thaddeus Stevens to the humblest member in this House, and from William P. Fessenden to the humblest Senator, warned his country against the dangers that might follow, and pledged his honor that at the earliest possible moment the country should be brought back to the old, safe, established doctrine of the fathers.

When they made the law creating the greenbacks they incorporated into its essential provisions the most solemn pledge men could devise that they would come back to the doctrines of the Fathers. The very law that created the greenback provided for its redemption and retirement; and every time the necessities of war required an additional issue new guaranties and new limitations were put upon the new issues to insure their ultimate redemption. They were issued upon the fundamental condition that the number should be so limited forever that under the law of contracts the courts might enforce their sanctions. The men of 1862 knew the dangers from sad experience in our history; and, like Ulysses, lashed themselves to the mast of public credit when they embarked upon the stormy and boisterous sea of inflated paper money, that they might not be beguiled by the siren song that would be sung to them when they were afloat on the wild waves.

But the times have changed; new men are on deck: men who have forgotten the old pledges; and now only twelve years have passed (for as late as 1865 this House, with but 6 dissenting votes, resolved again to stand by the old ways and bring the country back to sound money), and what do we find? We find a group of the orists and doctrinaires who look upon the wisdom of the Fathers as foolishness. We find some who advocate what they call "absolute money"; who declare that a piece of paper stamped a "dollar" is a dollar; that gold and silver are a part of the barbarism of the past, which ought to be forever abandoned. We hear them declaring that resumption is a delusion and a snare. We hear them declaring that the eras of prosperity are the eras of paper money; and they point us to all times of inflation as the periods of blessing to the people, prosperity to business; and they ask us no more to vex their ears with any allusion to the old standard, the money of the Constitution. Let the wild crop of financial literature that has sprung into life within the last twelve years witness how widely and how far we have drifted. We have lost our old moorings, have thrown overboard our old compass; we sail by alien stars, looking not for the haven, but are afloat on an unknown sea.

Now, what are the obstacles to resumption in accordance with the law we have passed? The first great obstacle stated by gentlemen who have argued the question is this: that we have not enough currency in the country for its business and that some measure of contraction will be likely to attend the further execution of the provisions of the resumption law. Before I enter directly upon that objection I desire to state a fact for the consideration of those who hear me. In that prosperous era of 1860, when there was free banking in most of the States and the banks were pushing all the currency they could into circulation without limit, there were just two hundred and seven millions of paper currency, and that was the largest volume that this country had ever known.

Now, the amount of coin in the country in 1860 was $200,000,000. Add that sum to the two hundred and seven millions of paper circulation and you have four hundred and seven millions of currency, paper and silver and gold. How much have we to-day? On the first day of this month we had seven hundred and twenty-seven millions of greenbacks, banking notes, fractional currency, and fractional silver, and if you add the nine millions of copper and nickel money now outstanding it makes a present volume of seven hundred and thirty-six millions of currency, counting no gold whatever, although the Pacific coast uses a large amount.

Now, I put it to the judgment of this House if under free banking in 1860 four hundred and seven millions was the limit of possible currency that could be kept in circulation, how can it be said that almost twice that amount is needed and is hardly enough for the wants of 1877? Have the laws of value changed in seventeen years? Gentlemen who assert a dearth of currency at the present time must point out the new elements in our fiscal affairs that require three hundred and twenty millions more money than was needed in 1860.

No theory of currency that existed in 1860 can justify the volume now outstanding. Either our laws of trade, our laws of value, our laws of exchange, have been utterly reversed or the currency of to-day is in excess of the legitimate wants of trade. But I admit freely that no Congress is wise enough to determine how much currency the country needs. There never was a body of men wise enough to do that. The volume of the currency needed depends upon laws that are higher than Congress and higher than governments. One thing only legislation can do. It can determine the quality of the money of the country. The laws of trade alone can determine its quantity.

General Garfield then pointed to the British cash-resumption act of 1819 as supporting his contention that the American resumption act under consideration, if unrepealed, would prove a blessing to the country.

Mr. Garfield.—The evils which England suffered from 1821 to 1826 did not arise from the resumption of cash payments. I appeal to every great writer of acknowledged character in England for the truth of this position. I ask gentlemen to read the eighth chapter of the second book of Miss Martineau's "History of the Peace," where the case is admirably stated. I appeal also to the opinion of Parliament itself, especially to the House of Commons, which is as sensitive an index of public opinion as England knows. When they were within about eighteen months of resumption of specie payment, a motion was made, like the motion of my colleague from Ohio [Mr. Ewing], that the resumption-act bill be repealed or modified, because it was producing distress. And a number of gentlemen in the House of Commons made speeches of the same spirit as those which we have heard here within the past week. The distress among the people, the crippling of business, the alarm of the mercantile classes, all were paraded in the House of Commons, and were answered by those knights of finance whose names have become illustrious in English history. And at the end of a long debate on that proposition, on the 11th of April, 1821, a vote was taken, and the proposition was rejected by a vote of 141 to 27. In other words, by a vote of 141 to 27 the House of Commons resolved that their act for the resumption of specie payments was not causing distress and ought not to be repealed and ought not to be modified except to make it more effective. As a matter of fact, it was so modified as to allow resumption to take place much sooner than was provided in the act of 1819.

But this was not enough. On the 11th of June, 1822, a Mr. Western moved for the appointment of a committee of inquiry into the effect of resumption, and charged that it had caused a violent contraction of the currency and an injury to the business of the country. Again the subject was fully debated, and the arguments against the resumption act completely answered, by a vote of 192 to 30. The motion of Mr. Western was rejected, and the Commons resolved that they would not alter the standard of gold or silver, in fineness, weight, or denomination.

Still, gentlemen tell us that the great distress in England was caused by the resumption act. I commend those gentlemen to such great writers as Tooke, who in his "History of Prices" has gone over this ground most thoroughly and ably. He says it was the corn law which produced the great evils from which England suffered in those years.

A law had been passed to prevent the price of wheat from falling below eighty shillings per quarter, by prohibiting all foreign importations whenever the price fell below that figure. In other words, England proposed to build a Chinese wall around the island so as to make wheat one of the most profitable crops for her farmers. Stimulated by that law, the agriculturists of England undertook the growing of wheat on a scale before unknown. And when they had expended millions in reclaiming waste lands and sowing an unusual breadth of wheat, they found their own harvest and the colonial importations had flooded the markets and lowered the price, and bankrupted thousands of English farmers. In spite of the law, wheat went down to forty-seven shillings and nine pence per quarter, and brought great distress upon the agricultural population.

That this fall in the price of wheat was not caused by the resumption act is conclusively shown by the fact that the three great harvests of 1820, 1821, and 1822 were general throughout Europe, and throughout the Continent the price of wheat declined almost as much as in England itself.

In 1822 a committee of the House of Commons was appointed to inquire into all the causes of the distress. I have read that report in full, and there is not a word in it that attributes any part of the distress to the resumption act of 1819; but the causes given are those which I have named.

Before quitting this point I beg leave to refer to a paper of the late Secretary of the Treasury, Hugh McCulloch, in the *North American Review.* He said that every great crisis in this country has been preceded by an enlargement of paper circulation. I affirm that to be true, and I challenge any man to controvert it. It was true in England always. It has been true in this country always. We had a great crisis in 1797; another in 1817; another in 1837; another in 1857; and our last in 1873—almost exactly twenty years apart.

These crises are periodic and return as the result of causes springing up among the mass of our business people; and they have all been preceded by overtrading, speculation, an enlargement of credits, an undue expansion of the instruments of credit; and they have all resulted in the same sad uniformity of misery that has followed their culmination.

I now proceed to notice the second point that has been made in favor of this bill. It is assumed that specie payment will injure the debtor class of this country and thereby oppress the poor; in other words, that the enforcement of the resumption law will oppress the poor and increase the riches of the rich. It is assumed that the laboring men are in debt and that the rich men constitute the creditor class. I deny this proposition *in toto.* I affirm that the vast majority of the creditors of this country are the poor people; that the vast majority of the debtors of this country are the well-to-do people, in fact, people who are moderately rich.

As a matter of fact the poor man, the laboring man, cannot get heavily in debt. He has not the security to offer. Men lend their money on security, and in the very nature of the case poor men can borrow but little. What then do poor men do with their small earnings? When a man has earned out of his hard work a hundred dollars more than he needs for current expenses he reasons thus: "I cannot go into business with a hundred dollars; I cannot embark in trade; but as I work I want my money to work." And so he puts his small gains where they will earn something. He lends his money to a wealthier neighbor or puts it in the savings bank. There were in the United States on the 1st of November, 1876, forty-four hundred and seventy-five savings banks and private banks of deposits, and their deposits amounted to $1,377,000,000, almost three-fourths of the amount of our national debt. Over two and a half millions of the citizens of the United States were depositors. In some States the deposits did not average more than $250 each. The great mass of the depositors are men and women of small means: laborers, widows, and orphans. They are the lenders of this enormous aggregate. The savings banks, as their agents, lend it to whom? Not to the laboring poor, but to the business men who wish to enlarge their business beyond their capital. Speculators sometimes borrow it. But in the main well-to-do business men borrow these hoardings. Thus the poor lend to the rich.

Gentlemen assail the bondholders of the country as the rich men who oppress the poor. Do they know how vast an amount of the public securities are held by poor people? I took occasion, a few years since, to ask the officers of a bank in one of the counties of my district, a rural district, to show me the number of holders and amount held of United States bonds on which they collected the interest. The total amount was $416,000. And how many people held them? One hundred and ninety-six. Of these just eight men had over $20,000 apiece, and the other one hundred and eighty-eight ranged from $50 up to $2,500. I found in that list fifteen orphan children and sixty widows, who had a little left them from their fathers' or husbands' estates, who had made the nation their guardian. And I found one hundred and twenty-one laborers, mechanics, ministers, men of slender means, who had kept what they had and put it in the hands of the United States that it might be safe. And they were the "bloated bondholders" against whom so much eloquence is fulminated in this House.

There is another way in which poor men dispose of their money. A man says, I can keep my wife and babies from starving while I live and have my health, but if I die they may be compelled to go over the hills to the poorhouse; and, agonized by that thought, he saves out of his hard earnings enough to take out and keep alive a small life insurance policy, so that, if he dies, there may be something left, provided the insurance company to which he intrusts his money is honest enough to keep its pledges. There are of course some rich men insured in these companies, but the majority are poor people, for the policies do not average more than $2,200 each. What is done with the assets of these companies? They are loaned out. Here again the creditor class is the poor and the insurance companies are the agents of the poor to lend their money for them. It would be dishonorable for Congress to legislate either for the debtor class or for the creditor class alone. We ought to legislate for the whole country. But when gentlemen attempt to manufacture sentiment against the resumption act by saying it will help the rich and hurt the poor, they are overwhelmingly answered by the facts.

Suppose you undo the work that Congress has attempted—to resume specie payment—what will result? You will depreciate the value of the greenback. Suppose it falls ten cents on the dollar. You will have destroyed 10 per cent. of the value of every deposit in the savings banks, 10 per cent. of every life insurance policy and fire insurance policy, of every pension to the soldier, and of every day's wages of every laborer in the nation.

Daniel Webster never uttered a greater truth in finance than when he said that of all contrivances to cheat the laboring classes of mankind none was so effective as that which deluded them with an irredeemable paper money. The rich can take care of themselves, but the dead weight of all the fluctuations and loss falls ultimately on the poor man who has only his day's work to sell.

I admit that in the passage from peace to war there was a great loss to one class of the community, to the creditors; and in the return to the basis of peace some loss to debtors was inevitable. This injustice was unavoidable. The loss and gain did not fall upon the same. The evil could not be balanced nor adjusted. The debtors of 1862-'65 are not the debtors of 1877. The most competent judges declare that the average life of the private debts in the United States is not more than two years. Now, we have already gone two years on the road to resumption, and the country has been adjusting itself to the new condition of things. The people have expected resumption, and have already discounted most of the hardships and sufferings incident to the change. The agony is almost over; and if we now embark again upon the open sea we lose all that has been gained and plunge the country into the necessity of trying once more over the same boisterous ocean, with all its perils and uncertainties. I speak the deepest convictions of my mind and heart when I say that, should this resumption act be repealed and no effectual substitute be put in its place, the day is not far distant when all of us, looking back on this time from the depth of the evils which will result, will regert, with all our power to regret, the day when we again let loose the dangers of inflation upon the country.

Gentlemen speak of the years of high prices as years of prosperity. It is true there was a kind of prosperity in the day of high prices; but do not gentlemen know that war prices cannot be kept up forever? Nothing but the extraordinary calamities of war can produce such prices as we knew from 1865 to 1870. To our foreign and domestic markets was added the war market. War sat like a grim monster swallowing up the accumulated wealth of the country. More than a million men were taken out of the ranks of the producers and added to the ranks of the consumers, and all prices went up; but does anybody dream that these prices can be kept up forever, when the soldiers are mustered out and the war has closed and business has begun to resume its normal level of peace? Oh, no, gentlemen, it was inevitable that the country must come down from the level of war prices, and the attempt to get it back is to fight against fate. Unless we bring ourselves steadily and surely by the strong courage and guidance of law back to resumption, we shall reach that level by a disastrous fall; but down to it we must come.

I do not undervalue the greenback or its great services to the country; but when the gentleman from Pennsylvania [William D. Kelley] spoke of the greenback as being the thing that put down the rebellion, I thought if I had been on the other side I would have said: We had a much more liberal supply of paper money than you had, why did it not put you down? [Laughter.] Our money was better than yours in one respect, for ours set a day of resumption, which was six months after the independence of the Confederate States should be acknowledged. [Laughter.] I think, sir, that those gentlemen who are familiar with the financial history of the Confederacy would not join the gentleman in his eulogy on paper currency which is cut loose from the coin standard.

Our country needs not only a national but an international currency. Let me state a fact of vast importance in this discussion. The foreign trade of this country—its exports and imports—amounts to $1,500,000,000 in value; and every dollar of that trade must be transacted in coin. We cannot help ourselves. Every article of the exports we send abroad is measured by and sold for coin. Every dollar of imports we must pay for in coin. We must translate these coin prices into our currency, and every fluctuation in the value of the greenback falls upon us and not upon the countries with which we trade. Therefore the commercial interests of America demand that the international and national value of money shall be one, so that what is a dollar in Ohio shall be a dollar the world over. Our money must be international as well as national, unless we wish to isolate this country and have no trade or commerce, or glory on the sea.

The trouble with our greenback dollar is this: it has two distinct functions, one a purchasing power and the other a debt-paying power. As a debt-paying power it is equal to one hundred cents; that is, to pay an old private debt. A greenback dollar will by law discharge one hundred cents of debt. But no law can give it purchasing power in the general markets of the world unless it represents a known standard of coin value. Now, what we want is that these two qualities of our greenback dollar shall be made equal; its debt-paying power and its general purchasing power. When these are equal the problem of our currency is solved and not till then.

We who defend the resumption act propose not to destroy the greenback but to dignify it, to glorify it. The law that we defend does not destroy it, but preserves its volume at $300,000,000 and makes it equal to and convertible into coin. I admit that the law is not entirely free from ambiguity. But the Secretary of the Treasury, who has the execution of the law, declares that section 3579 of the Revised Statutes is in full force, namely:

> When any United States notes are returned to the treasury, they may be reissued, from time to time, as the exigencies of the public interest may require.

Although I do not believe in keeping greenbacks as a permanent currency in the United States, although I do not myself believe in the Government becoming a permanent banker, yet I am willing for one that, in order to prevent the shock to business which gentlemen fear, the $300,000,000 of greenbacks shall be allowed to remain in circulation as long as the wants of trade show manifestly that they are needed. Now, is that a great contraction? Is it contraction at all?

Why, gentlemen, when you have brought your greenback up two and one-half cents higher in value, you will have added to your volume of money $200,000,000 of gold coin which cannot circulate until greenbacks are brought to par.

Let those who are afraid of contraction consider that and answer it.

Summing it all up in a word: the struggle now pending in this House is on the one hand to make the greenback better, and on the other to make it worse. The resumption act is making it better every day. Repeal that act and you make it indefinitely worse. In the name of every man who wants his own when he has earned it, I demand that we do not make the wage of the poor man to shrivel in his hands after he has earned it; but that his money shall be made better and better, until the plowholder's money shall be as good as the bondholder's money; until our standard is one, and there is no longer one money for the rich and another for the poor.

This is the era of pacification. We believe in the pacification of the country. That is, we seek to pass out of the storm center of war that raged over this country so long and enter the calm circle of peace. We believe in the equality of States, and the equality of citizens before the law. In these we have made great progress.

Let us take one step further. Let us have equality of dollars before the law, so that the trinity of our political creed shall be equal States, equal men, equal dollars throughout the Union. When these three are realized we shall have achieved the complete pacification of our country.

We are bound for three great reasons to maintain the resumption of specie payments: First, because the sanctity of the public faith requires it; second, because the material prosperity of the country demands it; and, third, because our future prosperity demands that the agitation shall cease and that the country shall find a safe and permanent basis for financial peace.

The elements are now all in our favor. The Secretary of the Treasury tells us in his report laid upon our table this morning that he has $66,000,000 of gold coin, unpledged for any other purpose, waiting as reserve for the day of resumption. He is adding to that stock at the rate of $5,000,000 a month. Our surplus revenue of $35,000,000 a year will all be added to his reserve. Foreign exchange is now in our favor. We are selling to other nations almost $200,000,000 a year more than we are buying. All these elements are with us. Our harvests have been more bountiful than ever before. The nation is on the returning wave of prosperity. Everywhere business is reviving, and there is no danger except from the Congress of the United States. Here is the storm center; here is the point of peril. If we can pass that point and not commit ourselves to the dangerous act now threatened, we shall soon see resumption complete.

I notice that gentlemen do not move to strike out the first

section of the resumption act. Why? Two years ago my colleague [Mr. Ewing], in his debate with Governor Stewart L. Woodford, laughed at silver resumption, so far as the postal currency was concerned, as absurd and as impossible.

He spurned the proposition to destroy our paper scrip which cost but little, and replace it with silver change which had some value. He argued that every silver coin issued would be hidden away and none would go into circulation. But since that debate silver resumption under the first clause of the bill is completed, except that we have not yet been able to fund all the old scrip, so lazily do the people exercise their right of redemption. But gentlemen think that now, if we resume under this section, the currency will all be taken up.

General Ewing.—In the debate with Governor Woodford, in 1875, I did make the statement to which the gentleman refers. But that was before the people of this country, or I presume the people of the world generally, knew of the furtive and rascally act of demonetization of silver in the adoption of our Revised Statutes. It was before the immense fall of silver. It was when the silver dollar was at a high premium over the greenback dollar. Speaking from conditions then existing and the price of silver at that time, the statement was reasonable that the fractional silver currency would be taken up and sold, and not go into general circulation.

General Garfield.—The trouble with the statement of my friend is that, the fractional silver currency being 12 per cent. below the value of the silver dollar, there was not the slightest danger, at the time he speaks of, that the silver coin after being issued would pass out of circulation. My friend did not believe in silver resumption until that metal became so depreciated as to be worth vastly less than paper.

Gentlemen think there is danger that the people will present all their greenbacks and demand the coin, if resumption is enforced. Let us see. Remember how slow they have been in giving up their scrip. Suppose that a farmer in one of your Eastern States sells his farm for $10,000. He wants to remove to the great West. He gets ten greenbacks of the denomination of $1,000 each. This is easy to carry; he can put it in his vest pocket. Do you think as a mere matter of convenience he will go to the assistant treasurer in New York and get for those greenbacks forty pounds' weight of gold coin to carry in his pockets, or, if the silver dollar should be restored, six hundred and forty pounds of silver? No, gentlemen, the moment your greenback is equal to gold, it is better than gold; for it is more convenient; and it will remain in circulation until the business of the country demands its withdrawal.

In conclusion, Mr. Speaker, if any of the substitutes offered to this bill will make resumption more safe, more certain, and will more carefully protect the business interests of the country, such amendment shall have my vote; but any measure that takes back the promise, that gives up what we have gained, that sets us afloat on the wild waves from which we have so nearly escaped, I will oppose it to the utmost, confidently trusting to the future for the vindication of my judgment. [Applause.]

On November 22 General Ewing spoke in support of his bill.

Mr. Speaker, it is characteristic of republican governments that the people confine their attention and interest to one great question until it is thoroughly settled. For six years preceding the war, nothing of public interest was generally considered but the slavery question. During the war the means of its successful prosecution absorbed all attention. Since its close, the status of the negro race as components of our political life, and the terms of rehabilitation of the revolted States, have been the controlling questions in every campaign. Now that the last of the Southern questions is happily settled by the triumph of the democratic principle of local self-government, there loom up, as paramount in importance and interest, the questions of the debt and the currency.

Happy would it have been for the people had they considered these questions twelve years ago. They would have been saved the infliction of five gigantic wrongs in their finance policy. They would have had a paper currency composed solely of greenbacks, and have avoided $350,000,000 of unnecessary bonded debt caused by dividing the circulation with national banks—a saving which would by this date have equaled one-third of our national burden. They would not have suffered the maladroit and mischievous funding in long bonds of the $1,200,000,000 of interest notes, the chief part of which were legal-tenders and performed the double office of investment and currency; which were dispersed throughout the country, and little felt as a burden because of the ebb and flow of payments from the treasury to the people as interest, and from the people back to the treasury as taxes. The funding of those notes largely contracted the effective currency just as our business wants were immensely increased by the return of the South to our industrial life; and substituted for them a credit system which occasioned the panic of 1873.

So, too, if the people had been awake to these questions, the act of repudiation and extortion in 1869 would never have become a law, by which $500,000,000 were in effect taken from them and given to the bondholders without consideration; nor the silver swindle of 1873 and 1874 by which we were deprived of the power to pay our public debts in the coin of the contract, the metal of which America is the great producer; nor the crowning villainy of the act of 1875, by which about ten thousand millions of currency debts were made payable in gold, by which the great wealth-producing classes are being robbed of their accumulations for the benefit of usurers, and our land in the midst of the abundance of God's bounties is filled with the cries of hunger and despair.

Mr. Speaker, I wish it to be understood that the bill has no connection with the question whether the system of free banking established by the resumption law shall stand or fall. It will leave the bank system just where it now is, open to all in any locality who may choose to establish banks of issue. This measure will merely stop the redemption and destruction of greenbacks, and the purchase and accumulation of coin for that purpose. When it shall have been disposed of, it will be for Congress to determine whether the sovereign prerogative of furnishing the money of the people shall be exercised by the Government alone, or divided with private corporations.

Mr. Speaker, no greater wrong can be inflicted on a people by government than a contraction of the volume of currency to which their values are adjusted. The prices of commodities, whether land, product, or labor, are determined absolutely by the effective volume of the currency. An increase of the volume raises the price of all commodities; but, if not carried beyond the wants of business, does injury to only a comparatively small class, whose wealth or dependence is chiefly in money securities, fixed rents, annuities, or salaries. Yet, while it injures them in one way it helps them in another: it lightens the burden of taxation, promotes industry, stimulates exchanges, multiplies opportunities for safe and profitable investments, and thus indirectly compensates them for the diminution of the relative value of their money. Thus, during the war of the rebellion, so great were the general benefits from the increased volume of the currency, and so many the new opportunities for successful investment, that even the small creditor class suffered little by the decrease of the purchasing power of money.

On the other hand, a contraction of the currency, by diminishing the price of land, labor, and commodities, spreads ruin among the masses. It oppresses debtors, by reducing the price of those commodities by the sale of which money is raised to pay debts. It in like manner lays increased burdens on taxpayers. It checks business, because neither the maker nor the exchanger of values can work profitably on a falling market; and, by diminishing business, forces wage people into idleness and starvation.

David Hume, in his "Essay on Money," says:

> The policy of the good magistrate consists in keeping the money of the nation if possible still *increasing;* because by that means he keeps alive a spirit of industry and increases the stock of labor, in which consist all real power and riches. Accordingly we find that, in every kingdom into which money begins to flow in greater abundance than formerly, everything takes a new face: labor and industry gain life, the merchant becomes more enterprising, the manufacturer more diligent and skillful, and even the farmer follows his plow with greater alacrity and attention.
>
> On the other hand, a nation whose money decreases is actually at that time weaker and more miserable than another nation which possesses no more money but is on the increasing hand. The workman has not the same employment from the manufacturer and merchant; the farmer cannot dispose of his corn and cattle, though he must pay the same rent to his landlord. The poverty and beggary which must ensue are easily foreseen.

Mr. Speaker, this resumption law found the prices of land, labor, and products in the United States adjusted to a volume of $733,000,000 of money, exclusive of fractional currency. I do not include silver or gold, for they were not then, and are not now, any part of the actual currency. This volume was not excessive. It was but $17.50 *per capita,* including the fractional currency. Compare it with the money of other nations. Take England, which has by various estimates from $27 to $34 *per capita,* or Germany, which has $23 *per capita.* These are small nations, comparable only in area with our States; they are covered with networks of railways and their exchanges are swiftly made; while we are spread over a vast continent, imperfectly developed, and our exchanges are comparatively slow. It was the deliberate judgment of General Grant's Administration in December, 1873, as expressed in his message—an opinion concurred in by the public generally—that our currency was then too small for our business in the dullest seasons of the year.

Now, the immediate evil of this resumption law is that it necessarily involves a destruction of from one-half to three-fourths of our paper money; that the gold with which the paper will be redeemed will not go into general circulation, and that therefore the execution of the law will result in a reduction of all values in substantially the proportion of the contraction of the currency, carrying with it an enormous increase of the burdens of debt and taxation, the widespread ruin of industry, and the pauperization of millions of our people.

This law was in fact devised by the money power to double their wealth through contraction and the consequent shrinkage of values, and at the same time to take from the people all control of the currency; to drive in the circulation of the country banks, and establish a dominion of the money power, through a few banks in the large cities, over the business and fortunes of the great wealth-producing classes and sections.

Under this law every greenback redeemed must be destroyed. My colleague [Mr. Garfield] says that Mr. Sherman now thinks they may be reissued. If so, he has changed front. He intimated most distinctly in the Senate, when the resumption bill passed, that redemption meant cancellation. But, whatever may be his opinion, the law stands, and whoever may be Secretary must execute its evident purpose. Section 3579 of the Revised Statutes, which Mr. Sherman is now reported to interpret as authorizing a reissue, was in force in 1875, when he expressed the opposite opinion. It provides that "when any United States notes are *returned* to the treasury they may be reissued." Certainly notes *returned*—that is, received *in payment of public dues*—may be reissued. The act of receiving such notes is not *redemption*—which is payment of a public debt, and involves extinction of the evidence of the debt unless otherwise expressly provided by law.

But Mr. Sherman's latest phrase of opinion on this question is not only unsustained by the law, but actually multiplies the difficulties and dangers of resumption. It compels redemption in gold not only once but over and over again, and requires the treasury to be the perpetual supplier of gold to all who need it; while it puts in the hands of the Secretary the power to expand or contract the currency by reissuing or hoarding greenbacks at his discretion.

Mr. Bristow, when Secretary of the Treasury declared the purpose and effect of the law in his report for December, 1875, saying, "the faith of the Government now stands pledged to the final redemption and *removal from the currency of the country* of the legal-tender notes as fast as they shall be presented for redemption." Mr. Morrill, his successor, reiterated it in his report in 1876, saying that the law "declared in effect *a monetary system composed of coin and national bank notes* redeemable in coin.'' The Treasury Department has declared it every month by the destruction of fractional currency redeemed under the same language of the same law. The act itself declares it by providing for the ''redemption'' of fractional currency ''until the whole amount *outstanding shall be redeemed*''; and by providing that legal-tenders shall be redeemed before January 1, 1879, ''until there shall be outstanding $300,000,000 of such legal-tender notes *and no more*''—both these provisions plainly showing that ''redemption'' means final extinction and removal from the currency of the country.

Mr. Speaker, no nation ever maintained a redeemable paper currency equal to the volume of coin in the country. France with $1,200,000,000 in coin according to the estimate of Victor Bonnet, and $1,600,000,000 according to Mr. Carey, has not yet felt able to resume specie payments on $491,000,000 of paper. England with $700,000,000 of coin can maintain a redeemable paper currency of only about two hundred and sixty millions. Before the war, we had two hundred and eighty-five millions of coin in the United States, and our banks never had a paper circulation in excess of two hundred and fifteen millions. The reason is obvious: when coin becomes actually current, two-thirds of its volume, at least, is absorbed by the people or hoarded as reserves by banks of deposit only: and it is not possible for banks of issue or the Government to get control of over one-third or a fourth of the coin in the country as a redemption fund. Thus, before the war, the banks never held to exceed eighty-three millions of the two hundred and eighty-five millions of coin in the country. The British banks hold about one hundred and thirty millions of the seven hundred millions in Great Britain, and the Bank of France holds four hundred and forty-three millions of the twelve hundred to sixteen hundred millions of coin in France.

Hence, if our own experience and that of other nations are to guide us to permanent resumption, we must increase our coin, or cut down our paper, or both, until the amount of coin in the country shall far exceed the amount of paper money. It should exceed it about threefold to make resumption as safe as in England or France; and should exceed it one-third to get back to the merely spasmodic resumption we had before the war.

Now, what is our present supply of coin and bullion? According to a number of estimates made for me, by persons who have the means of information attainable, we have one hundred and sixty millions of gold and silver coin and bullion in the Treasury, the banks, and among the people.

But we have had two hundred and eighty-five millions of gold and silver coin and bullion in 1860, and in the seventeen years since we have produced from our mines one thousand and seven millions of gold and two hundred and fifty-five millions of silver; about half of which, or six hundred and thirty-one millions, have gone into coinage. What has become of this vast sum of coin?

It has flowed abroad to pay our debts. Much more than half of our national debt is owned in Europe. The interest on our national bonds held abroad is exceeded by the coin interest on State, city, railway, and other American securities held there; so that the aggregate coin interest annually due from the people of the United States to Europe is estimated at from one hundred to one hundred and fifty millions of dollars. Add to this from forty to fifty millions per year paid for foreign shipping, and a sum equally great for expenses of foreign travel, and we have an aggregate annual drain of from one hundred and eighty to two hundred and fifty millions of dollars in payment of debts and expenditures abroad.

How have we paid this enormous annual foreign demand?

First, by the shipment of coin and bullion. From 1860 to 1876, both inclusive, we shipped abroad one thousand and fourteen millions of gold and silver more than we imported, being an average of over fifty-six millions a year. The balance of the foreign demand upon us we have paid in part by an occasional balance of trade in our favor; but always, in whole or in part, by selling more bonds abroad, thus each year increasing the annual drain of the precious metals and making it more impossible for us to get or keep any large sum of coin in our country.

I do not ignore the consideration that our disuse of gold and silver as money would of itself have caused them to flow abroad. But I claim that our foreign debts and expenditures make the drain imperative, whether we do or do not use the coin as a foundation for a home currency. Our great specie product of the past seventeen years has become the property of creditor nations who have built their business on it. We can neither bring it back, nor hold future accumulations here, by creating a demand for it at home, be it ever so imperative; for with nations, as with individuals, "the borrower is servant to the lender." No nation greatly in debt abroad ever did, or can, have a redeemable paper currency for domestic business. Russia, Austria, and Italy, who are like us greatly in debt abroad, are also like us compelled to forego specie payments.

But my colleague [Mr. Garfield] says in effect that this bad condition is all changed now, and resumption made easy by our favorable balance of trade. So far from the balance of trade helping us to coin, the report of the Bureau of Statistics of August 21, 1877, shows that we shipped abroad for the year ending June 30, 1875, seventy-two millions of coin and bullion more than we received; in 1876 forty-one millions, and in 1877 sixteen millions. So that, notwithstanding the unexampled balance of trade in our favor, and our great effort to accumulate gold for resumption, we have in the past three years exported one hundred and twenty-nine millions more of coin and bullion than we have received from abroad. How, then, has the balance of trade helped resumption?

Mr. Speaker, this vast and increasing drain of the precious metals makes a maintenance of specie payments absolutely impossible on one-third of our present volume of paper currency. Until the financial policy which has taken our debt from our own people to send it abroad shall be wholly reversed, and the debt is held at home; until the usury which forbids vessels built here, where money costs 10 per cent., from competing with those built on the Clyde, where money costs but 3, shall have been abated by a money policy which shall give money and moneyed securities a less exorbitant interest; we can no more arrest this outgoing drain of the precious metals than we can stop the waters warmed by an American sun in the Gulf from flowing to lave and enrich the British Isles.

The Administration has had in its hands for three years past the whole credit resources of our nation for the purchase of coin wherewith to prepare for resumption. It has been authorized to sell bonds bearing 4, 4½, and 5 per cent. interest. Three-fourths of the time allotted for preparation has already elapsed. The Secretaries of the Treasury have exerted themselves to the utmost to accumulate gold. The national banks have no doubt been fairly diligent in getting and hoarding it. The problem before the treasury and the banks has been to get gold enough to keep seven hundred and thirty-three millions of paper afloat, or to take up the paper with gold and destroy it. How successful have they been? We find from a report of the Secretary of the Treasury made to this House last Thursday that the United States had succeeded in obtaining to October 31, 1877, but $57,436,071 of gold, from which is to be deducted, however, accruing interest, amounting at that date to $24,840,093—leaving but $32,595,978 of gold applicable to resumption. Whether any of that small sum is what Jim Fisk would have called "phantom gold"—say subscriptions by the national banks for bonds *payable* in gold, but not yet paid—does not distinctly appear. In addition to the thirty-two and a half millions in the treasury, the national banks hold $19,948,407 of silver and gold combined. How much of this is silver and how much gold does not appear from the bank statement. No doubt the chief part is subsidiary silver coin, which is of no use for resumption.

William M. Springer [Ill.].—If the gentleman will allow me, I would say that, according to the last statement of the Comptroller of the Currency—that for November—there are but five millions of gold coin in the national banks, the other specie in the banks being in silver and United States gold certificates.

General Ewing.—After nearly three years of preparation, what have we accomplished? We have effected a net destruction of over seventy-five millions of greenbacks and bank notes combined; but have accumulated in the banks and the treasury less than fifty millions of gold and ten millions of silver applicable to resumption. Here we are, then, with resumption day not fourteen months distant, with not one-fifteenth of the amount of gold and silver indispensable to float six hundred and fifty-eight millions of paper money now outstanding—with no stock of the precious metals in the United States to draw from—with the outgoing drain still kept up—with our foreign creditors and the great banks of Europe determined to prevent the shipment of gold to America; holding in effect a mortgage on every dollar of the coined product of our mines; and able to drain the petty accumulations in our treasury or the banks at will by simply demanding coin payment of the interest on our public and private securities, or by sending them home for sale. Under these conditions, how utterly futile it is to hope that we can maintain resumption without the swift destruction of much the greater part of the present currency of the country!

If we were wholly out of debt to Europe, if our foreign commerce floated under our own flag, if there were no system of absenteeism among our wealthy classes, expending their wealth abroad, resumption in gold, or even in gold and silver, would be impossible on our present volume of paper currency for many years to come. In the proportion of coin in England to redeemable paper money, it would require about eighteen hundred millions in our country to maintain resumption on the six hundred and fifty-eight millions of paper money outstanding. In the proportion of France's paper money to her coin, we would require an accumulation of sixteen hundred millions. Take even the proportion of coin in our country in 1860 to the highest volume of paper money then in circulation and nominally redeemable, and it would require nearly nine hundred millions of coin to float our present paper money.

How can we accumulate such a vast sum of gold? The coined product of our mines, if it were all retained here, would not yield it in forty years. If we were free from debt to-day and were to offer 6 per cent. bonds in the markets of Europe in exchange for gold, we could not get a hundred millions. Recollect, sir, that England, France, and Germany never suffer a shipment of gold from their shores, if by any artifice or power they can prevent it. All the vast sales of bonds abroad for fifteen years past have brought us nothing but our own securities or merchandise. England refused to pay the Geneva award of fifteen and a half millions in gold, but paid it in securities. An export of ten to fifteen millions of gold will always produce a panic there. It is the base of the pyramid of currency and credits in every specie-paying country, and the withdrawal of any part of the base shakes the industrial fabric resting on it. Hence every monarch of Europe guards his country's gold as he does his crown or scepter.

Hence resumption can only be *maintained* by the destruction of the greater part of the present paper currency. To accomplish that purpose the means provided in the law are probably adequate. Mr. Sherman says they are. He ought to know. His plan probably will be to limit the amount of redemption per day to, say, two millions; to require all the greenbacks to be presented through a chosen syndicate which can pay him two millions of gold per day for 5 per cent. bonds, and present two millions of greenbacks per day and receive the gold back. It could probably be managed so that most of the gold thus used would be merely diverted from European and American money markets long enough to flow through the treasury and back to the same markets, causing comparatively little disturbance, and accomplishing in effect merely a *funding* of most of the greenbacks into gold-bearing bonds.

My colleague [Mr. Garfield] says the people will not want the gold when greenbacks are at par. True, the masses will not. They never have wanted it in preference to greenbacks, which they always have regarded as being, in the language of President Grant's message in 1873, "the best paper money they ever had." But the *people* generally will have no more to do or say as to the redemption and cancellation of their currency than they have had with the finance policy of the Government for the past twelve years; than they had with the establishment of the national bank system; or the funding of the $1,200,000,000 of interest-bearing treasury notes; or the passage of the infamous act of 1869; or the rascally sleight of hand by which silver was demonetized; or the enactment of that sum of financial villainies—the resumption law. The national banks, the importers, the gold rings in New York, the desperadoes of Wall street, the money kings of Europe to whom we are financially enslaved, *they* will present the greenbacks for redemption and destruction as fast as the gold can be paid over the counters of the treasury.

But we are assured there will be little more contraction, because gold will take the place of the redeemed greenbacks in the business of the country. That is a most fallacious conjecture. The dearth of gold here, the present large demand for it, the immeasurably increased demand arising from the fact that considerably more than two thousand millions of national, savings, and other bank deposits will then be payable in gold; that seven or eight billions of other debts, corporate and private, and seven hundred and fifty millions of annual taxes, now payable in currency, will then be payable only in gold; that every banking institution in the land will be at the mercy of the millionaire gamblers who may hoard it to burst the banks and place the business of the country at their feet, will create a general scramble for coin which will keep every dollar of it out of general circulation.

After our currency shall have been contracted over a half by destruction of the greenbacks, the bank circulation must also be largely reduced to maintain resumption. The national banks, since the resumption law was enacted, have made a net reduction of forty-eight millions of their circulation. Whatever other causes may have led to it, the obvious impracticability of maintaining even the present volume of bank currency redeemable in gold was the main cause. Over three hundred national banks have already surrendered their circulation in whole or in part. They are chiefly the banks of the country districts, that know perfectly well that it will be impossible for any banks to maintain their circulation except those situated in the great importing centers, where whatever of gold may remain in the country will accumulate, and where alone redemption will be practicable.

The destruction of over seventy-five millions of greenbacks and national bank notes under the operation of the resumption law has of itself caused much of the business distress we have witnessed; but the obviously impending destruction of more than half of what is left is the storm cloud which covers our heavens and fills all communities with alarm.

Sir, the assertion that the distresses that our country is now undergoing are due to the large volume of currency, and to the wastes of the war, is contradicted by our experiences, and by the parallel experience of England's twenty years of continental war and irredeemable paper money. British industry was greatly wasted by that protracted war, but the loss was more than made up by the industrial prosperity which attended her full, stable, but irredeemable paper currency. It was in that season that she established her manufacturing and commercial supremacy over the world. Every sea was whitened with her commerce; every market filled with her wares. Napoleon said in his exile at St. Helena, "Great Britain conquered me with her spindles"—with spindles kept in motion by a prosperity due to the fact that she had during that period of suspension a fuller, better, and more stable currency than any which can be built on the quicksands of gold and silver.

So *we* had, during the rebellion and for some time afterward, a full and satisfactory currency which stimulated industry, and compensated to a large extent for the ravages of war. If the distress which now afflicts our country were due to the increased volume of paper money, how is it that during the period of the fullest currency bankruptcies were almost unknown? How is it that that period, though marked by extremely heavy taxation, was one of comparatively little accumulation of municipal or private debt?

Mr. Speaker, the records of commercial failures in the United States indisputably show that business distress was least when the currency was fullest, and that the contraction of the currency, by funding legal-tender interest notes, arrested prosperity and caused an enormous increase of bankruptcies throughout the nation. In place of this currency withdrawn was substituted a mountain of debt which toppled over in the panic of 1873. But in the year following the panic those records show, and our recollections attest, that the business of the country revived. The return of prosperity was stopped by this resumption law, which was an emphatic warning to moneyed men to withdraw or withhold their money from all industrial pursuits, and to hoard it in anticipation of a contraction and shrinkage of values unparalleled in our history. Had our home debt and our currency been let alone, the prosperity that accompanied and followed the war would no doubt have continued, prices would have gradually settled to a salutary level through a relative shrinkage of the currency resulting from the extension of business, and we would have been to-day richer, freer from debt, and far, far nearer a practicable resumption than now.

My colleague [Mr. Garfield] attempts to prove that our present disasters are the result of the increase of the currency during the war, by citing the hard times from 1837 to 1842 and from 1857 to 1859 as instances of the evils of redundant currency. Sir, the volume of currency was no larger at those periods than it was in 1860, which has been cited by the gentleman as the most solidly prosperous year in our history. Those panics were caused by the fact that the specie reserves of the banks were necessarily small, and that to accommodate the business of the country they issued more paper than they could get coin to redeem with, and therefore specie payments collapsed. To get back to redemption, the banks were compelled by their charters to do just what the resumption law now compels the treasury and the national banks to do, that is, contract their paper to the little measure compatible with coin redemption. That contraction, and that alone, caused the business distress which characterized the years following those panics.

But my colleague tells us that greenbacks are within 2½ per cent. of gold, and by the 1st of January, 1879, we will glide into resumption as a ship is launched from the stocks. Sir, that is the same jack-o'-lantern which beguiled the British people into the bog of resumption in 1819. Ricardo and other oracles assured the people that, as gold was at but 4 per cent. premium, resumption was an easy step, and that the fall of values caused by resumption would not exceed the 4 per cent. premium then existing on gold. Their assurances were credited, the law was passed, and the shrinkage of the currency and the fall of values which followed exceeded tenfold the predictions of these oracles of finance. This theory, which Ricardo himself subsequently admitted to be fallacious, is referred to now by the resumptionists with as much assurance as if it were a demonstrated maxim of finance. The fact is the premium on gold is no measure whatever of the extent of contraction necessary to resumption.

Equalization is not resumption. Equalization can occur without disturbance of the volume of the currency or of domestic business, for it leaves all who want gold to exchange greenbacks for it in the market. Resumption involves redemption and destruction of the home currency to the extent of the demand for gold, regardless of the disasters to business attending such destruction.

The reduction of the premium on gold is due to causes which may cease or be counteracted at any time. The depression of industries in Germany through contraction by silver demonetization; and in England through a falling off of exports to the

United States, and through the cheapening of silver, which has enabled the residents of British India to manufacture goods there at less cost than they can be manufactured in England (thus cutting off her greatest market), has tended to lessen the demand for gold in Europe, while the decrease of our own imports has lessened demand for it at home. Hence its fall in price in our markets.

A revival of commercial prosperity in those nations, increasing the export demand for our gold; a money panic abroad; a large crop in England next year; a short crop here; or even the termination of the European war, opening the Dardanelles for export of Russian wheat, may turn the balance of trade against us and send gold up to 10 or 20 per cent. premium before resumption day. Any one of these incidents, after resumption, would probably drain the little accumulations from the treasury and the banks, and throw them into insolvency.

But we are told that silver will be remonetized, and then resumption will be practicable without further contraction. That, in my judgment, is an egregious error. The total supply of silver coin and bullion in the United States, exclusive of subsidiary coin, is stated on excellent authority not to exceed from five to ten millions of dollars. There is no great stock of silver in the world on which we may draw for the enormous sum needed as an auxiliary to resumption; the only one large accumulation being the demonetized coin of Germany, which does not exceed $80,000,000. Remonetization by us will strengthen the already strong tendency in Germany to restore its silver, and will go far to remove the restrictions on that coinage in France, Italy, Spain, and the other states of the Latin Union. Mints have been established to coin it in Japan and India, and are about to be established in China with a view to the substitution of silver for copper in the domestic business of those countries, which is vast enough to absorb all the silver of the world. If our paper currency should be contracted no further, and if every contingency were to result in our favor, we could not possibly accumulate in the next twenty years enough of the precious metals to maintain even the sham redemption we had before the war. The only alternatives, therefore, are an indefinite postponement of resumption, or contraction of the volume of paper money to less than the attainable supply of coin, say $200,000,000.

Mr. Speaker, there is no law of political economy more universally recognized than that the reduction of the effective volume of a currency, by which the values of a country are measured, causes a ratable reduction of all values of land, labor, and product. It was strikingly illustrated in the history of the British resumption law. When that act had been in force three years, and resumption day was but a year distant, Mr. Atkins showed on the floor of the House of Commons—and Tooke's "Tables of Prices" confirms his statement—that the reduction of the bank paper 45 per cent. as a necessary preparation for resumption caused an equally great reduction of all values on the island.

I think it safe to say that the combined effect of withdrawal of over seventy-five millions of the paper currency under the resumption law, and the hoarding caused by the threat of resumption, have together reduced its effective volume at least one-third, resulting in an average fall of values in like proportion.

Now, Mr. Speaker, what is the extent of injury thus inflicted? How have taxpayers suffered? We pay more taxes each year than the aggregate volume of our currency—seven hundred and fifty millions—for the support of national, State, and local governments. That is, a tax of $17.50 per head for every man, woman, and child in the United States—an enormous burden, far surpassing any borne by any people on earth. The British pay $11.09 per head; the French, $11.41; the Germans, $9.24; the Austrians, $7.22. This burden is insupportable, unless industries prosper. The resumption law has broken down industries and reduced one-third the average values of land, labor, and products, by the sale of which alone taxes are paid, and in effect has thus increased the tax burden 50 per cent. The burden has thus been made, in heavily taxed communities, absolutely insupportable. Several great States, and many counties and cities, have already sought relief in repudiation. Continue that process of reduction of values, bring them down much more, as will inevitably be done if this law be not repealed, and one-half of the corporate and municipal debts in the United States will be repudiated. The greed of the money power, in thus seeking to enhance so enormously the value of the dollar, is only equaled by its arrogant and dogged stupidity.

Consider, Mr. Speaker, the wrong done to individual debtors by this contrived shrinkage of values. The aggregate of private debts in the United States, including railway mortgages, is probably not less than seven and one-half billions of dollars, or three and one-half times the sum of our national debt. They are owed generally by the young, energetic, driving business men of the country, who are seeking to rise from poverty to competence, or from competence to wealth. They comprise two-thirds of the merchants, manufacturers, and exchangers of values, and give employment to two-thirds of the wage men of the country. This law breaks down their business, strips them of their property, and casts out of employment millions of laborers dependent on them.

Above all, Mr. Speaker, consider the effect of the shrinkage of values on wage laborers and their families; on the millions who are compelled to eat up in idleness the little accumulations of thrifty industry; on the millions who have no accumulations, but rely only on daily labor for daily bread, and who are now unemployed, or half employed, or living on pauper wages. The president of the Springfield and Pomeroy Railway Company, Mr. Emmett, who is struggling to construct a railway across Southern Ohio, told me recently that he had plenty of laborers offering to build his road without other compensation than enough bread and meat to keep the poor machines of their bodies in working order—asking nothing for clothes, nothing for wives or children, nothing to lay up in store for winter—and this too in the midst of bounteous harvests, in a region one of the fairest ever fashioned by the Almighty for the abode of man—

> O God! that bread should be so dear,
> And flesh and blood so cheap!

Suppose, Mr. Speaker, that resumption were attainable without further fall of values and depression of industries, and that after January 1, 1879, prosperity should promptly return. Let us make a rough estimate of the cost of resumption. It will have cost the people at large, through the enforced idleness of factories, an enormous sum, probably surpassing several times the aggregate of our national debt.

The debtor class, instead of paying seven billions, which they owe, would have to pay one-half more by the shrinkage of former values; that is, the enormous sum of about three and three-quarters billions of dollars would be wrongfully taken from them, so far as they have power to pay it, and given to the creditor class, without consideration and in violation of the spirit of the contracts.

The census of 1870 indicates that there are not less than ten millions of wage people in the United States, men, women, and children. If there be no increase of demand for labor by resumption day, we may safely put the loss of labor, unemployed, or only partly employed, at a daily average of three millions of days' labor; and, putting wages at an average of a dollar a day, the loss, from want of employment alone, will have been nine hundred millions a year for about three years—an aggregate of $2,700,000,000 wrung from the poorest class of our people.

The loss to taxpayers in depreciation of property with which taxes are paid, while the sum of taxes remains the same, would be three hundred and fifty millions a year, or over a thousand millions in the three years; and the increase of bonded debt in purchase of gold and silver to pay and cancel the greenback and fractional currency will be four hundred and sixteen millions more. Thus, under the specious pretext that national honor requires us to add 10 per cent. to the value of three hundred and fifty-four millions of greenbacks, the contrivers of this scheme will have wrested from the people many times the sum of our vast national debt.

But the shrinkage of the currency and of all values cannot stop here, if the resumption scheme be not arrested. The entire industrial system of this country has been pushed to the verge of destruction. Savings banks and insurance companies are now failing everywhere through depreciation of real estate mortgaged to them. Yet my colleague [Mr. Garfield] appeals to us, in the name of the workingmen whose means are in these failing companies, to adhere to the policy of contraction, which involves the loss of their savings in addition to loss of employment. There is not a savings or other bank in the United States which can possibly prepare for resumption by January 1, 1879. All the banks owe, by the estimate of the Comptroller of the Currency, about nineteen hundred and seventy-four millions to depositors, which will be payable in effect in gold on that day, in addition to three hundred and seventeen millions of bank notes. Those institutions have not to-day one million of gold for each two hundred millions payable fourteen months hence. When they shall have drifted on a few months longer, their helpless condition will become generally understood, and a panic will ensue which will involve the whole banking system and with it the entire industries of the country, to be followed by an enormous increase of suffering among wage people and by civil commotions, riots, and disasters which will shake the firm foundations of order and property.

Mr. Speaker, this is no phantom of the imagination, but a prediction of fact founded on the necessary effects of the law in the situation in which we are, as illustrated by the experience of England in her fatal scheme of forced resumption.

Our legislators slavishly borrowed this scheme from British

statute books, while shutting their eyes to every lesson its history taught the world. They are blind to the fact that, while resumption was possible in England, it is wholly impossible here. When she attempted resumption the paper money to which her values were adjusted was about $232,000,000; ours, seven hundred and thirty-three millions. She had far more gold in the country than we have. All the world owed her; we owe all the world. The precious metals flowed to her from every land; they flow out from us at every port. With her small volume of paper money, her comparatively large accumulation of coin, her supreme command as the creditor, the merchant, and manufacturer of the world, resumption might well have seemed practicable to her statesmen. With our large volume of paper money, our petty and diminishing supply of coin, in our helpless situation as the financial slave of the world, unable either to get or keep coin as the foundation of a redeemable paper currency, the attempt at forced resumption is theory or craft run mad.

England carried through the scheme of her theorists and usurers, stripped her laboring class of their homes and little accumulations, robbed debtors of their property, and suppressed with slaughter the cries of her starving wage men. Our theorists and usurers have a far more gigantic job on hand. Its monstrous immortality and injustice are understood by the people, who will not submit to be robbed and enslaved by it. The alliances of workingmen everywhere—their action in the late elections—the civil commotions of last spring—are but portents of a coming storm. Look at the multitudes in the streets of our cities fast being driven by hunger to despair! I saw hundreds last summer clubbed by policemen out of the parks in New York at night—homeless, starving workingmen, who had gone there to find a resting place on the grass under a pitying sky. I warn you, this scheme has been pushed just as far as it can go. Stop! or the spoliation of the masses, accomplished and still threatened, may arouse an avenging spirit which will not be content with merely righting wrongs.

Mr. Speaker, what are we to gain by this resumption scheme to compensate for the enormous calamities it has afflicted and will yet inflict? The answer is, "We will get a better and more stable currency redeemable in gold and silver, and shall then have a sound and lasting prosperity." Sir, I deny it, and confidently assert that we will get no currency at all comparable to that we have had for ten years past.

The most that can be said of it is that it will be in some respects a better and in others a worse currency than we had before the war. It will be better than then, because the State bank money had not uniform security or value. It will be a worse currency in this, that before the war we were comparatively out of debt abroad, and had more coin in the country and greater power to hold it than we can have for many years to come; and because the enormous aggregation of money and of money securities since then has created money kings and wreckers, who own and control the great banks and can contract and expand bank issues, make hard times and good times at pleasure, and rob the people at every change of values.

Imagine us back to an exclusive bank paper redeemable in coin. Let us view the inverted pyramid! We see $3 of bank paper built on each dollar of coin in the vaults and $3 of deposits on top of each dollar of paper, making $12 of paper and deposits, largely payable on demand, resting only on $1 of coin. Then suppose any year an abundant crop of cereals in Europe, and a consequent diminished export of grain from the United States, necessarily followed by increased coin shipments. The withdrawal of twenty-five millions of coin from the banks would involve a contraction of seventy-five millions of paper, taking the foundation from under two hundred and twenty-five millions of deposits—bringing on inevitably a general panic, just as the withdrawal from our banks in 1857 of seven millions of coin for shipment abroad caused the crash of that year. A war between any two great nations; a commercial crisis in any one of them; a combination of half a dozen of our largest creditors in London or the Netherlands; a combination of two or three great speculators at home; any one of a dozen incidents may occur in any month after resumption, causing the withdrawal from the banks for shipment abroad, or for making a corner at home, of coin enough to cause a disastrous panic.

The British have something approaching honest coin redemption, for there can only be $45,000,000 of bank paper in excess of coin in the vaults of the Bank of England; yet, there, with near seven hundred millions of coin in the country, "the export of ten to fifteen millions of coin," says Mr. Patterson in his "Science of Finance," "will produce a serious commercial crisis."

In the United States we have never had, and for many years cannot have, sufficient coin attainable by the banks to establish an honest redemption of one-third of the paper money which the necessities of business imperatively demand. Before the war the deposits but little exceeded the bank paper, while now they are three times the sum of our whole volume of paper currency, being near two thousand millions; yet then we had redemption only when coin was not generally wanted, but when the banks were called on for it the fact that $1 of coin will not redeem $3 of paper and $9 of deposits always threw them into insolvency. The system would have been a juggle if it were not a transparent lie. It is to get back to something even worse than this old system of insidious swindling that the American people are now undergoing the tortures of the damned.

But the gentleman from New York [Simeon B. Chittenden] declares with great vehemence that the greenback was originally merely a debt payable on a day not named; that the resumption law made it payable January 1, 1879; and that to repeal that law, and change the day of payment so fixed, is downright repudiation. Mr. Speaker, if the gentleman's statement be true that the greenbacks were payable on a day not named, then they were payable on *demand.* Then the resumption act postponing payment four years was an act of repudiation, and to now repeal that act is to restore as far as possible the original contract. Hence, by his own logic, he was a patriot when he voted against the resumption law in 1875. and is now a repudiator in sustaining it.

My colleague [Mr. Garfield] says the greenback was a forced loan. I deny it. It was issued as *money;* and solely because the people had not enough coin or other safe currency with which to prosecute the business of the war. I care not for the form of the contract, but for its meaning; not for the letter, but the spirit. It was and is only a pledge by the whole people to each successive holder that it shall be money; the money of the Constitution and law; the money of taxes, judgments, and contracts, in the transactions of domestic business; and that the function of money shall inhere in it until considerations of *public interest alone* require its redemption in coin.

A favorite scheme of the bullionists—those guardians of national honor—recommended repeatedly by Grant's Administration and the leading resumptionists of this House, has been and is to break this pledge of national faith by destroying the legal-tender character of the greenbacks in the hands of the people. They and they only are the repudiators; while those advocating the retention of the money, with all its faculties unimpaired, respect alike the obligations of national honor incurred in its issue and the considerations of national interest which demand its retention as the safest and best possible currency.

Sir, the resumption law was a trick and a fraud; hatched in the dark; its real purpose and effect concealed from all but the initiated in the mystery of money; and put through Congress without explanation or debate, because its authors well knew that the people would never consent to increase the bonded debt or destroy the greenback, and that if the effect of the bill had been known it would have been instantly strangled on this floor.

That law is itself a repudiation of the compact by which the greenback became the measure of all contracts in the myriad transactions of domestic business. It sought to destroy the greenback and to increase by stealth the values of $10,000,000,000 of contracts, public and private, measured by it. To repeal that law, and thus restore as far as possible the just measure of those contracts, is demanded alike by the people to whom the greenbacks belong and by every consideration of interest and honor.

If a repeal of this law be repudiation, as the gentleman from New York [Mr. Chittenden] so loudly asserts, who are the hapless sufferers? Not the people at large, for they hold the money to-day and pay it out to-morrow, and a change in its purchasing power is not so instantaneous as to affect hand to hand transactions. Is it the few men who have hoarded greenbacks on the pledge of the law? They diverted the money from the uses for which it was issued and have already made exorbitant profit by it. Is it not enough for them that $6 in greenbacks will now buy ten dollars' worth of labor or property? Does justice or honor demand that we give the hoarders of one or two hundred millions of greenbacks the power to double or treble their wealth by purchasing the people's labor and property at mere nominal prices, and that to accomplish this the industries, the property, the happiness of the masses shall be sacrificed?

No, sir! no public debt, however clear or obligatory, would justify a sacrifice so stupendous. In the language of Edmund Burke—

> It is to the property of the citizen, and not to the demand of the creditor of the State, that the original faith of society is pledged. The claim of the citizen is prior in time, paramount in title, superior in equity.

I have not attempted, Mr. Speaker, to reply to all the arguments on the other side, or to sound a tenth part of the depths and shoals of this subject, which is as boundless as the sea. No greater question was ever presented to an American Congress for its action. It touches the prosperity, the happiness, the future, of three-fourths of the men, women, and children of this land. Countless homes have already been desolated by this robber law. Thousands of men have been drivin by it to insanity or suicide. Hundreds of thousands have been cast down from competence to poverty. Millions have been deprived of that employment for their labor on which rest the hope and dependence of their families. It is now too late to right these wrongs, but greater evils may be averted from the most of these victims, and from millions more, by the prompt action of Congress and the President.

I do not appeal to that money power which intrigues for its own aggrandizement over the wrecked fortunes of the unwary multitude—a power to which our unhappy civil war gave birth, which has grown so enormous through unjust finance legislation, and now "bestrides this narrow world like a colossus"; which subsidizes the press, the great organs of public opinion; which captures statesmen and parties, and makes them its subservient tools; which vilifies and seeks to crush every public man who dare raise his voice against it. That power, in the flush and arrogance of its enormous and ill-gotten gains, has a heart of stone, not to be touched by human sympathy or compassion. I appeal to the masses; to their faithful representatives of both parties on this floor; to all who think that the true aim of government is the greatest good of the greatest number; who believe there is a faith due to the people as well as to the holders of public securities; and that whoever by covert legislation changes the value of contracts is as accursed as he who moves his neighbor's landmarks.

For twelve years past the finance policy of this country has been dictated in Lombard street or Wall street, and the people have been plundered by every fresh enactment. They have suffered the fate of the giant Gulliver tied down by the Liliputians. Thank God! they are now about to rise, to burst the bonds their petty foes have fastened on them sleeping, and to walk abroad again in their own majesty. [Great applause.]

None of the material amendments to the bill were agreed to. The bill passed by a vote of 133 to 120. The Senate referred the bill to the Committee on Finance, which did not report it during the session.

During the following session it was brought forward in the Senate, and debated at great length. A number of amendments to it were made, and it was passed on June 13, 1878, by a vote of 45 to 15. On June 17 the House voted on suspending the rules and concurring in the Senate amendments—yeas 140, nays 112. A two-thirds majority being required to suspend the rules, the motion was lost. The matter was not brought up again during this session.

Date Due
